CHINA'S RISE AND INTERNATIONALIZATION

Regional and Global Challenges and Impacts

Editors

Filip Abraham
Catholic University of Leuven, Belgium

Zhaoyong Zhang
Edith Cowan University, Australia

World Scientific

NEW JERSEY · LONDON · SINGAPORE · BEIJING · SHANGHAI · HONG KONG · TAIPEI · CHENNAI · TOKYO

Published by

World Scientific Publishing Co. Pte. Ltd.

5 Toh Tuck Link, Singapore 596224

USA office: 27 Warren Street, Suite 401-402, Hackensack, NJ 07601

UK office: 57 Shelton Street, Covent Garden, London WC2H 9HE

Library of Congress Cataloging-in-Publication Data

Names: Abraham, Filip, author. | Zhang, Zhaoyong, author.
Title: China's rise and internationalization : regional and global challenges and impacts /
    Filip Abraham, Zhaoyong Zhang.
Description: First Edition. | Hackensack : World Scientific Publishing Co. Pte. Ltd., 2020. |
    Includes bibliographical references and index.
Identifiers: LCCN 2020006518 | ISBN 9789811210907 (hardcover) |
    ISBN 9789811212239 (ebook)
Subjects: LCSH: China--Economic policy--1976-2000. | China--Economic policy--21st century. |
    China--Economic conditions--1976-2000. | China--Economic conditions--21st century. |
    Economic development--China.
Classification: LCC HC427.92 .A27 2020 | DDC 330.951--dc23
LC record available at https://lccn.loc.gov/2020006518

British Library Cataloguing-in-Publication Data
A catalogue record for this book is available from the British Library.

For any available supplementary material, please visit
https://www.worldscientific.com/worldscibooks/10.1142/11568#t=suppl

Desk Editor: Lum Pui Yee

Typeset by Stallion Press
Email: enquiries@stallionpress.com

Printed in Singapore

Contents

Part II: The Financial Aspects of China's Growth and Development

Chapter 1

Introduction — China's Rise and Internationalization: Challenges and Impacts

Filip Abraham* and Zhaoyong Zhang†

*KU Leuven and Vlerick Business School, Belgium
†Edith Cowan University, Australia

Over the past 40 years China's path-breaking initiatives of reforms have successfully transformed the country from a poor, closed nation into an important trading nation and manufacturing center in the world. Since launching the market-oriented reforms and opening up to foreign trade and investment in late 1978, China's economic development has been miraculous. According to the World Bank, China's GDP grew from US$149.5 billion in 1978 to US$13.6 trillion by 2018, with real GDP growth averaging nearly 10% a year despite the recent slowdown. And its GDP per capita rose 25.3-fold to US$7,755 in 2018 from US$307 in 1978 (at constant 2010 US$), lifting China from a low-income economy to an upper middle-income country and with more than 850 million people out of poverty. Since 2010, China has surpassed Japan to become the world's second largest economy by nominal GDP and overtaken the United States as the world's largest economy in terms of purchasing power parity (PPP) since 2014. There is no doubt that China's astonishing, unprecedented economic performance since 1978 is a miracle, which is described by the World Bank as "the fastest sustained expansion by a major economy in history".

In sharp contrast to the radical or "big-bang" reforms in Eastern Europe and the former Soviet Union, China adopted a gradual, pragmatic approach to reform its economic system, which is essentially experimental in nature, or "crossing the river by groping the stones" as described by Deng Xiaoping, the "chief architect" of China's economic reforms. China's economic reforms began in the agricultural sector in late 1978 and then extended gradually to the urban areas since the middle of the 1980s, marking the start of the full-scale, comprehensive, and in-depth reforms. Through such a gradual and experimental approach, China has undergone a highly dynamic, profound, yet smooth, internal institutional transition toward a system of socialist market economy over the past four decades, which "unleashed the standard forces of incentives, hard budget constraints, and competition for growth" (Qian, 1999) and contributed to its economic miracle. Studies have reported that China's household responsibility system (HRS) reform in the agricultural sector led to an increase in agriculture output by over 61% in 1979–1984, while 49% of agriculture output growth and 78% of the increase in productivity in the agricultural sector was due to the HRS reform (McMillan *et al.*, 1989; Lin, 1992). Equally impressive has been the contribution of TFP to China's economic growth, increasing from 11% before 1978 to more than 40% afterward (Perkins and Rawski, 2008; Xu, 2011) and over 43% on average in 2001–2018 (The Conference Board, 2019).

The opening up of the Chinese economy for foreign trade, investment, technology, and managerial skills began in 1979. As an integral part of the economic reform program, China's open-door policy centered on breaking the state monopoly of foreign trade, promoting exports with incentives- and subsidies-based measures, reducing import tariffs, establishing special economic zones (SEZs), and implementing the dual exchange rate system, which was later replaced by a unified rate in 1994. Since China's accession to the World Trade Organization (WTO) on December 11, 2001, it has effectively implemented a number of market-oriented reforms and measures to advance trade and investment liberalization and facilitation, foster the legal and investment environment, broaden the market access, and improve the market-based RMB exchange rate formation mechanism and convertibility.

These series of market opening-up measures and reforms have led to the emergence of China as the world's largest exporter in 2010 and the largest trading nation in goods in 2013, surpassing the United States, with a total international trade value of US$4.62 trillion in 2018, accounting for about 12% of the world's total trade (WTO, 2019). China has the largest foreign exchange reserves in the world, totaling US$3.2 trillion in June 2019 (SAFE, 2019), and is also the largest foreign direct investment (FDI) recipient in the developing countries and the second largest worldwide, with FDI inflows rising from almost zero dollar in 1978 to US$139 billion in 2018 (UNCTAD, 2019). Equally remarkable, China's Outward Direct Investment (ODI) has increased substantially since the country launched the "Going Global" strategy in 2002. In 2015, China hit a new record high in non-financial ODI amounting to US$118.02 billion, which marked the 13th consecutive year of rapid growth with an annual growth rate of 33.6%. This is also the year that China's ODI exceeded inbound FDI for the first time, symbolizing the successful transformation of China from a pure FDI recipient to a source country (Qi *et al.*, 2019). The recent UNCTAD report shows that China has become the world's second-largest investor in 2016, after FDI outflows surged by 44% to US$183 billion, 36% more than the amount of its inflows, though fully returned to the 2015 level since then (UNCTAD, 2017, 2019).

It is believed that China's astonishingly rapid rise and its increasing economic prominence will reshape the international financial system and drive greater regional financial and economic integration (De Grauwe and Zhang, 2016). The recent Belt and Road initiative — proposed by China — and measures to promote the internationalization of Chinese RMB and enterprises are expected to further foster greater inter-continental growth and cross-border trade flows and investment and deepen regional cooperation and integration among the countries involved. The early signs of RMB internationalization are already visible when banks in Hong Kong started to offer RMB retail banking services in 2004 and the dim sum bond market was established in Hong Kong in 2009. To facilitate the use of RMB in cross-border trade settlement and investment, China has signed bilateral currency-swap agreements with several Belt and Road countries. More recently, the Shanghai–Hong Kong Stock Connect in 2014 and the Shenzhen–Hong Kong Stock Connect arrangement in 2016 marked a new milestone in the process of RMB internationalization and financial market integration with the world (Ho *et al.*, 2016). RMB has ranked 5th as the most traded currency in 2014 and was added to the IMF's Special Drawing Right (SDR) basket in 2016, reflecting China's expanding role in global trade and the substantial increase in the international use and trading of the Chinese RMB. So far, over a dozen cities, including Hong Kong, London, Paris, and Sydney, have officially announced the establishment of offshore RMB centers, with Hong Kong being the largest center for offshore RMB banking business (Jin, 2012; PBC, 2013; Ho *et al.*, 2016, 2017). The rising significance of the RMB is viewed as a natural response to the growing weight of China's trade and investment flows in the world economy and also a result of China's rapid economic and financial integration with the rest of the world, especially with its East Asian neighbors (Ho *et al.*, 2017, Yeh, 2012).

In recent years, economic integration in the East Asian region has evolved into a new form of international specialization, characterized by intricate global production sharing and trade in intra-regional networks. These networks have enabled firms to exploit comparative advantage by slicing up long production processes and allocating the production blocks throughout the East Asian region, with China being the manufacturing center mainly for assembly by lower-skilled workers and exports of finished products throughout the world (De Grauwe and Zhang, 2012, 2016). On the contrary, China's financial development and deepening promote the use of the RMB in international transactions, hence facilitating the process of RMB internationalization.

All those developments together with the recent Belt and Road Initiative will not only offer opportunities for new complementarities but also reshape the patterns of trade, investment, and infrastructure development in the region.

However, the emergence of China as a regional and global economic power has raised widespread concerns over the nature and implications of China's rise and its influence. Those concerns relate to the dynamic impact of China's rise both regionally and globally, the sustainability of China's economic growth, and the future path of regional integration. Questions are being asked about how far the Chinese economy has been transitioned to market, how to maintain China's economic dynamism, and how to understand China's rising impact both regionally and globally. This volume brings together leading experts on European integration and the Chinese economy from Australia, Belgium, Canada, China, Hong Kong, South Korea, and the UK to analyze these important issues from different perspectives. All the 13 chapters in this volume were solicited from a recent international conference on China's Rise and Internationalization held in Ningbo, China on December 7–8, 2018.

Part I contains four chapters, addressing issues related to the rise of China in global trade and foreign direct investment. Chapter 2 by Filip Abraham, Yannick Bormans, and Jan Van Hove analyzes the EU–China international trade and investment relationship taking a European perspective in the current context of deglobalization and increasing protectionism. After a comprehensive and thorough analysis of the EU–China dynamic relationship, the authors identify several similarities in their strategic objectives and interests and propose several options for the EU and China to make progress in building a closer relationship notwithstanding the current tide of rising protectionism and unilateralism around the globe. They conclude that both the EU and China could join forces in the financing and implementation of Belt and Road projects that affect EU member states and could work together in strengthening the multilateral system by committing to open markets and globalization.

The Belt and Road Initiative, launched in 2013, is an ambitious development campaign through which China wants to boost trade and stimulate economic growth across Asia and beyond. This initiative has generated a mix of optimism and apprehension around the world. In Chapter 3, Chengyu Que, Fan Zhang, Junru Zhang, and Zhaoyong Zhang provide a comprehensive assessment of the overall trade interdependence and the dynamics of trade relationship between China and the Belt and Road countries. They find evidence confirming the existence of structural complementarity in trade flows between China and the Belt and Road countries at both the industry level and the country level, suggesting the absorptive capacity of their mutual products and the potential for further trade expansion. Their results also suggest that industrial upgrading will promote future trade development between China and its trade partners along the Belt and Road route.

How is the collapse of international trade related to the occurrence of a banking crisis? In Chapter 4, Yifei Mu, Qiushu Yin, and Antonio Alleyne investigate to what extent the drop in trade can be explained by a country's declining wealth during banking crises from both a global and Chinese perspective as well as from the perspective of both exporters and importers. The results show that banking crises are highly correlated with bilateral trade flow fluctuations, and most of the impacts from banking crises go through the importers. They also find that there is a relatively constant negative impact on import prior to the crises, and the decline in import tends to intensify during the post-crisis period. They conclude with a remark that the impact of a banking crisis on trade is also correlated with a country's financial development. A country with higher credit availability and a well-developed financial sector is expected to have a better performance in foreign trade.

In Chapter 5, Yibing Ding and Yingjie Fu argue that producer service FDI can affect the industrial structure upgrading in the manufacturing sector of a host country through vertical industrial linkages and industrial spillovers. The authors empirically examine the impact of producer service FDI inflow on the upgrading of China's manufacturing sector using provincial and industrial-level data. The results show that producer service FDI can significantly promote the upgrading of industrial structure in the eastern region of China but has little effect on the middle and west of China. The authors further employ a spatial Durbin model to confirm that producer service FDI can also generate spatial technological spillover effects across regions.

Part II contains five chapters with the financial aspects of China's growth and development as a common theme. Chapter 6 deals with the effects of China's growth surge on financial integration. In their contribution, Rod Tyers and Yixiao Zhou define two types of financial integration — Type 1 reflects the scale of cross-border flows as proportions of domestic saving or investment, while Type 2 refers to the weakness of capital controls. Using a well-developed parsimonious global macroeconomic model that incorporates bilateral linkages across six regions via both trade and financial flows, they find robust evidence that China's growth surge contributed substantially to integration of Type 1 but not of Type 2. With more Type 2 integration, the surge effects within China would have been substantially smaller, while the global impacts on yields and inflation would have been larger.

Chapter 7 by Xinmiao Zhou, Kai Zhang, and Huihong Liu empirically investigates the macroeconomic factors and financial security environment that affect systemic risk in China with a particular focus on the non-performing loans of commercial banks. With some carefully designed composite indexes for financial security, they conclude that China has formed a real-estate market bubble and suggest that slow credit expansion can prevent the rapid expansion of the credit bubble. They advise China to further promote financial market integration with the world, to develop the derivatives markets, and to encourage diversified forms of capital flows.

Kenneth S. Chan, Vinh Q. T. Dang, and Erin P. K. So, in Chapter 8, empirically investigate whether there exists a long-run relationship between the two government budget variables of expenditures and revenues in a way that would maintain fiscal deficits and debt at a sustainable level. In their work, they use a non-stationary panel data analysis of China's provincial governments in the period 1994–2013. The results suggest that provinces in the central and western regions do not achieve fiscal sustainability on their own or even with central government transfers. They find that provinces in the more developed eastern region overall achieve fiscal sustainability in the weak form, and the government budget in only four provinces is strictly sustainable on its own. These findings have important policy implications for China's macroeconomic stability.

The Chinese stock market has experienced remarkable growth since its two exchanges were established in the early 1990s. Nevertheless, it still remains relatively segmented. Investors often face several challenges such as problems of liquidity and short-selling constraints. Those factors could have contributed to several significant asset pricing anomalies, related to size, in the Chinese stock market. In Chapter 9, Kin-Yip Ho, Jiyoun An, and Zhaoyong Zhang explore the significance of the size anomaly in the Chinese stock market and its relation to a variety of asset pricing factors. They find robust results confirming that the size anomaly in the Chinese stock market is still significant after taking into account the impact of various asset pricing factors, such as idiosyncratic volatility, liquidity, and the book-to-market value. These findings have important implications for a better understanding of the dynamic relationships of the firm-level predictors and for the influence of liquidity on future stock returns and market dynamics in Chinese financial markets.

Chapter 10, authored by Zhaohui Wang, Xiangqun Zhang, and Hongya Li, also focuses on the Chinese stock market. They empirically test the hypothesis whether institutional investor's active portfolio weight change can make the stock market more stable. They develop several portfolio weight change measures such as the overall portfolio weight change, active portfolio weight change, and passive portfolio weight change, using weekly data of 111 hybrid funds from 2006 to 2015. The results show that institutional investor's active portfolio weight changes directly affect the stock returns and cause stock market volatility. Institutional investors can therefore not be considered as stock market stabilizers, but they conclude that financial derivatives and hedge funds may play this role.

The final part, Part III, contains four chapters dealing with issues related to innovation and sustainable growth in the Chinese economy. Chapter 11 by Hui-hong Liu and Xin-miao Zhou employs both empirical models and game-based approach to analyze the relationship between market competition and innovation behavior of firms in China at various technology levels. Their results show that the relationship varies with respect to firm levels of technology, exhibiting an inverted-U pattern. Market competition tends to encourage industry innovation when it is at a low level, but rather discourages innovation at a high level. They make several policy suggestions on how to encourage firms, especially the leader firms, to innovate.

The last three chapters address development and environmental issues in China. Chapter 12 by Lin-ju Chen and Cong-lei Tan employs a multi-objective model combined with input–output analysis to empirically estimate the macroeconomic costs of CO_2 emission reduction in the province of Zhejiang, China. They find that the abatement cost in 2020 is estimated to be between 1507 and 3505 RMB/ton CO_2 depending on the different GDP growth rates. Several industrial sectors such as textile, general, and special machinery industry are found to have a huge potential to further reduce carbon emissions. The authors provide several important policy recommendations for managing issues related to environmental protection and economic development.

Chapter 13 by Limin Liu, Minjie Wang, Ziyuan Xie, and Malviskate Ekia Ambonaya adopts a gravity model of international trade to empirically test the Pollution Haven Hypothesis (PHH) for China's manufacturing industry. They use panel data of bilateral trade in manufacturing between China and selected countries to assess the impacts of the environmental policy stringency gap between China and its trading partners on bilateral trade at the industry level. The results show that China's manufacturing industry can be regarded as a pollution haven, and the environmental policy stringency gap has different impacts on gross exports, net exports, and the domestic value-added component of manufacturing exports, depending on the type of industry.

The paper by Yunhua Zhang and Dan Luo assesses how local government expenditures affect local economic growth, consumption and private investment using data from Zhejiang Province, which has the largest domestic private economy. They find that the local fiscal expenditures have no effect on local economic growth and consumption, but show evidence of leading effect on private investment. They also argue that the different types of fiscal expenditures matter. In particular, the maintenance expenditures are found to have a significant positive impact on private investment, but other types of fiscal expenditures have either negative or no significant impacts on the private investment in Zhejiang Province.

The collection of papers in this volume provides important insights into the challenges and impacts of China's rapid rise and internationalization. We hope these contributions will stimulate further research in issues related to the dynamics of the Chinese economy and its rising international influence.

Acknowledgments

We wish to thank Chuanyong Le, Donald Lien, Kiyotaka Sato, and Xinmiao Zhou for their support and contribution to this project. We also specially thank Professor Xinmiao Zhou and his team for their tireless efforts in hosting the 4th International Conference on China's Rise and Internationalization on December 7–8, 2018 and to the Business School of Ningbo University for financial support to this conference.

References

De Grauwe, P. and Zhang, Z. Y. (2012). "Monetary Integration and Exchange Rate Issues in East Asia," *The World Economy*, **35**(4), 397–404.

De Grauwe, P. and Zhang, Z. Y. (2016). "The Rise of China and Regional Integration in East Asia," *Scottish Journal of Political Economy*, **63**(1), 1–6.

Ho, K. Y., Shi, Y. L. and Zhang, Z. Y. (2016). "It Takes Two Tango: A Regime-Switching Analysis of the Correlation Dynamics between the Mainland Chinese and Hong Kong Stock Markets," *Scottish Journal of Political Economy*, **63**(1), 41–65.

Ho, K. Y., Shi, Y. L. and Zhang, Z. Y. (2017). "Does News Matter in China's Foreign Exchange Market? Chinese RMB Volatility and Public Information Arrivals," *International Review of Economics & Finance*, **52**, 302–321.

Jin, Z. (2012). "The Use of RMB in International Transactions: Background, Development and Prospect." Presentation at Sasana Kijiang, Kuala Lumpur, Bank Negara Malaysia.

Lin, J. (1992). "Rural Reforms and Agricultural Growth in China," *American Economic Review*, **82**(March), 34–51.

McMillan, J., Whalley, J. and Zhu, L. (1989). "The Impact of Chinas Economic Reforms on Agricultural Productivity Growth," *Journal of Political Economy*, **97**(4), 781–807.

PBC (2013). Annual report. URL: http://www.pbc.gov.cn/english/130739/index.html.

Perkins, D. H. and Rawski, T. G. (2008). "Forecasting China's Economic Growth to 2025," in L. Brandt and T. G. Rawski (eds.), *China's Great Economic Transformation*, Cambridge University, Cambridge and New York, pp. 829–886.

Qi, J. H., Liu, H. and Zhang, Z. Y. (2019). "Exchange Rate Uncertainty and the Timing of Chinese Outward Direct Investment," *International Review of Economics & Finance*, https://doi.org/10.1016/j.iref.2019.11.008.

Qian, Y. Y. (1999). "The Institutional Foundations of China's Market Transition." Paper prepared for the Annual World Bank Conference on Development Economics, Washington, D.C., April 28–30, 1999 (http://www.worldbank.org/research/abcde/pdfs/qian.pdf).

SAFE (2019). The Time-series data of Balance of Payments of China. URL: http://www.safe.gov.cn/en/BalanceofPayments/index.html.

The Conference Board (2019). Total Economy Database, April, The Conference Board, New York.

UNCTAD (2017, 2019). World Investment Report 2017 & 2019. https://unctad.org/en/pages/PublicationWebflyer.aspx?publicationid=2460.

WTO (2019). International Trade Statistics. https://data.wto.org/.

Xu, C. G. (2011). "The Fundamental Institutions of China's Reforms and Development," *Journal of Economic Literature*, **49**(4), 1076–1151.

Yeh, K.-C. (2012). "Renminbi in the Future International Monetary System," *International Review of Economics Finance*, **21**(1), 106–114.

Part I

The Rise of China in Global Trade and Foreign Direct Investment

Chapter 2

EU–China Trade and Investment Relations in Turbulent Times: A European Perspective

Filip Abraham*, Yannick Bormans[†], and Jan Van Hove[‡]

*KU Leuven and Vlerick Business School, Belgium
[†] VIVES, KU Leuven, Belgium
[‡] KBC Group and KU Leuven, Belgium

This study analyzes the EU–China international trade and investment relationship taking a European perspective and identifies similarities and differences in the strategic objectives and interests of the EU and China. It proposes several options for making progress in building a closer relationship, notwithstanding the current tide of rising protectionism and unilateralism around the globe.

1. Introduction

We live in turbulent times. International trade relations are rapidly changing. The world economy is experiencing a period of deglobalization and increasing protectionism, resulting in frequent trade and investment tensions between the major trading blocs. The Trump presidency has replaced the traditional US support for the multilateral trading policy by an activist trade agenda of putting America first. The US and China are involved in a struggle for current and future global leadership. Emerging economies are demanding a growing role in the world economic system. Meanwhile, the European Union (EU) is struggling with slowing economic growth, Brexit, and migration from Syria, Afghanistan, and several African countries.

The relationship with regional partners such as Russia and Turkey is tense.

In these uncertain times, the EU has been reorienting its global trade and investment strategy. Europe can no longer rely on the unconditional support of its main ally, the United States. Further enlargement of the EU or substantial trade expansion with nearby neighbors is a distant prospect at best. Instead, the EU has sped up its efforts to conclude comprehensive free trade agreements (FTAs) with trading partners such as Canada, Japan, Australia, Singapore, and selected ASEAN countries.

When talking to EU trade negotiators, the elephant in the FTA room is clearly the relationship with China. This should not come as a surprise. China has become a global leader that has a major impact on the world economy. The dynamic transition of the Chinese economy toward a technology-driven economy creates both opportunities and challenges for European companies and policymakers. In fact, China is the EU's second largest trading partner (behind the US) and the EU is China's largest trading partner. Therefore, the EU–China relationship matters for both trading partners. Considering that the combined GDP of China and the EU accounts for more than a third of world GDP, their relationship matters for the rest of the world as well.

In spite of the potential for win–wins, China and the EU are not involved in negotiations for an FTA. In China, the EU is often perceived as a bureaucratic and inefficient organization. In the Chinese view, it is often more productive to strike *ad hoc* deals with individual EU member states. As a condition to engage in far-reaching deals with China, the EU wants to ensure that China opens up its market, respects intellectual property rights, and meets its obligations as a member of the World Trade Organization (WTO). Underlying the cautious EU approach is the fear that trade and investment integration may strengthen the position of Chinese companies in knowledge-based sectors at the expense of their European competitors.

Given this mutual reluctance, we argue in this chapter that a further strengthening of the EU–China collaboration requires a gradual building of trust based on a profound understanding of both common interests and different perspectives. In doing so, we will take the perspective of the EU which is where our expertise lies. As a starting point, Section 2 presents some stylized facts about EU–China trade and investment flows. In Section 3, we focus on the strategic objectives that define the EU's position toward China. Section 4 explores the options for a deeper collaboration in the years to come.

2. Facts and Figures About EU–China Trade and Foreign Direct Investment

In the past 15 years, the importance of China for EU imports and exports of goods has risen significantly. As seen in Figure 1, the Chinese share in total EU imports from non-EU countries has doubled from nearly 10% in 2002 to 20% in 2017. In that same period, EU exports to China more than doubled from less than 5% to approximately 10% of total extra-EU exports.[1]

The EU benefits from the expansion of exports to China. The corresponding increase in imports from China is the other side of the international trade coin. The growing market share of China in extra-EU imports has come at the expense of long-standing EU trading partners such as the US and Japan. The EU shows a bilateral trade deficit in goods with respect to China, which has been growing in the 2002–2017 period. It amounted to €176.6 billion in 2017 (see Figure 2).[2] The build-up of Chinese trade surpluses causes some concern in Europe but is a less sensitive issue than in the US. The reason is that in recent years the EU has realized a small trade balance surplus in its total trade with the rest of the world.[3]

---

[1]In this chapter, extra-EU exports and imports refer to the export and import flows between the EU28 countries and the rest of the world (the non-EU countries).

[2]Throughout the chapter, we provide data in nominal terms and hence do not adjust for inflation. Nominal amounts are usually expressed in €. At the time of writing this chapter, the following exchange rates prevailed 1€ = 1.13 USD and 1€ = 7.74 CNY.

[3]Note that the EU realized a small trade surplus in services with respect to China of €8.8 billion in 2016.

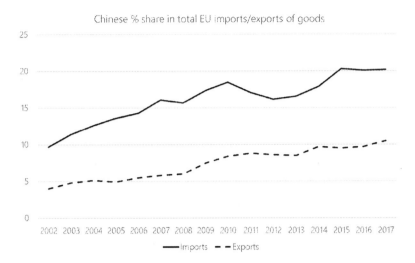

Figure 1. Evolution of the Chinese percentage share in total extra EU imports/exports of goods.

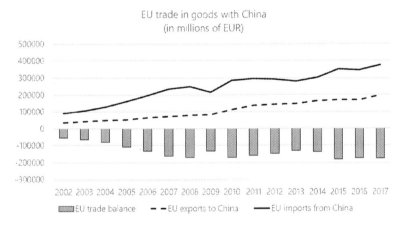

Figure 2. EU trade and trade balance in goods with China (in millions of €).
Source: KBC Economic Research.

The importance of China as an export destination varies considerably across EU member states. Figure 3 documents the share of exports to China in the GDP of the 28 EU member countries. This share went up significantly in the last two decades. The striking

Exports to China in % of GDP (goods trade)

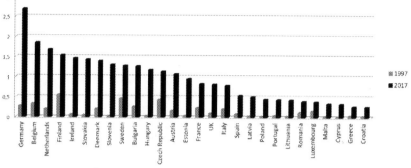

Figure 3.   Exports to China as a % of GDP of EU28 member countries.
Source: KBC Economic Research (2018), based on IMF.

feature of Figure 3 is the heterogeneity across member states. Simplifying a bit, the Chinese market matters more for a group of Northern EU countries, linked to the German economy, than for EU member states in the East or the South of Europe.

The relationship between the EU and China cannot be fully understood without delving into the sectoral composition of the trade flows. Table 1 gives an overview of the share of the top five import and export sectors in the total trade between the EU and China. Admittedly, this is a very rough decomposition of sectoral trade flows. But it contains some interesting information. One key finding is that intra-industry trade appears to play an important role in bilateral trade transactions. The sectors of machinery and appliances, chemicals and related products, and basic metals are among the top five in both EU import and export flows with China. On the contrary, there is also evidence of inter-industry specialization. The EU is a prominent exporter of transport equipment and optical and photographic instruments to China. Producers of textiles and miscellaneous manufacturing figure prominentely in Chinese exports to the EU.

The industry of machinery and appliances accounts for 49.9% of EU imports from China and for 30.8% of EU exports to China. This sector consists of a very broad category of industrial activities.

Table 1. Top five sectors in EU trade with China (in percentage of total imports or exports).

EU imports from China	%	EU exports to China	%
Machinery and appliances	49.9	Machinery and appliances	30.8
Textiles	10.0	Transport equipment	23.1
Other manufacturing	9.3	Chemicals and related products	10.3
Basic metals	6.3	Optical and photographic instruments	6.5
Chemicals and related products	4.4	Basic metals	6.3
Total top five sectors	79.9	*Total top five sectors*	77.0

Source: KBC Economic Research.

In what follows, we zoom in on high-tech products, which include sub-categories such as electronics, telecommunications, aerospace, computers, and electrical machinery. As we will argue later in the chapter, a strong presence in high-tech trade is a strategic objective for both China and the EU.

Figure 4 shows that China has become the largest provider of high-tech products exporting €120 billion to the EU. The US is the second largest supplier accounting for nearly €100 billion of EU imports of high-tech products. All other trading partners export far less. A further analysis of the trade data reveals that Chinese high-tech exports are heavily concentrated in electronics, telecommunication equipment and electronic machinery.

Once again, there are two sides to the trade coin. Figure 5 ranks the main export destinations of EU high-tech products. China takes the second position in this ranking after the US. In 2017, the EU exported products worth approximately €40 billion to China which is less than half of the amount sold in the US. More detailed data show that the sectoral pattern of EU high-tech exports to China is more diversified across sectors than the sales of Chinese technological products in the EU. The most important sectors are electronics and telecommunication, aerospace, pharmaceutical products, and scientific instruments.

While trade flows between China and the EU are going in both directions, the data for 2017 point to a EU trade balance deficit of

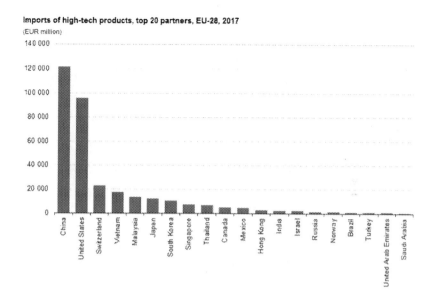

Figure 4. EU imports of high-tech products in 2017 (in millions of €).
Source: Eurostat (Comext database DS-018995).

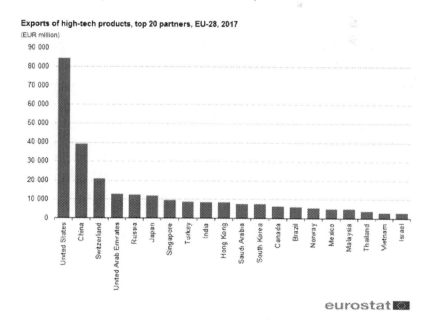

Figure 5. Main destinations of EU high-tech exports in 2017 (in millions of €).
Source: Eurostat (Comext database DS-018995).

approximately €80 billion. This accounts for 45% of the total EU trade deficit in goods with respect to China. With the rapid transition of China to a knowledge-based society, the trade gap in technological goods will most likely not narrow in the years to come. It remains to be seen how Europe's position in high-tech services will evolve. For those who view technology as one of Europe's comparative advantages, there are reasons to be worried.

The economic relationship between China and the EU goes beyond international trade flows. Figure 6 focuses on the flows of Chinese FDI into the EU in the period 2000–2018. The data show the spectacular rise of Chinese investment after the financial crisis of 2007–2008, dwarfing EU FDI in 2016–2017. Chinese FDI reached a maximum value of USD37.2 in 2016, but decreased in 2017 and 2018.

As seen in Figure 7, the picture for EU FDI in China is very different. The gradual expansion of investments in the Chinese market by EU companies ends in 2012 and shows a downward trend afterward.

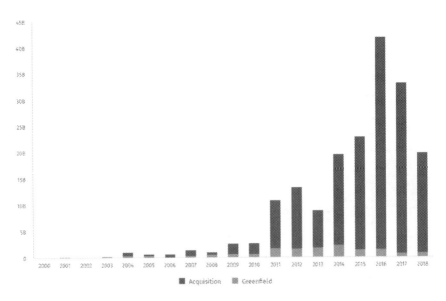

Figure 6. Annual value of Chinese FDI into the EU: 2000–2018 (in billions of USD).

Source: Rhodium Group.

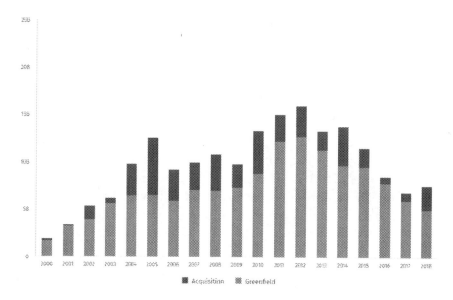

Figure 7. Annual value of EU FDI into China: 2000–2018 (in billions of USD). *Source*: Rhodium Group.

Rightly or not, European observers often attribute this decline to market entry barriers imposed by the Chinese government against foreign companies.

The surge of Chinese FDI raises concerns about the growing Chinese influence in strategic industries. More detailed sectoral data show that many FDI transactions target transport, utilities, and infrastructure as well as information and communications technology. This sectoral pattern is a sensitive issue in Europe.

Another key development in FDI is the ambitious Belt and Road initiative (BRI) of the Chinese government that aims at establishing a closer connection between China and Europe through both a land and a sea route. The BRI involves massive investments in infrastructure. As it looks at this moment, the central and eastern EU countries would be affected most by the land route. The effects of the sea route would be mostly felt in the Southern EU countries around the Mediterranean, such as Greece. Hence, the geographical pattern of EU countries impacted by the BRI is quite different from the ranking of member states according to their export dependence on the Chinese market.

3. Strategic Objectives in EU Trade and Investment Relations with China

In this section, we discuss the EU perspective toward trade and investment relations with China. As a starting point, we take the speech of President Xi Jinping on globalization, delivered at the World Economic Forum meeting of 2017 in Davos. This speech was well received in Europe because it accords well with the EU view on globalization. Analyzing the EU priorities through the views expressed by the Chinese president offers an interesting perpective on the European and Chinese positions.

Excerpts of the Davos Speech by President Xi Jinping

"The problems troubling the world are not caused by globalization."

"Pursuing protectionism is like locking oneself in a dark room. While wind and rain may be kept outside, that dark room will also block light and air. No one will emerge as a winner in a trade war."

"Countries should view their own interest in the broader context and refrain from pursuing their own interest at the expense of others."

"China will keep its doors wide open. We hope that other countries will also keep their doors open to Chinese investors."

3.1. *Globalization is not the problem, protection is...*

The first two quotes of the speech deal with the benefits of globalization and the threats of protectionism. While criticism on

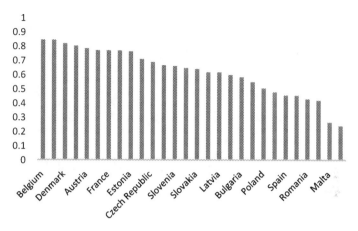

Figure 8. Correlation coefficient between annual global trade growth and annual real GDP growth in EU countries (1998–2017).

Source: KBC Economic Research (2018).

globalization is growing,[4] most European countries continue to support the expansion of international trade. This is not surprising because European growth and living standards are strongly dependent on open markets. In Figure 8, we compute the correlation coefficients for the 1988–2017 period between the annual growth of global trade and the growth of real GDP in the 28 EU member countries. Those correlation coefficients are very high, in particular for many of the higher income and smaller countries. It follows that European economies would be severely hurt by a full-fledged trade war.

The importance of international trade explains the continued EU support for multilateralism. Having said this, EU policymakers are well aware that new multilateral initiatives have little chance of success in a world where national strategic interests dominate global trade relations. They realize, as Mattoo and Staiger argue, that the United States is initiating a change from "rules-based" to "power-based" tariff bargaining and is selecting countries with which it runs bilateral trade deficits as the most suitable targets of its bargaining

---

[4]See Abraham (2017) for an analysis of European views toward globalization.

tariffs (Matto and Staiger 2019). For this reason, EU global trade policy is increasingly oriented toward negotiating comprehensive and deep free trade agreements with major trading partners, such as South Korea (2016),[5] Canada (2017), Japan (2019), and Singapore.[6]

3.2. *Strategic interests in EU trade and investment policy*

The speech by Xi Jinping mentions that countries should pursue their own interests. In recent months, the EU has become more active in pursuing its own strategic interests. This shift is taking place under the pressure of hardliners who argue that the EU has been too soft and naïve in defending its own interests. The rise and growing competition of China and other emerging economies undoubtedly plays a role, so does the "America First" approach of the Trump presidency.

There are quite some similarities between the strategic objectives of China and the EU. Just like China, the EU aims at a *strong position in technological and knowledge-intensive sectors*. It wants to remain a strong exporter of technological and high value-added goods and services, which are at the core of the European comparative advantage. The rise of China as a technological leader is greeted with mixed feelings. On the one hand, closer relations with China may facilitate market access to the Chinese market for European firms and expand intra-industry trade in technological products. On the other hand, the sizeable bilateral deficit in technological products is seen as a sign that European companies are rapidly losing ground with respect to their Chinese competitors.[7]

Another similarity with Chinese strategic thinking is that the *EU does not want to be overly dependent on foreign companies for its critical technology and infrastructure*. At least partially, the surge of

---

[5]Provisional application since 2011.
[6]This agreement was signed in 2018, but the ratification process in EU member states is still going on.
[7]Research by Abraham and Van Hove shows the strong impact of China's global rise on the market position of EU firms (Abraham and Van Hove, 2016).

the Chinese share in EU high-tech imports comes at the expense of trading partners such as the US, Switzerland, Japan, South Korea, Malaysia, and Vietnam. This makes Europe increasingly dependent on China. It also creates the impression for other European trading partners that closer trade cooperation between China and the EU will come at their expense.

The strategic independence argument in technology and critical infrastructure extends to FDI flows. The sectoral focus of Chinese FDI on information technology, infrastructure, and utilies, documented in Figure 7, raises national security concerns in Europe. News stories about alleged improper activities by companies such as Huawei add to this uneasy feeling. The response of a growing number of European countries is to screen FDIs from China and other countries in sensitive sectors.

Those national initiatives are complemented by the recent EU framework for screening investments that was accepted on November 20, 2018. This framework enables the European Commission and EU member states to screen FDIs on the grounds of security of public order. The criteria for this screening are as follows: (i) effects on critical infrastructure, (ii) security of supply of critical inputs, (iii) access to or ability to control sensitive information, (iv) effects on critical technology, and (v) the full or partial control of the investing company by the government of a non-EU country. The focus on European strategic interests was made very clear in the speech of EU Commission president Jean-Claude Junckcr at the launch of the agreement. Juncker declared that "Europe must always defend its strategic interests and that is precisely what this new framework will help us to do. This is what I mean when I say that we are not naïve free traders. We need scrutiny over purchases by foreign companies that target Europe's strategic assets."

A third and final similarity relates to *unity in diversity* in economic policy. The EU and China have the ambition to be a dominant player in their part of the world. China has become the driver of regional economic integration among East Asian countries based on a growing economic interdependence, intensifying cooperation, and intricate value chains (De Grauwe and Zhang, 2016). The EU plays a similar role in the European context. The European and East Asian intra-regional networks are both characterized by strong differences in the economic performance of the countries involved. Those internal differences have to be taken into account when deciding on a common economic policy. In the EU governance model, this is an important and delicate issue that requires a coming together of national and EU-wide interests.

We mentioned earlier that trade and investment links with China vary considerably across EU countries. All other things equal, the EU values a relationship with China that benefits most, if not all, member states. It supports initiatives that close the gap in economic performance between them. For example, the EU is eager to participate in the financing of BRI projects that improve the infrastucture of lagging EU economies. But it opposes Chinese BRI-related loan schemes that substantially raise the debt burden of weaker member states. And it considers the recently concluded BRI agreements between China and the member states, such as Italy, Greece, Hungary, and Portugal, as a Chinese strategy to undermine a common EU approach.

3.3.   *The broader context of EU strategic interests*

The speech of Xi Jinping states that countries should view their own interest in a broader context and refrain from pursuing their interests at the expense of others. How does this fit in with EU policy?

The EU policy is aimed at obtaining foreign market access for European firms. In doing so, it does not take a mercantilist approach that attempts to maximize exports and minimize imports at the expense of its trading partners. In fact, the EU accepts moderate trade deficits with major trading partners.

The goal of the European strategy is to establish sustainable long-term relationships with as many trading partners as follows. Therefore, the EU is hesitant to get involved in trade conflicts between non-EU countries. Currently, the big challenge is not to get sucked in a trade war between China and the US. When given the choice, Europe wants to maintain good relations with both countries. In any case, it prefers to be neutral if a full-fledged trade war between the global superpowers would erupt. A recent paper by Herrero points out that such a neutral position would minizime the economic costs for the EU (Herrero, 2019).

3.4. *Reciprocity*

A key feature of EU trade and investment policy is the principle of reciprocity. The EU is willing to grant access to its own market provided that its companies obtain access to the market of its trading partners. Or to put in President Xi Jinping words, Europe will keep its doors wide open. It hopes that other countries will also keep their doors open to European investors.

For Europe, adherence to reciprocity is crucial. It guarantees the willingness of trading partners to achieve a balance between benefits and commitments. And it helps to build a common level playing field in multilateral and bilateral relationships. On the multilateral stage, the EU links the reciprocity principle to the application of WTO rules on market access, intellectual property, subsidies, and non-discimination. The EU commits itself to follow those rules and expects its trading partners to do the same. In bilateral trade and investment relations, the EU views reciprocity as a fundamental principle in the conclusion of free trade agreements and in the screening of FDI.

In its relations with China, the EU is worried about the access to the Chinese market and the requirement that foreign companies are obliged to share their technological know-how with Chinese partners. There is also a growing concern about the resurgent state dominance, which has begun to diminish the role of the market and private firms in China's economy. Xi Jinping's economic policy favors companies owned by or related to the Chinese government through subsidies, credit facilities, and other forms of support (see Lardy, 2019).

From the European perspective, this government support distorts competition in the Chinese and the global market.

4.   Toward a Closer Collaboration between the EU and China

The first part of this chapter gave an overview of the trade and investments links between the EU and China. The second section identified several similarities in the views on trade and investment relations. An important message from this analysis is that both sides could benefit from more collaboration. But such closer relationship is not evident because the strategic objectives of the EU and China may clash, leading to a conflict that may spin out of control.

4.1.   *Opportunities for closer cooperation*

The main priority for the coming years is to take advantage of the existing opportunities for stronger bilateral trade and investment ties while avoiding excessive protection and a technology conflict.

Fueled by massive investments in innovation, China is making big strides forward in the development of new technologies while Europe seems to be lagging behind. The risk of a strategic clash is real when both sides pursue active policies to support their own high-tech companies. The probability of a conflict can be reduced by seizing the opportunities for collaboration in the development and implementation of new technologies. Chinese companies are very apt in valorizing novel technologies in products that sell well. Europe performs well in the fine-tuning of existing technologies. This complementary technological profile opens perspectives for enhanced cooperation in the technological area.

Technological cooperation is particularly valuable in areas where China and Europe face common societal challenges. Health care is one example because European and Chinese societies are rapidly graying. Technology is equally important for addressing environmental pollution and the impact of climate change.

As explained in Section 2, sectoral trade flows between China and the EU are characterized by two-way trade in goods and intra-industry specialization. With China rapidly moving up the technological ladder, the scope for intra-industry trade is likely to widen to a larger number of industries. This creates opportunities for further growth in bilateral trade flows.

Trade between the EU and China is not limited to the exports and imports of goods. Services matter as well. In 2016, trade in services accounts for less than 15% of trade in goods. With the Chinese economic structure gradually evolving toward a service-driven economy, the prospect for an expansion of trade in services looks promising.

Finally, both sides have nothing to gain from a closing of the home market for direct investment by foreign companies. The mutual sensitivity about FDI can be mitigated by clear rules and participation in joint investment projects.

4.2. *The next steps forward*

We see several ways to turn the current uncertainty into opportunities for enhanced cooperation. As the EU and China both have a stake in open markets, a first step is to work together in strengthening the multilateral trading system. This involves a commitment from each side to consistently apply WTO rules. It also implies joint initiatives against trading partners that undermine the multilateral system and do not play according to the multilateral rules.

A second step is to bring the negotiations on the EU–China Investment Agreement to a fruitful end. Those negotiations started in 2014 and the last (19th) round took place on October 29–30, 2018.

According to the website of the European Parliament, the objectives of the agreement are to (European Parliament, 2019):

(1) "provide for new opportunities and improved conditions for access to the EU and Chinese markets for Chinese and EU investors;

(2) address key challenges of the regulatory environment, including those related to transparency, licensing and authorization procedures;

(3) establish guarantees regarding the treatment of EU investors in China and of Chinese investors in the EU, including protection

against unfair and inequitable treatment, unlawful discrimination and unhindered transfer of capital and payments linked to an investment;

(4) ensure a level playing field by pursuing, *inter alia*, non-discrimination as a general principle subject to a limited number of clearly defined situations and

(5) support sustainable development initiatives by encouraging responsible investment and promoting core environmental and labor standards."

A successful agreement on this ambitious agenda would undoubtedly take away many of the hurdles that plague EU–China investment relations today. But it is remains to be seen whether this is possible in the light of the growing European sensitivity about the recent evolution in FDI flows from and to China.

The EU–China Investment Agreement is embedded in the broader EU–China 2020 Strategic Agenda for Cooperation adopted by both parties in 2014. This agenda bundles a wide range of domains for cooperation that go far beyond international trade and investment (European External Action Service, 2019). Few initiatives have been realized so far and 2020 is approaching fast. We may be wrong, but we do not expect any breakthroughs in the coming months.

During the last EU–China summit meeting in April 2019, both partners committed to a deepening of their strategic partnership beyond 2020. By their next summit meeting at the latest, a new agenda beyond 2020 would be defined.

In our opinion, a cornerstone of this agreement should be the negotiation of a deep and comprehensive EU–China FTA.[8] This would revitalize the bilateral relationship. Both sides have extensive experience in concluding FTAs. We mentioned earlier that the EU signed far-reaching FTA's with several of China's neighboring countries incorporating topics such as trade in goods and services, public procurement, regulatory issues, and sustainable development.

---

[8]The 2020 Strategic Cooperation Agenda mentions a deep and comprehensive FTA, once the conditions are right, as a longer term perspective.

Likewise, China negotiated a comprehensive FTA with Switzerland, one of the EU's closest neighbors. Why would a similar agreement between the EU and China be out of reach?

The trade focus in the new cooperation agreement does not exclude other issues. Cooperation should include a wider range of topics while avoiding the broad catalogue of ideas contained in the 2020 Cooperation Agenda. Fertile areas for collaboration could involve technological research, environmental pollution, climate change, and health.

A third and final issue is related to the BRI. Since several European countries are directly or indirectly affected, enhanced cooperation between the EU and China in BRI-related projects seems logical and desirable. The creation of the China–EU Co-investment Fund in 2017 represents an important decision in this regard. This fund is expected to provide €500 million, jointly backed by the European Investment Fund and the Silk Road Fund, to support equity investment. It will help to further develop synergies between the China's BRI and the Investment Plan for Europe, the so-called Juncker Plan.

5. Conclusion

This chapter discusses the EU–China international trade and investment relationship taking a European point of view. We present data about bilateral trade and investment flows between the EU and China. We identify the strategic objectives that define the EU's position toward China. And we offer some suggestions about moving forward in the bilateral relationship.

Looking at the data first, we find that bilateral trade and investment flows are substantial and growing over time. China has become the EU's second largest trading partner and the EU is China's most important trading partner. Exports and imports of goods expanded strongly in recent years involving both intra- and inter-industry trade. China has made big strides forward as an exporter of high-tech products, resulting in a significant bilateral trade surplus with respect to the EU. Likewise, Chinese FDI in the EU has grown spectacularly, in particular in sensitive sectors as transport, utilities and infrastructure and information and communication technology. By contrast, direct investments of EU companies in China have stagnated and even declined since 2012.

A comparison between the strategic interests of China and the EU reveals several similarities. Both trading partners have a common interest in supporting globalization and avoiding trade wars. They strive for a strong position in technology- and knowledge-intensive sectors. They do not want to be overly dependent on foreign companies for their critical technology and infrastructure. And they prefer that international trade and FDI strengthen internal cohesion by benefiting as many regions and/or member countries as possible.

Further expanding and deepening the EU–China relationship requires focusing on common interests that benefit both partners. This is not evident. Strategic interests of the EU and China may clash, especially when high-tech and critical infrastructure are involved. Moreover, the current tide of rising protectionism around the globe does not favor new multilateral and bilateral initiatives. Building trust and seizing the opportunities for mutually beneficial cooperation remain the main challenges for EU–China relations in the coming years.

What does Europe expect from its trading partners? The EU requires them to support and adhere to the multilateral rules on market access, subsidies, and intellectual property. It sees reciprocity in bilateral relations as a condition for opening its market for foreign companies. Furthermore, the EU is a proponent of deep and comprehensive FTA's that go beyond trade liberalization in goods by incorporating services and agriculture, public procurement, regulatory cooperation, and sustainable development.

How can the EU and China make progress in building a closer relationship in the next couple of years? A starting point is to complete what has been left undone. After nearly 5 years of negotiations, it is time to successfully conclude the EU–China Investment Agreement. A second priority is to revitalize the China–EU Cooperation Agreement for the period beyond 2020. This agreement could involve an FTA and enhanced cooperation in innovation, health care, and environmental sustainability. In addition, both parties could join forces in the financing and implementation of Belt and Road projects that affect EU member states. Last but not least, China and the EU could work together in strengthening the multilateral system by committing to open markets and globalization.

References

Abraham, F. (2017). "Revisiting Trade Integration in Uncertain Times. A European Perspective," *CDR*, **5**(2), 31–44.

Abraham, F. and Van Hove, J. (2016). "David versus Goliath? Smaller European Exporting Firms Facing Asian Competition on Global Markets," *Scottish Journal of Political Economy*, **63**(1), 18–40.

De Grauwe, P. and Zhang, Z. (2016). "The Rise of China and Regional Integration in East Asia," *Scottish Journal of Political Economy*, **63**(1), 1–6.

European Parliament (2019). "A Balanced and Progressive Trade Policy to Harness Globalization," http://www.europarl.europa.eu/legislative-train/theme-a-balanced-and-progressive-trade-policy-to-harness-globalisation/file-eu-china-investment-agreement.

European External Action Service (2019). "EU–China 2020 Strategic Agenda for Cooperation," http://eeas.europa.eu/archives/delegations/china/documents/news/20131123.pdf.

Herrero, A. G. (2019). "Europe in the Midst of CHINA-US Strategic Economic Competition: What Are the European Union's Option," Bruegel Working Paper, Issue 03, April 2019.

Lardy, N. R. (2019). *The State Strikes Back: The End of Economic Reform in China*, Peterson Institute for International Economics, 164 pp.

Matto, A. and Staiger, R. W. (2019). "Trade Wars: What Do They Mean? Why Are They Happening Now? What Are the Costs?" NBER Working Paper No. 25762, April 2019.

Chapter 3

Trade Interdependence and Comparative Advantage Between China and Countries Along the Belt and Road

Chengyu Que[*,¶], Fan Zhang[†,‖], Junru Zhang[‡,**]
and Zhaoyong Zhang[§,††]

Dalian Jiaotong University, China
†Dongbei University of Finance & Economics, China
‡School of Accounting, Curtin Business School, Curtin University, Australia
§School of Business & Law, Edith Cowan University, Australia
¶qcy@djtu.edu.cn
‖zhxiaofan@126.com
***alex.zhang1@curtin.edu.au*
††Zhaoyong.zhang@ecu.edu.au

The objective of this study is to provide an empirical assessment of the dynamic trade relationship and interdependence between China and the countries along the Belt and Road (B&R) routes during the period 2000–2017. The results show that the changes in the comparative advantage explain the remarkable growth of China's bilateral trade with these countries. There is also evidence confirming the existence of structural complementarity in trade between China and the B&R countries both at the industry level and at the country level. This has important implications for the absorptive capacity of the products from China and its trade partners along the B&R routes and provides benefits for further trade expansion. The study also shows that industrial upgrading will promote future trade development among these countries.

1. Introduction

The Belt and Road Initiative (BRI), launched in 2013, has provoked both enthusiasm and skepticism around the world. While the international community acknowledges China's remarkable economic growth and development and its increasing economic influence, it is also increasingly concerned with the likely threat and challenge posed by a rising China from both economic and geopolitical perspectives. From the perspective of China, the BRI is its solution to cope with the complex and dynamic international environment and for the purpose of building high-quality, sustainable, risk-resistant, reasonably priced, and inclusive infrastructure, which will result in "high-quality" growth for every country along the routes. As the biggest trader and second largest economy in the world, several studies have documented that China's economic strategy has a significant impact on its trading partners and the world economic system. For instance, Yu (2017) found that the Asian Infrastructure Investment Bank facilitates and accelerates infrastructure improvement in the Belt and Road (B&R) Region, and the BRI provides a channel for Chinese companies to invest in other countries through leveraging in infrastructure development. Kaczmarski (2017) suggests that BRI has improved the trading relationships jointly with the Eurasian Economic Union since early 2010s in their respective impactful endeavours. However, the prospect of the BRI is closely associated with the conditions of economic interactions between the concerned countries. For trade relations, the Belt and Road countries (BRCs) each have a diverse trade pattern with China, reflecting their level of economic development and trade interdependence.

As a grand open cooperation framework, the BRI covers an extensive range of countries with different culture and diversified trade structures. On the imports side, manufactured products are the most important products in most countries' imports. On the exports side, some BRCs mainly export primary commodities. For instance, fuels accounted for a share of 59.0% in Russia's total exports and 67.3% in its exports to China. The trade volume between Russia and China has expanded over 14 times from 2000 to 2017, exceeding their respective trade growth rate during the same period. Other countries concentrate more on the exports of manufactured products, showing similar structures with China. As observed in South Korea, manufactured goods accounted for 89.3% in total exports and 91.8% in exports to China in 2017. Despite the similarity in trade structure, the South Korea–China trade still increased over six-fold during 2000–2017. Similarly, the trade between other BRCs and China grew impressively and accounted for an increasing portion of each other's total trade. The assessment of their comparative advantage suggests that there exists trade complementarity in certain product categories, which explains the rapid bilateral trade growth with China and implies the basis for future development.

The purpose of this study is to assess the overall interdependence of foreign trade between China and the BRCs during the period 2000–2017, and examine the dynamics in comparative advantage and development of trade relationship between China and the BRCs. As highlighted by some existing studies (see Huang, 2016; Liu and Dunford, 2016) that the manufactured products play a critical role in the development of bilateral trade relations between China and the BRCs, we will also investigate the impact of industrial upgrading on their comparative advantage and future trade relations with China.

The rest of this chapter is structured as follows. Section 2 presents an overview of the BRI. Section 3 studies the trade patterns of China and the BRCs and compares the similarities and differences in their trade structures. Section 4 assesses the interdependence between China and the BRCs and the bilateral trade development. In Section 5, we examine the structural change of trade relations between China and the BRCs by classifying the commodities into five main groups and nine sub-groups according to their technological complexity and their revealed comparative advantage during the sample period in 1990–2017. The final section concludes with some policy implications.

2.   Overview of the Belt and Road Initiative

During President Xi Jinping's visits to Kazakhstan and Indonesia in 2013, he introduced the concept of the Silk Road Economic Belt and 21st Century Maritime Silk Road, which was later known as the

Belt and Road Initiative. Geographically, the overland "Belt" has three routes: the first route is from northwest and northeast China through Central Asia and Russia to Europe and the Baltic Sea; the second route starts from northwest China and passes through Central and Western Asia into the Persian Gulf and the Mediterranean Sea; and the third route is from southwest China, through the Indo-China Peninsula, to the Indian Ocean. The "Maritime Silk Road" has two routes: one crosses the South China Sea through the Chinese coastal ports, then Southeast Asia, the Indian Ocean, Africa, and Europe, while the other crosses the South China Sea extending in the South Pacific Ocean. On the overall framework, China summarizes the BRI into six corridors, six means of communication, multiple countries, and multiple ports. The six corridors include the New Eurasian Land Bridge Economic Corridor, the China–Mongolia–Russia Economic Corridor, the China–Central Asia–West Asia Economic Corridor, the China–Indo-China Peninsula Economic Corridor, the China–Pakistan Economic Corridor, and the Bangladesh–China–India–Myanmar Economic Corridor. The six means of communication are rail, highways, seagoing transport, aviation, pipeline, and aerospace integrated information network, which comprise the main targets of infrastructure connectivity.[1] "Multiple countries" refer to the emphasis on cooperating with demonstrative countries along the Belt and Road. "Multiple ports" mean linking key cities and ports along the B&R to enable reliable sea passages. The grand initiative has developed into a major Chinese foreign cooperation framework, which facilitates and accelerates effectively the cooperation in infrastructure construction, trade, investment, finance, cultural, and social areas along the B&R, with various sources of funding such as Asian Infrastructure Investment Bank (AIIB) and Silk Road Fund. At the current stage, infrastructure construction is the core activity of BRI, including international transportation systems, energy pipelines, and supporting financial facilities. Based

---

[1]Office of the Leading Group for the Belt and Road Initiative, 2017.

on the available data, the number of Chinese contracted projects in 123 BRCs have increased sharply from 5,890 in 2013 to 12,505 in 2016. India exceeded all other countries with 1,154 contracts in 2016.

By March 2019, there were 130 BRCs listed on the Chinese official website,[2] including 43 in Asia, 37 in Africa, 24 in Europe, 16 in Latin America and the Caribbean, and 10 in Oceania. China has signed cooperation documents with 122 countries under the framework of BRI. The full list of countries is given in Appendix A. The AIIB currently has a total of 93 members and approved 34 projects since its commencement in 2016. Eleven new projects were approved in 2018 worth US$7.3 billion. Appendix B shows the list of AIIB-approved projects in 2017 and 2018. As the second largest economy and the biggest trader in the world, China's BRI has caused both enthusiasm and skepticism across the world. Essentially, according to the Chinese government (NDRC, 2015), the aim of the BRI is "to promote the connectivity of Asian, European and African continents and their adjacent seas, establish and strengthen partnerships among the countries along the Belt and Road, set up all-dimensional, multi-tiered and composite connectivity networks, and realize diversified, independent, balanced and sustainable development in these countries". Through the connectivities of policy coordination, facilities, unimpeded trade, financial integration, and people-to-people relationships, it is believed that the BRI will help to align and coordinate the developmental strategies of the countries along the Belt and Road, enhance mutual understanding and trust, and enable them to live in harmony, peace, and prosperity (Huang, 2016). The BRI is China's ambitious economic vision of the opening up of and cooperation among the BRCs, manifesting China's strategic response to the changing global environment and for promoting balanced domestic growth and industrial upgrading. However, the reality is that China and BRCs vary substantially in terms of economic size, growth rate,

---

[2]BELT AND ROAD PORTAL, URL://www.yidaiyilu.gov.cn/.

Table 1.   Indicators of BRCs' and China's economies, 2017.

Country	GDP US$ billion	GDP growth (%)	Trade/GDP ratio (%)	Population (million)
The largest five BRCs				
India	2,600.8	6.7	41.1	1,339.2
Russia	1,577.5	1.5	46.7	144.5
South Korea	1,530.8	3.1	80.8	51.5
Australia	1,323.4	2.0	41.9	24.6
Indonesia	1,015.5	5.1	39.5	264.0
The smallest five BRCs				
Vanuatu	0.9	4.5	—	0.3
Samoa	0.8	2.7	77.6	0.2
Dominica	0.5	−9.5	113.7	0.1
Tonga	0.4	2.7	95.7	0.1
Micronesia	0.3	3.2	—	0.1
China	12,237.7	6.9	37.8	1,386.4

Source: World Bank World Development Indicators (2018).

business environment, and market openness.[3] The delivery of this initiative largely depends on the characteristics of the trade and investment.

Table 1 presents the major economic indicators for China and the BRCs in 2017. As shown in Table 1, China, with a population of over 1.3 billion and GDP of US$12.2 trillion in 2017, is a giant for most BRCs. Chinese GDP in 2017 accounted for 15.2% of the world total GDP, compared with the combined GDP of 24.7% of the world total for the 128 BRCs. India, Indonesia, South Korea, Russia, and Australia have reached a trillion-level GDP. Excluding these five countries, the rest of the Belt and Road countries have a share of 14.7% of the world GDP, even lower than that of China.

---

[3]Zhang and Ow (1996) and Qin *et al.* (2016) report that the diversity between China and the ASEAN countries in terms of economic size, system, and development strategy at the country level is both a "pushing" force to stimulating the development of bilateral trade relations between these economies and a "resisting" force to limiting the trade expansion. The implementation of the BRI will offer opportunities for new complementarities and further reshape the patterns of trade, investment, and infrastructure development in the region and the BRCs.

China has maintained average annual nearly double-digit real GDP growth over the last three decades. Despite the recent slow-down, this pace is described by the World Bank as "the fastest sustained expansion by a major economy in history" and more than 800 million people were lifted out of poverty. The magnificent GDP growth has made China one of the most dynamic economies in the world. Among the B&R countries, the average annual GDP growth rate was about 3.6% during the period. In 2017, there were 12 countries that experienced negative growth, 71 countries grew faster than the previous year, and 15 countries grew faster than China. Interestingly, these 15 countries performed quite differently compared with their past trends. For instance, Romania was the only developed country that has had a growth rate faster than that in China for the first time in 20 years. Libya experienced a growth rate of 26.7%, which is the highest among all the countries. However, Libya had suffered from economic recession for many years and is now still recovering from the war. Likewise, the developed countries in Europe are still recovering from the shock of global financial crisis, while countries in Asia are relatively more dynamic.

Despite occasional external disputes, China has maintained peace and stability for decades, which has led to the relatively steady economic growth. However, BRCs are rather diverse. In Asia, there are some countries with stable development such as South Korea and Singapore, whereas other countries are constantly disturbed by domestic political changes. Countries like Afghanistan, Iraq, and Syria are still suffering from domestic turmoil and military conflicts. According to the Ease of Doing Business Rank[4] by the World Bank, China ranked 46th out of 190 countries. A high ease of doing business ranking means the country's regulatory environment is more conducive to the starting and operation of a local firm. Thirty-two BRCs scored better than China. New Zealand, Singapore, South Korea, Georgia, and Macedonia held the top five spots among the BRCs.

China is the world's second largest economy, next to the United States, and the largest trading nation in goods with the world's

---

[4]World Bank (2018), URL://www.doingbusiness.org/en/rankings.

largest foreign exchange reserves of US$3.2 trillion. However, China's market is still relatively less open compared with most countries along the B&R, despite its multistage market-oriented economic reforms. During the period 1978–2006, China's trade/GDP ratio increased from 9.7% to 64.5%. Then it declined after the global financial crisis in 2008 and reached 37.8% in 2017. This ratio is much lower than the average ratio of 89.3% among the 110 BRCs. In particular, seven BRCs are less trade dependent than China, while 44 countries have a trade/GDP ratio above the average value, and 36 countries have ratio over 100%.

3. Trade Patterns of China and BRCs

In 2017, China's total trade volume amounted to over US$4.1 trillion, of which China exported US$2.3 trillion in goods and services while importing US$1.8 trillion (IMF, 2018). Over the past several decades, China has run large trade surpluses. China trades mostly with the Asian countries. In 2017, 48.1% of Chinese exports and 56.2% of Chinese imports were conducted with its Asian neighboring countries. In the same year, North America accounted for 20.2% of China's total exports and 9.5% of China's total imports, Europe accounted for 18.8% of China's total exports and 17.8% of China's imports, and the combined shares of Africa, Latin America, and Oceania in China's total exports and imports are, respectively, 12.1% and 16.9%.

As indicated in Table 2, China is more dependent on advanced economies. In 2017, over 65% of its exports and 59% of imports were with advanced economies. The United States, Japan, South Korea, and Euro area countries are the main outlet for Chinese exports. From 1980 to 1993, Japan was the largest export destination for China. Since then, the US market has become increasingly important, and overtaken Japan to be China's largest export market. After the establishment of diplomatic relations between China and South Korea in 1992, South Korea started to take a steady proportion in China's total exports. In 2017, the share of the US, Japan,

Table 2. China and representative BRCs: Trade distribution by major destination (%).

		Advanced economies			Emerging and dev. countries	
		Total	Euro area	USA	Total	China
Exports						
China	2000	83.9	12.3	20.9	15.9	—
	2010	70.3	14.9	18.0	29.4	—
	2017	65.2	11.6	19.0	34.5	—
South Korea	2000	66.1	10.3	22.0	33.8	10.7
	2010	42.0	8.2	10.7	57.9	25.1
	2017	42.0	6.3	12.2	58.0	25.1
India	2000	64.6	18.0	21.4	31.8	1.8
	2010	44.9	14.6	10.6	53.5	7.9
	2017	48.5	12.7	15.6	50.8	4.2
Singapore	2000	59.7	11.0	17.3	40.2	3.9
	2010	45.4	7.5	6.5	54.6	10.4
	2017	45.9	7.5	6.6	54.1	14.7
Russia	2000	63.8	38.0	7.8	36.1	5.1
	2010	56.4	37.8	3.2	30.0	5.3
	2017	52.5	33.9	3.1	47.3	10.9
Poland	2000	85.7	64.7	3.2	14.1	0.3
	2010	80.7	57.5	1.8	19.2	1.0
	2017	81.4	57.0	2.6	18.4	1.0
Australia	2000	69.8	7.8	9.8	28.5	5.7
	2010	51.3	4.1	4.0	47.9	25.1
	2017	43.7	3.0	3.9	53.7	33.4
Imports						
China	2000	75.3	10.7	9.9	21.5	—
	2010	59.0	10.2	7.3	31.9	—
	2017	59.4	10.7	8.5	33.2	—
South Korea	2000	60.7	7.7	18.3	39.2	8.0
	2010	46.7	7.6	9.5	53.3	16.8
	2017	46.2	9.8	10.5	53.6	20.5
India	2000	49.1	14.3	6.3	27.4	2.9
	2010	39.2	9.6	5.5	60.2	11.8
	2017	35.9	8.3	5.4	62.3	16.2

(*Continued*)

Table 2. (*Continued*)

		Advanced economies			Emerging and dev. countries	
		Total	Euro area	USA	Total	China
Singapore	2000	59.0	9.1	15.1	40.6	5.3
	2010	47.7	9.5	11.5	52.3	10.8
	2017	49.1	9.8	10.7	50.9	13.9
Russia	2000	49.7	29.8	8.0	49.3	2.8
	2010	54.5	32.3	4.5	43.6	18.0
	2017	49.9	29.3	5.6	50.1	21.2
Poland	2000	79.5	55.0	4.4	20.4	2.8
	2010	75.8	57.5	1.7	23.8	5.2
	2017	74.8	58.2	2.0	25.0	7.9
Australia	2000	73.2	14.2	20.1	26.3	7.8
	2010	54.2	13.5	11.1	42.8	18.7
	2017	49.6	13.0	10.8	44.9	22.9

Source: Calculated from Direction of Trade Statistics data provided by IMF.

and South Korea was 19%, 6%, and 5%, respectively. The Euro area countries together accounted for 12% of Chinese exports. Import-wise, these countries also hold the largest proportion. A remarkable change is the reduction of trade reliance on advanced economies in China's trade structure. In 2000, about 83.9% of its total exports and 75.3% of its imports were conducted with advanced economies, while both were reduced to 65.3% and 59.4%, respectively, in 2017. In contrast, the share of emerging and developing economies increased from 15.9% to 34.5% in export and from 21.5% to 33.3% in import during the same period.

It is also interesting to note the structural changes of China's trade pattern at the product level. During the period in 1995–2017, the share of primary products in China's total exports has decreased dramatically while manufactured products have dominated. Table 3 shows the export and import structures of China and representative BRCs for the selected years of 2000–2017. As seen from Table 3, 93.4% of China's exports were manufactured products in 2017, of which machinery and transport equipment accounted

Table 3. China and representative BRCs: Trade structure by main categories (%).

SITC		All food items (0 + 1 + 22 + 4)	Agricultural raw materials (2 − (22 + 27 + 28))	Fuels (3)	Ores and metals (27 + 28 + 68)	Manufactured goods ((5 to 8) − (667 + 68))	of which		
							Chemi prod. (5)	Other manuf. ((6 + 8) − (667 + 68))	Machi. and equip. (7)
Exports									
China	2000	5.4	1.1	3.2	1.8	88.0	4.9	50.0	33.1
	2010	2.8	0.5	1.7	1.4	93.4	5.5	38.4	49.5
	2017	3.0	0.4	1.6	1.2	93.4	6.2	39.2	48.0
South Korea	2000	1.5	0.9	5.4	1.2	89.9	8.0	23.7	58.2
	2010	1.1	0.9	7.0	2.1	88.3	10.5	21.2	56.6
	2017	1.3	0.9	6.3	2.0	89.3	12.3	17.9	59.1
India	2000	12.8	1.3	3.4	2.8	61.4	10.3	43.9	7.3
	2010	8.3	2.2	17.2	7.6	52.4	10.7	27.2	14.5
	2017	11.7	1.5	12.2	4.0	61.0	13.9	30.5	16.6
Singapore	2000	2.1	0.5	9.5	1.0	82.9	7.7	10.0	65.2
	2010	2.0	0.3	18.2	1.1	70.9	13.4	9.4	48.1
	2017	2.6	0.5	14.6	0.9	72.3	15.3	10.3	46.7
Russia	2000	1.2	3.1	50.6	9.1	24.1	6.0	11.9	6.2
	2010	1.9	1.9	65.6	5.5	13.5	4.0	6.7	2.8
	2017	5.7	2.5	59.0	6.4	20.4	5.2	9.7	5.5
Poland	2000	7.9	1.8	5.2	5.0	80.1	6.7	39.0	34.4
	2010	10.8	1.2	4.2	4.7	79.1	8.6	28.9	41.6
	2017	13.0	1.2	2.5	3.2	79.8	9.6	32.5	37.6

(*Continued*)

Table 3. (*Continued*)

SITC		All food items (0 + 1 + 22 + 4)	Agricultural raw materials (2 − (22 + 27 + 28))	Fuels (3)	Ores and metals (27 + 28 + 68)	Manufactured goods ((5 to 8) − (667 + 68))	Chemi prod. (5)	of which	
								Other manuf. ((6 + 8) − (667 + 68))	Machi. and equip. (7)
Australia	2000	19.7	6.1	20.9	19.6	23.2	4.3	7.6	11.3
	2010	10.6	2.5	28.9	34.0	12.8	3.5	4.0	5.3
	2017	14.1	3.0	30.2	31.5	11.6	2.9	3.8	4.9
Imports									
China	2000	4.0	4.7	9.2	5.9	75.1	13.4	20.9	40.8
	2010	4.3	3.5	13.5	13.3	63.7	10.7	13.7	39.4
	2017	6.2	3.7	13.5	10.6	62.0	10.4	11.6	40.0
South Korea	2000	4.8	3.2	23.7	5.5	61.3	8.4	16.1	36.8
	2010	4.5	1.7	28.8	8.1	56.4	9.6	17.8	29.0
	2017	5.9	1.4	23.0	6.7	62.5	10.1	18.2	34.1
India	2000	5.9	3.7	19.6	5.4	45.6	11.5	12.0	22.1
	2010	3.9	1.6	28.4	4.9	41.7	10.9	10.3	20.5
	2017	5.5	1.8	27.4	5.5	44.2	11.0	10.7	22.5
Singapore	2000	3.5	0.5	11.0	1.7	80.2	5.4	14.6	60.2
	2010	3.4	0.4	24.9	1.7	64.0	6.7	12.2	45.1
	2017	3.9	0.4	23.1	1.4	64.3	7.9	12.6	43.8

(*Continued*)

Table 3. (*Continued*)

SITC	All food items (0+1+22+4)	Agricultural raw materials (2-(22+27+28))	Fuels (3)	Ores and metals (27+28+68)	Manufactured goods ((5 to 8)-(667+68))	of which		
						Chemi prod. (5)	Other manuf. ((6+8)-(667+68))	Machi. and equip. (7)
Russia								
2000	18.7	2.1	3.5	3.9	67.1	11.0	27.7	28.3
2010	15.1	1.0	1.7	1.7	78.7	12.7	25.6	40.3
2017	12.2	1.0	1.1	2.3	81.8	13.7	26.1	42.0
Poland								
2000	6.0	2.0	11.0	2.9	77.9	14.1	26.6	37.2
2010	7.6	1.8	10.9	3.3	74.2	14.2	25.5	34.5
2017	8.8	1.5	7.4	3.6	77.1	14.4	27.4	35.3
Australia								
2000	4.5	1.4	8.2	1.1	82.6	11.2	25.3	46.0
2010	5.3	0.7	13.6	1.7	72.4	10.7	22.8	39.0
2017	6.5	0.7	10.3	1.4	73.7	10.0	23.0	40.8

Source: Calculated from Merchandise Trade Matrix data provided by UNCTAD (2018).

for 48.0%, and other manufactured goods and chemical products accounted for 39.2% and 6.2%, respectively. The increasing proportion of machinery and transport equipment might be influenced by China's structural optimization of foreign trade and its industrial upgrading program toward the higher end of the global value chain. Accompanying this transformation is the change of China's exports pattern from the traditional resource-intensive and labor-intensive products to technology-intensive and capital-intensive manufactures. Similarly, the import structure of China is also dominated by manufactured products. The imports of manufactured goods showed a slight downward trend, dropped from 75.1% in 2000 to 62.0% in 2017, which mainly come from the decrease in other manufactured goods, while the imports of fuels, ores, and metals increased from 15.1% to 24.1% during the same period.

Along the B&R, the total trade volume of 128 countries was US$11.5 trillion in 2017, which accounted for 32.5% of the world's total trade and over half were contributed by Asian countries. There were large disparities between countries, with the top 25% of these countries making up 83.9% of the aggregated volume of 128 countries. The top 10 countries in terms of total trade are South Korea, India, Singapore, Russia, Poland, United Arab Emirates, Thailand, Australia, Vietnam, and Malaysia, whose combined trade volume took up over 50% of BRCs' total trade. In particular, South Korea's total exports amounted to US$562.0 billion, which was the largest, followed by Singapore and Russia with the export value of US$366.1 billion and 355.7 billion, respectively. On the import side, South Korea has maintained the leading position with a total value of US$472.6 billion, followed by India and Singapore. Turning to overall trade structures, Table 3 shows that manufactured products and fuels made up a relatively larger proportion in export distribution. As for imports, manufactured commodities, especially machinery and transport equipment, were the main imports.

The total trade volume of 43 Asian countries totalled over US$6.6 trillion in 2017, of which countries in Southeastern Asia accounted for 38.6%, Western Asia for 27.3%, Eastern Asia for 15.8%,

Southern Asia for 16.4%, and Central Asia for 1.9%. The imports of all these countries are predominantly manufactured goods. By contrast, their export structures are more diversified. In Central Asia and Western Asia, the Commonwealth of Independent States (CIS) mainly export resource-based primary goods. Among these countries, the exports of Kazakhstan, Turkmenistan, and Azerbaijan concentrate more on fuels. Similarly, the oil-rich Persian Gulf nations also heavily rely on fuels exports, which constitute the principal source of world oil supply. However, other countries in this area, like Turkey, lay more emphasis on the exports of manufactured commodities. In Southern Asia, countries represented by India mainly export manufactured products, especially labor-intensive goods. In Southeastern Asia, ASEAN countries have redirected their trade increasingly from the developed countries to the emerging and developing economies, especially to the Chinese market, during the period 2000–2017. For ASEAN countries, manufactured goods are predominant in export structure except for Brunei, Laos, and Myanmar. Brunei traditionally depends on the export of fuels, which made up 91.8% of its total exports in 2017. Laos and Myanmar distribute some proportion to primary products. In Eastern Asia lies the largest trader along the B&R, which is South Korea. As indicated in Table 3, its exports depend heavily on manufacturing. In 2017, manufactured goods accounted for 89.3% of its total exports, of which 59.1% was machinery and transport equipment. During 2000–2017, both export and import of South Korea have shifted from advanced economies to emerging and developing economies.

In Europe, the combined trade volume of 24 BRCs was about US$3.1 trillion in 2017. Most of these countries trade predominantly with the industrial countries. In particular, the 14 EU members and six Balkan countries trade mostly with countries in the Euro area, with manufactured goods taking the largest proportion in both exports and imports. However, the case is different for CIS countries. Belarus, Moldova, and Ukraine rely more on emerging and developing trade partners, while Russia has a relatively even distribution. As shown in Table 3, manufactured goods are also dominating their imports. On the export side, primary goods account for an important proportion in these countries, and fuels have become the main exports of Russia.

The exports of African countries along the B&R consist of mainly primary commodities. The export of fuels is particularly important for those countries endowed with rich oil resources, such as Algeria, Angola, Chad, Congo (the Republic of), Gabon, Libya, and Nigeria. In 2017, only four countries' exports are predominated by manufactured commodities, including Egypt, Morocco, South Africa, and Tunisia. For other countries, the share of primary goods ranged from 49.1% for Guinea to 100% for Angola. While on the import side, manufactured products generally account for the majority of these countries' total imports.

Among the eight BRCs in Oceania, Australia and New Zealand are the two largest trading countries, with the former alone accounting for 82.7% of the region's total trade in 2017. Excluding Australia, New Zealand's share would jump to 82.0%. As seen in Table 3, primary products represent the majority of Australia's top exports, while manufactured products represent the top goods imports. In 2017, 61.6% of Australia's exports were fuels, ores, and metals, and manufactured commodities accounted for 73.7% of its total imports, of which machinery and transport equipment accounted for 40.8%, other manufactured goods for 23.0%, and chemical products for 10.0%. New Zealand has a similar pattern in import structure while exporting a larger share of food items than Australia. There has been a shift in both countries' trade patterns from the traditional European and North American markets largely to the East and Southeast Asian region since the 1980s. By 2018, Australia's trade with Asia accounted for 66% of Australia's total trade, with China being Australia's largest two-way goods and services trading partner and accounting for 31% of Australia's total exports and 18% of its imports.

In Latin America and the Caribbean, about 60% of these BRCs' trade was with Chile, Venezuela, and Ecuador in 2017. These three countries share similar concentration on manufactured commodities in imports and primary commodities in exports. Chile distributes a larger share in ores and metals export while Ecuador exports mainly food items. Venezuela, as an OPEC member, has been dependent on the export of fuels since 1995. As for other economies in this area, there are some manufacturing exporters, but their trade volume is relatively low.

To compare the overall trade structures of China and the BRCs, one notable feature is the extensive similarity of the import structures. Manufactured products are predominantly the main products for all countries' imports, of which other manufactured goods, machinery, and transport equipment account for a substantial proportion. The dependence on manufactured products can also be observed in many BRCs' export structure. In contrast, a number of countries along the B&R export largely the primary commodities, revealing some complementary features compared with China.

4. Trade Interdependence

The growth of bilateral trade between China and BRCs is remarkable. From 2000 to 2008, BRCs' total trade with China increased from US$134.6 billion to 910.0 billion at an average annual rate of roughly 27%. After the 2008 global financial crisis, the bilateral trade maintained an overall upward trend, although the growth rate had ups and downs. The total trade reached US$1564.1 billion in 2017, more than 11 times that of 2000. During 2000–2017, BRCs' exports to China increased from US$72.5 billion to US$680.8 billion, while their imports from China increased from US$62.1 billion to US$883.3 billion. In addition, bilateral trade between China and BRCs has both increased. The trade with China accounted for 14% of BRCs' total trade in 2017, which has grown from 4% in 2000. During this period, BRCs' share in China's total trade also increased from 28% to 38%. In particular, BRCs shipped 4.4% of their total exports to China and sourced 4.1% of their total imports from China in 2000. By 2017, the shares of such exports and imports further increased to 12.0% and 15.2%, respectively.

Table 4. Trade interdependence between China and representative BRCs (%).

	Exports to China as % of total Chinese imports			Imports from China as % of total Chinese exports		
	2000	2010	2017	2000	2010	2017
Asia	25.51	25.55	25.25	17.37	21.05	26.35
South Korea	8.20	8.38	7.71	5.13	4.53	4.25
Europe	3.09	2.35	3.19	2.86	6.10	5.36
Russia	2.32	1.42	2.12	0.38	2.47	2.11
Africa	1.36	3.08	2.52	1.35	2.75	2.93
South Africa	0.15	0.58	0.47	0.42	0.77	0.71
Latin America	0.47	1.71	1.50	0.70	1.32	1.42
Chile	0.40	1.24	1.04	0.38	0.63	0.68
Oceania	1.77	4.09	4.71	2.61	2.78	2.68
Australia	1.60	3.81	4.19	2.25	2.43	2.29

	Exports to China as % of the exporting country's total exports			Imports from China as % of the importing country's total imports		
	2000	2010	2017	2000	2010	2017
Asia	5.86	12.48	14.15	5.17	12.50	17.93
South Korea	10.72	25.05	25.12	7.98	9.44	11.50
Europe	1.88	2.50	3.75	1.84	7.36	8.07
Russia	5.09	5.30	10.94	2.81	4.37	5.24
Africa	2.29	9.16	12.16	2.86	9.50	13.88
South Africa	1.53	8.89	9.59	3.74	4.18	5.22
Latin America	1.30	11.77	15.43	2.35	10.67	16.90
Chile	4.69	24.36	27.58	5.13	5.69	6.48
Oceania	5.16	22.97	31.29	7.41	18.02	22.12
Australia	5.67	25.09	33.45	7.82	8.77	10.07

Source: Calculated from Direction of Trade Statistics data provided by IMF.

Table 4 reports the trade interdependence between China and selected BRCs. As it can be seen in Table 4, BRCs' trade dependence on China is relatively heavier than the latter's dependence on them during 2000–2017. Among many BRCs, China remains as an important trade partner in imports rather than in exports. However, only a few countries show exceptions, including South Korea, Australia, and Chile, where their exports are more dependent on China. For instance, South Korea, as the largest trader, has a relatively high dependence on China. The share of South Korea's exports to China grew from 10.7% in 2000 to 25.1% in 2017, accounting for 8.2% and 7.71% of the Chinese total imports, respectively. Also, the share of South Korea's imports from China grew from 8.0% to 20.5% during this period, accounting for 5.1% and 4.3% of Chinese total exports, respectively.

Overall, the trade interdependence between China and most BRCs are greater than before. The resource-rich countries like Russia, Saudi Arabia, and Australia have an expanding bilateral trade with China, which facilitated by their relatively complementary trade structures with China. However, trade with China also increased substantially in countries whose trade structures are quite similar to that of China, such as South Korea, India, Singapore, and Poland. These findings are further supported by the analysis of changes in comparative advantage in Section 5.

5.   Changes in Comparative Advantage

While manufactured goods are the major products in the trade of China and the BRCs, the trend is shifting from other manufactured products to machinery and transport equipment. This may suggest that technology is playing a more important role in trade patterns. In addition, the B&R includes both the developed and the developing economies. The conventional method that uses factor endowments as the main determinants of comparative advantage is limited to examine the comparative advantage pattern of China and the BRCs. As such, following the grouping method of Lall (2000), we divide commodities at SITC three-digit level into five main groups and nine sub-groups according to their technological complexity. This classification allows us to investigate the comparative advantage pattern of these countries even if they have similar endowments of labor, capital, or skills. We adopt the "revealed" comparative advantage index introduced by Balassa (1965) to calculate the RCA of China and top 30 traders along the B&R. This sample has a relatively balanced geographical distribution and high representativeness.[5] Table 5 illustrates the revealed comparative advantage of China and the representative BRCs for selected years of 1990–2017.

As shown in Table 5, China has been losing its comparative advantage in primary products and gaining comparative advantage in HT products during 1990–2017, while its comparative advantage in LT products remained at the same level. Looking into sub-categories, the advantage of LT1 and HT1 was more significant in LT and HT. MT3 also developed a comparative advantage over time. These features have determined China's exports structure and are in line with what we observed about the changes in exports composition during the period. The highest RCAs are in LT1, showing China's comparative advantage in manufactured products like textile, garment, and footwear. The relatively highly skilled, low-wage labor force in China is believed to be the main pull factor for FDI inflow, inducing MNEs to shift their operations to China. The labor-intensive processes have benefited China substantially for its export growth in this industry. The growing RCAs in MT3 and HT1 indicate China's push up the technology ladder. However, it is notable that electronic and electrical products in HT1 have labor-intensive final assemblies. The growth in this category is also related to the undertaking of the labor-intensive assembly in the production of technology-intensive commodities. However, the comparative advantage in engineering products and the changes of RCAs in other sub-category manifest a certain extent of quality upgrade in Chinese exports during the period.

Focusing on the BRCs, Saudi Arabia, Russia, Australia, and other resource-rich countries have sustained high RCAs in primary products during 1990–2017, which suggests that their export structures are resource-intensive products. The complementarity between these countries and China supports large-scale bilateral trade and further expansion. As for South Korea, India, Singapore, and other

---

[5]The list of the 30 countries' RCA indices is not reported but is available upon request.

Table 5. China and representative BRCs: Indices of revealed comparative advantage, 1990–2017.

		PP	RB			LT			MT				HT		
			Total	RB1	RB2	Total	LT1	LT2	Total	MT1	MT2	MT3	Total	HT1	HT2
China	1990	1.40	0.68	0.59	0.78	2.45	3.91	1.20	0.63	0.63	0.69	0.60	0.35	0.34	0.35
	2000	0.53	0.63	0.62	0.65	2.81	3.91	1.92	0.66	0.18	0.87	0.86	0.97	1.11	0.48
	2010	0.19	0.48	0.54	0.45	2.26	3.14	1.71	0.87	0.32	0.73	1.22	1.78	2.29	0.57
	2017	0.24	0.52	0.52	0.00	2.04	2.56	1.72	0.83	0.44	0.78	1.08	1.59	2.04	0.61
South Korea	1990	0.23	0.42	0.45	0.40	2.33	3.39	1.43	0.91	0.36	1.54	0.94	1.34	1.84	0.23
	2000	0.17	0.81	0.47	1.09	1.11	1.40	0.89	1.12	1.03	1.47	1.02	1.56	1.94	0.21
	2010	0.14	0.78	0.46	0.95	0.69	0.48	0.82	1.57	1.65	1.40	1.62	1.60	1.72	1.29
	2017	0.19	0.84	0.42	0.00	0.63	0.34	0.82	1.37	1.24	1.44	1.41	1.55	1.89	0.80
Singapore	1990	0.37	1.60	0.61	2.54	0.54	0.57	0.52	0.66	0.11	0.69	0.96	2.35	3.19	0.48
	2000	0.16	0.86	0.33	1.28	0.43	0.31	0.53	0.57	0.07	0.75	0.78	2.55	3.14	0.51
	2010	0.10	1.32	0.36	1.82	0.41	0.14	0.58	0.68	0.17	0.89	0.84	2.20	2.78	0.82
	2017	0.11	1.26	0.50	0.00	0.40	0.20	0.52	0.72	0.10	1.13	0.90	1.90	2.37	0.90
India	1990	1.35	1.69	0.24	3.09	2.22	4.22	0.53	0.30	0.18	0.54	0.24	0.29	0.16	0.58
	2000	1.03	2.08	0.42	3.42	2.64	4.53	1.12	0.38	0.23	0.84	0.25	0.22	0.11	0.59
	2010	0.72	2.31	0.45	3.27	1.60	2.29	1.16	0.68	0.57	1.09	0.52	0.37	0.22	0.73
	2017	1.06	1.91	0.56	0.00	1.70	2.39	1.25	0.74	0.61	1.16	0.61	0.39	0.15	0.91
Russia	1990	—	—	0.00	0.00	—	0.00	0.00	—	0.00	0.00	0.00	—	0.00	0.00
	2000	3.54	1.34	0.77	1.80	0.34	0.10	0.53	0.40	0.09	1.05	0.28	0.16	0.07	0.48
	2010	3.14	1.43	0.59	1.87	0.14	0.03	0.20	0.29	0.04	0.88	0.11	0.06	0.06	0.07
	2017	4.02	1.67	0.89	0.00	0.20	0.06	0.29	0.39	0.11	1.14	0.19	0.12	0.09	0.18

(*Continued*)

Table 5. (*Continued*)

		PP	RB			LT			MT				HT		
			Total	RB1	RB2	Total	LT1	LT2	Total	MT1	MT2	MT3	Total	HT1	HT2
Poland	1990	1.77	0.99	0.93	1.04	1.11	0.86	1.31	0.79	0.30	1.21	0.87	0.50	0.49	0.51
	2000	0.80	1.22	1.80	0.75	2.00	1.48	2.41	1.14	1.09	1.05	1.22	0.35	0.37	0.29
	2010	0.58	1.08	2.00	0.60	1.54	0.73	2.05	1.32	1.85	1.03	1.20	0.75	0.90	0.39
	2017	0.70	1.08	1.96	0.00	1.59	0.81	2.09	1.23	1.41	1.15	1.15	0.60	0.63	0.54
Australia	1990	3.43	1.57	0.66	2.46	0.24	0.17	0.30	0.25	0.15	0.35	0.25	0.26	0.21	0.37
	2000	3.41	1.53	0.84	2.08	0.29	0.27	0.30	0.36	0.35	0.39	0.37	0.28	0.19	0.62
	2010	2.48	2.07	0.57	2.85	0.14	0.07	0.18	0.21	0.18	0.24	0.22	0.19	0.10	0.42
	2017	3.68	2.05	0.60	0.00	0.15	0.08	0.19	0.16	0.09	0.19	0.19	0.17	0.10	0.32

Notes: PP: primary products, RB: resource-based manufactured products (RB1: agriculture-based, RB2: other), LT: low-technology manufactured products (LT1: textile, garment, and footwear, LT2: other), MT: medium-technology manufactured products (MT1: automotive, MT2: process, MT3: engineering), HT: high-technology manufactured products (HT1: electronic and electrical, HT2: other).

Source: Calculated from UN Comtrade data provided by UNCTAD (2018).

manufacturing exporters, their RCAs in primary products are relatively low. Compared with China, these countries have similar trade structures, but their comparative advantages differ in certain product groups. This allows them to maintain a dynamic economic relationship with China.

Table 5 indicates that South Korea' comparative advantage has shifted from LT to MT and HT products from the 1990s to the 2000s, which may suggest that South Korea had made substantive technology progress. South Korea once competed with China in the textile industry back in the 1990s. However, after 2000, South Korea's RCA in LT1 completely dropped below that of China, while South Korea's import dependence on China increased sharply. The rapid growth of FDI from South Korea to China in the early 2000s also corroborated this change of comparative advantage. While entering the 2010s, China, benefiting from a relatively low labor-cost, acquired a higher comparative advantage in HT1. The FDI from South Korea to China increased substantially during 2011–2016. However, we are limited to assess the relationship between FDI and the changes in comparative advantage in more depth due to the lack of data on the distribution of sectoral investment. The bilateral trade dependence remained at the same level during this period. The dynamic trade and investment relationship between South Korea and China is directly influenced by the different comparative advantages among products. However, with China's increasing labor-cost and growing emphasis on technology and innovation, future changes of comparative advantage may change the trade structure between these two countries. National policies on technology will be increasingly important in the development of South Korea–China comparative advantage and interdependence.

The comparative advantage of Singapore, the Philippines, Thailand, and Malaysia mainly lies in HT1. By comparison, China's comparative advantage lies mainly in LT products. However, China's RCA index in HT products is increasing and approaching that of Singapore, the Philippines, and Malaysia. Hence, it may suggest a unidirectional ASEAN's dependence on China rather than vice versa.

The European manufacturing exporters generally have a comparative advantage in MT products. MT products require complex technologies, advanced skills, and long learning periods. For developed economies, MT is usually the core of their industry. Taking Poland as example, Table 5 shows that its comparative advantage mainly exists in MT products compared with China, and it directly influences the trade structure and the trade growth of Poland, even though its recent trade interdependence is still low. The comparative advantage pattern between China and the BRCs in Europe suggests the potential of further expansion in trade and FDI. This may further suggest that the interdependence is likely to be strengthened with China's intension to promote Sino-European economic cooperation.

Of the 30 countries in our study, half of them are China's sources of supply for primary products (especially fuels). Their complementary comparative advantage with China has shown evidence to support trade growth and potentials for further cooperation. In comparison, the other countries are trading manufactured products with China as complementarity exists in certain technological categories. We also find that industrial upgrading will be increasingly important for comparative advantage and trade development.

6. Conclusion

Although the economies of the BRCs and China differ significantly in terms of economic size, growth rate, business environment, and market openness, their trade interdependence has been progressing remarkably over the last two decades. It has been shown that the BRCs' trade dependence on China is relatively greater than China's trade dependence on the BRCs. For most of the BRCs, China is more important as a source of supply for their imports than as an outlet for their exports. Given the complementarity of their trade structures and patterns of revealed comparative advantage, it is not surprising to see the growth of trade between China and the BRCs like Russia and Australia. For the BRCs with similar trade structures to China, manufactured products are the main trading products between them. The revealed comparative advantage shows that complementarity exists in certain technological categories. This determines the dynamic nature in their economic interaction. Among the BRCs, the major manufacturing exporters are located in Asia and Europe. It is interesting to note the difference between them. During the period, the changes of revealed comparative advantage in Asian countries are greater than those in European countries, which makes the Asian area a competitive manufacturing cluster. In comparison, there has been fewer changes of the revealed comparative advantage in all categories of European countries. Their comparative advantages mainly exist in medium-technology products.

The changes in comparative advantage during the examined period show a rapid trade growth between China and the BRCs, while the current patterns of revealed comparative advantage provide a basis for further expansion. The long-run trade interdependence is closely associated with the industrial upgrading in China and the BRCs. Under the framework of BRI, bilateral cooperation agreements and active infrastructure construction can contribute to facilitating foreign trade and investment and improving the efficiency of factor allocation. However, whether this can be realized depends on the conditions of economic interactions between the related countries. This remains to be examined in future work.

Appendix A. BRCs Classified by Geographical Location

Geographical location	BRCs
Asia	
Eastern Asia	South Korea, Mongolia
Southeastern Asia	Brunei, Cambodia, Indonesia, Laos, Malaysia, Myanmar, Philippines, Singapore, Thailand*, Timor-Leste, Vietnam
Southern Asia	Afghanistan, Bangladesh, Bhutan*, India*, Iran, Maldives, Nepal, Pakistan, Sri Lanka

(Continued)

(*Continued*)

Geographical location	BRCs
Western Asia	Armenia, Azerbaijan, Bahrain, Georgia, Iraq, Israel*, Jordan*, Kuwait, Lebanon, Oman, Qatar, Saudi Arabia, Syria*, Turkey, United Arab Emirates, Yemen*
Central Asia	Kazakhstan, Kyrgyzstan, Tajikistan, Turkmenistan*, Uzbekistan
Europe	
Eastern Europe	Belarus, Bulgaria, Czechia, Hungary, Poland, Moldova, Romania, Russia, Slovakia, Ukraine
Southern Europe	Albania, Bosnia and Herzegovina, Croatia, Greece, Macedonia, Malta, Montenegro, Portugal, Serbia, Slovenia
Western Europe	Austria
Northern Europe	Estonia, Latvia, Lithuania
Africa	
Northern Africa	Algeria, Egypt, Libya, Morocco, Sudan, Tunisia
Eastern Africa	Burundi, Djibouti, Ethiopia, Kenya, Madagascar, Mozambique, Rwanda, Seychelles, Somalia, South Sudan, Uganda, Tanzania, Zambia, Zimbabwe
Southern Africa	Namibia, South Africa
Western Africa	Cabo Verde, Côte d'Ivoire, Gambia, Ghana, Guinea, Mauritania, Nigeria, Senegal, Sierra Leone, Togo
Middle Africa	Angola, Cameroon, Chad, Congo, Gabon
Latin America and the Caribbean	Antigua and Barbuda, Barbados, Bolivia, Chile, Costa Rica, Dominica, Dominican Republic, Ecuador, El Salvador, Grenada, Guyana, Panama, Suriname, Trinidad and Tobago, Uruguay, Venezuela
Oceania	Australia, Cook Islands, Fiji, Micronesia, New Zealand, Niue, Papua New Guinea, Samoa, Tonga, Vanuatu

Notes: *Countries that have not signed cooperation documents with China. Countries are classified according to United Nations–Statistics Division–Geographic Regions.
Source: YIDAIYILU.GOV.CN.

Appendix B. AIIB-Approved Projects, 2017–2018

Project name	Country	Estimated total project cost (US$ million)	Total AIIB financing (US$ million)
2018			
AIIB Asia ESG Enhanced Credit Managed Portfolio	Regional	500	500
Andhra Pradesh Urban Water Supply & Septage Management Improvement Project	India	570	400
Mandalika Urban and Tourism Infrastructure Project	Indonesia	316.5	248.39
TSKB Sustainable Energy and Infrastructure On-lending Facility	Turkey	200	200
Sustainable Rural Sanitation Services Program	Egypt	694	300
Andhra Pradesh Rural Roads Project	India	666	455
Strategic Irrigation Modernization and Urgent Rehabilitation Project	Indonesia	578	250
Turkey Gas Storage Expansion Project	Turkey	2,375	600
National Investment and Infrastructure Fund Phase I	India	600	100
Madhya Pradesh Rural Connectivity Project	India	502	140
Bangladesh Bhola IPP	Bangladesh	271	60
2017			
Beijing Air Quality Improvement and Coal Replacement Project	China	761.1	250
Oman Broadband Infrastructure Project	Oman	467	—
Bangalore Metro Rail Project — Line R6	India	1,785	335
Metro Manila Flood Management Project	Philippines	500	207.6
IFC Emerging Asia Fund	Emerging Asia	640	150

(Continued)

(*Continued*)

Project name	Country	Estimated total project cost (US$ million)	Total AIIB financing (US$ million)
Transmission System Strengthening Project (Tamil Nadu)	India	303.47	100
Egypt Round II Solar PV Feed-in Tariffs Program: Al Subh Solar Power	Egypt	70–75	17.5–19
Gujarat Rural Roads (MMGSY) Project, Phase I	India	658	329
Nurek Hydropower Rehabilitation Project, Phase I	Tajikistan	350	60
India Infrastructure Fund	India	750	150
Batumi Bypass Road Project	Georgia	315.2	114
Andhra Pradesh 24 × 7 — Power For All	India	571	160
Natural Gas Infrastructure and Efficiency Improvement Project	Bangladesh	453	60
Dam Operational Improvement and Safety Project II	Indonesia	300	125
Regional Infrastructure Development Fund Project	Indonesia	406	100
Trans Anatolian Natural Gas Pipeline Project	Azerbaijan	8,600	600

Source: Asian Infrastructure Investment Bank.

References

Balassa, B. (1965). "Trade Liberalisation and Revealed Comparative Advantage," *The Manchester School*, **33**(2), 99–123.

Huang, Y. (2016). "Understanding China's Belt & Road Initiative: Motivation, Framework and Assessment," *China Economic Review*, **40**, 314–321.

International Monetary Fund (2018). Direction of Trade Statistics, viewed December 2018, ⟨http://data.imf.org/?sk=9D6028D4-F14A-464C-A2F2-59 B2CD424B85&sId=1409151240976⟩.

Kaczmarski, M. (2017). "Two Ways of Influence-Building: The Eurasian Economic Union and the One Belt, One Road Initiative," *Europe-Asia Studies*, **69**(7), 1027–1046.

Lall, S. (2000). "The Technological Structure and Performance of Developing Country Manufactured Exports, 1985–98," *Oxford Development Studies*, **28**(3), 337–369.

Liu, W. and Dunford, M. (2016). "Inclusive Globalization: Unpacking China's Belt and Road Initiative," *Area Development Policy*, **1**(3), 323–340.

National Development and Reform Commission (2015). Vision and Actions on Jointly Building Silk Road Economic Belt and 21st-Century Maritime Silk Road [Press release]. Retrieved from http://beltandroad2019.com/english/n100/2017/0410/c22-45.html.

Office of the Leading Group for the Belt and Road Initiative (2017). *Building the Belt and Road: Concept, Practice and China's Contribution*, Foreign Languages Press, Beijing.

Qin, F. M., Xu, T. and Zhang, Z. Y. (2016). "Economic Cooperation and Interdependence between China and ASEAN: Two to Tango?," in Young-Chan Kim (ed.), *Chinese Global Production Networks in ASEAN*, Springer International Publishing, Switzerland, pp. 255–288, https://www.springer.com/gp/book/9783319242309.

UNCTAD (2018). Merchandise Trade Matrix, viewed January 2019 ⟨https://unctadstat.unctad.org/wds/ReportFolders/reportFolders.aspx⟩.

UN Comtrade Database (2018). Trade Statistics, viewed February 2019 ⟨https://comtrade.un.org/data⟩.

World Bank (2018). World Development Indicators, viewed February 2019 ⟨https://databank.worldbank.org/data/reports.aspx?source=2&series=NY.GDP.MKTP.CD#⟩.

Yu, H. (2017). "Motivation Behind China's 'One Belt, One Road' Initiatives and Establishment of the Asian Infrastructure Investment Bank," *Journal of Contemporary China*, **26**(105), 353–368.

Zhang, Z. Y. and Ow, C. H. (1996). "Trade Interdependence and Foreign Direct Investment between China and ASEAN," *World Development*, **24**(1), 155–170.

Chapter 4

Banking Crises' Impacts on Bilateral Trade

Yifei Mu[*], Qiushu Yin[†], and Antonio Alleyne[‡,§]

*Dongbei University of Finance and Economics,
Dalian, P. R. China
†Jilin University, Institute of Economics,
Changchun, P. R. China
‡Department of Economics, The University of the West Indies,
Cave Hill Campus, St. Michael BB11000, Barbados
§ar.alleyne@hotmail.com

Since the 2007 banking crisis and the onset of the Great Recession, there have been a number of insights linking the Great Recession with the collapse of trade. This study focuses on how banking crises may impact the bilateral trade flows over time, with a special interest in Chinese performance. It disentangles the financial shocks' impacts on trade flows from the perspective of both exporters and importers. This study uses the data covering 223 countries and across 21 years and produces relatively robust results for the correlation between banking crises and bilateral trade flow fluctuations. Most of the impacts from banking crises go through the importers, both on a global and Chinese perspective. Largely, there is a relatively constant negative impact on import for the time periods in advance of the onset of crises. After the crisis is over, the decline in import tends to intensify during the immediate years. However, Chinese imports indicate no lasting impact following a crisis.

1. Introduction

Following the financial crisis, which began in 2007, the global economy contracted greatly. During this time period,[1] the trajectory for

---

[1]According to the United Nations Conference on Trade and Development.

67

world trade flows was on a dramatic decline. For example, European trade flows fell by nearly 19.3% from the fourth quarter of 2008 to the fourth quarter of 2009. The decline in trade flows was not particular to Europe, and Asia's exports to the rest of the world declined by 22.6% and North America's exports fell by 19.3%. Trade within regions seemingly contracted faster than trade between regions. Trade within Europe declined by 25.5%. Trade within Asia decreased at three-quarter the rate, while trade within North America fell by a staggering 28.1%.

This research explores whether such large trade declines may be explained by countries' declining wealth during banking crises. Most trade models predict that a country's trade flow will have a one-to-one expansion or recession[2] according to its GDP. However, during the 2008 crisis, trade declined more sharply than GDP. For example, during the years 2008 and 2009, the US export/GDP ratio decreased from 13% to 11.4%, while the import/GDP ratio decreased from 18% to 14.2%. China, Japan, and Germany's export/GDP ratio decreased from 35%, 17.7%, and 48% down to 26.7%, 12.6%, and 41.9%, respectively, while their import/GDP ratio also decreased from 27.3%, 17.5%, and 41.8% down to 22.3%, 12.3%, and 37%. It seems the change of the trade flow is more aggressive than the change of GDP, therefore contradicting a theorized one-to-one relationship between trade and GDP movements.

As a result of the impact on trade from the Great Recession, there have been a number of research articles that have provided links from the financial crisis to the decline in trade. Manova's (2013) model of trade and financial credit contains expressions of how financial conditions can impact trade. And, from an empirical perspective, research by Chor and Manova (2012) and Amiti and Weinstein (2011) on the 2007 banking crisis suggest that financial shocks impact international trade to a greater extent than they do the domestic market.

---

[2]Work by Kaboski argues the decline will be larger.

While these papers provide insights into the relationship between the Great Recession and the fall in trade, limited insight is known about how, on average, a banking crisis may impact trade flows. Thus, the focus of this research is whether banking crises across time have a similar impact on trade flows as what was observed during the Great Recession. More specifically, the question we investigate is as follows: "Is there a robust correlation between banking crises and trade flow fluctuations? How do banking crises influence exporters and importers?" Two channels are identified to induce the correlation between banking crises and trade flows. One occurs through the producers. Due to credit constraint, producers may have limited access to credit during a banking crisis, causing a fall in production. In addition, if the producers (or agents in the source country) are reliant on credit to finance trade, the impact of a banking crisis on trade can be magnified (Manova, 2013). Another channel is by way of the consumer: it may be the case that trade is financed by the importing country. During a banking crisis, limitations to the destination country's ability to finance imports are likely to arise. And, assuming the tradable sector is composed largely of durable and capital goods, import demand may be relatively more income sensitive.

Alternatively, Anderson and van Wincoop (2004) argued that the disproportionate change in trade is as a result of poorer countries facing higher cost, adding that the financing options (bank, non-bank and private) only add to impact the variation. In this study, we disentangle whether declines in trade are robustly correlated with banking crises and how much of the decline can be "attributed" to the source and destination countries.

As a measure of caution, the number of periods a banking crisis can be expected to impact trade is also investigated. It is unclear how long a financial crisis impacts the availability of credit in an economy. As such, a banking crisis that occurs in one period may impact trade in the years that follow the constrained period. Figure 1 shows the import goods and services as a ratio of GDP for a select group of countries with banking crises with a duration of 2 years. Banking

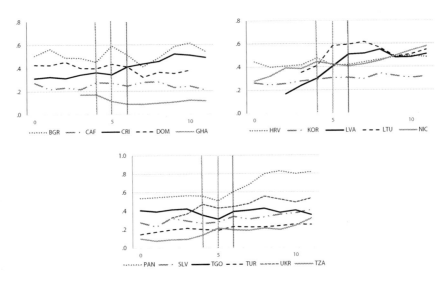

Figure 1. Import goods and services as a ratio of GDP for a select group of countries with banking crises with a duration of 2 years.

Notes: BGR — Bulgaria, CAF — Central African Republic, CRI — Costa Rica, HRV — Croatia, DOM — Dominican Republic, SLV — El Salvador, GHA — Ghana, KOR — Republic of Korea , LVA — Latvia, LTU — Lithuania, NIC — Nicaragua, PAN — Panama, TZA — United Republic of Tanzania, TGO — Togo, TUR — Turkey, UKR — Ukraine.

crises start at some time between two red lines and end between the second red line and blue line. There is no obvious discernible trend present before or after the crisis. One present object is to estimate, on average, what is and how large the influence on the trade is, due to banking crises spanning different time periods.

The remainder of the study is organized as follows. Section 2 provides a concise review of the relevant literature. Section 3 introduces the empirical model used in the analysis, which is followed by an assessment of the data and its sources in Section 4. Section 5 presents the empirical findings and discusses the implications of the findings. The final section provides some concluding remarks.

2. Literature Review

Several studies use high-frequency data to analyze the influence of the 2007 Great Recession on trade. Levchenko *et al.* (2010) used disaggregated quarterly US trade data and found a great collapse in trade, especially for intermediate goods. Industries with a larger reduction in domestic output also had larger reductions in trade. Chor and Manova (2012) used monthly US import data to analyze the trade collapse after the 2007 crisis, finding that credit constraints had an impact on trade and that the exports of industries with a larger dependence on the external financial market will tend to be more vulnerable and sensitive to financial shocks. Similarly, Bricongne *et al.* (2012) use monthly data from France and also found out that the firms depending more on external financing were more affected in the recent global crisis. Lacovone and Zavacka (2009) use annual data to show that the industries which are more dependent on financial markets in more financially developed countries saw larger declines in trade during the banking crisis.

There is also some theoretical research on financial shocks and their effects on trade. Eaton *et al.* (2008) developed a variation of the model from Melitz (2003), which embeds an idiosyncratic shock for each firm and the importer's market, as well as a common shock for importer's market. This leads to the changes in productivity of export and foreign market entry. When the Pareto distribution is utilized in this model, trade volumes depend not only on the cost, economy size, inward, and outward multilateral resistances but also on the variance of the entry shock, the variance of the demand shock, and the covariance of the two. In the context of banking crises, shocks arise from the financial sectors. In Monova (2013), she adds a credit constraint to the exporter, embedding the probability of default into the cut-off productivity of export. In this model, the financial condition of one country could impact both the extensive and intensive margins of trade. Limited financial development will lead to fewer foreign markets and lower the aggregate trade volume.

There is also some research focusing on a trade collapse through other channels. Alessandria *et al.* (2010) study the correlation between a trade decline and inventory adjustment. Gopinath *et al.* (2012) study the trade price fluctuation in different categories of goods during the 2007 banking crisis.

3. Model

3.1. *Background context*

Assume a world with N countries with varieties of goods. All consumers have identical constant-elasticity-of-substitution (CES) preference[3]:

$$U_j = \left[\sum_{i=1}^{N} C_{ij}^{\frac{\sigma-1}{\sigma}} \right]^{\frac{\sigma}{\sigma-1}} , \quad j = 1, \ldots, N, \tag{1}$$

where U_j is the utility of consumers in country j, C_{ij} is the goods consumed by people in country j imported from country i, σ is the elasticity of substitution, and $\sigma > 1$.[4] Maximizing utility subject to a budget constraint can explain the demand for the goods consumed in country j import from country i, X_{ij}:

$$X_{ij} = \left(\frac{p_i \tau_{ij}}{P_j} \right)^{1-\sigma} Y_j. \tag{2}$$

Here, p_i is the price of the good's price sold within the importer i. τ_{ij} is the trade cost for goods shipped from country i to country j. Y_j is the GDP of country j, and P_j is the CES price index such that:

$$P_j = \left[\sum_{j=1}^{N} (p_i \tau_{ij})^{1-\sigma} \right]^{1/(1-\sigma)} . \tag{3}$$

---

[3]See Anderson and van Wincoop (2003) for details.
[4]The preference exhibits "love of variety".

Assume firms maximize profit and all markets are clear, we can write an expression for bilateral trade flow as

$$X_{ij} = \left(\frac{\tau_{ij}}{\Pi_i P_j}\right)^{1-\sigma} \left(\frac{Y_i Y_j}{Y_w}\right), \qquad (4)$$

where Y_w is the world gross GDP and

$$\Pi_i = \left[\sum_{j=1}^{N}(\theta_j/\tau_{ij}^{\sigma-1})P_j^{1-\sigma}\right]^{1/(1-\sigma)}, \qquad (5)$$

$$P_j = \left[\sum_{i=1}^{N}(\theta_i/\tau_{ij}^{\sigma-1})\Pi_i^{1-\sigma}\right]^{1/(1-\sigma)}, \qquad (6)$$

where θ_i denotes Y_i/Y_w, that is, the share of country i's GDP relative to the world. Π_i and P_j are usually known as multilateral resistance. Π_i is the outward multilateral resistance which measures how difficult it is for country i to export goods relative to the rest of the world. P_j is the inward multilateral resistance that measures how difficult it is for country j to import goods relative to the rest of the world. Anderson and van Wincoop (2003) noticed that when the influence on trade is estimated, it is critical to include both inward and outward multilateral resistances into the regression.

Taking the natural log of both side of Equation (4), we get

$$\ln(X_{ij}) = (1-\sigma)[\ln(\tau_{ij}) - \ln(\Pi_i) - \ln(P_j)]$$
$$+ \ln(Y_i) + \ln(Y_j) - \ln(Y_w). \qquad (7)$$

This measures the relation between trade flow on the left side and trade cost, multilateral resistance, and GDP on the right side within some time period. When the trade crosses some time periods, Equation (7) can be presented as

$$\ln(X_{ijt}) = (1-\sigma)[\ln(\tau_{ijt}) - \ln(\Pi_{it}) - \ln(P_{jt})]$$
$$+ \ln(Y_{it}) + \ln(Y_{tj}) - \ln(Y_{wt}). \qquad (8)$$

3.2.   Unilateral effects estimation with one-stage model

In Anderson and van Wincoop (2003) detail of various trade costs, the authors argued that costs financed through the banking system will be impacted by a banking crisis. However, the impact is likely to be asymmetric across importers and exporters. When a financial shock (BC) is treated as a unilateral effect, the trade cost (τ_{ijt}) can be written in the following exponential form:

$$\tau_{ijt} = d_{ij}e^{\gamma_1 \cdot g_{ij} + \gamma_2 \cdot BC_{it} + \gamma_3 \cdot BC_{jt} + u_{ijt}}. \tag{9}$$

Baier and Bergstrand (2009) introduced the method to linearly approximate the multilateral resistances. For the bilateral trade costs, those resistance terms in Equations (5) and (6) can be presented as

$$\ln(\Pi_{it}) = \left[\sum_{j=1}^{N} \theta_j \ln(\tau_{ijt}) - \frac{1}{2} \sum_{k=1}^{N} \sum_{m=1}^{N} \theta_k \theta_m \ln(\tau_{km}) \right], \tag{10}$$

$$\ln(P_{jt}) = \left[\sum_{i=1}^{N} \theta_i \ln(\tau_{ijt}) - \frac{1}{2} \sum_{k=1}^{N} \sum_{m=1}^{N} \theta_k \theta_m \ln(\tau_{kmt}) \right]. \tag{11}$$

Plugging in Equations (10) and (11) back into Equation (8) and taking the linear expansion to $\ln(\tau_{ijt})$ and combining with Equation (9), the regression changes to

$$\ln(X_{ijt}) = \alpha_0 + \beta_1 \widetilde{\ln(d_{ij})} + \beta_2 \widetilde{\text{border}}_{ij} + \beta_3 \widetilde{\text{lang}}_{ij} + \delta_1 BC_{it}$$

$$+ \delta_2 BC_{jt} + \varphi_1 \ln(Y_{it}) + \varphi_2 \ln(Y_{tj}) + \varphi_3 \ln(Y_{wt})$$

$$+ \beta_1 \overline{\ln(d_{ij})} + \beta_2 \overline{\text{border}}_{ij} + \beta_3 \overline{\text{lang}}_{ij} + \varepsilon_{ijt}, \tag{12}$$

where

$$\widetilde{\ln(d_{ij})} = \ln(d_{ij}) - \sum_{j=1}^{N} \theta_j \ln(d_{ij}) - \sum_{i=1}^{N} \theta_i \ln(d_{ij}), \tag{13}$$

$$\widetilde{\text{border}}_{ij} = \text{border}_{ij} - \sum_{j=1}^{N} \theta_j \text{border}_{ij} - \sum_{i=1}^{N} \theta_i \text{border}_{ij}, \tag{14}$$

$$\widetilde{\text{lang}_{ij}} = \text{lang}_{ij} - \sum_{j=1}^{N} \theta_j \text{lang}_{ij} - \sum_{i=1}^{N} \theta_i \text{lang}_{ij}, \tag{15}$$

$$\overline{\ln(d_{ij})} = \sum_{k=1}^{N} \sum_{m=1}^{N} \theta_k \theta_m \ln(d_{km}), \tag{16}$$

$$\overline{\text{border}_{ij}} = \sum_{k=1}^{N} \sum_{m=1}^{N} \theta_k \theta_m \text{border}_{ij}, \tag{17}$$

$$\overline{\text{lang}_{ij}} = \sum_{k=1}^{N} \sum_{m=1}^{N} \theta_k \theta_m \text{lang}_{ij}, \tag{18}$$

where border_{ij} measures contiguity and lang_{ij} measures common language between countries. $\overline{\ln(d_{ij})}$, $\overline{\text{border}_{ij}}$, and $\overline{\text{lang}_{ij}}$ are world averages of the distance, contiguity, and language, which are constant within each year. The use of year fixed effect will absorb all individual effects of these variables, including $\ln(Y_{wt})$, which represents the annual world GDP. ε_{ijt} represents the estimated error term, which is assumed to be equal to the unexplained residuals (u_{ijt}) for the population. The regression will be estimated as follows:

$$\ln(X_{ijt}) = \alpha_0 + \beta_1 \widetilde{\ln(d_{ij})} + \beta_2 \widetilde{\text{border}_{ij}} + \beta_3 \widetilde{\text{lang}_{ij}} + \delta_1 BC$$
$$+ \delta_2 BC_{jt} + \varphi_1 \ln(Y_{it}) + \varphi_2 \ln(Y_{tj}) + \varphi_3 I_t + \varepsilon_{ijt}. \tag{19}$$

Here, I_t is year fixed effect.

3.3. *Unilateral effects estimation with a two-stage model*

The effects of a unilateral financial shock, i.e. a shock to the banking system within the confines of one trading partner, are also assumed to be completely captured by multilateral resistance. Hence, we can construct a two-stage approach to assess such a situation.

In the first stage, the model expressed in Equation (8) without BC_{ijt} using exporter-year fixed effects (I_{it}) and importer-year fixed

effects (I_{jt}). The coefficients of I_{it} and I_{jt} will capture all information about multilateral resistance and other information that are
unchanged in the country-year dimension.

Estimated coefficients of I_{it} capture the impacts of unilateral
financial shock specific to exporters, importers' share-weighted GDP
bilateral effects,[5] some of the average trade cost cross the world,[6]
exporter's GDP, and a portion of the world's GDP. The second stage
regression is as follows:

coefficients from $I_{it} - \ln(GDP_{it})$

$$= \alpha_0 + \delta_1 BC_{it} + \beta \sum_{j=1}^{N} \theta_j \tau_{ijt} + \varphi_1 I_t + \varepsilon_{ijt}. \qquad (20)$$

Expressed in Equation (8), the theory tells us that the coefficient
of the log exporter's GDP becomes negative (-1) when moved to
the left side. The exporter–importer fixed effects (I_t) will capture
all bilateral impacting effects, world-average trade cost effects, and
world GDP for year t.

Similarly, for importer-year fixed effect, the following second-stage
regression is used:

coefficients from $I_{jt} - \ln(GDP_{jt})$

$$= \alpha_0 + \delta_1 BC_{jt} + \beta \sum_{i=1}^{N} \theta_i \tau_{ijt} + \varphi_1 I_t + \varepsilon_{ijt}. \qquad (21)$$

4. Data Source

4.1. *Value of trade*

The value of total bilateral trade for 223 countries for the years 1995–
2016 is taken from the CEPII database. It is reported as HS92 6 digit
and aggregated at the country level. The value is measured in thou-

---

[5]Which is $\sum_{j=1}^{N} \theta_j \tau_{ijt}$.
[6]Which is $\frac{1}{2} \sum_{k=1}^{N} \sum_{m=1}^{N} \theta_k \theta_m \tau_{ijt}$.

sands of US dollars in the current year. The inflation of the currency will be captured by importer-year fixed effect and exporter-year fixed effect.

4.2. *Geography data*

Geography data are used to measure traditional trade cost. The study uses the bilateral value of the distance, contiguity, and common official language as measures of the traditional trade cost. The data are from the CEPII database.[7] Both contiguity and common language are dummy variables. Contiguity is equal to unity if two trade partners share the common border, and zero otherwise. Common official language is equal to unity if two trade partners use the same official language and zero otherwise. CEPII provides both simple great circle distance and the population-weighted distance between countries. This study uses the population-weighted distance.[8]

4.3. *Banking crises data*

The Leaven and Valencia banking crises database provides annual banking crisis data for the period 1976–2014, which included 151 occurrences of systemic banking crises across individual countries. According to Leaven and Valencia (2012), a banking crisis is defined as systemic if two conditions are met:

(1) Significant signs of financial distress in the banking system (as indicated by significant bank runs, losses in the banking system, and/or bank liquidations).
(2) Significant banking policy intervention measures in response to significant losses in the banking system.

Here, significant bank runs indicate a 5% or greater drop in deposits within 1 month during the time period.

---

[7]The data can be obtained from http://www.cepii.fr/CEPII/en/bdd_modele/bdd.asp.
[8]Using other measurements of distance will yield similar results.

For policy interventions in the banking sector to be significant, at least three out of the following six measures must have been used:

(1) extensive liquidity support (5% of deposits and liabilities to non-residents),
(2) bank restructuring gross costs (at least 3% of GDP),
(3) significant bank nationalizations,
(4) significant guarantees put in place,
(5) significant asset purchases (at least 5% of GDP), and
(6) deposit freezes and/or bank holidays.

In this study, the crises lag variables capture the impact on trade for the years after the banking crises. In order to clarify whether bilateral trade is impacted pre-crisis, forward crises variables will also be used. In total, the panel dataset contains trade vales, banking, and geographic data for 223 countries for the period 1995–2016. See Table 1 for a further description of the data.

Table 1. Summary statistics.

	No of obs.	Mean	Std. dev.	Min.	Max
Trade (1,000 current US dollars)	497,673	4.7E+05	4.6E+06	1	4.6E+08
Country's GDP (exporter, 1,000 current US dollars)	497,673	4.4E+08	1.5E+09	1.1E+04	1.9E+10
Distance	497,673	7325.5	4476.8	10.5	19904.5
Contiguity	497,673	0.022	0.147	0	1
Common language	497,673	0.155	0.362	0	1
Banking crisis (exporter)	497,673	0.071	0.257	0	1
One country of the trade pair has banking crisis	497,673	0.121	0.326	0	1
Both countries of the trade pair have banking crises	497,673	0.006	0.080	0	1
One country of the trade pair ever had banking crisis	497,673	0.653	0.476	0	1
Both countries of the trade pair ever had banking crises	497,673	0.067	0.250	0	1

5. Results

As mentioned previously, there are likely two channels through which a banking crisis can influence trade flows. If the banking crisis's impacts occur through the producer channel,[9] one could expect that there should be a negative shock arising via exports, with the recovery extending well after the crisis is over. If the impacts occur through consumers, there should be a negative shock on trade flow at (current) time t of the importer's banking crisis. It is likely that negative effects may follow after an importer's banking crises has ended. Similarly, there might be significant influences prior to the crisis.

5.1. *One-stage results for exporters and importers*

In Table 2, the dependent variable is the log of the trade value. The log of the distance between country pairs is represented by ln(distance). Contiguity and common language are the binary variables for two trade partners who share the same border or the same official language. GDP-share-weighted log of distance, contiguity and common language is the linear approximation of the inward multilateral resistance and outward multilateral resistance. Variables "Banking crisis (exporter)" and "Banking crisis (importer)" are dichotomous variables representing an exporter and importer banking crisis, respectively, at year t. The variable N years forward of exporter/importer represents the binary variables for the nth year prior to the beginning of the exporter/importer banking crisis, which means these variables are equal to unity if the current year is n years before the beginning of a banking crisis for the exporter/importer. The variables N years lag of exporter/importer are the binary variables for the nth year's lag from the exporter/importer banking crisis ending-year, which means these variables are equal to unity if the current year is n years after the ending of a banking crisis for the exporter/importer. We also include dichotomous measures if the exporter country or importer country had at least one banking crisis during the period 1995–2016. Additionally, a binary distinction was

---

[9] As mentioned in Manova (2013).

Table 2. Linear approximations for multilateral resistance and banking crises with the country ever experiencing a banking crisis.

	Dep var ln(trade)				
Ln(distance) minus importers' share weighted log-distance minus exporters' share weighted log-distance	−0.789*** (0.00358)	−0.790*** (0.00358)	−0.790*** (0.00358)	−0.790*** (0.00358)	−0.791*** (0.00358)
Common language minus importers' share weighted language minus exporters' share language	0.844*** (0.0101)	0.844*** (0.0101)	0.844*** (0.0101)	0.844*** (0.0101)	0.844*** (0.0101)
Contiguity minus importers' share weighted contiguity minus exporters' share weighted contiguity	1.643*** (0.0221)	1.643*** (0.0221)	1.642*** (0.0221)	1.646*** (0.0221)	1.643*** (0.0221)
Ln(export's GDP)	0.987*** (0.00189)	0.987*** (0.00189)	0.987*** (0.00190)	0.987*** (0.00189)	0.987*** (0.00190)
Ln(import's GDP)	0.821*** (0.00184)	0.821*** (0.00184)	0.820*** (0.00184)	0.821*** (0.00184)	0.820*** (0.00184)
Exporting OECD countries	0.755*** (0.00939)	0.755*** (0.00939)	0.754*** (0.00941)	0.755*** (0.00940)	0.753*** (0.00948)
Importing OECD countries	0.682*** (0.00960)	0.685*** (0.00961)	0.680*** (0.00963)	0.686*** (0.00961)	0.670*** (0.00970)
5 years forward of banking crisis for exporter					0.0194 (0.0375)
4 years forward of banking crisis for exporter					0.00626 (0.0372)

(Continued)

Table 2. (*Continued*)

	Dep var ln(trade)				
3 years forward of banking crisis for exporter					0.0343
					(0.0335)
2 years forward of banking crisis for exporter					0.0435
					(0.0299)
1 year prior to banking crisis					0.0344
					(0.0285)
Banking crisis for exporter	0.0198	0.0236*	0.0275*	0.0213	0.0257*
	(0.0140)	(0.0142)	(0.0143)	(0.0143)	(0.0146)
1 year after to banking crisis		0.0412*	0.0449*	0.0386*	0.0432*
		(0.0229)	(0.0230)	(0.0230)	(0.0231)
2 years lag of banking crisis for exporter		0.0117	0.0150	0.00884	0.0136
		(0.0220)	(0.0221)	(0.0221)	(0.0223)
3 years lag of banking crisis for exporter		0.0180	0.0212	0.0157	0.0203
		(0.0214)	(0.0215)	(0.0215)	(0.0216)
4 years lag of banking crisis for exporter				0.000411	0.00481
				(0.0209)	(0.0210)
5 years lag of banking crisis for exporter				−0.0428**	−0.0380*
				(0.0216)	(0.0217)
5 years forward of banking crisis for importer					0.279***
					(0.0381)
4 years forward of banking crisis for importer					0.275***
					(0.0378)
3 years forward of banking crisis for importer			0.159***		0.162***
			(0.0339)		(0.0340)
2 years forward of banking crisis for importer			0.186***		0.186***
			(0.0304)		(0.0305)

(*Continued*)

Table 2. (*Continued*)

	(1)	(2)	(3)	(4)	(5)
Dep var ln(trade)					
1 year prior to banking crisis			0.159***		0.160***
			(0.0290)		(0.0291)
Banking crisis for importer	−0.0499***	−0.0744***	−0.0554***	−0.0915***	−0.0563***
	(0.0142)	(0.0144)	(0.0146)	(0.0146)	(0.0148)
1 year after to banking crisis		−0.126***	−0.108***	−0.144***	−0.111***
		(0.0232)	(0.0233)	(0.0233)	(0.0234)
2 years lag of banking crisis for importer		−0.150***	−0.134***	−0.167***	−0.134***
		(0.0223)	(0.0223)	(0.0223)	(0.0225)
3 years lag of banking crisis for importer		−0.139***	−0.124***	−0.155***	−0.125***
		(0.0217)	(0.0217)	(0.0218)	(0.0219)
4 years lag of banking crisis for importer				−0.155***	−0.125***
				(0.0211)	(0.0212)
5 years lag of banking crisis for importer				−0.126***	−0.0952***
				(0.0217)	(0.0219)
Exporter ever had a banking crisis	0.288***	0.284***	0.281***	0.286***	0.282***
	(0.00789)	(0.00810)	(0.00829)	(0.00823)	(0.00857)
Importer ever had a banking crisis	0.0558***	0.0742***	0.0588***	0.0875***	0.0591***
	(0.00798)	(0.00836)	(0.00836)	(0.00831)	(0.00863)
Both crisis ever	0.120***	0.122***	0.120***	0.124***	0.120***
	(0.0144)	(0.0144)	(0.0144)	(0.0144)	(0.0144)
Constant	−30.16***	−30.15***	−30.16***	−30.15***	−30.16***
	(0.0550)	(0.0550)	(0.0550)	(0.0550)	(0.0550)
Observations	470,416	470,416	470,416	470,416	470,416
R-squared	0.637	0.637	0.637	0.637	0.638
Year Fixed Effect	YES	YES	YES	YES	YES

Note: Standard errors in parentheses ( ); ***$p < 0.01$, **$p < 0.05$, *$p < 0.10$.

made for the OECD members on account of their unique financing capabilities.

The pattern of how the banking crisis influences trade flows in different time period reveals interesting results. For exporters, irrespective of the time prior to a banking crisis, and at the year of crisis, there appears to be no real significant (negative) influence. However, weak indications of adverse influences can be seen during the fifth year after the crisis period.

For importers, trade flows appear to decrease slightly, on average, as time draws closer to a banking crisis. During the banking crisis period, the negative impact ranges from 5% in the first column with no lag or forward to 9% in the fourth column with 5 years of lag and no forward year assessment. Based on the results in column five, trade flow suffered a significant 5% drop compared to the year prior to the crisis. After a crisis ended, the negative impact intensified to the second lag year followed by a slow recovery turnaround.

For both exporters and importers, if the country ever had experienced a banking crisis, simultaneously or during individual periods, the influence on bilateral trade flows appears positive. From the first column, which does not include any forwards and lags, to the fifth column including five forwards and five lags, countries that ever had a banking crisis tend to experience an increase in trade, with an additional boost when dual crises were ever encountered. Despite adding more information (lags and forward) about the banking crisis into the regression, this coefficient remains relatively constant for both the exporter and the importer. This result supports previous assertions that for a country with prior banking crisis experience is correlated with higher financial development, thus leading to greater trade.

Overall, the results from Table 2 reflect that the time pattern for banking crises seems robust, with countries which ever had experienced a banking crisis tending to trade more.

5.2. *Two-stage results for exporters and importers*

Due to some variations between the results and our initial expectations, this study uses a two-stage model approach to test and confirm the previous outcome. In the first stage, Table 3 uses the same controlling factors as in the previous estimations. Here, the coefficients for exporter-year fixed effect and importer-year fixed effect capture all the non-bilateral effects for importers and exporters. These unilateral effects across time contain the information pertaining to the outward/inward multilateral resistance, exporters/importers' GDP, and effect from financial shocks.

Table 4 uses coefficients of exporter-year fixed effects from Table 3 minus log of exporters' GDP as the dependent variable to analyze the unilateral effect of the banking crisis on exporters' side. Importers' GDP-share-weighted distance, common language, contiguity, and OECD classification are the linear approximations of outward multilateral resistance. Comparing with the exporter's results from Table 2, the results in Table 4 indicate noticeable variations particularly during the crisis period and during the subsequent years.

From column one of Table 4, when the exporter is facing a banking crisis period, there is a positive 5.1% increase in trade value. However, the inclusion of forwards and lags time periods into the equation

Table 3.   First stage of the regression.

Dep. var. ln(trade)	
Ln(distance)	-1.483^{***}
	(0.0035)
Common language	0.879^{***}
	(0.0075)
Contiguity	0.891^{***}
	(0.0195)
Importer-year fixed effect	Yes
Exporter-year fixed effect	Yes
Constant	20.53^{***}
	(0.0303)
R-square	0.751
No. of obs.	497,673

Note: Standard errors in parentheses ( );
$^{***}p < 0.01$, $^{**}p < 0.05$, $^{*}p < 0.10$.

Table 4. Exporter-year fixed effect and exporters' banking crisis.

Coefficient of exporter-year fixed effect from Table 4			
5 years forward of banking crisis for exporter			0.0345***
			(0.0122)
4 years forward of banking crisis for exporter			0.0191
			(0.0121)
3 years forward of banking crisis for exporter			−0.00224
			(0.0110)
2 years forward of banking crisis for exporter			0.00772
			(0.00985)
1 year forward of banking crisis for exporter			0.0187**
			(0.00945)
Banking crisis for exporter	0.0512***	0.0793***	0.0823***
	(0.00467)	(0.00478)	(0.00490)
1 year lag of banking crisis for exporter		0.117***	0.120***
		(0.00781)	(0.00788)
2 years lag of banking crisis for exporter		0.0952***	0.0979***
		(0.00753)	(0.00760)
3 years lag of banking crisis for exporter		0.120***	0.122***
		(0.00735)	(0.00740)
4 years lag of banking crisis for exporter		0.112***	0.114***
		(0.00712)	(0.00718)
5 years lag of banking crisis for exporter		0.0539***	0.0564***
		(0.00740)	(0.00746)
Exporter ever had a banking crisis	0.358***	0.339***	0.337***
	(0.00323)	(0.00330)	(0.00339)
Constant	−6.452***	−7.290***	−7.305***
	(0.198)	(0.200)	(0.201)
Importers' GDP share-weighted OECD	Yes	Yes	Yes
Importers' GDP share-weighted distance	Yes	Yes	Yes
Importers' GDP share-weighted language	Yes	Yes	Yes
Importers' GDP share-weighted contiguity	Yes	Yes	Yes
Observations	356,059	356,059	356,059
R-squared	0.910	0.910	0.910

Note: Standard errors in parentheses ( ); ***$p < 0.01$, **$p < 0.05$, *$p < 0.10$.

suggests an even greater positive impact on trade. With five lagged years (column 3), the impact increases to 7.9%. After similar forwards are added to the analysis, the impact reaches 8.2%, despite having predominantly insignificant forwards. There is a clear pattern with the average effects of around 7%. Though providing a stronger level of evidence, the lagged years show similar findings as in Table 2. At least the four immediate years before a banking crisis forward present no signs of a significant impact. For exporters that ever had a banking crisis, the trade value tends to be slightly above 35% higher than the countries that lack the experienced of a banking crisis.

Overall, the results in Table 4 are small in magnitude; positive impacts during the current year and lag-years are quite small. Whereas, the impact on exporters that experienced a banking crisis is significantly larger and comparable to the findings in Table 2.

Similar to Table 4, Table 5 uses coefficients of importer-year fixed effect from Table 3 minus log of importers' GDP as the dependent variable to analyze the unilateral effect of banking crises from the importers' perspective. Column one shows a 2.5% decline in the period the importer is experiencing a banking crisis. Extending the model to include forward and lag time periods, seen in column three, our analysis indicates a greater decline of 3.4% during the crisis period at time t. Compared to the initial results in Table 2, Table 5 confirms all importer findings at a marginally lesser magnitude of impact.

The second column of Table 5 also exhibits an increasing decline until the second years following the crisis period. For the second year lag period, the decline in trade is around 9.8%; the highest level of any lag year. By the fifth and final lag year in our assessment, the decline in trade is around 4.1%. This pattern remains after the inclusive of five forwards and lags; however, the magnitude of the trend is again slightly reduced. The forward time period also exhibits a dominantly positive trend, which is similar to the forward trends in the fifth column of Table 2, excluding the fourth year, but again at lesser impact magnitudes.

For importers that ever had a banking crisis, the results in Table 6 replicate the results in the previous single-stage model. Across all two-stage unilateral results for the importer, countries ever experiencing a banking crisis tend to trade at least an additional

Table 5. Importer-year fixed effect and importers' banking crisis.

	Coefficient of importer-year fixed effect from Table 4		
5 years forward of banking crisis for importer			0.0420***
			(0.0108)
4 years forward of banking crisis for importer			0.0541***
			(0.0107)
3 years forward of banking crisis for importer			−0.0125
			(0.00967)
2 years forward of banking crisis for importer			0.0841***
			(0.00871)
1 year forward of banking crisis for importer			0.0844***
			(0.00835)
Banking crisis for importer	−0.0252***	−0.0445***	−0.0338***
	(0.00412)	(0.00421)	(0.00430)
1 year lag of banking crisis for importer		−0.0753***	−0.0656***
		(0.00682)	(0.00686)
2 years lag of banking crisis for importer		−0.0976***	−0.0884***
		(0.00656)	(0.00660)
3 years lag of banking crisis for importer		−0.0730***	−0.0641***
		(0.00640)	(0.00644)
4 years lag of banking crisis for importer		−0.0676***	−0.0590***
		(0.00621)	(0.00625)
5 years lag of banking crisis for importer		−0.0405***	−0.0321***
		(0.00640)	(0.00644)
Importer ever had a banking crisis	0.131***	0.147***	0.138***
	(0.00235)	(0.00245)	(0.00255)
Constant	−1.031***	−0.613***	−0.680***
	(0.138)	(0.139)	(0.139)
Exporters' GDP share-weighted OECD	Yes	Yes	Yes
Exporters' GDP share-weighted distance	Yes	Yes	Yes
Exporters' GDP share-weighted language	Yes	Yes	Yes
Exporters' GDP share-weighted contiguity	Yes	Yes	Yes
Observations	470,416	470,416	470,416
R-squared	0.914	0.914	0.914

Note: Standard errors in parentheses ( ); ***$p < 0.01$, **$p < 0.05$, *$p < 0.10$.

Table 6. Linear approximations for multilateral resistance and banking crises with the country ever experiencing a banking crisis with country pair effects (robustness check).

	Dep var ln(trade)					
Ln(export's GDP)	0.517***	0.514***	0.521***	0.521***	0.512***	0.521***
	(0.00116)	(0.00116)	(0.00116)	(0.00116)	(0.00116)	(0.00116)
Ln(import's GDP)	0.764***	0.753***	0.753***	0.753***	0.742***	0.745***
	(0.00103)	(0.00103)	(0.00103)	(0.00103)	(0.00103)	(0.00104)
Exporting OECD countries	1.646***	1.651***	1.643***	1.643***	1.655***	1.646***
	(0.00545)	(0.00546)	(0.00547)	(0.00546)	(0.00546)	(0.00551)
Importing OECD countries	0.318***	0.352***	0.354***	0.354***	0.379***	0.381***
	(0.00546)	(0.00547)	(0.00547)	(0.00546)	(0.00546)	(0.00551)
5 years forward of banking crisis for exporter						-0.125***
						(0.0200)
4 years forward of banking crisis for exporter						-0.148***
						(0.0198)
3 years forward of banking crisis for exporter			-0.139***			-0.166***
			(0.0179)			(0.0180)
2 years forward of banking crisis for exporter			-0.201***			-0.225***
			(0.0159)			(0.0160)
1 year prior to banking crisis			-0.144***			-0.166***
			(0.0153)			(0.0153)
Banking crisis for exporter	0.0186**	0.0125	-0.0106		0.00753	-0.0302***
	(0.00757)	(0.00766)	(0.00775)		(0.00773)	(0.00791)
1 year after to banking crisis	-0.0178	-0.0178	-0.0385***		-0.0240*	-0.0584***
	(0.0126)	(0.0126)	(0.0126)		(0.0126)	(0.0127)

(Continued)

Table 6. (Continued)

Dep var ln(trade)

2 years lag of banking crisis for exporter		−0.0391*** (0.0121)	−0.0575*** (0.0122)	−0.0456*** (0.0122)	−0.0781*** (0.0123)
3 years lag of banking crisis for exporter		−0.0267** (0.0118)	−0.0434*** (0.0119)	−0.0325*** (0.0119)	−0.0628*** (0.0119)
4 years lag of banking crisis for exporter				−0.00924 (0.0115)	−0.0371*** (0.0116)
5 years lag of banking crisis for exporter				−0.0682*** (0.0119)	−0.0949*** (0.0120)
5 years forward of banking crisis for importer					−0.0221 (0.0203)
4 years forward of banking crisis for importer					−0.0285 (0.0202)
3 years forward of banking crisis for importer		−0.0474*** (0.0181)	−0.0514*** (0.0182)		−0.0718*** (0.0182)
2 years forward of banking crisis for importer		−0.00693 (0.0162)	−0.0123 (0.0163)		−0.0303* (0.0164)
1 year prior to banking crisis		−0.0137 (0.0156)	−0.0172 (0.0156)		−0.0343** (0.0157)
Banking crisis for importer	−0.0368*** (0.00773)	−0.0590*** (0.00791)	−0.0589*** (0.00791)	−0.0698*** (0.00788)	−0.0770*** (0.00806)
1 year after to banking crisis		−0.0822*** (0.0128)	−0.0819*** (0.0128)	−0.0962*** (0.0128)	−0.102*** (0.0129)
2 years lag of banking crisis for importer		−0.105*** (0.0123)	−0.105*** (0.0123)	−0.118*** (0.0123)	−0.124*** (0.0124)

(Continued)

Table 6. (*Continued*)

	Dep var ln(trade)				
3 years lag of banking crisis for importer		−0.0959*** (0.0120)	−0.0959*** (0.0120)	−0.109*** (0.0120)	−0.115*** (0.0121)
4 years lag of banking crisis for importer				−0.120*** (0.0116)	−0.126*** (0.0117)
5 years lag of banking crisis for importer				−0.0653*** (0.0120)	−0.0706*** (0.0121)
Exporter ever had a banking crisis	0.823*** (0.00451)	0.828*** (0.00462)	0.838*** (0.00472)	0.833*** (0.00469)	0.849*** (0.00487)
Importer ever had a banking crisis	0.0563*** (0.00453)	0.0825*** (0.00473)	0.0820*** (0.00473)	0.101*** (0.00471)	0.103*** (0.00488)
Both crisis ever	0.799*** (0.00797)	0.805*** (0.00797)	0.805*** (0.00797)	0.810*** (0.00797)	0.810*** (0.00797)
Constant	−19.51*** (0.0466)	−19.33*** (0.0466)	−19.44*** (0.0467)	−19.16*** (0.0465)	−19.32*** (0.0468)
Observations	470,416	470,416	470,416	470,416	470,416
R-squared	0.887	0.887	0.887	0.887	0.887
minus importers' share-weighted distance minus exporters' share-weighted distance	Yes	Yes	Yes	Yes	Yes
minus importers' share-weighted language minus exporters' share language	Yes	Yes	Yes	Yes	Yes
minus importers' share-weighted contiguity minus exporters' share-weighted contiguity	Yes	Yes	Yes	Yes	Yes
Year fixed effect	Yes	Yes	Yes	Yes	Yes
Importer-exporter fixed effect	Yes	Yes	Yes	Yes	Yes

Note: Standard errors in parentheses ( ); ***$p < 0.01$, **$p < 0.05$, *$p < 0.10$.

10%. The above results estimated in the single model are displayed in Table 2. Overall, the results of the two approaches depict similar patterns of impact from a banking crisis.

5.3. *Robustness check*

This study replicates the regressions in both the one-stage model and the two-stage model by adding country pair dummy variable, which will absorb all non-time-varying country-pair fixed effects.

As a robustness check for the one-stage results, the fifth column of Table 6 exhibits different patterns relative to Table 2's fifth column for exporters. Export value declines prior to the beginning of a banking crisis. When a crisis occurs, the decline almost doubles when compared with a year before the crisis. The negative pattern remains unclear after the ending of the crisis. Though varying from our initial outcome, these results are parallel to our expectations of banking crises' impacts via exporter channel. For importers, results from Table 6 are quite robust compared with the results from Table 2. The trade decline around 8% during the banking crisis recover slowly around the following fifth year.

For the two-stage model, this study includes importer-exporter fixed effect in the first stage. Similar to Tables 4 and 5, we regress the exporter/ importer banking crises on the coefficient of exporter-year/importer-year fixed effect. Displayed in Table 7 (Exporters) and Table 8 (Importers), this research can confirm that, by added increased restrictions, the impact of a banking crisis channeled through the producer/exporter (Table 7) does result in negative influences toward trade flows (i.e. it corroborates our earlier expectations). However, the pattern of this influence is unclear, as the impact magnitudes fluctuates between periods before and after a crisis. In addition, our opinions regarding the importers/consumer channel remain unchanged. The third column of Table 8 exhibits that an 11% decline for importer during the banking crisis. Compared with a 4% decline in the third column of Table 5, the impact is relatively larger. There is a similar pattern that trade recovers slowly in the fifth year.

Table 7.   Exporter-year fixed effect and exporters' banking crisis (robustness check).

	Coefficient of exporter-year fixed effect from Stage 1 regression inclusive of three fixed-effects		
5 years forward of banking crisis for exporter			−0.0307*** (0.00558)
4 years forward of banking crisis for exporter			−0.0412*** (0.00555)
3 years forward of banking crisis for exporter			−0.0773*** (0.00503)
2 years forward of banking crisis for exporter			−0.139*** (0.00451)
1 year prior to banking crisis			−0.0889*** (0.00433)
Banking crisis for exporter	−0.0157*** (0.00215)	−0.0351*** (0.00219)	−0.0515*** (0.00224)
1 year after to banking crisis		−0.0836*** (0.00359)	−0.0988*** (0.00361)
2 years lag of banking crisis for exporter		−0.0867*** (0.00346)	−0.101*** (0.00348)
3 years lag of banking crisis for exporter		−0.0556*** (0.00337)	−0.0695*** (0.00339)
4 years lag of banking crisis for exporter		−0.0424*** (0.00326)	−0.0558*** (0.00328)
5 years lag of banking crisis for exporter		−0.0901*** (0.00339)	−0.103*** (0.00341)
Exporter ever had a banking crisis	0.0854*** (0.00126)	0.101*** (0.00131)	0.114*** (0.00136)
Constant	−17.06*** (0.0773)	−16.65*** (0.0778)	−16.60*** (0.0777)
Importers' GDP share-weighted OECD	Yes	Yes	Yes
Importers' GDP share-weighted distance	Yes	Yes	Yes
Importers' GDP share-weighted language	Yes	Yes	Yes
Importers' GDP share-weighted contiguity	Yes	Yes	Yes
Observations	497,673	497,673	497,673
R-squared	0.708	0.709	0.710

Note: Standard errors in parentheses ( ); ***$p < 0.01$, **$p < 0.05$, *$p < 0.10$.

Table 8. Importer-year fixed effect and exporters' banking crisis (robustness check).

Coefficient of importer-year fixed effect from Stage 1 regression inclusive of three fixed-effects			
5 years forward of banking crisis for importer			0.0603***
			(0.00533)
4 years forward of banking crisis for importer			0.0604***
			(0.00529)
3 years forward of banking crisis for importer			−0.0156***
			(0.00478)
2 years forward of banking crisis for importer			0.00753*
			(0.00431)
1 year prior to banking crisis			0.0190***
			(0.00413)
Banking crisis for importer	−0.0673***	−0.109***	−0.105***
	(0.00205)	(0.00208)	(0.00213)
1 year after to banking crisis		−0.177***	−0.173***
		(0.00337)	(0.00339)
2 years lag of banking crisis for importer		−0.172***	−0.168***
		(0.00324)	(0.00326)
3 years lag of banking crisis for importer		−0.155***	−0.151***
		(0.00316)	(0.00318)
4 years lag of banking crisis for importer		−0.162***	−0.158***
		(0.00307)	(0.00309)
5 years lag of banking crisis for importer		−0.102***	−0.0982***
		(0.00316)	(0.00318)
Importer ever had a banking crisis	0.00724***	0.0407***	0.0374***
	(0.00117)	(0.00121)	(0.00126)
Constant	−18.36***	−17.47***	−17.49***
	(0.0690)	(0.0689)	(0.0690)
Exporters' GDP share-weighted OECD	Yes	Yes	Yes
Exporters' GDP share-weighted distance	Yes	Yes	Yes
Exporters' GDP share-weighted language	Yes	Yes	Yes
Exporters' GDP share-weighted contiguity	Yes	Yes	Yes
Observations	470,416	470,416	470,416
R-squared	0.716	0.721	0.721

Note: Standard errors in parentheses ( ); ***$p < 0.01$, **$p < 0.05$, *$p < 0.10$.

Overall, the results from the single-stage model and the two-stage model are robust with each other. Exhibited is a negative impact on exporters by adding country-pair fixed effects. This is consistent with the expectation that the banking crisis will influence the trade via the producer/exporter channel. However, the fluctuation pattern still remains unclear. For importers, the pattern is relatively clear and the results are robust across Tables 2–8. There is a relatively large decline in trade during the banking crisis and slow recovery after 5 years of the ending of it.

5.4. *Chinese exporters and importers*

Following a single-stage approach, we investigated the isolated effects of a banking crisis on the Chinese exporter and imports. Using previous controlling factors, Tables 9–11 present the findings. Analyses of the banking crises' impact on the Chinese trade flow across the time period indicate a lesser impact on China, relative to the global average. For China's exporters, there appears to be no real significant influence, with limited and sporadic years indicating any significance. When isolating Chinese bilateral exports, during years three, four, and five following the crisis (Table 10), Chinese exports displayed increasing patterns of impact, both in significance level and in size. Noting the absence of any Chinese banking crisis during the period of investigation, this suggests a delayed impact for the Chinese producers.

For Chinese imports, the impact appears far less intrusive. With the exception of a negative impact during the period of the regression, banking crises appear to have no significant effects on the patterns of Chinese imports. During the banking crisis period, a negative impact ranges from 14% in the first column with no lag or forward to 19% in the fourth column with 5 years of lag and no forward year assessment. However, all effects can only be identified at a 5%, or higher, level of significance and these are followed by an immediate control of the effect.

Regarding China's banking crises experience, as an exporter or an importer, our results are unable to conclusively support any identified relationship with trade.

Table 9. Linear approximations for multilateral resistance and banking crises for China's trade.

	Dep var ln(China trade)				
Ln(distance) minus importers' share-weighted log-distance minus exporters' share-weighted log-distance	-0.531^{***} (0.0489)	-0.530^{***} (0.0488)	-0.531^{***} (0.0489)	-0.529^{***} (0.0488)	-0.531^{***} (0.0489)
Common language minus importers' share-weighted language minus exporters' share language	1.832^{***} (0.142)	1.830^{***} (0.142)	1.826^{***} (0.142)	1.828^{***} (0.142)	1.822^{***} (0.142)
Contiguity minus importers' share-weighted contiguity minus exporters' share-weighted contiguity	0.359^{***} (0.0915)	0.359^{***} (0.0914)	0.364^{***} (0.0914)	0.359^{***} (0.0914)	0.366^{***} (0.0914)
Ln(export's GDP)	1.325^{***} (0.0121)	1.326^{***} (0.0121)	1.327^{***} (0.0121)	1.326^{***} (0.0121)	1.327^{***} (0.0121)
Ln(import's GDP)	0.979^{***} (0.0116)	0.978^{***} (0.0116)	0.979^{***} (0.0116)	0.978^{***} (0.0116)	0.979^{***} (0.0116)
Exporting OECD countries	-0.396^{***} (0.0777)	-0.395^{***} (0.0777)	-0.389^{***} (0.0778)	-0.394^{***} (0.0777)	-0.374^{***} (0.0785)
Importing OECD countries	-0.0871 (0.0781)	-0.0812 (0.0780)	-0.0732 (0.0781)	-0.0796 (0.0780)	-0.0690 (0.0788)
5 years forward of banking crisis for exporter					-0.323 (0.330)
4 years forward of banking crisis for exporter					-0.365 (0.325)
3 years forward of banking crisis for exporter			-0.175 (0.229)		-0.219 (0.230)

(*Continued*)

Table 9. (*Continued*)

	Dep var ln(China trade)				
2 years forward of banking crisis for exporter			−0.0460 (0.208)		−0.0864 (0.209)
1 year prior to banking crisis			−0.0760 (0.198)		−0.114 (0.199)
Banking crisis for exporter	0.0148 (0.106)	−0.00482 (0.107)	0.00377 (0.109)	−0.0264 (0.108)	−0.0375 (0.111)
1 year after to banking crisis		−0.00574 (0.157)	−0.00108 (0.158)	−0.0294 (0.158)	−0.0412 (0.159)
2 years lag of banking crisis for exporter		−0.240 (0.150)	−0.236 (0.151)	−0.263* (0.151)	−0.275* (0.152)
3 years lag of banking crisis for exporter		−0.0807 (0.149)	−0.0788 (0.149)	−0.100 (0.149)	−0.114 (0.150)
4 years lag of banking crisis for exporter				−0.241* (0.143)	−0.256* (0.144)
5 years lag of banking crisis for exporter				−0.0745 (0.146)	−0.0979 (0.148)
5 years forward of banking crisis for importer					−0.103 (0.330)
4 years forward of banking crisis for importer					−0.168 (0.325)
3 years forward of banking crisis for importer			−0.406* (0.228)		−0.441* (0.229)
2 years forward of banking crisis for importer			−0.344* (0.208)		−0.373* (0.209)

(*Continued*)

Table 9. (*Continued*)

	Dep var ln(China trade)				
1 year prior to banking crisis			-0.206 (0.197)		-0.236 (0.198)
Banking crisis for importer	-0.270*** (0.105)	-0.333*** (0.106)	-0.385*** (0.108)	-0.345*** (0.107)	-0.412*** (0.110)
1 year after to banking crisis		-0.327* (0.154)	-0.375** (0.155)	-0.338** (0.155)	-0.402** (0.157)
2 years lag of banking crisis for importer		-0.321* (0.148)	-0.363** (0.149)	-0.328** (0.148)	-0.388*** (0.150)
3 years lag of banking crisis for importer		-0.321* (0.145)	-0.358** (0.146)	-0.332** (0.146)	-0.384*** (0.147)
4 years lag of banking crisis for importer				-0.213 (0.142)	-0.260* (0.143)
5 years lag of banking crisis for importer				0.0534 (0.145)	0.0177 (0.147)
Exporter ever had a banking crisis	0.0199 (0.0638)	0.0330 (0.0651)	0.0319 (0.0664)	0.0494 (0.0660)	0.0671 (0.0684)
Importer ever had a banking crisis	-0.0971 (0.0642)	-0.0493 (0.0655)	-0.0134 (0.0669)	-0.0412 (0.0663)	0.0101 (0.0689)
Both crisis ever	0.180*** (0.0668)	0.179*** (0.0667)	0.180*** (0.0667)	0.179*** (0.0667)	0.171** (0.0670)
Constant	-32.33*** (0.391)	-32.30*** (0.391)	-32.34*** (0.392)	-32.28*** (0.391)	-32.33*** (0.392)
Observations	7,813	7,813	7,813	7,813	7,813
R-squared	0.788	0.788	0.788	0.788	0.789

Note: Standard errors in parentheses ( ); ***$p < 0.01$, **$p < 0.05$, *$p < 0.10$.

Table 10. Linear approximations for multilateral resistance and banking crises where China is the exporter.

	Dep var ln(China exports)				
Ln(distance) minus importers' share-weighted log-distance minus exporters' share-weighted log-distance	−0.236*** (0.0445)	−0.235*** (0.0445)	−0.235*** (0.0445)	−0.235*** (0.0445)	−0.235*** (0.0445)
Common language minus importers' share-weighted language minus exporters' share language	2.010*** (0.131)	2.008*** (0.131)	2.007*** (0.131)	2.008*** (0.131)	2.006*** (0.131)
Contiguity minus importers' share-weighted contiguity minus exporters' share-weighted contiguity	0.539*** (0.0837)	0.538*** (0.0837)	0.540*** (0.0837)	0.538*** (0.0837)	0.540*** (0.0838)
Ln(export's GDP)	0.831*** (0.0416)	0.822*** (0.0418)	0.819*** (0.0421)	0.822*** (0.0418)	0.819*** (0.0421)
Ln(import's GDP)	0.939*** (0.00919)	0.939*** (0.00918)	0.940*** (0.00919)	0.939*** (0.00918)	0.940*** (0.00920)
Importing OECD countries	0.110* (0.0590)	0.113* (0.0589)	0.116* (0.0591)	0.114* (0.0590)	0.117*** (0.0593)
5 years forward of banking crisis for exporter					
4 years forward of banking crisis for exporter					
3 years forward of banking crisis for exporter					
2 years forward of banking crisis for exporter			−0.216** (0.109)		−0.218** (0.109)

(Continued)

Table 10. (*Continued*)

	Dep var ln(China exports)				
1 year prior to banking crisis			−0.0806 (0.108)		−0.0800 (0.108)
Banking crisis for exporter	−0.00915 (0.106)	−0.00733 (0.106)	−0.0119 (0.106)	−0.00540 (0.106)	−0.00994 (0.107)
1 year after to banking crisis		0.0145 (0.105)	0.0101 (0.105)	0.0161 (0.105)	0.0119 (0.106)
2 years lag of banking crisis for exporter		0.164 (0.103)	0.160 (0.103)	0.162 (0.103)	0.158 (0.104)
3 years lag of banking crisis for exporter		0.189* (0.102)	0.184* (0.102)	0.186* (0.102)	0.180* (0.102)
4 years lag of banking crisis for exporter				0.226** (0.101)	0.220** (0.101)
5 years lag of banking crisis for exporter				0.346*** (0.0996)	0.340*** (0.102)
5 years forward of banking crisis for importer					0.00871 (0.216)
4 years forward of banking crisis for importer					−0.0653 (0.216)
3 years forward of banking crisis for importer			−0.154 (0.195)		−0.165 (0.195)
2 years forward of banking crisis for importer			−0.0451 (0.175)		−0.0539 (0.176)
1 year prior to banking crisis			0.0267 (0.165)		0.0177 (0.165)

(*Continued*)

Table 10. (*Continued*)

	Dep var ln(China exports)				
Banking crisis for importer	-0.146^*	-0.180^{**}	-0.185^{**}	-0.186^{**}	-0.194^{**}
	(0.0774)	(0.0786)	(0.0795)	(0.0793)	(0.0809)
1 year after to banking crisis		-0.182	-0.186	-0.188	-0.196
		(0.123)	(0.123)	(0.123)	(0.124)
2 years lag of banking crisis for importer		-0.176	-0.180	-0.181	-0.188
		(0.117)	(0.117)	(0.117)	(0.118)
3 years lag of banking crisis for importer		-0.175	-0.178	-0.180	-0.187
		(0.114)	(0.115)	(0.115)	(0.115)
4 years lag of banking crisis for importer				-0.104	-0.110
				(0.111)	(0.112)
5 years lag of banking crisis for importer				0.0161	0.0105
				(0.114)	(0.115)
Exporter ever had a banking crisis					
Importer ever had a banking crisis	-0.0847^*	-0.0594	-0.0553	-0.0546	-0.0478
	(0.0454)	(0.0465)	(0.0474)	(0.0472)	(0.0490)
Both crisis ever	0.0358	0.0351	0.0344	0.0345	0.0329
	(0.0605)	(0.0605)	(0.0606)	(0.0605)	(0.0608)
Constant	-21.37^{***}	-21.16^{***}	-21.11^{***}	-21.17^{***}	-21.11^{***}
	(0.906)	(0.910)	(0.916)	(0.910)	(0.917)
Observations	4,006	4,006	4,006	4,006	4,006
R-squared	0.865	0.865	0.865	0.865	0.865
Year Fixed Effect					

Note: Standard errors in parentheses ( ); $^{***}p < 0.01$, $^{**}p < 0.05$, $^*p < 0.10$.

Table 11. Linear approximations for multilateral resistance and banking crises where China is the importer.

	Dep var ln(China imports)				
Ln(distance) minus importers' share-weighted log-distance minus exporters' share-weighted log-distance	−0.831***	−0.830***	−0.833***	−0.829***	−0.832***
	(0.0879)	(0.0878)	(0.0879)	(0.0879)	(0.0879)
Common language minus importers' share-weighted language minus exporters' share language	1.646***	1.643***	1.636***	1.640***	1.629***
	(0.253)	(0.253)	(0.253)	(0.253)	(0.253)
Contiguity minus importers' share-weighted contiguity minus exporters' share-weighted contiguity	0.179	0.180	0.187	0.179	0.191
	(0.164)	(0.164)	(0.164)	(0.164)	(0.164)
Ln(export's GDP)	1.372***	1.372***	1.373***	1.372***	1.374***
	(0.0192)	(0.0192)	(0.0192)	(0.0192)	(0.0192)
Ln(import's GDP)	0.597***	0.586***	0.569***	0.587***	0.565***
	(0.0832)	(0.0834)	(0.0840)	(0.0834)	(0.0840)
Exporting OECD countries	−0.616***	−0.611***	−0.597***	−0.608***	−0.579***
	(0.116)	(0.116)	(0.116)	(0.116)	(0.116)
5 years forward of banking crisis for exporter					−0.445
					(0.419)
4 years forward of banking crisis for exporter					−0.480
					(0.418)
3 years forward of banking crisis for exporter			−0.432		−0.502
			(0.376)		(0.378)
2 years forward of banking crisis for exporter			−0.347		−0.408
			(0.338)		(0.339)

(*Continued*)

Table 11. (*Continued*)

Dep var ln(China imports)					
1 year prior to banking crisis			−0.311 (0.318)		−0.370 (0.320)
Banking crisis for exporter	−0.104 (0.151)	−0.154 (0.153)	−0.194 (0.155)	−0.181 (0.155)	−0.254 (0.158)
1 year after to banking crisis		−0.166 (0.246)	−0.204 (0.247)	−0.193 (0.247)	−0.263 (0.248)
2 years lag of banking crisis for exporter		−0.396* (0.233)	−0.429* (0.234)	−0.420* (0.234)	−0.486** (0.235)
3 years lag of banking crisis for exporter		−0.252 (0.232)	−0.282 (0.232)	−0.276 (0.232)	−0.337 (0.234)
4 years lag of banking crisis for exporter				−0.352 (0.218)	−0.409* (0.220)
5 years lag of banking crisis for exporter				−0.0335 (0.224)	−0.0901 (0.225)
5 years forward of banking crisis for importer					
4 years forward of banking crisis for importer					
3 years forward of banking crisis for importer					
2 years forward of banking crisis for importer			−0.333 (0.226)		−0.337 (0.227)
1 year prior to banking crisis			−0.0664 (0.223)		−0.0667 (0.223)

(*Continued*)

Table 11. (*Continued*)

	Dep var ln(China imports)				
Banking crisis for importer	−0.440**	−0.427**	−0.457**	−0.415*	−0.443**
	(0.217)	(0.217)	(0.218)	(0.218)	(0.218)
1 year after to banking crisis		−0.277	−0.304	−0.267	−0.295
		(0.214)	(0.215)	(0.215)	(0.216)
2 years lag of banking crisis for importer		0.0944	0.0662	0.0944	0.0616
		(0.209)	(0.209)	(0.209)	(0.210)
3 years lag of banking crisis for importer		−0.0852	−0.113	−0.0954	−0.132
		(0.205)	(0.206)	(0.206)	(0.206)
4 years lag of banking crisis for importer				0.221	0.187
				(0.204)	(0.205)
5 years lag of banking crisis for importer				0.560***	0.575***
				(0.200)	(0.206)
Exporter ever had a banking crisis	0.0191	0.0563	0.0861	0.0758	0.138
	(0.0868)	(0.0890)	(0.0906)	(0.0903)	(0.0938)
Importer ever had a banking crisis					
Both crisis ever	0.307**	0.307**	0.311**	0.307**	0.296**
	(0.121)	(0.121)	(0.121)	(0.121)	(0.121)
Constant	−25.14***	−24.90***	−24.55***	−24.91***	−24.45***
	(1.827)	(1.833)	(1.845)	(1.833)	(1.845)
Observations	3,807	3,807	3,807	3,807	3,807
R-squared	0.734	0.734	0.735	0.735	0.735
Year Fixed Effect					

Note: Standard errors in parentheses ( ); $^{***}p < 0.01$, $^{**}p < 0.05$, $^{*}p < 0.10$.

6. Conclusion

After the Great Recession, the literature focused increasingly on the impact of the financial sector on trade flows and the magnitudes of this impact. This analysis uses data that cover most of the countries involved in global trade for a time period of 24 years. The results are relatively robust where the average correlation between banking crises and trade fluctuations is concerned.

An unexpected result in the level of influence from the financial sector on the importers' side of the trade was identified, despite the vast literature focusing on the exporters' side. In a two-stage analysis, there is some exporter significance, but almost all the effects are small and after imposing sharper restrictions, such outcome better aligns with expectations. On the contrary, there is a robust correlation between banking crises and imports, considering a trade being largely durable and capital goods being likely more income sensitive. Also, almost all the impacts for different time periods, especially for the current year of the banking crisis and the years after it, are significantly negative.

Combining the different influences from the exporter and the importer side, one potential explanation exists to explain the 2007 Great Recession influence on the global trade collapse. Previously, financial shocks occurred in countries at different income levels, in varied time periods. Thus, from a demand perspective, the financial shocks only caused a marginal disturbance in the flow of trade with the global market remaining, on average, at stable levels. However, during the Great Recession, a large number of high-income countries, for example, major OECD countries, were simultaneously affected. The combined collapse of such influential countries within the global system of trade led to a significant drop in demand, which resulted in a collapse of the overall trade market.

This study also shows that the impact of the financial shock on the trade flow for importers follows a certain pattern. Before the importer experienced a banking crisis, imports were already in a marginal but persistent declining trend compared with other countries, which might be caused by the tighter credit constraints faced by the importers prior to the onset of the banking crisis. When the crisis begins, the decline in imports continues. After the banking crisis, the global average decline in trade intensified, which led to a slow recovery in the following years. However, Chinese imports showed no long-term effects from the banking crises as no consecutive years of significant decline were identified. Unlike global export trends, the isolated pattern on Chinese imports suggests a 2-year lag for exporters to the mainland before any significant impact is revealed.

Most of the results also support the fact that countries with previous banking crisis experience are likely to trade more, globally. These results support the assumption that a banking crisis is also correlated with financial development, i.e. the availability of credit, and countries with advanced financial sectors are expected to present greater trade performance.

Acknowledgements

Funding: This work was supported partly by the Ministry of Education of China Youth Fund Program (Grant No. 17YJC790110) and partly by the Department of Education of Liaoning Province's Youth Fund Program (Grant No. LN2017QN017).

References

Alessandria, G., Kaboski, J. and Midrigan, V. (2010). "The Great Trade Collapse of 2008–2009: An Inventory Adjustment," *IMF Economic Review*, **58**, 254–294.

Amiti, M. and Weinstein, D. E. (2011). "Exports and Financial Shocks," *The Quarterly Journal of Economics*, **126**(4), 1841–1877.

Anderson, J. E. and van Wincoop, E. (2003). "Gravity with Gravitas: A Solution to the Border Puzzle," *American Economic Review*, **93**(1), 170–192.

Baier, S. L. and Bergstrand, J. H. (2009, February). Bonus vetus OLS: A Simple Method for Approximating International Trade-cost Effects using the Gravity Equation. *Journal of International Economics*, **77**(1), 77–85.

Bricongne, J.C., Gaulier, F. L., Taglioni, D. and Vicard, V. (2012). "Firms and the Global Crisis: French Exports in the Turmoil," *Journal of International Economics*, **87**, 134–146.

Chor, D. and Manova. K. (2012). "Off the Cliff and Back? Credit Conditions and International Trade during Global Financial Crisis," *Journal of International Economics*, **87**, 117–133.

Eaton, J., Kortum, S. and Kramarz, F. (2008). "An Anatomy of International Trade, Evidence from French Firms." NBER Working Paper No. 1461.

Gopinath, G., Itskhoki, O. and Neiman, B. (2012). "Trade Prices and the Global Trade Collapse of 2008–2009," *IMF Economic Review*, **60**, 303–328.

Lacovone, L. and Zavacka, V. (2009). "Banking Crises and Exports: Lessons from the Past." World Banking Policy Research Working Paper No. 5016.

Laeven, L. and Valencia, F. (2012). "Systemic Banking Crises Database: An Update." IMF Working Paper No. 12/163.

Levchenko, A. A., Lewis, L. T. and Tesar, L. L. (2010). "The Collapse of International Trade during the 2008–2009 Crisis: In Search of the Smoking Gun," *IMF Economic Review*, **58**, 214–253.

Manova, K. (2013). "Credit Constraints, Heterogeneous Firms, and International Trade," *The Review of Economic Studies*, **80**(2), 711–744.

Melitz, M. J. (2003). "The Impact of Trade on Intra-industry Reallocations and Aggregate Industry Productivity," *Econometrica*, **71**(6), 1695–1725.

Scott L. Baier, Jeffrey H. Bergstrand (2009). Bonus vetus OLS: A Simple Method for Approximating International Trade-Cost Effects using the Gravity Equation, *Journal of International Economics*, **77**(1), 77–85.

Chapter 5

Does Producer Service FDI Promote the Upgrading of China's Manufacturing Sector?

Yibing Ding* and Yingjie Fu[†,‡]

*School of Economics, Jilin University,
Changchun, P. R. China
†International Economics & Trade School,
Center of Post-doctoral Research,
Dongbei University of Finance and Economics,
Dalian, P. R. China
‡fuyingjie@dufe.edu.cn

As an important part of China's supply-side reform, it is significant to promote the transformation and upgrading of the industrial structure in the manufacturing sector. In theory, producer service FDI can affect the industrial structure upgrading in the manufacturing sector of the host country through the vertical industrial linkages and industrial spillovers. By using provincial and industrial-level data, this empirical study about the impact of producer service FDI inflow on the upgrading of China's manufacturing sector shows that producer service FDI can significantly promote the upgrading of industrial structures in the east of China, but has little effect on the middle and west of China. Furthermore, the spatial Durbin model is used to show that producer service FDI not only has direct effect on each province but also leads to spatial spillover effects on geographically close provinces.

1. Introduction

Under the "new normal" of China's economy, the industrial structure in the manufacturing sector is an important aspect of economic quality. How to effectively realize its transformation and upgrading is an important issue to be studied and solved. Meanwhile, as an important factor in the Chinese economy, since the beginning of the economic reform, foreign capital has played a key role in promoting technological progress and economic growth. With the increasing demand for the upgrading and optimization of China's industrial structure, new demands will be placed on the structure and quality of foreign capital inflows. It is of great practical significance to clarify how foreign capital inflows affect the industrial structure, especially in the manufacturing sector.

Producer services are the services that are utilized by the producers as the intermediate inputs. This conception was first proposed by Greenfield (1966). Later, Browning and Singelman (1975) and others further discussed this conception. When the market and economy are less developed, the producer services are normally provided by the enterprises themselves. As the economy becomes more developed, there emerged independent firms which provided only the producer services like logistics and accounting; they mainly provided these services to the manufacturers. And as the manufacturing sector upgraded, it needs more professional and high-level producer services.

Conventional research has focused on the impact of overall FDI on industrial structure development (Wen *et al.*, 2009). With the rapid transformation and upgrading of China's manufacturing in recent years, some scholars have begun to evaluate the impact of FDI inflows on the process of transformation and upgrading (Ge and Luo, 2015). However, few scholars have evaluated the impact of FDI in the producer service industries on the transformation and upgrading of industrial structure in the manufacturing sector. Given the rising demand for services as intermediate inputs, producer services are among the main driving forces of economic growth and development in various countries and regions. At present, for many developed countries, advanced producer service industry is quite important for the formation of strong international competitiveness in the manufacturing sector. In theory, the opening up of the producer service industry has a potential positive effect on the productivity improvement of most technology-intensive manufacturing industries, while the protection of the producer service industry will put the manufacturing sector at a competitive disadvantage (Francois and Woerz, 2008).

Since 2010, FDI in service industries has surpassed FDI in manufacturing industries and become the largest component of foreign direct investment in China. And the growth rate of FDI in producer service industries is higher than that in other service industries. However, FDI in the producer service industries shows an unbalanced distribution across the regions and industries in China. Is the current development and the structure of China's producer service industry desirable? Does it have a positive effect on restructuring China's manufacturing sector? If this positive role exists, is there a regional difference and a spatial spillover effect? The answers to these questions can provide new insights on the relationship between FDI in producer services and the structural change in the manufacturing sector. It will also have important policy implications for countries like China to better utilize foreign capital and improve the quality of foreign investment inflow. This study examines the impact of FDI inflows in producer service industries on the structural changes in the manufacturing sector in the context of the overall opening of China's services sector through the theoretical and empirical analyses. On this basis, we can provide the conclusions and policy recommendations accordingly. The contributions of this study are as follows: first, it extends the studies about the effects of the producer service FDI inflow and provides a better understanding about the relations between this kind of FDI and the development of manufacturing sector. Second, this study examines the spatial spillover effect of the producer service FDI inflow's impact, which is also an extension of the current studies.

The study is structured as follows: in Section 2, we analyze China's FDI inflow in producer services and show the structural change in manufacturing sector since 2006 when China began to enter a comprehensive opening stage. In Section 3, we theoretically analyze the impact of FDI in producer service industries on the upgrading of manufacturing sector. In Section 4, we estimate and test the effect of FDI in producer service industries based on panel data model and spatial data model by using China's provincial data. Finally, we draw conclusions and highlight some policy implications in Section 5.

2. FDI Inflow in Producer Services and Changes of Manufacturing Structure in China

2.1. *The development of China's FDI inflow and the producer service FDI inflow*

China's FDI inflow in recent four decades experienced four stages. The first stage is from 1979 to 1991. In this stage, FDI in China was mainly allocated in the coastal area and invested into the labor-intensive sector. The second stage is from 1992 to 2001. In this stage, FDI flow into China experienced a drastic increase with an annual growth rate at 33%. Since 2002–2018, as China entered the WTO, FDI inflow became more stable with an annual growth rate at around 10%, and services sector attracted more and more FDI inflow. From 2019, as the new law concerning the FDI was passed, a new stage of FDI inflow into China started, and the administration in China will be more positive for FDI inflow in new areas.

Figure 1 shows the sectoral distribution of FDI in China in 2005–2017. As can be seen from Figure 1, the proportion of FDI flowing into China's manufacturing industry has been decreasing since 2005, while the proportion of FDI flowing into the services industry has

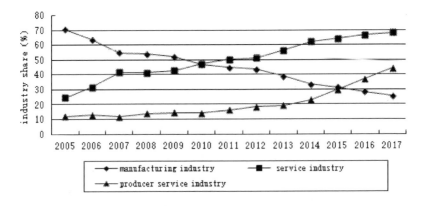

Figure 1. FDI inflow of China's manufacturing and service industries.

been increasing gradually. Since 2010, the proportion of FDI in the services industry in the total inflow of foreign capital has begun to surpass that in the manufacturing industry, becoming the industry with the largest amount of FDI inflow. At the same time, the figure shows that the proportion of producer service FDI in total inflow of foreign capital has increased year by year. Since 2016, the proportion of producer service FDI surpassed the FDI in manufacturing. This indicates that FDI in services industry, especially producer services, plays an increasingly important role in the foreign investment in China. Its influence on China's economic development is worth researching.

Figure 2 presents the breakdown of FDI in producer services. It can be seen from the figure that FDI in producer services absorbed by China is not evenly distributed. During the period 2005–2014, FDI in leasing and commercial services dominated, accounting for about 40–50% of all the FDI inflow in producer services. The proportion of FDI in the financial sector was less than 10%, which is relatively low. However, since 2009, the proportion of FDI in the financial sector has increased rapidly, which is closely related to China's further opening of the financial sector to foreign investment. The proportion of transportation, warehousing, and postal services fell from 25% in 2005 to 9.6% in 2017. FDI in information transmission, computer services, software industry, scientific research, technical services, and geological exploration has increased slowly since 2005.

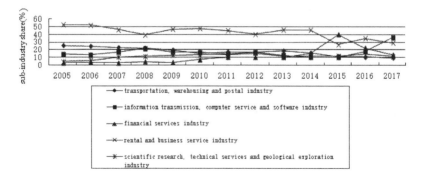

Figure 2.   FDI inflow within China's producer services.

Table 1. FDI inflow of producer services in representative provinces of China in 2017 (unit: $100 million).

East				Central			West	
Guang-dong	Zhe-jiang	Jiangsu	Shan-dong	Anhui	Hubei	Henan	Chong-qing	Guizhou
86.02	72.34	47.64	37.29	3.21	2.75	2.48	12.17	4.24
		41.49%			8.44%		2.83%	

Data source: 2018 China statistical yearbook and statistical yearbook of corresponding provinces.

Table 1 shows the regional distribution of FDI in producer services in China. It is not difficult to find that FDI in producer services mainly concentrated in developed areas along the east coast of China, while the proportion of FDI in the central and western regions is small, resulting in the imbalance in regional distribution of FDI in producer services. Foreign enterprises, especially manufacturing business, are the main customers of foreign investment in the service industry. Because producer services multinationals tend to follow their original customers and competitors, and the manufacturing FDI mostly focused in the coastal areas in China, the producer service FDI also focused in the coastal areas. The reason that the coastal areas attracted more manufacturing FDI is that these areas not only provide more skilled labor force but also have more market-oriented and FDI-friendly environment.

2.2. *Changes in the structure of China's manufacturing sector*

Figure 3 shows the changes of manufacturing structure in different regions of China.[1] As can be seen from the left panel in Figure 3,

---

[1]The eastern region includes Beijing, Tianjin, Hebei, Liaoning, Shanghai, Jiangsu, Zhejiang, Fujian, Shandong, Guangdong, Guangxi, and Hainan. The central region includes nine provinces and autonomous regions: Shanxi, Inner Mongolia, Jilin, Heilongjiang, Anhui, Jiangxi, Henan, Hubei, and Hunan. The western region covers 10 provinces, autonomous regions, and municipalities directly under the central government, including Sichuan, Chongqing, Guizhou, Yunnan, Tibet, Shaanxi, Gansu, Ningxia, Qinghai, and Xinjiang.

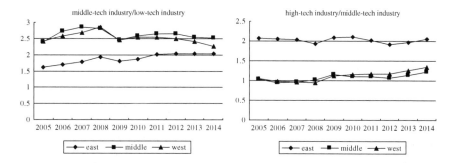

Figure 3. Structural change of manufacturing industry in China.

the output of the middle-technology industries relative to the low-technology industries in the three regions of China has been increasing in the past decade, among which the central region and the western region account for a higher proportion than the eastern region. It shows that in the process of industrial upgrading, the central and western regions have the ability to develop from low-technology industries to middle-technology industries. However, a further comparison of the proportions of output of high-technology industries and mid-technology industries shows that the proportion of high-technology industries in the eastern region is significantly higher than that in the central and western regions. The industrial structure of the central and western regions needs to be further developed to have more high-technology industries.

3. The Mechanism of FDI in Producer Service Industries Influencing the Manufacturing Sector Upgrading

The importance of producer services as inputs for the manufacturing industries has been widely examined (Katouzian, 1970; Park, 1989; Mariotti *et al.*, 2013). In theory, producer service FDI mainly affects the industrial structure upgrading in the manufacturing sector of the host country through the inter-industrial vertical linkage effect and inter-industrial spillover effect.

From the perspective of inter-industrial vertical linkage effect, the increase of FDI inflow in producer services can provide higher quality and more diversified producer services, for firms in both upstream industries and downstream industries. This will reduce the costs of these firms. Cost reduction will improve the efficiency of these firms and finally promote the upgrading of manufacturing sector. In particular, foreign producer service firms establish forward linkages by providing services to downstream local manufacturing enterprises (Fernandes and Paunov, 2012). Compared with the relatively low technology level and the lack of advanced human resources in some local producer service firms in the host countries, multinational companies in the producer service industry often have more advanced technology and more knowledge reserves, which can provide high-quality services and technological support. A large number of diversified producer services can reduce the cost of quality adjustment in downstream manufacturing and also enable some local manufacturing firms at the lower position in the industrial system to obtain services with high quality and reasonable price from foreign producer service enterprises at the higher position in the industrial system. Therefore, the inflow of FDI in producer services is related to the local manufacturing sector, which will promote the development of the host country's manufacturing sector. In addition, when foreign producer service enterprises enter the host country, sometimes they need the local manufacturers in the host country to provide intermediate input, thus forming backward linkages (Mariotti *et al.*, 2013). Due to the increasingly fierce economic competition in various countries, many multinational corporations use the localization strategy to cope with the challenges. This localization improves the backward linkages of FDI in producer services, thus causing some backward technology spillover effect on local manufacturers. Hence, FDI can help to promote the transformation of industrial structure in the manufacturing sector through its technological spillover effect on the efficiency of manufacturing in the host countries.

Based on the perspective of industrial spillovers, investors in producer services usually have relatively abundant capital, advanced human resources, and more experience. They can interact with the local manufacturers in the host country to generate spillovers of management and technical knowledge through competition, human capital flow, imitation-demonstration effect and other ways, thus promoting the development of local manufacturing (Blomström and Persson, 1983; Aitken *et al.*, 1997; Fons-Rosen *et al.*, 2017). More specifically, as for the competition effect, producer services FDI from developed countries can help improve the quality of overall producer services, reduce the price of producer services, and enhance the competitiveness of the host country's producer services industry. Under the pressure of external competition, local producer service enterprises have to strengthen their capacity of independent innovation to provide more cost-effective and diversified services for manufacturing in order to gain a favorable position in competition. Through this competition effect, local manufacturers can effectively save their costs in searching for high-quality producer services, so that they can focus on their own progress. As for the human capital flow, multinational producer service companies can introduce new service technologies and new standards, thus improving the quality of their local employees in the host country, and through the movements of these employees, the overall quality of employees in the producer service industry would be improved. As for the imitation-demonstration effect, domestic firms can benefit from observing and imitating the successful innovative managerial experience of the multinational producer service companies, which can then help improve the productivity level of the whole industry and eventually the development and upgrading of local manufacturing industry through industrial linkages.

4. Empirical Analysis of FDI in Producer Services on Upgrading China's Manufacturing Sector

4.1. *Econometric model setting and variable selection*

The basic static model is specified as follows:

$$y_{it} = x'_{it}\beta + \lambda_t + u_i + \varepsilon_{it},$$

where y_{it} refers to the upgrading of manufacturing industry in each province of China; x_{it} refers to the core independent variable, i.e. FDI in producer service industry and control variables; λ_t refers to time fixed effects; u_i refers to individual fixed effects and ε_{it} refers to the error term.

The upgrading of manufacturing structure in this chapter mainly refers to the increasing of the proportion of the industries with higher technology in the manufacturing sector. According to the OECD manufacturing classification, this study further divides the manufacturing industry into three categories: high technology, middle technology, and low technology (Fu and Ye, 2014).[2] Middle-/low-technology industry, high-/middle-technology industry, and high- and middle-/low-technology industry are defined to measure the upgrading of manufacturing structure.

As there is no international agreement on the classification of producer services, this study adopts the classification of the 13th Five-Year Plan for Economic and Social Development of the People's Republic of China, by including transportation, warehousing and postal service, information transmission, computer services and software industry, finance, leasing and business services, scientific research, technical services, and geological services as the producer services. FDIs in these sectors from China's 15 provinces[3] or municipalities directly under the central government are used to proxy producer services FDI in China from 2006 to 2015.

We choose control variables as follows: first, according to Michaels *et al.* (2012), the higher the level of urbanization, the more likely

---

[2]The high-technology industry includes general equipment, special equipment, transportation, electrical machinery and equipment, communication electronics, instrumentation and cultural office machinery, chemical and pharmaceutical industries. Middle-technology industry includes petroleum processing, coking and nuclear fuel processing industry, rubber, plastic, nonmetal mineral products, ferrous smelting, mid-end/low-end technology industry, high-end/mid-end technology and nonferrous metal smelting and metal products, and other industries. Low-technology industry includes food manufacturing, beverage, tobacco, textile, leather, lumber, furniture, papermaking, printing, and stationery and other manufacturing industries.

[3]Restricted by the availability of data, the provinces (municipalities directly under the central government) included in this study are Beijing, Liaoning, Hebei, Shangdong, Guangdong, Jiangsu, Zhejiang, Heilongjiang, Anhui, Jiangxi, Henan, Hubei, Chongqing, Guizhou, and Shanxi province.

that manufacturing industries could transfer toward relative high-technology industries. Thus, we utilize the percentage of urban population in each province as the indicator of urbanization (Wang, 2010). Second, from Acemoglu and Guerrieri (2008), we know that capital deepening plays an important role in the structural change of manufacturing industry. Therefore, the ratio of fixed asset investment to the GDP in each province is taken as the indicator of capital deepening in our empirical model. Third, if one province has more non-state-owned employments, it usually means this province owns more active economy. And the more active the economy, the more conducive the upgrading of manufacturing industry. So we choose the ratio of the employment of the non-state-owned enterprises to the total employment in each province as the indicator of employment structure.

In addition, considering the global financial crisis in 2008–2009 may have an impact on the structural change of manufacturing industry, the dummy variable of crisis is added. At the same time, as the impact of producer services FDI on the upgrading of manufacturing structure may be regional differences, the regional dummy variables are also included in the model. Specific definitions and descriptions of variables are shown in Table 2.

4.2. *Basic regression results*

This study applies static panel model to test the impact of FDI inflow in producer services on the upgrading of manufacturing structure. According to the Hausman test, the fixed effect model was selected as the basic model for estimation. According to regression results, FDI inflow in producer services has a positive impact on the upgrading of the manufacturing production from the middle-technology industry to the high-technology industry in the eastern area of China, while it has little impact in the central and western areas. For the transition from the low-technology industry to the middle-technology industry, it has no impact for the whole sample. For more details, column (1) in Table 3 shows no significant impact of producer service FDI on the upgrading of middle-technology industrial structure. Column (2) shows a positive significant impact of FDI on the upgrading of

Table 2. Variable definition and description.

Variables	Name of variables	Variable description
Dependent variable	Upgrading of manufacturing structure	The ratio of the output of middle-(high-) technology industries to the low-(middle-) technology industries in the provinces. *Data source*: *China Industrial Economic Statistical Yearbook*, Provincial statistical yearbook, denoted as y.
Independent variables	Producer services FDI	The ratio of producer service FDI to manufacturing FDI in the provinces. *Data source*: Statistical yearbook of each province (city), denoted as x
Control variables	Urbanization level	Percentage of urban population in each province (city). *Data source*: Statistical yearbook of each province (city), denoted as urban.
	Investment	The ratio of fixed asset investment to the GDP in the provinces. *Data source*: Statistical yearbook of each province (city), denoted as invest.
	Employee	The ratio of the employment of the non-state-owned enterprises to the total employment in the provinces. *Data source*: Statistical yearbook of each province (city), denoted as employee.
	Crisis dummy	1 for years 2008 and 2009, 0 for others, denoted as crisis.
	Regional dummy	Denoted as middle*FDI, west*FDI.

high-technology industrial structure. As for the western and middle area, the dummy result is not significant, implying that the positive effects of producer service FDI on the upgrading in the manufacturing sector are mainly from the eastern area of China. When using the ratio of the combined output of middle- and high-technology industries to the low-technology industries as the dependent variable, it was found that the FDI in producer services promoted mainly the development of middle-technology industries, rather than both middle- and high-technology industries.

Table 3. Basic regression results.

	Static model			Dynamic model		
	(1) Middle-/low-technology	(2) High-/low-technology	(3) Middle and high-/low-technology	(4) Mid-end/low-end	(5) High-end/mid-end	(6) Middle and high-/low-technology
l.y				0.6271*** (0.0000)	0.9523*** (0.0000)	0.7781*** (0.0000)
FDI	−0.1443 (0.1770)	0.2809*** (0.0000)	0.0918 (0.6080)	−0.1128 (0.1870)	0.1102** (0.0110)	−0.0685 (0.6940)
Middle*FDI	−0.5903 (0.4140)	−0.0531 (0.8860)	−1.36 (0.2630)	0.8555 (0.3960)	0.4428 (0.3440)	1.145 (0.4590)
West*FDI	−0.0557 (0.8180)	0.0946 (0.4480)	0.2348 (0.5640)	0.7343 (0.2120)	−0.0600 (0.9000)	0.6010 (0.1940)
Urban	0.0770*** (0.0000)	0.0178* (0.0790)	0.2023*** (0.0000)	0.0336*** (0.0000)	−0.0016 (0.9280)	0.0281*** (0.0000)
Invest	−1.9508*** (0.0020)	−0.6868** (0.0300)	−5.3130*** (0.0000)	−0.1126 (0.8270)	0.4388 (0.4850)	−2.3620*** (0.0000)
Employee	14.4271*** (0.0030)	9.5321*** (0.0000)	−7.443 (0.3490)	−1.059 (0.8150)	5.8960*** (0.0010)	6.0935** (0.0610)
Crisis	0.1695* (0.0520)	−0.0166 (0.7080)	0.2454* (0.0930)	−0.1740*** (0.0000)	0.0637* (0.0050)	
Hausman test	0.0070	0.0001	0.0008			

Note: Standard errors in parentheses ( ); $^{***}p < 0.01$, $^{**}p < 0.05$, $^{*}p < 0.10$.

Considering the time lag effect in industrial structure adjustment, the dynamic panel model[4] was further used to investigate the effect of FDI in producer services on the upgrading of China's manufacturing structure. The results of two-step estimations are almost the same as those of the static panel model. Producer service FDI plays a positive role in the development of the high-technology manufacturing industries in the eastern region, but has no significant impact on the central and western regions. At the same time, the industrial structure adjustment has a remarkable lag effect, and previous industrial structure change can affect the current industrial structure. For the control variables, an increase in urbanization is found to significantly promote the upgrading of the industrial structure, especially from the low-technology to the middle-technology industries, while for promoting the transfer toward the high-technology industries, the effect of urbanization is much weaker. Investment has a negative effect on the upgrading of manufacturing structure, which indicates that fixed asset investment does not necessarily bring about the upgrading of the manufacture structure. The development of Chinese manufacturing structure no longer relies on the physical capital investment for upgrading alone. As for employment, the increase in the number of non-state-owned enterprises can promote the upgrading of the industrial structure to some extent. It shows that the more employees involved in foreign capital enterprises and private enterprises, the better promotion of the structural upgrading and transformation of the manufacturing sector.

4.3. *Robustness test*

As the more developed the manufacturing structure, the more likely it is to attract related producer service FDI. There might be an endogenous relationship between producer service FDI and the upgrading of the manufacturing structure. For robustness check, we

---

[4]To ensure the validity of the estimation results, instrumental variables should be used as little as possible and explanatory variables with a lag of up to three periods should be used as instrumental variables.

use the one-period lagged FDI in producer services as the instrumental variable to run the regressions for the ratio of high-technology industries to the middle-technology industries. The results shown in columns (1) and (2) in Table 4 are consistent with the results in column (2) in the basic regression (Table 3) and the results in columns (5) and (6) are consistent with the conclusions of the column (5) in the basic regression, accordingly. Columns (3) and (4) in Table 4 are the results using the ratio of FDI in producer services to GDP as the dependent variable.

The results show that the relative scale of the producer service FDI as compared with GDP cannot promote the development of the high-technology industries in eastern China. From the results we can see that it is the quality of the FDI rather than the quantity, i.e. the industrial distribution of FDI inflows in the eastern region, that plays a pivotal role for the development of high-technology manufacturing industries. On the contrary, the expansion of the scale of the producer service FDI can promote the upgrading of manufacturing structure in western China. It is likely due to the relatively small scale of producer service FDIs in western China, when the scales are relatively small. This finding is consistent with the results of (Liu *et al.*, 2011), who used the quantile regression.

4.4. *Spatial spillover effect*

According to the findings of He *et al.* (2012) and Jiao (2014), producer service FDI has a technological spillover effect spatially. To extend the benchmark study, we investigate whether FDI in producer services can promote the development of the high-technology manufacturing industries in eastern China through the spatial spillover effect of FDI. The results of the benchmark model estimation show that producer service FDI has a statistically significant spatial influence among the eastern provinces. In this study, the spatial Durbin model was used to investigate the spatial impact of producer service FDI on upgrading manufacturing in eastern China. According to the results of the Hausman test, the fixed effect model is adopted for regression. Table 5 shows the regression results. Three types of spatial

Yibing Ding & Yingjie Fu

Table 4. Robustness test.

	(1)	(2)	(3)	(4)	(5)	(6)
l.y					0.9086***	0.8308***
					(0.0000)	(0.0000)
FDI	0.1634**	0.3531***	-0.4699***	-0.0061***	0.0687**	0.0969***
	(0.0300)	(0.000)	(0.005)	(0.001)	(0.059)	(0.0000)
Middle*FDI	0.0048	-0.2191	0.5875	0.0063	0.022	0.2484
	(0.994)	(0.576)	(0.126)	(0.128)	(0.953)	(0.4900)
West*FDI	-0.081	-0.013	0.7083***	0.0078***	0.0484	0.112
	(0.688)	(0.92)	(0.001)	(0.001)	(0.901)	(0.21)
Urban	0.0236*	0.0185*	0.0243**	0.0265**	0.0084	0.0124***
	(0.076)	(0.084)	(0.029)	(0.029)	(0.536)	(0.001)
Invest	-0.7181*	-0.4388	-0.7197**	-0.4026	0.388	
	(0.091)	(0.179)	(0.041)	(0.284)	(0.474)	
Employee	11.977***		12.17***			6.3694***
	(0.0000)		(0.0000)			(0.0000)
Crisis	0.0038	-0.0141	-0.0072	-0.0001		0.0748**
	(0.947)	(0.765)	(0.883)	(0.998)		(0.0000)
Hausman test	0.0001	0.075	0.0165	0.0231		
Sargan test					0.9561	0.9757
AR(2) test					0.1369	0.1679

Note: Standard errors in parentheses ( ); $^{***}p < 0.01$, $^{**}p < 0.05$, $^{*}p < 0.10$.

Table 5. Regression results of spatial Durbin model.

	(1) Spatial adjacency	(2) Spatial adjacency	(3) Geographic distance	(4) Geographic distance	(5) Economic distance	(6) Economic distance
FDI	0.2994** (0.038)	0.3172** (0.026)	0.2665* (0.081)	0.3832*** (0.02)	0.2607* (0.098)	0.3517** (0.028)
Urban	0.2218*** (0.000)	0.2775*** (0.000)	0.1978*** (0.000)	0.4225*** (0.000)	0.2248*** (0.000)	0.1661*** (0.000)
Invest	−5.4907*** (0.001)	−6.448	−5.5101*** (0.001)	−9.22	−3.79106** (0.016)	
Employee	38.4797*** (0.000)	39.7468*** (0.000)	37.4953*** (0.000)		32.6023*** (0.001)	41.5656*** (0.000)
Direct effect	0.2286* (0.0900)	0.2279 (0.1030)	0.2417* (0.0760)	0.3173*** (0.0320)	0.2853** (0.0590)	0.3692** (0.0160)
Spatial spillover effect	0.3978** (0.016)	0.3298** (0.033)	0.7209** (0.03)	0.9845** (0.015)	−0.65 (0.494)	−0.9934 (0.331)
Fixed effect	Y	Y	Y	Y	Y	Y
Time fixed effects	N	Y	N	Y	N	N

Note: Standard errors in parentheses ( ); $^{***}p < 0.01$, $^{**}p < 0.05$, $^{*}p < 0.10$.

weight matrix are applied here. The first is the spatial adjacency
matrix, in which the value between adjacent provinces (or municipalities directly under the central government) is 1, and the remaining values are 0. To ensure the robustness of the results, the spatial
geographical distance weight matrix (W2) and the spatial economic
distance weight matrix (W3) are also introduced. Among them, the
spatial distance weight ($1/d$) is the reciprocal of the geographical
distance between each municipality or provincial capital, and geographic distance data come from the national bureau of surveying
and mapping. The economic distance weight is defined as

$$e_{ij} = \frac{1}{\left| \overline{Y_i} - \overline{Y_j} \right|}, \quad i \neq j,$$

and

$$\overline{Y_i} = \frac{1}{t_1 - t_0 + 1} \sum_{t=t_0}^{t_1} Y_{it}, \quad e_{ij} = 0, \quad i = j,$$

where Y_{it} is real per capita income of region i in year t. The data
were collected from the provincial statistical yearbook.

From the results of direct impact, producer service FDI can significantly promote the high-technology manufacturing industries in
eastern China. This result is consistent with the benchmark regression results. For spatial spillovers, the results in columns (1)–(4)
show that FDI inflow in producer services can positively affect the
upgrading of manufacturing structure in geographically neighboring
provinces. The results in columns (5) and (6) show little impact,
which means that there is almost no spillover effect of producer service FDI between provinces with similar economic development level,
because the competitiveness between provinces with similar economic
development level is strong, so there could be no spatial spillover
effect among them.

5.   Conclusions and Policy Implications

In the context of the overall opening of China's service industry,
this study has examined the impact of the FDI inflow in producer

services on the structural changes of China's manufacturing sector from 2006 to 2015. The main findings are as follows: first, the FDI inflow in the producer service industry promotes the upgrading of the manufacturing structure in the eastern part of China significantly and substantially, but has little impact in the central and western regions. A second conclusion is that the quality of FDI inflow rather than quantity, i.e. the industrial distribution of FDI inflow, has a key impact on the development of high-technology manufacturing industries in eastern China. Third, in eastern China, the inflow of FDI in producer services does not only promote the development of high-technology manufacturing industries in the host province but also generates a significant and positive spatial spillover effect in geographically adjacent areas. Fourth, due to the small scale of FDI in producer services in the western region of China, expanding the FDI will help promote the structural upgrading of manufacturing sector in the region.

Based on these findings and the development status of the producer service industry in China, the following policy suggestions are proposed.

First, the government should further encourage the inflow of FDI into the producer service industry and fully utilize the potential of China's producer service industry. China's producer service industry has a relatively short time of opening and a low degree of openness. As the role of Chinese manufacturing in the global value chain increases, the demand for producer services will gradually expand. Further opening up the producer service industry and improving the efficiency of the FDI inflow into this industry, it will be conducive to better promote the development of China's manufacturing and enhance their international competitiveness. At the same time, due to the relatively low overall development level of the domestic service industry, the inflow of foreign capital in the producer service industry can lead to supplementary demonstration effects, which will help to promote the growth of China's producer service industry and thus provide better services for the manufacturing sector.

Second, due to the economies of scale in the producer service industry, FDI in this sector has the potential risk of foreign monopolization and the exclusion of domestic enterprises. Therefore, the government departments need to design a reasonable mechanism for the further opening of this sector. On the one hand, foreign-invested manufacturing enterprises can be required to increase the procurement of domestic service inputs. On the other hand, the government can promote competition and eliminate barriers to entry in these industries, so as to encourage the entrance of private capital and to promote the growth of domestic producer services. In addition, the spillover effects of FDI should be fully utilized to improve the economic efficiency of the industry.

Finally, the limited impact of current producer service FDI on the industrial upgrading of the central and western regions in China represents a challenge. In order to avoid this regional disparity and to solve the problem of differences in regional openness, China should make full use of the policy support of the "Belt and Road" initiatives to promote the openness of the central and western regions, guiding the inflow of foreign capital rationally towards the overall improvement of the economic situation of the central and western regions.

Acknowledgements

Funding: This work was supported partly by the Ministry of Education of China Youth Fund Program (Grant No. 17YJC790036) and partly by China Postdoctoral Science Foundation Project (Grant No. 2017M621143).

References

Acemoglu, D. and Guerrieri, V. (2008). "Capital Deepening and Nonbalanced Economic Growth," *Journal of Political Economy*, **116**(3), 467–498.

Aitken, B., Hanson, G. H., and Harrison, A. E. (1997). "Spillovers, Foreign Investment, and Export Behavior," *Journal of International Economics*, **43**(1–2), 103–132.

Blomström, M. and Persson, H. (1983). "Foreign Investment and Spillover Efficiency in an Underdeveloped Economy: Evidence from the Mexican Manufacturing Industry," *World Development*, **11**(6), 493–501.

Browning, H. and Singelman, J. (1975). "The Emergence of a Service Society: Demographic and Sociological Aspects of the Sectoral Transformation of the

Labor Force in the USA." National Technical Information Service, Springfield, VA.

Fernandes, A. M. and Paunov, C. (2012). "Foreign Direct Investment in Services and Manufacturing Productivity: Evidence for Chile," *Journal of Development Economics*, **97**(2), 305–321.

Fons-Rosen, C., Kalemli-Ozcan, S., and Sorensen, B. E. (2017). "Foreign Investment and Domestic Productivity: Identifying Knowledge Spillovers and Competition Effects," NBER working paper, No. 23643.

Francois, J. and Woerz, J. (2008). "Producer Services, Manufacturing Linkages, and Trade," *Journal of Industry, Competition and Trade*, **8**(3–4), 199–229.

Fu, Y. H. and Ye, X. S. (2014). "The Selection of Technology Progress Path of Manufacturing Structure Optimization," *China Industrial Economics*, **9**, 78–90.

Ge, S. Q. and Luo, W. (2015). "Multinational Enterprises Entry and Industrial Structural of Manufacturing Sector in China: Based on Global Value Chain Perspective," *Journal of Economic Research*, **11**, 34–48.

Greenfield, H. (1966). *Manpower and the Growth of Producer Services*, Columbia University Press, New York.

He, Q. S., Zhang, P. Y. and Bo, Y. S. (2012). "Study on the Spatial Econometric of Producer Service FDI Technology Spillover Effect," *The Problems of Economy Journal*, **1**, 83–86.

Jiao, P. (2014). "The Economic Growth Effect on FDI Agglomeration in Producer Services: By Using the Spatial Econometric Methods," *Foreign Economics and Relations Trade*, **8**, 66–68.

Katouzian, M. A. (1970). "The Development of the Service Sector: A New Approach," *Oxford Economic Papers*, **22**(3), 362–382.

Liu, B. Q., Wang, Y. Z. and Wen, F. H. (2011). "Modern Productive Service Industry, High-end Manufacturing Industry and Industrial Security Under the Open Economy," *Social Science*, **5**, 50–55.

Mariotti, S., Nicolini, M. and Piscitello, L. (2013). "Vertical Linkages Between Foreign MNEs in Service Sectors and Local Manufacturing Firms," *Structural Change and Economic Dynamics*, **25**, 133–145

Michaels, G., Rauch, F. and Redding, J. (2012). "Urbanization and Structural Transformation," *The Quarterly Journal of Economics*, **127**(2), 535–586.

Park, S. H. (1989). "Linkages Between Industry and Services and Their Implications for Urban Employment Generation in Developing Countries," *Journal of Development Economics*, **30**(2), 359–379.

Wang. L. X. (2010). "Urbanization Path and City Scale in China: An Economic Analysis," *Economic Research Journal*, **10**, 20–32.

Wen, D. W., Xian G. M. and Ma, J. (2009). "FDI, Industrial Structure Change and China's Export Competitiveness," *World Journal of Management*, **4**, 96–107.

Part II

The Financial Aspects of China's Growth and Development

Chapter 6

Financial Integration and China's Growth Surge

Rod Tyers[*,†,¶] and Yixiao Zhou[‡,§,‖]

*Business School, University of Western Australia,
Research School of Economics, Australia
† Centre for Applied Macroeconomic Analysis (CAMA),
Australian National University, Australia
‡ Crawford School of Public Policy,
Australian National University, Australia
School of Economics, Finance and Property,
§ Curtin Business School, Curtin University
¶ rod.tyers@uwa.edu.au
‖ yixiao.zhou@anu.edu.au

China's financial openness, as measured by cross-border flows and asset ownership, peaked during its 2000s growth surge, as did downward pressure on global interest rates and price levels. This was despite China's restriction of financial inflows to approved FDI and tight controls on private outflows. We therefore consider two different types of financial integration. The first, Type 1, reflects the scale of cross-border flows as proportions of domestic saving or investment. The second, Type 2, indicates the weakness of capital controls and, in particular, the ease of rebalancing the Chinese collective portfolio away from official foreign reserves and across foreign regions. China's growth surge contributed substantially to the integration of Type 1 but not Type 2. Results from global modelling are summarized showing that, with more Type 2 integration, surge effects within China would have been substantially smaller, while the global impacts on yields and inflation would have been larger.

1. Introduction

Central to the impacts of China's emergence on the rest of the world is the "unbalanced" nature of its growth surge after the 1990s, which peaked in the early 2000s and saw faster growth in the domestic supply of merchandise than in its domestic consumption. This had direct, and much analyzed, effects on the terms of trade facing other regions.[1] Yet, in addition to the deflationary forces unleashed in these regions, the associated excess supply of saving also changed the financial terms of trade, contributing to asset price inflation and the observed trend decline in asset yields over the same period.[2,3]

Since the global financial crisis (GFC), and more particularly after 2010, a decline in the level of imbalance in China's growth became apparent. China's production structure has been diversifying away from export-oriented light manufacturing to services to better meet home consumption demand (Lardy, 2006; Bowles, 2012). There has been relative growth in Chinese consumption and a decline in its excess saving, thus unwinding some of the global effects of the prior growth surge. Yet, the deflationary effects of the surge have been

---

[1]The literature on the terms of trade consequences for the advanced economies began in the 1990s with the debate over the poor performance of unskilled US workers (Bound and Johnson, 1992; Wood, 1994; Berman *et al.*, 1994; Leamer, 1996; Wood 2018) and extended into a more complex debate over the apparently declining performance of all but the most highly paid US workers (Haskell *et al.*, 2012; Helpmann *et al.*, 2010; Autor *et al.*, 2013). It has also included global modelling studies that kicked off with Krugman (1995) and proceeded to the decomposition studies by Tyers and Yang (1997) and Francois and Nelson (1998) with more detailed follow-up of labor effects by Tyers and Yang (2000), Winchester and Greenaway (2007), Francois and Wignaraja (2008), Harris *et al.* (2011), Harris and Robertson (2013), Levchenko and Zhang (2012), and Di Giovanni *et al.* (2013). Diversity in method notwithstanding, all the global modelling studies find net gains to the rest of the world transmitted via terms of trade effects.

[2]The terms of trade gain transmitted financially have been commonly referred to as the Asian "savings glut". See Bernanke (2005), Chinn and Ito (2007), Choi *et al.* (2008), Ito (2009), Chinn *et al.* (2012), and Arora *et al.* (2014).

[3]These changes abroad were superficially beneficial, though the evidence to date suggests that the gains have been at least partially offset by structural unemployment. For a survey and analysis of the neoclassical and Keynesian effects abroad, see Tyers (2015b).

persistent, albeit subsequently compounded by other global developments, including the retreat to money during the GFC and its effects on perceived investment risk, increased automation, the extraordinary global expansion of the largest of the information technology-based service companies, and an unanticipated energy supply glut, necessitating transitions to unconventional monetary policy (UMP) in Japan, the US, and Europe.

The role of financial integration is worth particular attention in analyzing the global effects of change in China. Its opening to trade was extensive, necessitated by a very high degree of specialization in labor-intensive manufacturing and hence the need to exchange this for products and services that would meet growing domestic demands. This commenced soon after its transitional reforms of the late 1970s and accelerated following its commitment to a modern taxation system and a *de facto* fixed exchange rate in 1994. Meanwhile, as reflected by the scale of cross-border financial flows, China appeared to open financially. Foreign direct investment (FDI) played a significant role in financing investment and there were substantial outflows of excess saving into global financial markets. Yet the FDI was state-vetted, entering under mandated partnerships with state-owned enterprises (SOEs). On the outflow side, private acquisitions of foreign assets were restricted and the domestic currency non-convertible. This meant that the foreign currency remaining in the banking system, due to the excess of export earnings over import expenditure, had to be acquired by the central bank and deposited abroad as official foreign reserves.

We therefore consider two different types of financial integration. The first, Type 1, reflects the scale of cross-border flows as proportions of domestic saving or investment. The second, Type 2, indicates the weakness of capital controls and, in particular, the ease with which the Chinese collective portfolio can be rebalanced away from official foreign reserves and across foreign regions. China's growth surge contributed substantially to integration of Type 1 but not of Type 2. While the financial effects of the surge are of significant interest to us, our focus in this study is on the differences in domestic and global effects of the surge that would have arisen had there also been financial integration of Type 2. To explore this, we use a parsimonious global macroeconomic model that incorporates bilateral linkages across six regions via both trade and financial flows.

The model includes a number of innovative elements. First, by allowing for asset differentiation it incorporates optimizing financial portfolio management in each region that serves to direct saving from each into investments across all regions. Second, the degree of asset differentiation is quantified, via an elasticity of asset substitution, to reflect financial integration of Type 2. Third, UMP is represented where relevant, placing direct demands on the global markets for long maturity assets that are endogenous to chosen targets. This tends to enhance the spillover effects of monetary policy (Chen *et al.*, 2016), which proves important because the UMP response raises long maturity asset prices and lowers yields. The consequent rebalancing of portfolios in favor of money then exacerbates the deflationary effects of China's growth surge.

Overall, the results suggest that the surge had significant implications for the advanced regions, transmitted via changes in both financial flows and the international terms of trade. This is consistent with empirical analyses that have revealed large macroeconomic effects.[4] Moreover, it emerges that the growth surge would have yielded net real income gains not only in China but also, albeit more modestly, in advanced regions. Meanwhile, we find that these effects are quite sensitive to the level of China's financial integration. Indeed, the domestic effects of the surge are shown to be considerably moderated in the presence of financial integration of Type 2, including the scale of the growth surge itself. On the other hand, foreign effects are seen to be amplified by such integration and particularly the deflationary pressures in the US.

---

[4] For empirical results that confirm the global significance of changes in China, see Eickmeier and Kuehnlenz (2018). Our modelling results are contrary, however, to those of N'Daye *et al.* (2010) and Genberg and Zhang (2010), who find that the international effects of changes in Chinese consumption are small. Their conclusions stem from the use of a model in which spillover effects stem primarily from trade, and financial flows are only weakly represented.

Section 2 places China's 2000s growth surge in the context of the evolution of its policy regimes, its economic structure, and coincident developments in the slower growing advanced economies. Section 3 reviews the corresponding changes in financial structure, openness, and external impact. Section 4 then presents the model used for quantitative analysis, and Section 5 offers numerical analysis of the foreign effects of China's growth surge. Section 6 considers the sensitivity of these effects to financial integration, and conclusions are offered in Section 7.

2.   The Surge and Its External Effects

Outside China, macroeconomic assessments of Asian growth have been dominated by critics worried about the imbalances associated with excess saving (the "savings glut") and the "upstream" financial flows that stem from it.[5] China's particular contribution to these upstream financial flows has been variously attributed to capital market distortions, exchange rate "manipulation", and myriad other interventions by the all-pervasive Chinese state to confer unfair advantage on Chinese firms and to raise exports and investment at the expense of household consumption.[6] To see both sides of these controversies, we need to place the growth surge in context.

2.1.   *Growth and trade*

Adopting the standard "East Asian" growth model, China was able to move workers from rural poverty to urban locations where they

---

[5] A substantial literature now either asserts, or depends upon, the "savings glut" hypothesis. Contributions include those by Bernanke (2005, 2011), Caballero *et al.* (2008), Caballero (2009), Chinn and Ito (2007), Choi *et al.* (2008), Chinn *et al.* (2012), Eichengreen (2004), and Lee and McKibbin (2007).

[6] The American literature critical of China's macroeconomic policies is also extensive. Bernanke (2005, 2011) offers the outline and Krugman (2010) declares that "China is making all of us poorer". The US macroeconomic position is put in more detail by, among others, Lardy (2006, 2012) and Bergsten *et al.* (2008). Similar advocacy of policy-induced "balance" in China's growth can be found, still more formally, in Blanchard and Giavazzi (2006), while it is also recognized that some of the US reaction is mercantilist (Ito, 2009).

could be combined with capital and imported technology, yielding rapid productivity growth (Song *et al.*, 2011). But the modest skills of these workers required that the product mix comprises only light (labor-intensive) manufactures, unbalancing it relative to consumption and investment demand and thus requiring a rapid expansion in trade. The speed of the growth, combined with lagging social institutions and industrial reform, also induced very high household saving rates and made state-owned enterprises very profitable, leading to high corporate saving (Bayoumi *et al.*, 2010). This had modest effects on the developed regions prior to the 2000s, before which the scale of China's economy did not rival their own. After China's post-WTO accession, however, an unprecedented accumulation of foreign investment combined with new access to markets in the advanced economies to deliver the growth surge.

As indicated by the real GDP series in Figure 1, the modern Chinese economy has in fact enjoyed three growth surges, the first following the "reform and opening up" from the late 1970s and the second following the implementation of the *de facto* peg to the US dollar and the taxation reforms of 1994. During the first surge, however, China contributed only 2% of the global economy. By 2000,

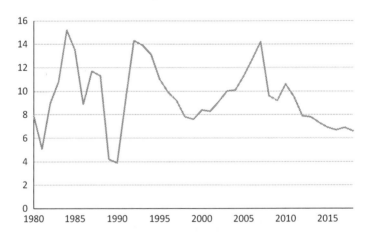

Figure 1.   Official real GDP growth of China, annual percent change, 1980–2018.
Source: IMF World Economic Outlook.

this was near 10%, with much larger shares of global manufactures production and trade.[7]

2.2. External financial effects

Implications of the surge for global finance follow from the recognition that, since 1980, Asian economies have contributed about half of the increment to global saving, with China contributing fully a third of the increment since 1990. This is evidence that the shift in global growth toward high-saving Asia, which occurred in the 1980s, accelerated the rate at which the global savings supply curve shifted to the right. If, as the data suggest, the corresponding global investment demand curve shifted by less, the Wicksellian (1898) "natural" rate of interest at the global level must have declined.[8]

Long maturity bonds in open and well-regulated financial markets arbitrage with other major instruments of private saving and investment and are extensively traded internationally. Their yields tend therefore to be more stable through time than business-cycle-driven short yields and their movements highly correlated across the advanced economies, as is evident from Figure 2 (Arora *et al.*, 2014). It is argued by Ito (2013, p. 8) that globalization has made domestic financial markets more susceptible to international factors, tending to decouple short-term and long-term interest rates.[9] Consistent with Bernanke (2005), he concludes that the long-term interest rate is tied down by global saving imbalances and hence reflects the natural rate of interest. This reasoning, and that of Rey (2013), both imply that, when there is free capital mobility, there is inter-regional arbitrage at the long end of the yield curve,

---

[7]These are proportions of global GDP in international dollars from the IMF, *World Economic Outlook Database.*

[8]*Ex ante* shifts in saving supply and investment demand cannot be observed. See Tyers (2015b) for a discussion of this.

[9]He and McCauley (2013) find evidence of "imperfect substitutability along the yield curve" and use it to explore monetary policy spillover effects, which they see as enlarged by the global integration of long bond markets.

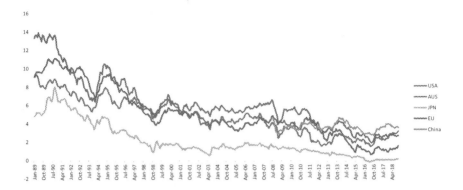

Figure 2.   Long-term bond yields in advanced economies.

Sources: Long-term interest rates refer to government bonds maturing in 10 years. Long-term interest rates in this figure are monthly averages of daily rates, measured as a percentage. Rates for USA, Australia, and Japan are obtained from the OECD Database. Rates for EU and China are obtained from the CEIC Database.

whereas the short end of the yield curve is conventionally controlled by monetary authorities.[10] It follows, then, that the rise in Asian saving is a possible explanation for the persistent downward trend in long-term bond rates since the 1980s that is apparent from Figure 2.[11]

Inside China, the excess saving stemmed from a decline in private consumption as a share of GDP between 2000 and 2008, with this share not picking up until after 2010, as shown in Figure 3. Also indicated in the figure are extraordinary rates of domestic saving from GDP. This suggests a major role for the Chinese financial sector in recycling half its GDP into investment. While investment from abroad has been important, as seed capital in the very early years and as a source of modern technology later (Sun, 2009), total investment has mostly followed the pattern of domestic saving through time.

---

[10]We thank Paul Luk for clarifying this point.

[11]The separation of the series for Japan is associated with its long-term current account surplus and the major Yen appreciation shocks of the late 1980s and early 1990s, which established a negative risk premium among Japanese savers. In all regions, inflation rates were low throughout the period shown in the figure and so the trend of nominal long rates reflects that of corresponding real rates.

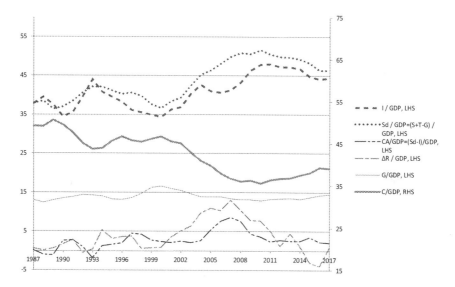

Figure 3. Saving, investment, and external balance of the Chinese economy (1987–2017).

Source: Authors' calculations based on data from the CEIC Database and State Administration of Foreign Exchange (SAFE). Data on current account and change of official reserve are obtained from SAFE. Other data are obtained from the CEIC Database.

Nonetheless, tremendous growth in the domestic economy and thus in recyclable saving has meant that, while inward FDI continued to expand beyond the 2000s surge, its share in total investment in China has been declining (Figure 4). Meanwhile, Chinese policy has ensured that FDI nonetheless retains the largest share of net capital inflow (Figure 5).

Gross flows on China's balance of payments are plotted in Figure 6, including its current account, capital account, change of official foreign reserves, and net flows on its financial account (which here excludes changes in official reserves). In this figure, credits refer to inflows of funds and debits to outflows. During the surge, the balance of payments shows a relative boom in current account net credits, offset mostly by a substantial rise in official foreign reserves. The subsequent fall in official foreign reserves stemmed from both

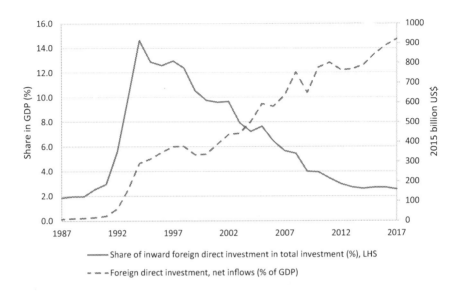

Figure 4. FDI inflow and its share of total domestic investment in China (%).

Source: Authors' calculations based on data from United Nations Conference on Trade and Development (UNCTAD) and the CEIC Database. From UNCTAD, data for inward foreign direct investment as a share of GDP in China are obtained. Based on data in the CEIC Database, we calculate total domestic investment as a share of GDP in China. We then calculate the share of FDI inflow in total domestic investment by dividing the former by the latter. For the red series, real GDP is calculated in constant 2015 US$ based on the IMF *World Economic Outlook Database*. Then this is multiplied by the share of inward FDI in GDP to obtain inward FDI in constant 2015 US$.

a reduction in the imbalance between Chinese production and consumption and hence a decline in the trade surplus, along with a slump in the net inflow of investment funds.

3. Quantifying Financial Integration

One way to understand financial integration is to see it as the process through which increases in cross-border arbitrage cause prices in domestic financial markets to adjust more in harmony with foreign markets (Lien and Zhang, 2018; Ho, 2009). China's comparatively high economic growth rate and the similarly high underlying rates of return it has offered to new capital suggest an increasing trend in capital flows

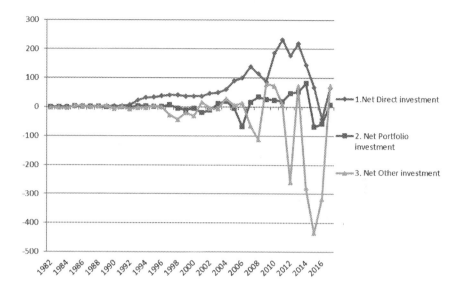

Figure 5. Net investment inflow, billion USD (1982–2017).

Source: Authors' calculations based on data on total credits and total debits of direct investment, portfolio investment, and "other investment" in "The Balance of Payments Table" from China's State Administration of Foreign Exchange (SAFE). Net investment of each type of asset is the difference between total credits and total debits of each type of asset.

both into and out of its economy.[12] In our view, this is a reflection of Type 1 financial integration, which depends only on the extent to which assets are traded and owned externally. Indeed, Type 1 financial integration might best be measured from flow data by a combination of the ratio of investment from abroad to total domestic investment or domestic GDP and the ratio of saving directed to investment abroad to total domestic saving or domestic GDP. From asset stock data, the corresponding measures are available.

By contrast, in Type 2 financial integration, the focus is on the flexibility with which inward flows can be directed across domestic investments and outward flows can be directed across a range of asset

---

[12]Huang *et al.* (2010) and Garcia-Herrero (2015) assert that the trend in such flows indicate that China's capital account has become more open in recent years, yet the gross flows in Figure 5 suggest a subsequent reversal of this trend.

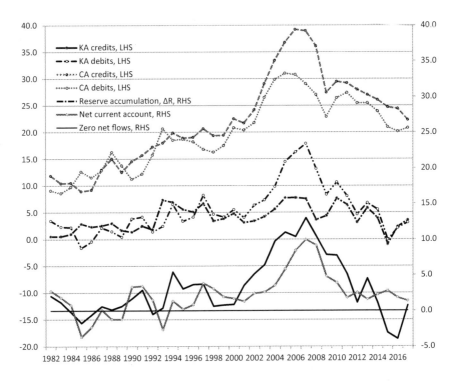

Figure 6.   Gross balance of payments flows, China, % of GDP (1982–2017).

Source: Authors' calculations based on data from "The Balance of Payments Table" from China's State Administration of Foreign Exchange (SAFE) and the CEIC Database. Data for the financial and capital accounts (consolidated here and referred to as "KA"), the current account, and the change of official foreign reserves are obtained from SAFE, and data for GDP are obtained from the CEIC Database.

types and destination economies. An economy that is open in this way is likely to have a more globally diversified collective asset portfolio. This is not achieved via officially sanctioned FDI on the inflow side and outflows driven by official foreign reserve accumulation, even though these yield high values for Type 1 integration. Type 2 financial integration yields freer arbitrage, allowing asset prices in domestic financial markets to adjust more in harmony with foreign markets.

Quantifying financial integration depends on both *de facto* and *de jure* measures, where *de jure* measures reflect official capital control policies and *de facto* measures indicate actual practice. A range of possible *de facto* measures for China is shown in Figure 7. These suggest that, during the surge period, there were substantial increases in Type 1 integration but that the pattern since then has been mixed. Considering stock measures, the foreign-owned capital stock rose as a share of GDP while the corresponding share of Chinese-owned capital abroad fell. The inward FDI stock fell while the outward FDI stock rose, though by contrast, the stock of inward portfolio assets rose while that of outward portfolio assets fell. This contrast is most evident after the growth surge, signalling important roles for the "belt and road" initiative and improved access by foreigners to portfolio assets on China's two stock markets (Lim, 2017).

Turning to flow measures that indicate Type 1 financial integration, the final graph in Figure 7 is constructed as the weighted sum of the quotient of financial outflows with total domestic saving and the quotient of financial inflows with total domestic investment. This shows a large peak during the growth surge and a decline thereafter, notwithstanding a modest recovery post-GFC. Meanwhile, also after the surge, there was significant diversification of assets away from the concentration on foreign reserves. The shares of the FDI stock, portfolio assets, other assets, and foreign reserves in total assets change from 7%, 7%, 15%, and 72% to 21%, 7%, 25%, and 46%, respectively.[13] These changes suggest increases in Type 2 financial integration, at least to the extent that they have allowed portfolio diversification.

More direct assessments of capital control are available from the two *de jure* measures of capital control offered in Figure 8. These are calculated based on the codification of information provided in the IMF's Annual Report on *Exchange Rate Arrangements and Restrictions* (AREAER). While there is no change in the Chinn–Ito Index (Chinn and Ito, 2007), that by Fernandez *et al.* (2016) does show

---

[13]Total assets consist of direct investment assets (FDI stock), portfolio investment assets, financial derivative assets, other assets, and reserve assets. The value of financial derivate assets is much smaller than other types of assets and is therefore omitted in Figure 7 and the discussion in the main text.

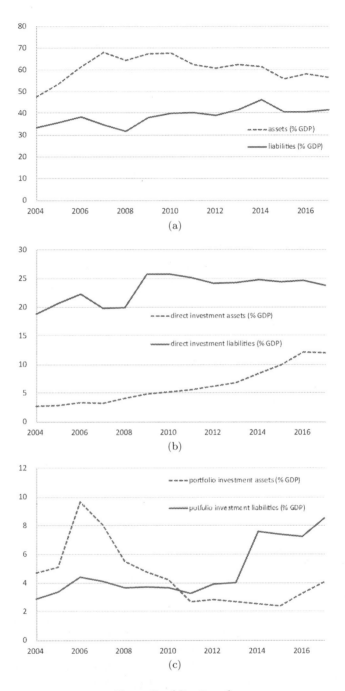

Figure 7. (*Continued*)

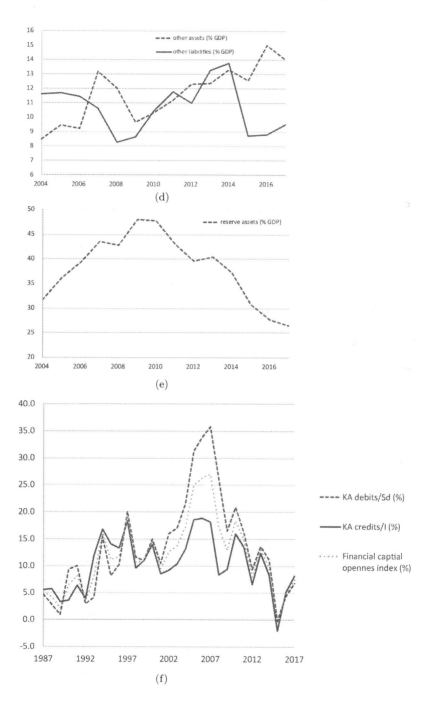

Figure 7. (*Continued*)

Figure 7. *De facto* measures of China's Type 1 financial openness. (First five relate to stocks of foreign assets and liabilities; the sixth depends on flows.) (a) Total assets and total liabilities as a share of GDP (%). (b) Direct investment assets and direct investment liabilities as a share of GDP (%). (c) Portfolio investment assets and portfolio liabilities as a share of GDP (%). (d) Other assets and other liabilities as a share of GDP (%). (e) Reserve assets as a share of GDP (%). (f) Financial capital openness index: debits on the capital and financial accounts to total domestic saving, credits on the capital and financial accounts to the level of gross domestic investment, and their arithmetic average.

Source: Authors' calculations based on data from State Administration of Foreign Exchange (SAFE). SAFE provides data on China's International Investment Position on an annual basis. These data cover foreign assets, foreign liabilities, and their detailed components direct investment assets, direct investment liabilities, portfolio investment assets, portfolio investment liabilities, other investment assets, other investment liabilities, and reserve assets as shares of GDP. The bottom right index is constructed based on Paranavithana *et al.* (2018). The index depends in every period on the ratio of gross capital outflows (debits on the capital and financial accounts) to total domestic savings (S_d) on the one hand and that of the gross value of financial capital inflows (credits on the capital and financial accounts) to the level of gross domestic investment on the other hand (I): Financial capital openness index $= \frac{1}{2} \left[\frac{|KA\ debits|}{|S_d|} + \frac{|KA\ credits|}{|I|} \right]$. When the value of gross capital inflows is close to the value of total domestic investments and the value of gross capital outflows is close to the total domestic savings, the average value of the financial capital openness index tends toward unity. The most extreme case would be where gross capital outflows represent very low values compared to total domestic savings and gross capital inflows represent very low values compared to total domestic investment expenditure. This occurs if non-resident and resident flows are controlled, in which case the financial openness index is near zero.

some relaxation of controls in recent years, though not during the growth surge.

These measures confirm that China opened significantly by Type 1 measures but did not act to raise the level of Type 2 integration until after the surge and the GFC. In our analysis that follows, we ask how the global effects of China's growth surge would have been different had the extent of Type 2 financial integration been greater.

Chinn-Ito Index of financial openness, 1984-2016

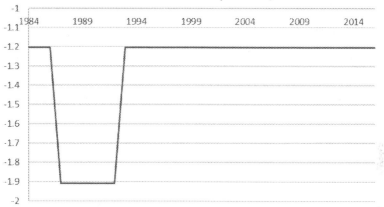

Source: Chinn and Ito (2007). The index is update to 2016 and is available from the Chinn–Ito Index Website at http://web.pdx.edu/~ito/Chinn-Ito_website.ht m. As is explained in detail in Chinn and Ito (2007), the Chinn–Ito Index is the first principal component of the original variables pertaining to regulatory controls over current or capital account transactions, the existence of multiple exchange rates, and the requirements of surrendering export proceeds in the Annual Report on Exchange Arrangements and Exchange Restrictions (AREAER) published by the International Monetary Fund. This index takes on higher values, the more open the country is to cross-border capital transactions. By construction, the series has a mean of zero.

Overall restrictions index (all asset categories), 1995-2015

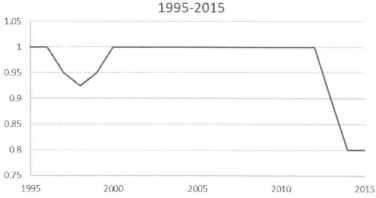

Figure 8. (*Continued*)

←———————————————————————————————————

Source: Fernández *et al.* (2016). The index is normalized to [0, 1], with higher values indicating higher restrictiveness. This index is a measures of *de jure* restrictions on cross-border financial transactions. It differs from Chinn–Ito Index in terms of the way information is extracted from the Annual Report on Exchange Arrangements and Exchange Restrictions (AREAER) published by the International Monetary Fund.

Figure 8.   *De jure* measures of Chinese financial integration.

4.   Modeling Financial Interdependence

A multi-region general equilibrium structure is used that centers on the global financial capital market.[14] It is assumed that the financial products of each region are differentiated and that portfolio managers assign new net saving across regions so as to maximize expected portfolio returns given this differentiation. This retains Feldstein–Horioka (1980) home bias while allowing significant redirections in financial flows at the margin. It also allows the level of global financial market integration to be parameterized by varying this degree of differentiation. The scale of short-run spillover effects associated with growth performance, excess saving, and monetary policy therefore depend on it.

Although there is a tendency for financial flows to move the global economy toward interest parity, this differentiation leaves this process incomplete in the lengths of run considered. At the same time, regional rates of return on equity investments depart from regional bond yields, the former reflecting expected rates of return on installed capital and the latter short-run equilibrium in regional financial markets reflecting expected rates of return between savers, indebted governments, and investors. Within each region, the demand for money is driven by a "cash in advance" constraint applying across the whole of GDP and a wealth effect whereby portfolio expansion requires a sustained liquid share, comprising non-yielding money. Thus, in every

———————————————————

[14]This section draws on an analysis presented in more detail by Tyers and Zhou (2019b). The model used represents all financial products, including government bonds, as regionally differentiated and so there is no perfectly integrated global market for any asset class.

region, home money is held in a portfolio with long maturity bonds, which are claims over physical capital and government debt across the regions.[15] The opportunity cost of holding money is the yield on these long bonds. On the supply side of the money market, in regions with unconventional monetary policy, expansions raise demand for long maturity bonds, reducing their yields and hence reducing the opportunity cost of holding money.

Six regions are identified: the US, the EU, Japan, China, Australia, and the Rest of the World, though the focus of this study is on the first four.[16] Each region supplies a single product that is also differentiated from the products of the other regions. On the supply side, there are three primary factors with "production" labor, a partially unemployed variable factor while the stocks of physical capital and skill remain fixed and fully employed. Collective households are net savers with reduced form consumption depending on current and expected future disposable income and the home interest rate. Aggregate consumption is subdivided via a single CES structure between the products of all the regions. The following offers detail on the aspects of the model central to this analysis.[17]

4.1. *Financial markets*

Here the modeling departs from convention by incorporating explicit portfolios of assets from all regions. Data on regional saving and investment for 2016 are first combined with those on international financial flows to construct an initial matrix to allocate total domestic saving in each region to investment across all the regions. From this is derived a corresponding matrix of initial shares of region i's net (private and government) saving that are allocated to the local

---

[15]Expectations are exogenous in the model, formed over future values of home nominal disposable income, the rate of inflation, the real post-tax rate of return on home assets and bilateral real exchange rate alignment.

[16]The EU is modelled as the full 26, and it is assumed that this collective has a single central bank.

[17]The routine components of the model, along with i, are available in the appendix in Tyers and Zhou (2018).

savings supply that finances investment in region j, i_{ij}^{S0}. When the model is shocked, the new shares are calculated so as to favor investment in region, j, with comparatively high after-tax yields, generally implying high expected real gross rates of return, r^{ce}. This is calculated as

$$r_i^{ce} = r_i^c + \hat{e}_i^e = \frac{P_i^P M P_i^K}{P_i^K} \left(\frac{\varphi_i^0}{\varphi_i} \right) + \hat{e}_i^e, \tag{1}$$

where P_i^K is the price of capital goods, which in this model is linked by an exogenous factor to P_i^P, the producer price of the region's generic good.[18] The (exogenous) expected proportional change in the real exchange rate is $\hat{e}_i^e$. A further adjustment is made using an interest premium factor, φ_i, that is defined relative to the US ($\varphi_{US} = 1$). This permits consideration of the effects of changes in sovereign risk in association with the fiscal balance. Increments to regional sovereign risk cause investments in those regions to be less attractive.

$$\varphi_i = \varphi_i^0 \left[\left(\frac{G_i}{T_i} \Big/ \frac{G_{US}}{T_{US}} \right) \right]^{\phi_i}, \quad \forall i \neq \text{``US''}, \tag{2}$$

where ϕ_i is an elasticity indicating sensitivity to sovereign risk.

In region i, then, the demand for investment financing depends on the ratio of the expected rate of return on installed capital, r_i^{ce}, and a domestic market clearing bond yield or financing rate, r_i:

$$\frac{I_i^D}{I_i^0} = \left(\frac{r_i^{ce}}{r_i} \right)^{\varepsilon_i^I}, \tag{3}$$

where ε_i^I is a positive elasticity enabling the relationship to reflect Tobin's Q-like behavior. This investment demand is then matched in each region by a supply of saving that incorporates contributions from all regional households.

---

[18]The producer price level is the factory door price of the regional good, which differs in this model from the GDP price level due to indirect taxation. See Tyers (2015a; Appendix 1) for further explanation of this.

Region i's portfolio manager allocates the proportion i_{ij}^S of its annual (private plus government) saving to new investments in regions j, such that $\sum_j i_{ij}^S = 1$.[19] Because the newly issued equity is differentiated across regions based on unmodeled and unobserved region-specific properties, their services are combined via a constant elasticity of substitution (CES) function specific to each regional portfolio manager. Thus, region i's household portfolio management problem is to choose the shares, i_{ij}^S, of its private saving net of any government deficit, $S_i^D = S_i^P + T^D + T^I - G$, which are to be allocated to the assets of region j so as to maximize a CES composite representing the value of the services yielded by these assets:

$$\max_{i_{ij}^S} U_i^F = S_i^D \left[\sum_j \alpha_{ij}(i_{ij}^S)^{-\rho_i} \right]^{-\frac{1}{\rho_i}} \quad \text{such that} \quad \sum_j i_{ij}^S = 1. \quad (4)$$

Here α_{ij} is a parameter that indicates the benefit to flow from region i's investment in region j. The CES parameter, ρ_i, reflects the preparedness of region i's household to substitute between the assets it holds. To induce rebalancing in response to changes in rates of return, α_{ij} are made to be dependent on ratios of after-tax yields in destination regions, j, and the home region, i, via the following equation[20]:

$$\alpha_{ij} = \beta_{ij} \left(\frac{r_j}{\tau_j^K} \middle/ \frac{r_i}{\tau_i^K} \right)^{\lambda_i} \quad \forall i, j, \ \lambda_i > 0 \ \forall i. \quad (5)$$

Here, τ_i^K is the power of the capita income tax rate in region i. This relationship indicates the responsiveness of portfolio preferences to

---

[19] The manager does not reoptimize over *total* holdings every year. This is because the model is deterministic and risk is incorporated only via exogenous premia, so the motivations for continuous short-run rebalancing, other than the arrival of new saving, are not represented.

[20] Note that region i's market bond yield, r_i, is determined concurrently and indicates the replacement cost of capital in region i and therefore the opportunity cost for region i's household of investment in region j.

yields, via the (return chasing) elasticity λ_i. The allocation problem, thus augmented, is:

$$
\max_{i_{ij}^S} U_i^F = S_i^D \left[\sum_j \beta_{ij} \left(\frac{r_j}{\tau_j^K} \middle/ \frac{r_i}{\tau_i^K} \right)^{\lambda_i} (i_{ij}^S)^{-\rho_i} \right]^{-\frac{1}{\rho_i}},
$$

$$
\text{such that } \sum_j i_{ij}^S = 1. \tag{6}
$$

Solving for the first-order conditions we have, for region i's investments in regions j and k:

$$
\frac{i_{ij}^S}{i_{ik}^S} = \left(\frac{\beta_{ij}}{\beta_{ik}} \right)^{\frac{1}{1+\rho_i}} \left(\frac{r_j}{\tau_j^K} \middle/ \frac{r_k}{\tau_k^K} \right)^{\frac{\lambda_i}{1+\rho_i}}. \tag{7}
$$

This reveals that region i's elasticity of substitution between the bonds of different regions is $\sigma_i^I = \lambda_i/(1+\rho_i) > 0$, which has two elements: the return-chasing behavior of region i's household (λ_i) and the imperfect substitutability of regional bonds, and therefore the sluggishness of portfolio rebalancing (ρ_i). For the purposes of this analysis, the values of σ_i^I are seen as indicating the extent of each region's integration with global financial markets.

The optimal share of the net domestic saving of region i that is allocated to assets in region j then follows from Equation (8) and the normalization condition that $\sum_k i_{ik}^S = 1$:

$$
i_{ij}^S = \frac{1}{\sum_k \left(\frac{\beta_{ik}}{\beta_{ij}} \right)^{\frac{\sigma_i^I}{\lambda_i}} \left(\frac{r_k/\tau_k^K}{r_j/\tau_j^K} \right)^{\sigma_i^I}}. \tag{8}
$$

The key matrix for calibration is $[\beta_{ij}]$. These elements are readily available, first, by noting that only relative values are required and hence, for each region of origin, i, one value can be set to unity, and second, by making the assumption that the initial database has the steady-state property that the net rates of return in regions j are initially the same as the market bond yield, r_j. Then, since in the base data $r_{ij}^{e0} = r_j^0$, $r_{ik}^{e0} = r_k^0$, the β_{ij}'s are available from a modified Equation (6).

4.2. *Regional money market equilibrium*

In each region, home money is held in a portfolio with regionally differentiated long maturity bonds, which are claims over physical capital and government debt across the regions. Since portfolios are dominated by long maturity assets, the opportunity cost of holding money is the long bond yield. In each region, this is derived from equilibrium in a weakly segmented global market for loanable funds. Central banks derive monetary expansions in regionally specific proportions from conventional monetary policy and from UMP, with reliance on the market segmentation theory of the yield curve (Johnson *et al.*, 2010) to ensure that conventional monetary policy has no direct impact on the market for long-term bonds. Short rates are therefore not modelled explicitly, rather the monetary base in each region is determined as being endogenous to the target of monetary policy and an exogenous parameter determines the share of any change in the monetary base that takes the form of a long asset balance sheet expansion. UMP expansions raise home long maturity asset prices and lower long yields, causing imperfect spillovers across regions due to global arbitrage that is only partially constrained by asset differentiation.

A cash-in-advance constraint is assumed to generate transactions demand for home money across all components of gross (including intermediate) output. Transactions demand is then augmented by the real purchasing power of financial wealth over domestic goods, to account for the observed dependence of money demand on portfolio size.[21] Portfolio rebalancing effects are driven by the opportunity cost of holding home money, which is the nominal after-tax yield on home long-term bonds.[22] Real money balances are measured in terms of

---

[21]The inclusion of financial wealth in the money demand equation follows Ragot (2014) and Mena and Tirelli (2017), who incorporate (Baumol, 1952; Tobin, 1956) behavior.

[22]Thus, it is assumed here that the opportunity cost of holding money is measured by the long bond yield. Short rates, at least as they have a role in conventional monetary policy, are here embedded in the determination of the monetary base. The assumption that all investment financing depends on the long maturity market is a simplifying abstraction in this global analysis.

purchasing power over home products at the GDP price, P^Y:

$$m_i^D = a_i^{MD}(y_i)^{\varepsilon_i^{MY}}(w_i^F)^{\varepsilon_i^{MW}}\left(\frac{r_i\left(1+\pi_i^e\right)}{\tau_i^K}\right)^{-\varepsilon_i^{MR}} = \frac{M_i^S}{P_i^Y} = \frac{\mu_i M_i^B}{P_i^Y}. \tag{9}$$

For region i, y_i is real, regional gross output, and distinct from real GDP since intermediates as well as goods and services entering final demand are transacted. Real financial wealth is w_i^F, τ_i^K is the power of the capital income tax rate in region i and π_i^e is the expected inflation rate of the consumer price level, P^C, defined as a CES aggregate of home and imported consumer prices. Real financial wealth or assets, w^F, is represented as the present value of an infinite stream of real dividends that are equal to after-tax returns on the capital stock, at the expected real rate of return on installed capital, r^{ce}, discounted at the current real financing rate, r. A price adjustment is also made for relative inflation or deflation of capital goods prices, which raises or lowers the purchasing power of financial wealth over home products:

$$w_i^F = \frac{r_i^{ce}\left(1-t_i^K\right)\left(P_i^K/P_i^Y\right)K}{r_i}. \tag{10}$$

Thus, money demand is driven by transactions (y), portfolio expansion (w^F), and portfolio rebalancing as it affects the liquid component (driven by the opportunity cost, r).

On the supply side of the money market, the proportion of expansions that occur via the purchase of long maturity assets (UMP) is parameterized. Conventional expansions directly affect the money supply, while UMP expansions affect both money supply and the long end of the yield curve. UMP expansions raise home long maturity asset prices and lower long yields, causing imperfect spillovers due to global arbitrage that is only partially constrained by asset differentiation.[23]

---

[23]By contrast, conventional monetary policy involves trade in short-term instruments that has no direct, immediate impact on the market for long-term bonds, which are major components of the global portfolio. Short rates are therefore

Regional financial market clearance requires that the home financial market in each region clears separately and this implies global financial market clearance. For region i, the nominal value of domestic investment, I_i^D, represents the sum total of all domestic long bond issues. This is then equated with demand for those bonds from home and foreign (net private and government) savings, along with demands for home long bonds that arise from the "quantitative easing" components of monetary expansions by both home and foreign central banks.

5.　Effects of the Growth Surge

To quantify the internal and external effects of China's growth surge, Tyers and Zhou (2019b) conduct a set of model experiments. Closures indicate underlying assumptions about the labor market, fiscal policy, financial market clearance, and monetary targeting, and a set of shocks that represent the drivers of the surge in its peak years. These vary with the lengths of run. The first set is short run, suggesting the effects within the year the shocks arise, and the second is long, allowing labor market clearance and capacity adjustments. They are detailed in Table 3. The growth surge shocks, listed in Table 2, are representative of empirical results centered on the Chinese economy in 2002–2007 to the extent that they indicate the underlying annual changes to productivity and factor endowments.[24] The shock to the consumption equations captures the observed decline in the share of consumption expenditure and the rise in the share of private savings in GDP that was occurring in the period.

The numerical results for the default parameterization of the model are summarized in Table 3. It can be seen from these that the

---

not modelled explicitly, rather the monetary base in each region is determined as being endogenous to the target of monetary policy and an exogenous parameter determines the share of any change in the monetary base that takes the form of a long asset balance sheet expansion.

[24]The capital accumulation and productivity shares of China's recent growth are controversial (Krugman, 1994). The numbers used here are broadly consistent with the meta-analysis by Wu (2011).

Table 1. Simulation closures.[a]

Closure	Short run	Long run
Labour market	Exogenous nominal low-skill wage with endogenous employment	Constant unemployment rate with endogenous low-skill wage
Fiscal policy	Exogenous nominal government spending on goods and services with endogenous government revenue at fixed rates of tax on income, consumption, and trade	Exogenous nominal government spending on goods and services and fiscal balance with endogenous rates of tax on consumption expenditure
Investment and capital	Exogenous physical capital stock with endogenous investment and expected rates of return	Endogenous physical capital stock and investment with exogenous expected rates of return
Monetary policy targets[b]	Advanced economies: Consumer price level	

Monetary policy targets[b]: Advanced economies: Consumer price level
China and the rest of the World: fixed exchange rates against the US$[c]
Alternate case to estimate counterfactual deflation: money supplies fixed in all regions[d]

Notes: [a]Since the model is a system of non-linear simultaneous equations and more variables are specified than equations in the system, there is flexibility as to the choice of those to make exogenous. This choice mirrors assumptions about the behavior of labor markets, fiscal deficits, investment, and monetary policy targets.
[b]Money supplies can be set to target any of the three price levels (consumer, producer, and GDP), nominal exchange rates against the US$ or nominal GDP levels.
[c]The US$ is the *numeraire* in the model, which calculates exchange rates against it and also the effective exchange rates.
[d]No changes in commercial bank reserve behavior are assumed so that money multipliers remain constant.

surge, and the associated imbalance between production and consumption in China, created excess supply in the advanced economies and so would have been deflationary in the absence of money supply adjustment. The results indicate the size of monetary expansions needed in China and in the advanced economies to avoid contractionary deflations. These are between 3% and 5% per year, which

Table 2. Growth surge shocks.[a]

%	
Total factor productivity, A^V	5
Total factor and input productivity, A^Y	2
Consumption constant, A^C	-10
Skill stock, S^K	6
Capital stock,[b] K	8

Notes: [a]All shocks are to the Chinese economy only.
[b]In the long run, the capital stock is endogenous to
fixed expected rates of return and so it is not shocked.
Source: Authors' approximations as to primary shocks
during the peak growth surge years 2002–2006.

is considerably faster than the growth of the advanced economies at
that time, yet still ignoring deflationary shocks other than those ema-
nating from China. As expected, given the discussions in Section 2,
the simulations confirm that the surge placed downward pressure
on long interest rates globally. This suggests two alternative ways
to think about the monetary expansions required to avoid deflation.
On the one hand the excess supplies raised the relative abundance
of goods relative to money and, on the other hand, the opportunity
cost of money components in portfolios caused rebalancing in favor
of liquidity, raising the demand for money relative to goods and thus
reducing the prices of goods in terms of money.[25]

Real appreciations of the advanced currencies relative to China's,
combined with consumption baskets that include imported products
that are excluded from the calculation of producer or GDP prices,
ensure that producer prices inflate relative to consumer prices. This
stimulates employment in the short run and capital accumulation
in the long run and drives moderate increases in real output in
regions outside China. Associated moderate increases in the purchasing power of disposable incomes at domestic consumer prices (our
measure of welfare) occur uniformly across the advanced regions.

---

[25]The use of UMP by Japan at the time of the surge also placed downward
pressure on global long yields, though this effect is small in these simulations.

Table 3.   Effects of the growth surge with moderate financial integration.[a]

% changes		US	EU (26)	Japan	China
Real bond yield, r	Short run	−2.3	−2.1	−2.2	−4.7
	Long run[b]	−2.2	−2.0	−2.4	−5.5
Money supply, M_S	Short run	3.7	2.8	5.0	4.2
	Long run[b]	3.8	3.0	4.5	4.0
Consumer price level, P^C	Short run	0.0	0.0	0.0	−8.7
	Long run[b]	0.0	0.0	0.0	−9.2
Consumer price level, P^C	Short run	−1.1	0.1	−2.0	−9.7
(M_S target all regions)	Long run[b]	−1.5	−0.2	−2.0	−10.5
Producer price level, P^P	Short run	0.6	0.2	0.9	−11.3
	Long run[b]	1.0	0.6	1.7	−13.1
Real effective exchange	Short run	3.5	2.0	3.5	−11.3
rate, e_R	Long run[b]	4.3	2.5	3.3	−13.1
Nominal effective	Short run	−0.1	0.9	−2.2	0.1
exchange rate, E	Long run[b]	0.0	1.2	−0.3	0.2
Real output (GDP), Y/P^Y	Short run	0.2	0.1	0.4	10.3
	Long run[b]	0.2	0.1	0.2	11.8
Real disposable income Y_D/P^C	Short run	0.8	0.4	1.4	8.4
	Long run[b]	1.4	1.0	2.1	7.6

Notes: [a]These results are from the model described in the text with the closures and shocks listed in Tables 3 and 4. In particular, the default monetary target for all the advanced economies is the domestic consumer price level while China and the rest of the world adopt the bilateral exchange rate with the US. Two sets of results for P^C are shown, with the second set emerging from the alternative monetary policy closure that has all regions targeting their money supplies. The "moderate" financial integration parameters referred to are values of the elasticity of substitution between assets for each region, σ_i^I. These are US: 15, EU: 15, Japan: 10, China: 5, Australia: 15, and rest of World: 5.
[b]The long-run simulations maintain constant employment while allowing financial flows to deliver changes in capital stocks and hence adjustments in production capacity. Fiscal balance is maintained by adjusting tax rates on consumption expenditure.
Source: Simulations of the model are described in the text.

Meanwhile, in China, the effects are obviously much larger. Because China is assumed to maintain a *de facto* peg to the USD, the substantial real depreciations that arise from its productivity gains and its excess supply of goods cause large deflations, though these are insufficient to restrict employment in the short run or capital growth in the long run and very high rates of growth are achieved.

6.   Sensitivity to Type 2 Financial Integration

Financial integration can be thought of in several ways, even within the confines of the model adopted here. The approach we use is to regard more financial integration as indicating more ready substitution of Chinese assets with those from all regions, reflected by a rise in China's elasticity of asset substitution, σ_i^I. Type 1 financial integration is endogenous in the simulations, occurring in response to shocks to Chinese consumption behavior and to endogenous reallocations of investment globally. What is added here is pure Type 2 financial integration, as defined in Section 3. It is represented here as the progression of China's σ_i^I between two and 20, while holding the levels for the advanced economies at 20, indicating high levels of financial integration.[26] Here the analysis sets the values for the advanced economies as constant at 20 and examines the effects of allowing China's elasticity to rise from 2 to 20.

For low values of σ_i^I, China's financial outflows are restricted to adhere to the original pattern of these flows reflected in the model's database. As the values rise, the distribution of these outflows across regional assets is more responsive to relative yield changes. This includes greater flexibility of the share in China's collective portfolio of its own domestic assets. To see the effect of this, the surge shocks are repeated for different values of this parameter. The effects of the shocks on regional bond yields, deflationary pressure, current account imbalance, real GDP, and "welfare" (the real purchasing power of regional income at consumer prices) are assessed for the advanced regions.

More flexible Chinese portfolio management alters the effects of the growth surge, causing them to depart from default values.

---

[26]The values of the substitution elasticity of advanced regional assets used in generating the results in the previous section are less extreme than these (15 for the US and EU, 10 for Japan, and 5 for China), representing other numerical measures of Type 2 financial integration (Tyers, 2015a, Appendix 2).

Table 4. Sensitivity of the effects of the growth surge to Type 2 financial integration.[a,b]

% changes due to $\sigma_i^I = 2.20$		US	EU (26)	Japan	China
Real bond yield, r	Short run	10	6	6	−25
	Long run[c]	13	7	6	−32
Money supply, M_S	Short run	9	5	4	−67
	Long run[c]	12	5	5	−77
Consumer price level, P^C	Short run	61	1010[d]	7	−20
(M_S target all regions)	Long run[b]	53	−121[d]	4	−35
CA balance, % *GDP*	Short run	12	7	5	15
	Long run[c]	14	7	9	18
Real output (GDP), Y/P^Y	Short run	7	2	2	−6
	Long run[c]	8	0	−4	−2
Real disposable income Y_D/P^C	Short run	7	2	2	−7
	Long run[c]	9	2	3	−16

Notes: [a]The numbers indicate the proportional change in the effects of the growth surge detailed in Table 3 due to the sweep of the Chinese elasticity of asset substitution between $\sigma_i^I = 2$ and $\sigma_i^I = 20$.
[b]These results are from the model described in the text with the closures and shocks listed in Tables 1 and 2. In particular, the default monetary target for all the advanced economies is the domestic consumer price level while China and the rest of the world adopt the bilateral exchange rate with the US. The results shown for P^C are, however, from the alternative monetary policy closure that has all regions targeting their money supplies. The "moderate" financial integration parameters referred to are values of the elasticity of substitution between assets for each region, σ_i^I. These are US: 15, EU: 15, Japan: 10, China: 5, Australia: 15, and rest of World: 5.
[c]The long-run simulations maintain constant employment while allowing financial flows to deliver changes in capital stocks and hence adjustments in production capacity. Fiscal balance is maintained by adjusting tax rates on consumption expenditure.
[d]The large proportional changes in EU deflation stem from very small denominators, due to the very small effects of the surge on EU price levels shown in Table 3.
Source: Simulations of the model are described in the text.

The proportions by which these results change, due to the full sweep of asset substitution elasticity values from 2 to 20, are indicated in Table 4. Not surprisingly, given that the shocks are to the Chinese economy only, the Chinese performance indicators are the most strongly affected by some distance. Increased integration makes investment abroad easier. Since the surge caused a substantial rise in excess saving, the more readily that saving can escape abroad, the smaller is its tendency to suppress Chinese home long bond yields. In the advanced regions, however, the arrival of additional Chinese saving in response to Type 2 integration ensures that long bond yields decline further than they otherwise would have. The expected movement toward convergence of bond yields between China and the advanced economies is evident from Figure 9, which suggests that full financial integration would cause a decline in yields in the advanced economies by about 3%. At the rates in the database, this suggests declines in 10-year bond yields of about 15 basis points.[27] The proportional effects of financial integration on US yields are a bit larger since the initial flows from China to Europe and Japan are small relative to those destined for the US. Even where proportional changes to initial shares of Chinese outflow to the EU and Japan are substantial, the small base tends to push most of the additional outflow to the US.

Turning to the deflationary effects of the surge, the monetary expansions that are needed to maintain the targets of monetary policy in China and the advanced economies are indicated in Figure 10. Not surprisingly, the sizes of these expansions also depend on China's level of Type 2 financial integration. When this increases, the deflationary pressure abroad also increases and, therefore, monetary expansions must be larger. This can be seen as driven by an increased presence of China's excess saving on global financial markets, suppressing yields and therefore opportunity costs of money holding, and so we observe portfolio rebalancing in favor of money. Increases in money demand then decrease the price levels of goods relative to money in foreign regions in the absence of supply expansions. In China, of course, the opposite is true. Its monetary target is its bilateral exchange rate with the US and expansions are needed to defend it, but these expansions are smaller, the more financially integrated the economy. More financial integration implies smaller real

---

[27]This is significant though small in relation to the changes in long yields due to excess saving by Japan and the petroleum exporters.

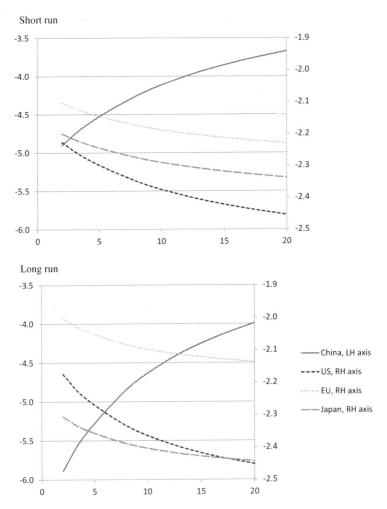

Figure 9. Growth surge effects on long yields with varying financial integration[a,b] (percent changes in regional long bond yields).

Notes: [a]The horizontal axis is the elasticity of substitution between Chinese and other global assets, σ^I.
[b]The simulations approximate the effects of a single year's change to the Chinese economy at the peak of its growth surge.
[c]The long-run simulations maintain constant employment while allowing financial flows to deliver changes in capital stocks and hence adjustments in production capacity. Fiscal balance is maintained by adjusting tax rates on consumption expenditure.

Source: Simulations of the model are described in the text.

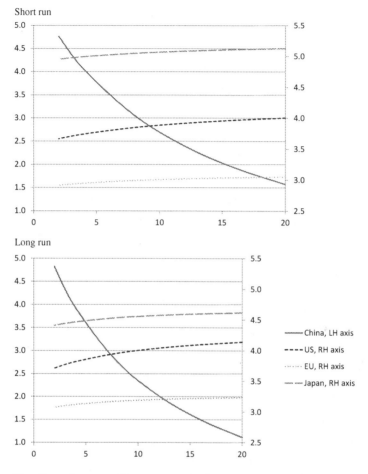

Figure 10. Growth surge effects on required monetary expansions with varying financial integration[a,b,c] (percent changes in regional money supplies).

Notes: [a]The horizontal axis is the elasticity of substitution between Chinese and other global assets, σ^I.

[b]The simulations approximate the effects of a single year's change to the Chinese economy at the peak of its growth surge.

[c]The targets of monetary policy in the advanced economies are set at zero consumer price inflation, while in China and the rest of the world, it is the US$ exchange rate.

[d]The long-run simulations maintain constant employment while allowing financial flows to deliver changes in capital stocks and hence adjustments in production capacity. Fiscal balance is maintained by adjusting tax rates on consumption expenditure.

Source: Simulations of the model are described in the text.

depreciations against the advanced economies and smaller declines in
domestic yields. Hence, the rise in portfolio demand for home money
within China is also smaller.

The scale of the deflations in the consumer price level that these
monetary expansions are intended to avoid and its sensitivity to
financial integration are indicated by Figure 11. Outside China, these
deflation forces are considerable — between one and two percentage
points per year for the US and Japan — and they increase with
greater financial integration. Indeed, for the US, the deflation pressure rises by almost a percentage point per year across the range
of asset substitutability postulated. Similarly, large effects occur on
current account balances. Financial openness encourages more Chinese saving to go abroad, raising investment relative to domestic
saving in foreign economies and thus enlarging their current account
deficits, as indicated in Figure 12. At the same time, this reduces
China's investment relative to its domestic saving and so drives its
current account surplus higher. For the US, China's financial integration causes a current account deficit expansion of up to 0.1% of GDP
while China's surplus would rise by between 0.3% and 0.5% of GDP.

The effects of financial integration on China's real GDP are to
moderate its performance, as indicated in Figure 13. This is because
greater integration causes more financial outflow from China, and
hence less domestic investment, and with its fixed nominal exchange
rate, more domestic deflation, which impairs employment in the short
run and capital growth in the long run. China's real exchange rate
depreciates more with greater integration, exacerbating the terms of
trade shift against it. Even so, the net Chinese effects of the surge
shocks remain substantially positive. Abroad, the US focus of China's
outflows tends to mean that financial integration and the USD are
positively correlated. With the consumer price level target of US
monetary policy, this exchange rate appreciation narrows the gap
between the consumer and producer prices and therefore raises producer prices the more integrated is the Chinese economy. The effect
of this on employment and capital growth, and therefore real GDP, is
positive but moderate. The net welfare effects by region are summarized in Figure 14. They show that Chinese welfare gains are smaller

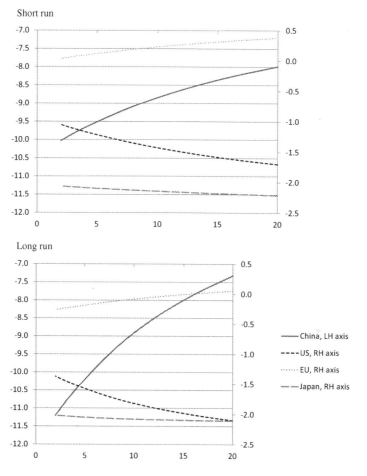

Figure 11. Growth surge effects on consumer price levels that would occur in the absence of monetary expansions, with varying financial integration[a,b,c] (percent changes in consumer price levels).

Notes: [a]The horizontal axis is the elasticity of substitution between Chinese and other global assets, σ^I.

[b]The simulations approximate the effects of a single year's change to the Chinese economy at the peak of its growth surge.

[c]Here, the targets of monetary policy are simply set to zero money supply growth in all regions.

[d]The long-run simulations maintain constant employment while allowing financial flows to deliver changes in capital stocks and hence adjustments in production capacity. Fiscal balance is maintained by adjusting tax rates on consumption expenditure.

Source: Simulations of the model are described in the text.

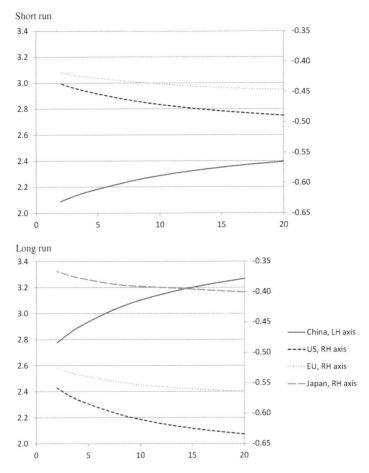

Figure 12.   Growth surge effects on current account balances, with varying financial integration[a,b] (Changes in the current account balances in percentage points
of GDP).

Notes: [a]The horizontal axis is the elasticity of substitution between Chinese and
other global assets, σ^I.
[b]The simulations approximate the effects of a single year's change to the Chinese
economy at the peak of its growth surge.
[c]The long-run simulations maintain constant employment while allowing financial
flows to deliver changes in capital stocks and hence adjustments in production
capacity. Fiscal balance is maintained by adjusting tax rates on consumption
expenditure.
[d]The results in the short run for the US and Japan are near coincidental; thus,
those for Japan are not distinguished.

Source: Simulations of the model are described in the text.

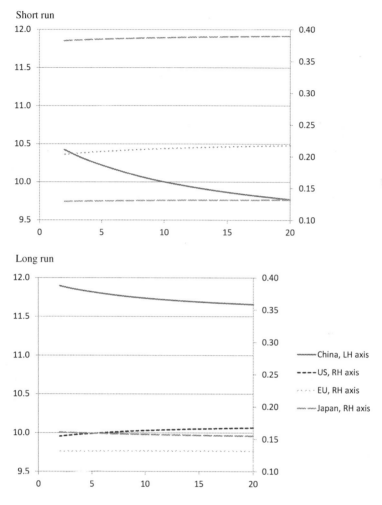

Figure 13. Growth surge effects on real GDP, with varying financial integration[a,b] (percent changes real GDP).

Notes: [a]The horizontal axis is the elasticity of substitution between Chinese and other global assets, σ^I.
[b]The simulations approximate the effects of a single year's change to the Chinese economy at the peak of its growth surge.
[c]The long-run simulations maintain constant employment while allowing financial flows to deliver changes in capital stocks and hence adjustments in production capacity. Fiscal balance is maintained by adjusting tax rates on consumption expenditure.

Source: Simulations of the model are described in the text.

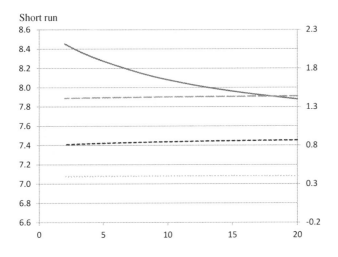

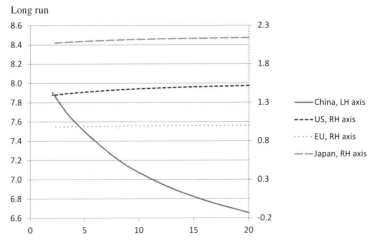

Figure 14. Growth surge effects on economic welfare, with varying financial integration[a,b] (percent changes in the real purchasing power of disposable income at consumer prices).

Notes: [a]The horizontal axis is the elasticity of substitution between Chinese and other global assets, σ^I.
[b]The simulations approximate the effects of a single year's change to the Chinese economy at the peak of its growth surge.
[c]The long-run simulations maintain constant employment while allowing financial flows to deliver changes in capital stocks and hence adjustments in production capacity. Fiscal balance is maintained by adjusting tax rates on consumption expenditure.

Source: Simulations of the model are described in the text.

than those in real GDP, despite the deflation, due to growth in real wages that is slower than that in real GDP and that, as with real GDP, these gains diminish with financial integration.

Overall, the effects of the surge are quite sensitive to the level of China's financial integration. The Chinese effects are considerably moderated in the absence of controls restricting the rebalancing of its collective portfolio, including the growth surge itself. On the contrary, the foreign effect, and particularly the deflationary pressures in the US, are amplified by such integration.

7. Conclusion

The 2000s growth surge stimulated global growth but provided the first of several shocks to the performance of global financial markets prior to the GFC. Measures to quantify financial openness in China suggest that the surge occurred at a time when the economy was at its most open financially, based at least on Type 1 measures that depend only on domestic and foreign asset acquisitions and holdings. In terms of Type 2 measures, which account for restrictions on portfolio diversity, during the surge, capital controls were strict and there was little formal integration. Changes in Type 2 measures did come later, as China's holdings abroad diversified beyond official foreign reserves.

Here, results from a global macroeconomic model with rebalancing national portfolios containing international assets are summarized. These help evaluate the international effects of these major changes in China and to assess, counterfactually, what the implications might have been had additional Type 2 financial integration been undertaken at the same time. This would have allowed Chinese portfolio managers more ready substitution of assets across investment destinations, reflected in the model by a rise in China's elasticity of asset substitution. It is shown that the economic effects on the advanced economies would have been larger the more these authorities might have allowed Type 2 integration. The surge itself was net beneficial to foreign economies, but it suppressed global bond yields, imposed deflationary pressure offset by extraordinary, and ultimately unsustainable, monetary expansions, and it caused current accounts to shift toward deficit. Such financial integration would have moderated the GDP and welfare gains accruing to the Chinese economy, but it would have increased the effects on foreign economies. Net welfare gains would have been larger but the negative effects would have been larger, particularly the declines in global bond yields and the deflationary pressures in the US.

Looking ahead, a reversal of China's external balance looms as it transitions to consumption-led growth and is faced with rising aged dependency (Golley *et al.*, 2017), while at the same time the government seeks to sustain the level of investment. As the rate of overall growth slows, the most efficient share of investment in GDP will necessarily fall, yet a political imperative is to sustain employment in what is the largest construction industry in the world. This could lead to further reforms in China, to the financial sector and in the protection of intellectual property rights of foreign investing firms. Deepening of Type 2 financial integration would then be necessary, as might be achieved through reduced controls on outward flows and the further expansion of global portfolio capital access through onshore bond and equity markets

With this Type 2 deepening, the net benefits from China's future expansion will flow more readily to foreign partner economies. Yet, because future Chinese growth will be slower and its excess product supply will be smaller, the further negative effects of this expansion abroad, in the form of deflationary forces and inequality, will be reduced. At the same time, the maturing of Chinese industry and the expansion of intra-industry trade with North America and Europe will see increased conflicts over property rights and investment conditions more generally and over assistance to state-owned enterprises.[28] Future financial uncertainty will therefore stem from the strategic interactions between industrial and macroeconomic policies in the world's two largest economies.

---

[28]The US–China trade conflict of 2018–2019 is a reflection of this issue and its resolution is likely to embody reforms to foreign investment conditions (Tyers and Zhou, 2019a).

Acknowledgement

Funding for the research described in this study is from Australian Research Council Discovery Grant No. DP0557885. Constructive comments received from discussant Junru Zhang at the 4th International Conference on China's Rise and Internationalization held in Ningbo China are acknowledged, along with suggestions made at seminars at the Australian National University and the Hong Kong Institute of Monetary Research. Thanks for assistance with data gathering for this research are due to Ying Zhang.

References

Arora, V., Tyers, R. and Zhang, Y. (2014). "Reconstructing the Savings Glut: The Global Implications of Asian Excess Saving," CAMA Working Paper No. 2014-02/20, Centre for Applied Macroeconomics, Australian National University, Canberra, February.

Autor, D. H., Dorn, D. and Hanson, G. H. (2013). "The China Syndrome: Local Labor Market Effects of Competition in the United States," *American Economic Review*, **103**(6), 2121–2168.

Baumol, W. (1952). "The Transaction Demand for Cash: An Inventory Theoretic Approach," *Quarterly Journal of Economics*, **66**, 545–556.

Bayoumi, T., Tong, H. and Wei, S. J. (2010). "The Chinese Corporate Savings Puzzle: A Firm-level Cross-country Perspective," NBER Working Paper No. 16423.

Bergsten, C. F., Freeman, C., Lardy, N. R. and Mitchell, D. J. (2008). "China's Rise: Challenges and Opportunities, Peterson Institute for International Economics, Washington DC.

Berman, E., Bound, J. and Griliches, Z. (1994). "Changes in the Demand for Skilled Labour within US Manufacturing: Evidence from the Annual Survey of Manufactures," *Quarterly Journal of Economics*, **109**(2), 367–397.

Bernanke, B. S. (2005). "Remarks by the Governor," Sandridge Lecture, Virginia Association of Economists, Richmond Virginia, Federal Reserve Board, March.

Bernanke, B. S. (2011). "Global Imbalances: Links to Economic and Financial Stability," Speech Given at the Banque de France Financial Stability Review Launch Event, Paris, France, February 18.

Blanchard. O. and Giavazzi, F. (2006). "Rebalancing Growth in China: A Three-handed Approach," China and the World Economy, Institute of World Economics and Politics," *Chinese Academy of Social Sciences*, **14**(4), 1–20.

Bound, J. and Johnson, G. (1992). "Changes in the Structure of Wages in the 1980s: An Evaluation of Alternative Explanations," *American Economic Review*, **82**(3), 371–392.

Bowles, P. (2012). "Rebalancing China's Growth: Some Unsettled Questions," *Canadian Journal of Development Studies*, **33**(1), 1–13.

Caballero, R. J. (2009). "The 'Other' Imbalance and the Financial Crisis," MIT Working Papers in Economics 9-32, Cambridge MA, December.

Caballero, R. J., Farhi, E. and Gourinchas, P. O. (2008). "An Equilibrium Model of 'Global Imbalances' and Low Interest Rates," *American Economic Review*, **98**(1), 358–393.

Chen, Q., Filardo, A., He, D. and Zhu, F. (2016). "Financial Crisis, US Unconventional Monetary Policy and International Spillovers," *Journal of International Money and Finance*, **67**, 62–81.

Chinn, M. D., Eichengreen, B. and Ito, H. (2012). "Rebalancing Global Growth," in O. Canuto and D. Leipziger (eds.), *Ascent after Descent: Regrowing Economic Growth after the Great Recession*, World Bank, Washington DC, pp. 35–86.

Chinn, M. D. and Ito, H. (2007). "Current Account Balances, Financial Development and Institutions: Assaying the World 'Saving Glut'," *Journal of International Money and Finance*, **26**, 546–569.

Choi, H., Mark, N. C. and Sul, D. (2008). "Endogenous Discounting, the World Saving Glut and the US Current Account," *Journal of International Economics*, **75**, 30–53.

Di Giovanni, J., Levchenko, A. A. and Zhang, J. (2013). "Global Welfare Effect of China: Trade Integration and Technical Change," *American Economic Journal: Macroeconomics*, **6**(3), 153–183.

Eichengreen, B. (2004). "Global Imbalances and the Lessons of Bretton Woods," NBER Working Paper No. 10497, National Bureau of Economic Research, Cambridge, MA.

Eickmeier, S. and Kuehnlenz, M. (2018). "China's Role in Global Inflation Dynamics," *Macroeconomic Dynamics*, **22**(02), 225–254.

Feldstein, M. and Horioka, C. Y. (1980). "Domestic Saving and International Capital Flows," *Economic Journal, Royal Economic Society*, **90**(358), 314–329.

Fernández, A., Klein, M. W., Rebucci, A., Schindler, M. and Uribe, M. (2016). "Capital Control Measures: A New Dataset," *IMF Economic Review*, **64**(3), 548–574.

Francois, J. F. and Nelson, D. (1998). "Trade, Technology and Wages: General Equilibrium Mechanics," *Economic Journal*, **108**, 1483–1499.

Francois, J. F. and Wignaraja, G. (2008). "Economic Implications of Asian Integration," *Global Economy Journal*, **8**(3), 1–48.

Garcia-Herrero, A. (2015). "Internationalizing the Currency While Leveraging Massively: The Case of China," Bruegel Working Paper No. 2015/12.

Genberg, H. and Zhang, W. (2010). "Can China Save the World by Consuming More?" VOX EU, April 25.

Golley, J., Tyers, R., and Zhou, Y. (2017). "Fertility and Savings Contractions in China: Long-Run Global Implications," *The World Economy*, **41**(11), 3194–3220.

Harris, R. G. and Robertson, P. E. (2013). "Trade, Wages and Skill Accumulation in the Emerging Giants," *Journal of International Economics*, **89**(2), 407–421.

Harris, R. G, Robertson, P. E. and Xu, J. (2011). "The International Effects of China's Trade and Education Booms," *The World Economy*, **34**(10), 1703–1725.

Haskel, J., Lawrence, R. Z., Leamer, E. E. and Slaughter, M. J. (2012). "Globalization and U.S. Wages: Modifying Classic Theory to Explain Recent Facts," *Journal of Economic Perspectives, American Economic Association*, **26**(2), 119–140.

He, D. and McCauley, R. N. (2013). "Transmitting Global Liquidity to East Asia: Policy Rates, Bond Yields, Currencies and Dollar Credit," Hong Kong Institute for Monetary Research Working Paper No. 15/2013, BIS Working Papers No. 431, Bank for International Settlements, China & World Economy, Wiley-Blackwell, October.

Helpman, E., Itskhoki, O. and Redding, S. J. (2010). "Inequality and Unemployment in a Global Economy," *Econometrica*, **78**(4), 1239–1283.

Ho, N. W. (2009). "Financial Integration: Concepts and Impacts," *Macao Monetary Research Bulletin*, **10**, 69–84.

Huang, Y., Wang, X., Wang, B. and Lin, N. (2010). "Financial Reform in China: Progresses and Challenges," PAFTAD Conference Paper, online available at http://www.paftad.org/files/34/07_HUANG_Fin%20Reform_nofig.pdf.

Ito, H. (2009). "US Current Account Debate with Japan then, and China Now," *Journal of Asian Economics*, **20**, 294–313.

Ito, H. (2013). "Monetary Policy in Asia and the Pacific in the Post, Post-Crisis Era," in Presented at the *36th Pacific Trade and Development (PAFTAD) Conference, "Financial Development and Cooperation in Asia and the Pacific,"* Hong Kong Monetary Authority, November 19–21.

Johnson, R. S., Zuber, R. A. and Gandar, J. M. (2010). "A Re-examination of the Market Segmentation Theory as a Pedagogical Model," *Journal of Financial Education*, **36**(1/2), 1–37.

Krugman, P. (1994). "The Myth of Asia's Miracle," *Foreign Affairs*, **73**(6), 62–78.

Krugman, P. (1995). "Growing World Trade: Causes and Consequences," *Brookings Papers*, **1**, 327–377.

Krugman, P. (2010). "Capital Export, Elasticity Pessimism and the Renminbi (Wonkish)," *New York Times* (blog), March 16.

Lardy, N. R. (2006). "Toward a Consumption-driven Growth Path," Policy Brief, 06-6, Peterson Institute for International Economics, Washington DC.

Lardy, N. R. (2012). "Sustaining China's Growth after the Global Financial Crisis," Peterson Institute for International Economics, Washington DC, January.

Leamer, E. E. (1996). "Wage Inequality from International Competition and Technological Change: Theory and Country Experience," *American Economic Review, Economic Association*, **86**(2), 309–314.

Lee, J. W. and McKibbin, W. J. (2007). "Domestic Investment and External Imbalances in East Asia," CAMA Working Paper No. 4-2007, Australian National University, Canberra.

Levchenko, A. A. and Zhang, J. (2012). "The Global Labor Market Impact of Emerging Giants: A Quantitative Assessment," Paper Presented at the *13th Jacques Polak Annual Research Conference*, hosted by the IMF, Washington D.C., November 8–9.

Lien, D. and Zhang, Z. (2018). "Introduction to China's Rise and Financial Market Integration in East Asia: Issues and Prospects," *The North American Journal of Economics and Finance*, **46**, 166–167.

Lim, R. E. (2017). "Reviewing Recent Developments in China's Capital Markets and Assessing the Relevance of the Proposed Shanghai International Board," *Capital Markets Law Journal*, **12**(1), 78–93.

Mena, L. and P. Tirelli (2017). "Optimal Inflation to Reduce Inequality," *Review of Economic Dynamics*, **24**, 79–94.

N'Daiye, P., Zhang, P. and Zhang, W. (2010). "Structural Reform, Intra-regional Trade, and Medium-term Growth Prospects of East Asia and the Pacific — Perspectives from a New Multi-region Model," *Journal of Asian Economics*, **21**, 20–36.

Paranavithana, H., Magnusson, L. and Tyers, R. (2018). "Assessing Monetary Policy Targeting Regimes for Small Open Economies", CAMA Working Paper, 33/2018.

Ragot, X. (2014). "The Case for a Financial Approach to Money Demand," *Journal of Monetary Econometrics*, **62**, 94–107.

Rey, H. (2013). "Dilemma Not Trilemma: The Global Financial Cycle and Monetary Policy Independence," Federal Reserve Bank of Kansas City Economic Symposium at Jackson Hole, August.

Song, L., Yang, J. and Zhang, Y. (2011). "State-owned Enterprises' Outward Investment and the Structural Reform in China," *China and the World Economy*, **19**(4), 38–53.

Sun, S. (2009). "How Does FDI Affect Domestic Firms' Exports? Industrial Evidence," How Does FDI Affect Domestic Firms' Exports? *Industrial Evidence*, **32**(8), 1203–1222.

Tobin, J. (1956). "The Interest Elasticity of Transactions Demand for Cash," *Review of Economics and Statistics*, **38**, 241–247.

Tyers, R. (2015a). "Pessimism Shocks in a Model of Global Macroeconomic Interdependence," *International Journal of Economics and Finance*, **7**(1), 37–59.

Tyers, R. (2015b). "International Effects of China's Rise and Transition: Neoclassical and Keynesian Perspectives," *Journal of Asian Economics*, **37**, 1–19.

Tyers, R. and Yang, Y. (2000). "Capital-Skill Complementarity and Wage Outcomes Following Technical Change in a Global Model," *Oxford Review of Economic Policy*, **16**, 23–41.

Tyers, R. and Yang, Y. (1997). "Trade with Asia and Skill Upgrading: Effects on Labor Markets in the Older Industrial Countries," *Review of World Economics*, **133**(3), 383–418.

Tyers, R. and Yang, Y. (2000). "Capital-Skill Complementarity and Wage Outcomes Following Technical Change in a Global Model," *Oxford Review of Economic Policy*, **16**, 23–41.

Tyers, R. and Zhou, Y. (2018). "Deflation Forces and Inequality," CAMA Working Paper No. 15/2018, Australian National University, April.

Tyers, R. and Zhou, Y. (2019a). "The US-China Trade Dispute: A Macro Perspective," CAMA Working Paper No. 11/2019, Australian National University.

Tyers, R. and Zhou, Y. (2019b). "Financial Integration and the Global Effects of China's Growth Surge," CAMA Working Paper No. 09/2019, Australian National University.

Wicksellian, K. (1898). Interest and Prices: A Study of the Causes Regulating the Value of Money (Translation from German, Macmillan, London, 1936).

Winchester, N. and Greenaway, D. (2007). "Rising Wage Inequality and Capital-skill Complementarity," *Journal of Policy Modeling*, **29**(1), 41–54.

Wood, A. (2018). "The 1990s Trade and Wages Debate in Retrospect," *The World Economy*, **41**(4), 975–999.

Wood, A. (1994). *North-South Trade, Employment and Inequality*, Clarendon Press, Oxford.

Wu, Y. (2011). "Total Factor Productivity Growth in China: A Review," *Journal of Chinese Economic and Business Studies*, **9**(2), 111–126.

Chapter 7

Systemic Risks, Macroeconomic Shocks, and Financial Security in China

Xinmiao Zhou, Kai Zhang, and Huihong Liu[*]

*Business School, Ningbo University,
818 Fenghua Road, Ningbo 315211, China*
[*]liuhuihong@nbu.edu.cn

The healthy development of China's economic and financial markets is crucial. This chapter discusses in depth the macroeconomic factors and financial security environment that affect the systemic risk in China, and focuses on the regional research and analysis. The study discusses the relationship between macroeconomic factors and financial market performance and simulates the fragility and security conditions of the financial market through the detailed empirical facts. The loan scale, the transaction volume in financial markets, and the price performance of real estate are taken as the most important influential macroeconomic shocks to the systemic risk in China. The composite index for financial security is calculated by fully considering systemic risk based on factor analysis and finds significant regional differences in China. Through the method of stress testing, this chapter measures the different effects of macroeconomic shocks under different economic environments, time periods, and regions and puts forward relevant suggestions for the healthy and stable development of financial markets in China.

1. Introduction

The impact of financial development on economic growth has always been an important issue in the academic circles. A financial crisis usually occurs after bubbles arise in asset price. In recent years, the financial crisis is more closely related to real estate, stock markets, and credit risk, such as the financial crisis arising from the real estate and stock market bubbles in Japan in the 1980s and 1990s and the global economic crisis arising from the sub-prime crisis in the United States in 2008. Since the bankruptcy of Lehman Brothers Holdings (the fourth largest investment bank in the United States) on September 15, 2008, the financial crisis has prevailed for 10 years. Over the past decade, economists have had more concrete reflections on the causes of the crisis. Financial liberalization and neo-liberalism have become the target of public criticism.

The international economic environment that the emerging economies were confronted with at that time was also undergoing some significant changes, such as the increasing flow of transnational capital and financial liberalization. As a result, most of the emerging economies have relaxed the original financial repression policy and have turned to financial moderation. The excessive and inadequate financial repression and financial liberalization are perceived to have damaged economic growth. Moderation refers to finding a balance between the two. In order to find a better solution to the problem of financial moderation in the process of economic development, various financial reforms in China's financial market have recently been implemented with positive results. However, the stock market crash in China's capital market in 2015 caused the market value of the Chinese stock market to lose a total of 22 trillion yuan in just 3 weeks, which has aggravated the accumulation of systemic risks in China's financial system. The related problems of financial security have become the focus of the economic debate.

With the rapid development of China's economy, as well as the urgent need for financial markets to integrate into the progress of globalization, it has become quite essential to fully understand the development environment of China's financial markets, the level of risk and the ability to resist risk, and other real conditions. Based on such macroeconomic context, this chapter attempts to carry out a comprehensive and crossover analysis of the impact of the economic shocks and the state of financial security on systemic risk in China. We adopt theoretical and empirical analyses to provide theoretical, data, and policy recommendations for the choice of a reasonable direction for adjustment and development of the financial structure in the future.

The chapter is organized as follows: Section 2 summarizes the review of related literature. Section 3 describes some empirical facts related to systemic risk in China. Section 4 builds the econometric models to calculate the composite index of financial security, and process macroeconomic stress tests to discuss the relationship among systemic risk, financial security and some key macroeconomic factors. Section 5 provides the concluding remarks and policy proposals.

2. Review of Related Literature

The outbreak of the financial crisis in 2008 once again triggered widespread concern and in-depth studies on systemic risks by scholars. But, in the past, a consensus has almost been reached on the understanding and definition of systemic risks in academic circles and industry. Systemic risk refers to an uncontrollable risk that begins with the partial disruption of the financial system and gradually spreads to the total system, resulting in system disorder. This rapidly affects the real economy, leading to an economic recession and depression of the whole society that cannot be reversed in the short term (FSB, IMF, and BIS, 2011). In the process of research on systemic risks, the default rate of clients in financial institutions tends to be regarded as an indicator (De Nicolo and Kwast, 2002). When the default rate of the client exceeds a certain cutoff point, the operations of financial institutions will become fragile and a slight economic shock will lead to their bankruptcy. In case defaults and bankruptcies occur to a large number of financial institutions simultaneously, the financial system will collapse completely. Thus, systemic risks are crucial to the regulators who are responsible for maintaining financial security. Unfortunately, the measurement and analysis of systematic risk have been controversial due to the difficulty in developing a set of effective methods. Some studies argue that the failure to evaluate and measure systemic risks in an effective way is also one of the causes of the financial crisis (Alessandri *et al.*, 2009).

One of the most important players concerned about systemic risks is the regulatory authority, which mainly regulates commercial banks (Dewatripont and Tirole, 1993; Freixas *et al.*, 1997). Regulators are more willing to take into account both systemic and financial security, that is, to examine and quantify risks from a macro-prudential perspective. They observe the degree of occurrence of risk and the process of crisis outbreak at any time and benefit from receiving warnings in a timely manner so that they can take preventive measures to restrain the further spread of risk well in advance or just in time. However, such an idealized measurement method has not been well implemented (Goodhart *et al.*, 2005).

Adrian and Shin (2010) pointed out that, "the financial crisis reminds us that data predicts and transmits important information". The amount of credit, leverage, and money and the overall situation of cross-border financial affairs reflect the exposure of systemic risks and thus affect financial stability. An effective macro-prudential policy should pay attention to relevant data from all important sectors and departments at any time. A number of studies have pointed out that the current banking regulation system lays particular stress on the individual financial institutions, while it has ignored to a great extent the externality and overall dynamics of the financial sector based on the macroeconomic cycles (Freixas *et al.*, 2015). The purpose of macro-prudential regulation is to protect the entire financial system, as well as to lower the damage to the entire financial system and the costs of bankruptcy of the real sectors involved by restricting the likelihood of the occurrence of a systemic crisis and regulating the crisis (Bhattacharya and Thakor, 1998; Freixas and Rochet, 2008), and to find specific solutions to the risks in the two dimensions of time and region (Borio, 2009; Bank of England, 2011).

At present, the measurement of systemic risks in the academic circles is mainly divided into two categories: Value at risk (VaR) based on the default correlations and empirical analysis of market data and stress testing. These two methods have made unprecedented achievements, and a number of frontier branches have been derived

(Liu *et al.*, 2012), such as the CoVaR method based on specific market conditions and returns (Adrian and Brunnermeier, 2009). Acharya *et al.* (2009) develop a model in which capital shortages of individual financial institutions in periods of distress generate systemic risk in the economy. Their measure is called the systemic expected shortfall and is a linear combination of the marginal expected shortfall and leverage. In addition, Brownlees and Engle (2015) constructed the SRISK index method, which aims to measure the anticipation of the future risk exposure of the financial intermediaries in the context of a downward trend in the market. These methods provide a strong theoretical support for the in-depth and effective recognition of systemic risks and the maintenance of financial security by regulators.

The VaR method lays more stress on the empirical analysis with fewer theoretical restrictions, and thus, it is more likely to be accepted by the practitioners and managers in the financial sector. Stress testing is an effective risk management tool to assess the potential impact of extreme events on the banking or financial system. Similar to the stress testing of portfolios by a single institution, macro-stress testing can be used to test the robustness of the macroeconomy as a whole when it encounters the impact of a certain external or tail event, which can be used to measure the size of systemic risks (Drehmann, 2018). The instrument of stress testing may be VaR (Pesaran *et al.*, 2006), or a macro-model related to the driving factors of market risks (Elsinger *et al.*, 2006). In the macro-model, we can simulate the impact of all kinds of economic factors to get an appropriate variety of risk contexts, and in doing so, we will better understand the ability of the macroeconomic environment or financial environment of a country to resist stress. After the financial crisis in 2008, the regulatory authorities in various countries imposed macro-stress testing on the banking industry. For example, the regulatory authorities in the United States require financial institutions to report the condition of stress testing every year (see the Dodd–Frank Act in 2010 for details). The China Banking Regulatory Commission also explicitly stipulates that the banks in China should take stress testing as an important part of their assessment procedures for internal capital adequacy since 2012.

A considerable number of papers have conducted a joint study on systemic risks, financial vulnerability, and macro-prudential management (Rochet and Tirole, 1996; Kiyotaki and Moore, 1997; Freixas *et al.*, 2000; Allen and Gale, 2000; Butzbach, 2016). Likewise, Chinese economists have carried out a number of studies and discussions regarding the characteristics of the financial market in China. Examples are the discussions concerning "Imbalance Adjustment, Macroeconomic Stability and Financial Risk Prevention" (Wang and Fan, 2017), the studies involving liquidity, stock market crash, and financial systemic risks (Zhang *et al.*, 2011), and the research on financial stability, systemic risks, and macro-prudential policies (Fan *et al.*, 2013); on financial development, real estate fluctuations, and monetary policy (Peng and Fang, 2016); on asset price bubbles, economic openness, and financial risk management (Lin *et al.*, 2014; Peng and Tan, 2017); and so on. However, financial security is seldom mentioned in the studies on the above issues. The existing research has acknowledged the importance of financial security, and Chinese studies have been mostly devoted to this topic (Xiao *et al.*, 2015; Wang, 2016, 2017; Nie and Zhou, 2017); this research focus is closely related to the fact that China's national strategy has always laid emphasis on financial security.

3.   Empirical Facts in China

According to the history of financial crisis in western countries, the final signal of risk outbreak is the bankruptcy of commercial banks, which is closely related to the high non-performing loan rate. The past experience of developed countries also proves that systemic risk is directly related to the scale of loans of financial institutions and the price bubbles of financial assets. Are these key economic factors equally important to China's systemic risk? In this section, we intend to study the performance of systemic risk in China through some intuitive statistical description.

In a strict sense, China has not experienced a devastating financial crisis. Even the 2015 stock market crash is still far from being a "devastating" crackdown. However, the uncoordinated development of the financial market in all aspects and the varying degrees of risks have hindered the high-quality economic development in China to a certain extent. With the acceleration of integration into the process of globalization, China faces new problems in the risks and resistance to stress of China's financial markets. In general, the non-performing loan rate is regarded as the most intuitive index to measure systemic risks. According to different regions and market environment, a certain safety value can be set, and the non-performing loan ratio beyond the warning line indicates the occurrence of a financial risk. We try to use WIND database of China's commercial banks and 2003–2017 China Statistical Yearbook data to perform a simple statistical analysis. Figure 1 shows the quarterly data of the average non-performing loan ratio of commercial banks in China, the Shanghai Stock Exchange Composite Index, and the size of loans of financial institutions during the period from December 2003 to December 2017. As shown in Figure 1, the loan scale of commercial banks continues to rise, the Shanghai Stock Exchange Index has experienced two peaks, and the peak period has been accompanied by a certain rise of the non-performing loan ratio.

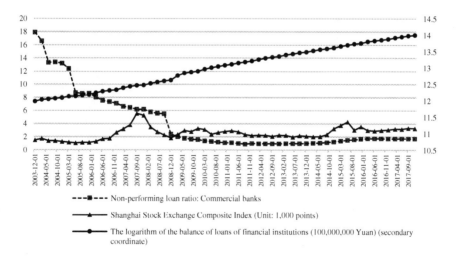

Figure 1. Major indicators of the financial market.

Source: Wind database.

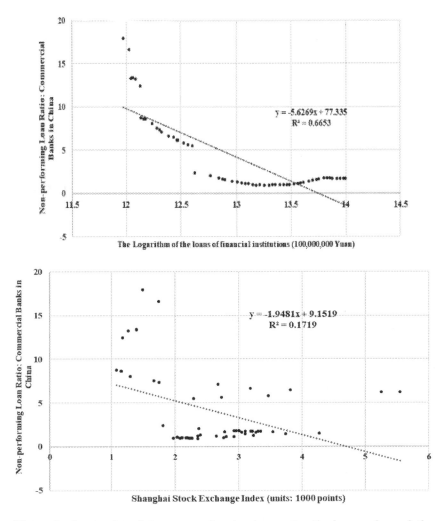

Figure 2. Scatterplot of the non-performing loan ratio, the loan scale, and the stock index.

As shown in the scatterplot in Figure 2, we can further examine whether the condition of the Chinese market is similar to the experience of western developed countries, that is, whether the size of loans and the price of financial assets exert a key impact on the non-performing loan ratio, and thus ultimately affect the systemic risks of the entire financial market.

In the regression equation in Figure 2, the dependent variables are the non-performing loan rates of commercial banks and the independent variables are the loan scale of financial institutions and the composite index of Shanghai Stock Exchange. The regression coefficients of independent variables in the two equations are significant at the 1% level. In case of an increase in the loan scale and the price of financial assets, the overall level of market default represented by the non-performing loan ratio will be reduced so that financial risks can be avoided. In theory, this can be explained by the fact that when the loan scale and asset price do not contain bubbles, the entire financial sector and the economy will automatically enter the mode of good development automatically. In such circumstances, appropriate financial liberalization will be conducive to the more efficient development of the Chinese economy. However, if the asset prices and loan expansion contain bubbles, the price of the financial assets and the credit scale have to be maintained at a higher level in order to avoid a high default rate. The hidden risk is that once the capital market collapses, a financial crisis cannot be avoided. The empirical facts of China are similar to those of developed countries, but the above analysis does not provide information about the level of financial security in the Chinese market. This needs to be further analyzed in what follows.

There has never been a long devastating financial crisis in the Chinese market, nor has there been bankruptcy of a bank in a strict sense. The financial regulation by the government and the central bank has always played an important role in the financial industry. Hence, it is difficult to define a critical value for financial security. But, some reference points can nevertheless be observed from Figure 1. In September 2007 and June 2015, two peaks occurred in the stock market and the asset bubble reached its peak. Once the relevant economic stimulus occurs, the bubble will be broken in the absence of harsh financial regulation, and then a financial crisis will break out. The non-performing loan ratios corresponding to these two periods are 6.17 and 4.27, respectively. Systemic risks lead to an unsafe situation when the non-performing loan ratio exceeds the level of 4.27. In accordance with the Core Indicators for the Risk Management of Commercial Banks (for Trial Implementation) posed by the China Banking Regulatory Commission (2005), the non-performing loan ratio of commercial banks should not be higher than 5%, which also indirectly supports the above analysis.

In order to have an additional understanding of the operational state of commercial banks in the Chinese market, we collected the data of 1,648 quarterly or annual non-performing loan ratios disclosed by 106 commercial banks from 1999 to 2017 in China, among which there are 31 listed banks, 31 urban commercial banks, and 44 rural commercial banks. Figure 3 shows the distribution of the non-performing loan ratio of these commercial banks. It shows a histogram and an empirical cumulative distribution function (CDF) diagram of "loss distribution excluding 10% extreme values", "10% extreme loss distribution", and "5% extreme loss distribution" from left to right, respectively.

In Figure 3, the non-performing loan ratios of 90% of commercial banks are all lower than 4%, and the shape of thick right tail and the slowly growing CDF chart offer a challenge to Chinese commercial banks to cope with extreme risk events. The extreme loss distributions show that 10% of the non-performing loan ratios of commercial banks have still exceeded 4% since 1999 and do not give the thin right tail feature of controllable losses. Among the extreme losses, more than 50% of the non-performing loan ratios exceed 5%, more than 20% of the non-performing loan ratios exceed 10%, and more than 5% of the non-performing loan ratios exceed 20%. Were it not for the fact that China has carried out financial repression policies for a long time, it would have been impossible for some vulnerable banks to avoid bankrupty.

The extreme imbalance of regional development in China is reflected in the development of the financial industry. To show that, we make a simple regional observation of the sample banks. Among them, a large number of banks, which have a long history, a large scale, and nationwide distribution in the business outlets, are classified as "national banks" because it is difficult to assign those banks to specific regions. The following are the four major

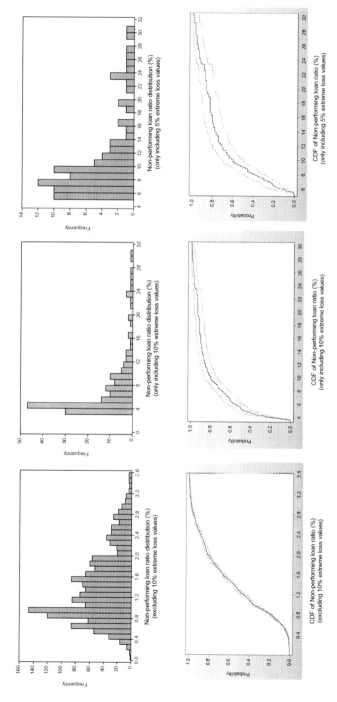

Figure 3.   Loss distribution of the non-performing loan ratios in commercial banks.

Source: Wind database.

banks in China: the Industrial and Commercial Bank of China, the Agricultural Bank of China, the China Construction Bank, and the Bank of China. Of the 1,648 banks in the sample, there are 622 commercial banks in the eastern region, 141 in the western region, 165 in the middle region, 68 in the northeast region, and 652 commercial banks nationwide. The cumulative empirical distribution of their non-performing loan ratios is shown in Figure 4 (the data of the northeastern region are not separately listed).

According to the critical value of the loss distribution extreme value, the eastern region is in the best operating situation. In the past 20 years, 90% of the non-performing loan ratios have been below 3.12%. In the western region, 90% of the non-performing loan ratios have been below 4%; this level exceeds the average loss level nationwide, and its financial environment is sobering. The national banks exhibit good operating situation.

To sum up, in the Chinese market, where the financial markets are not fully liberalized and financial repression plays a dominant

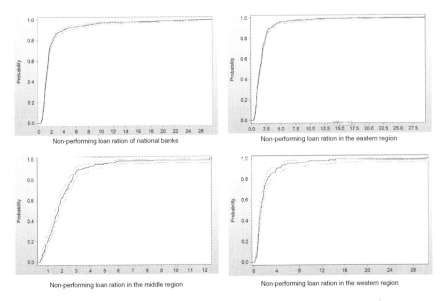

Figure 4. Empirical cumulative distributions of the non-performing loan ratios of regional commercial banks.

role, 10% of the non-performing loan ratios disclosed by commercial banks still exceed the required standard of the regulators throughout a long observation period.

In accordance with the 1996 Amendment of the Basel Committee on Banking Supervision, which was implemented in 1998, the banks are required not only to hold capital for credit risks but also to hold capital for market risks. The capital required for a bank's trading books is calculated by VaR on the basis of the historical values of catastrophic loss. If we followed this international practice, the non-performing loan ratio we have observed should be controlled within the range of 1–5% after taking into account the multiplier of at least three times.[1] Despite the absence of a major financial crisis in China's history, a gap with the international standards apparently exists.

4. Empirical Analysis

According to financial theory, there are a variety of economic factors that trigger or aggravate financial risks. Different financial markets involve different determining factors. The same financial factors may be beneficial to financial security in some financial environments but stimulate financial risks in other cases. In this section, we will take full account of all kinds of possible factors in China's financial market by combining the reality of China and the previous studies. We measure the relevant factors of systemic risks, the main indicators that constitute financial security, and the effects of the key macroeconomic factors on financial risks by means of an empirical analysis.

---

[1] The capital required by the bank is equal to the number of k multiplied by VaR (additional adjustments required for other special risks), and the "k" is determined by the regulators. The value of k varies between different banks, but in any case, the value of K will not be less than 3. For banks with a well-established VaR detection system, it is highly possible for the k value of the bank to approach the minimum value of 3. However, for the banks that fail to establish a perfect VaR system, the value of k is likely to be higher.

4.1. Building the basic systemic risk equation and single-factor influence equation

We define the non-performing loan ratio of commercial banks as the dependent variable of the basic equation of systemic risks. The independent variables are the loan scale, the transaction volume of the securities market, the value added in the real estate industry, and other macroeconomic factors of interest. The development level of GDP and other factors that affect the financial security environment are introduced into the panel equation as control variables. Based on the previous studies, a large number of financial security factors may be involved which may be correlated. If all these variables were introduced into the panel model as control variables, multicollinearity may hamper the estimation of the composite panel equation. Therefore, we first examine the impact of these factors on the non-performance loan ratio separately. Then we consider the overall impact of these factors to construct the composite index of financial security. Finally, we introduce the composite index as a control variable of aggregative indicator into the panel equation for analysis.

Through the analysis and comparison of the relevant statistics set by different models, this chapter adopts the mixed section–time fixed effect model of panel data for analysis. The specific model is as follows:

$$y_{it} = m + x'_{it}\beta + Y_t + \mu_{it}, \quad i = 1, 2, \ldots, N, \ t = 1, 2, \ldots, T, \quad (1)$$

where y_{it} refers to the non-performing loan ratio in the area i at time t and x_{it} refers to the value of the economic variable i at time t, and β is the regression coefficient. The estimation of parameters is detailed in Appendix A.

The data are mainly derived from the National Bureau of Statistics website and the WIND database. According to the availability of data, 372 groups of data are selected from 31 provinces between 2005 and 2016, of which there are 10 eastern provinces, six central provinces, 12 western provinces, and three northeastern provinces. The variables selected in this chapter are mainly used in the correlation factor analysis of systemic risks, the building of composite index of financial security, and the stress testing of macroeconomic shocks. The definitions and statistical descriptions of related variables are shown in Table 1. The calculation of the composite index for financial security F-S Index in the last line of Table 1 is described in detail in the next part of the analysis.

Table 1. Definitions and statistical descriptions of variables.

Variable (definition)	Mean	Standard deviation	Minimum	Maximum
Default: Non-performing loan ratio				
	3.81	4.90	0.23	24.74
LnLoan: The logarithm of the balance of loans (100,000,000 yuan)				
	9.27	1.15	5.19	11.62
LnExcha: The logarithm of the total transaction volume of securities market (100,000,000 yuan)				
	9.67	1.90	1.93	14.48
LnGDP: The logarithm of GDP (100,000,000 yuan)				
	9.19	1.09	5.52	11.30
LnReAdd: The logarithm of the added value of real estate market (100,000,000 yuan)				
	5.92	1.55	2.30	8.74
LnPCGDP: The logarithm of GDP per capita (yuan)				
	10.31	0.62	8.59	11.68
LnFAdd: The logarithm of the added value in the financial sector (100,000,000 yuan)				
	6.10	1.29	1.86	8.72
LnConsumLe: The logarithm of consumption level of residents (yuan)				
	9.26	0.59	7.96	10.81
LnTrade: The logarithm of total imports and exports (1,000 US dollars)				
	17.08	1.74	12.23	20.81
LnCA: The logarithm of total current assets of privately owned and state-owned enterprises (100,000,000 yuan)				
	8.04	1.25	3.13	10.17
F-S Index: Composite index for financial security				
	0.59	0.20	0	1

Eviews 8 software is used to conduct a significance test and regression analysis on the panel model. The application of the mixed "cross-section and time fixed" effect is supported to our analysis. The regression results are shown in Tables 2 and 3. Whether it is the regression result of the basic equation or that of the single-factor influence equation, most of the variables are closely related to the indicators of the default rate that mainly represent the systemic risks, and it is also consistent with our expectations. The basic equation (Table 2) shows that during the observation period, the gradual expansion of the loan scale and the increase of the added value in the real estate industry are important factors to predict the occurrence of default, which also means that once the loan scale is tightened, a significant decline in the housing prices is likely to trigger a systemic risk. The regression results also show that when the trading scale of the securities market reaches a certain degree, it will also stimulate the occurrence of default. This shows the sensitivity of systemic risks to the value of the stock market to a certain extent. As a controlled variable, LnGDP is significantly positive, and it is different from the usual anticipation. When the economic level improves to a certain extent, it will easily breed the bubbles in the loan scale and the real estate expansion, which will lead to financial risk. The negative correlation of the composite index for financial security, F-S Index, indicates the importance of creating a healthy,

Table 2. Regression results of the mixed "cross-section and time fixed" effect panel (basic equation).

Variable	Intercept	LnLoan	LnExcha	LnGDP	LnReAdd	F-S Index
Model 1	6.341**	−3.977***	1.113***	3.851***	−1.994***	
	(2.522)	(−6.564)	(4.122)	(6.697)	(−3.788)	
Model 2	3.656	−3.261***	1.206***	3.534***	−1.861***	−4.583*
	(1.241)	(−4.458)	(4.393)	(5.874)	(−3.508)	(−1.735)

Model 1: Adj.R^2 : 0.737; F-statistic: 70.17; D-W value: 0.703.
Model 2: Adj.R^2 : 0.738; F-statistic: 66.34; D-W value: 0.707.

Note: The period fixed effects are not listed in the table. The values in brackets are t statistics. *, **, and *** indicate that it is significant at the levels 10%, 5%, and 1%, respectively.

Table 3. Regression results of the mixed "cross-section and time fixed" effect panel (single-factor influence equation).

Variable	Model 1	Model 2	Model 3	Model 4	Model 5	Model 6
Intercept	23.02*** (7.142)	9.835*** (12.484)	25.61*** (8.166)	12.75*** (8.941)	8.123*** (7.973)	7.415*** (13.899)
LnPCGDP	−1.86*** (−5.967)					
LnFAdd		−0.988*** (−7.768)				
LnConsumLe			−2.356*** (−6.959)			
LnTrade				−0.524*** (−6.301)		
LnCA					−0.537*** (−4.279)	
F-S Index						−6.067*** (−7.000)
Adj.R^2	0.699	0.717	0.709	0.702	0.686	0.709
F-statistic	72.90	79.344	76.24	73.966	68.392	76.389
D-W statistic	0.641	0.650	0.660	0.632	0.616	0.647

Note: The period fixed effects are not listed in the table. The values in brackets are t-statistics. *, **, and *** indicate that it is significant at the levels 10%, 5%, and 1%, respectively.

orderly, and safe financial security environment to avoid systemic risks.

Based on the previous studies, we consider the combined effects of GDP per capita, the development level of the financial sector, the situation of residents' consumption, the trade scale, and the amount of liquid assets in enterprises as the important indicators to calculate the composite index of financial security.

4.2. Calculation of composite index for financial security

The purpose of calculating the composite index of financial security is to evaluate the state of the financial environment. We calculate it based on the method of factor analysis. We select all the variables in different categories that have a significant impact on the non-performing loan ratios in the single-factor influence equation in Table 4 for factor analysis. All the variables show a significant effect on the non-performing loan ratios. The composite index calculated by factor analysis is designed to follow the rule of "a higher value of the variable leads to a higher degree of financial security".

It is valued according to the common factor and processed by the 0–1 distribution in order to more intuitively observe the index more intuitively, so that the composite index for financial security can be obtained. The relevant statistical summary is shown in Table 1. The composite index for financial security is substituted into the basic equation and the single-factor influence equation separately, and the regression results prove that the composite index is set ideally. The regression results are shown in Table 2.

The composite index of financial security in this chapter is a macro-level index. Its size corresponds to the financial risk environment of a certain market. Our research will give different boundaries of the index, representing the financial security level of "excellent", "good", and "low". "Excellent" indicates the financial environment is healthy and risks can be well controlled. "Good" indicates the financial environment is normal and might need further improvement. "Low" implies the financial environment is risky and necessary measures should be taken to manage the risks.

This chapter links the different boundaries of financial security with the regulated non-performing loan ratio. In order to allow the security boundaries not only to be adjusted dynamically with the time but also to vary with different regions, we add the dummy variables of the eastern, central and western regions (the northeastern region is the reference group) in Model 6 of the single-factor influence equation in Table 3 and then conduct regression on the non-performing loan ratio again. The results show that the regional dummy variables and the F-S Index are both significant at the 1% level, and that the value of R^2 of the equation is 0.75 and the F-statistic is 69.96 (the coefficients of the variables in the equation can be seen in the notes of Figures 5–8). Therefore, we consider setting up a safe non-performance loan ratio and substituting it into our fitting equation. Finally, according to the requirements of different regions and time, we work out the safety margins of the financial

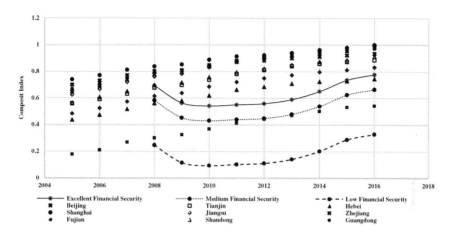

Figure 5.   Composite index of financial security in the eastern region of China. *Note*: The regional financial security safety margins in the figure are worked out based on the fitting equation of "the fitted value of default = 2.304* the eastern region −2.132* the middle region −3.026* the western region −7.433* F-S Index + 10.555 + period fixed effect". By setting the default value as 1.67 (excellent), 2.5 (medium), and 5 (low), the corresponding composite indexes for financial security can be worked out.

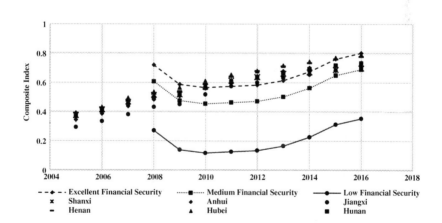

Figure 6.   Composite index of financial security in the middle region of China. *Note*: The regional financial security safety margins in the figure are worked out based on the fitting equation of "the fitted value of default = 2.304* the eastern region −2.132* the middle region −3.026* the western region −7.433* F-S Index + 10.555 + period fixed effect". By setting the default value as 1.67 (excellent), 2.5 (medium), and 5 (low), the corresponding composite indexes for financial security can be worked out.

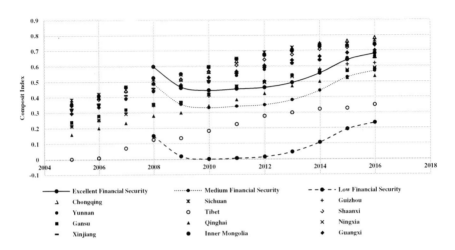

Figure 7. Composite index of financial security in the western region of China.
Note: The regional financial security safety margins in the figure are worked out based on the fitting equation of "the fitted value of default = 2.304* the eastern region −2.132* the middle region −3.026* the western region −7.433* F-S Index + 10.555 + period fixed effect". By setting the default value as 1.67 (excellent), 2.5 (medium), and 5 (low), the corresponding composite indexes for financial security can be worked out.

security indexes under different circumstances. According to the provision mentioned in the preceding text that the non-performing loan ratio in the indicators of credit risk regulation in commercial banks should not be higher than 5%, coupled with the regulatory requirements of the Basel Accord for the default rate multiplied by 3, we take one-third of 5%, namely 1.67%, as the ideal value of the "excellent" level of financial security and one half of 5%, namely 2.5%, as the intermediate value of the "good" level of financial security, and 5% as the warning value of the "low" level of financial security.

The scattered points in Figures 5–8 are the values of the composite indexes for financial security in various regions from 2005 to 2016, and the smoothed lines refer to the financial safety margins at different levels in different periods. We define the values of composite indexes for financial security between 0 and 1, and the higher the value is, the safer the financial environment of the region will be. However, for different regions, there are different requirements for the

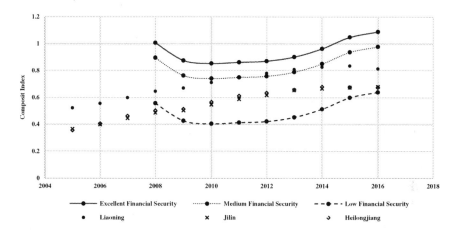

Figure 8.   Composite index of financial security in the northeastern region of China.

Note: The regional financial security safety margins in the figure are worked out based on the fitting equation of "the fitted value of default = 2.304* the eastern region −2.132* the middle region −3.026* the western region −7.433* F-S Index + 10.555 + period fixed effect". By setting the default value as 1.67 (excellent), 2.5 (medium), and 5 (low), the corresponding composite indexes for financial security can be worked out.

excellent, medium, and low levels of financial safety margins in different periods. Therefore, there are different regulatory requirements for different regions, and when the scattered points are above the corresponding smoothed lines, we believe that the region has safe financial environment. By observing the distribution of scattered points, it can be seen that the value of security index in the eastern region is relatively the highest, and the lowest values are more distributed in the western region. Next, by observing the smoothed lines of financial safety margins in different regions, it can be inferred that the eastern region has the lowest requirements for financial safety margins, which means that the eastern region has the largest number of provinces above the safety margins as well as indirectly indicates that the eastern region has a relatively mature and stable macroeconomic environment for financial development. However, in the northeastern region, it is seen that in order to ensure a relatively low default rate to fully avoid the occurrence of the systemic risks, it must satisfy a high financial safety margin to achieve such default rate, which also means that the northeastern region has the smallest number of provinces above the safety margins, thereby showing the relatively weak financial environment in the northeastern region. From the figures, we can also observe that, irrespective of which region it is, the highest requirements for the value of the boundaries of financial security are at different levels in 2008, 2015, and 2016, which is closely related to the outbreak of the financial crisis and the stock market crash in these 3 years (2016 is a continuation of the impact of 2015). And it also verifies the reliability of our estimate of the index once again.

In this section, we focus on the calculation of financial security composite index in different regions of China. The index is composed of per capita GDP, the added value in the financial sector, consumption level of residents, trade scale, and current assets of enterprises which are highly related to the default rate of commercial banks. The boundaries of "excellent", "good", and "low" are different for different time periods. The results show that most of the provinces in the eastern region are located on the upper side of the curves "good" and "excellent", followed by the middle region, the western region, and the northeastern region. This order denotes that the eastern region has the best healthy financial environment and the middle region has the better one. The western region and the northeastern regions are less optimistic.

4.3. *Macroeconomic shocks*

The stress testing model which combines the credit risk with the macroeconomic factors has been relatively mature (Virolainen, 2004). The core idea is to link macroeconomic factors with the default rate represented by the non-performing loan ratio. In case of a reasonable setting of the model, the corresponding changes in the default rate can be observed by generating a macroeconomic shock in the system, which is a simulation for the possible default rate in the future. The objective is to obtain the expected loss and extreme loss of a credit portfolio in the future under the prevailing macroeconomic conditions. This study refers to the model framework of Wilson (1997a, 1997b).

The first step is to assume that the average default rate of commercial banks in region i can be defined in the form of a logistic equation as follows:

$$p_{i,t} = \frac{1}{1 + \exp(y_{i,t})}. \tag{2}$$

The logistic distribution form has been widely used in the research models on bank failure, and it can ensure that the estimated default rate is in the interval $[0,1]$. $p_{i,t}$ is the average default rate of the region i at time t, and $y_{i,t}$ is the index of the level of the development and operation of a bank in a specific region. The better the operation and development of a commercial bank is, the higher the value of $y_{i,t}$ will be, and the lower the default rate $p_{i,t}$ will be, and vice versa. The expression for $y_{i,t}$ can be easily obtained in the form of the logistic equation through the logit conversion:

$$L(p_{i,t}) = \ln\left(\frac{1 - p_{i,t}}{p_{i,t}}\right) = y_{i,t}.$$

Since we can obtain the value of the default rate in the model represented by the non-performing loan ratio in advance, we can deduce the average value of the operating-level index of commercial banks in the region. If we fail to know the non-performance loan ratio, we can compile the operating level index and then estimate the default rate through the representative operating state of the commercial banks in the region.

In the model, $y_{i,t}$ is affected by a number of exogenous macroeconomic factors. In accordance with the mixed section–time fixed effect model adopted by the previously set panel equation, Equation (1) can be expanded as follows:

$$y_{it} = m + \beta_1 x_{1,it} + \beta_2 x_{2,it} + \cdots + \beta_n x_{n,it} + \gamma_t + u_{it}, \tag{3}$$

where β_is are the coefficients of the related macroeconomic factors, which are presented in this chapter as the loan scale, the value added of the real estate sector, the total trading volume of the securities market, and the composite index of financial security.

In the second step, similar to the approach of Virolainen (2004), we can predict the expected value of each macroeconomic factor in the next stage by using a set of univariate autoregressive equations of order 2 (AR(2)), based on the time series data of each macroeconomic factor:

$$x_{it} = k_{i0} + k_{i1}X_{i\,t-1} + k_{i2}X_{i\,t-2} + \varepsilon_{it}, \tag{4}$$

where k_i represents the regression coefficient of the ith macroeconomic factor. ε_{it} is a random error term, and it is assumed that it obeys the independent normal distribution.

Equations (2)–(4) define the relationship between the default rate and the macroeconomic factors in the form of a joint equation, with the residual vector E of $(j+i) \times 1$ dimensions, and the variance and covariance matrices Σ of the residual of $(j+i) \times (j+i)$ dimensions, which are defined as follows:

$$E = \begin{pmatrix} u \\ \varepsilon \end{pmatrix} \sim N(0, \Sigma) \quad \Sigma = \begin{bmatrix} \Sigma_u & \Sigma_{u,\varepsilon} \\ \Sigma_{\varepsilon,u} & \Sigma_\varepsilon \end{bmatrix}.$$

The last step is to simulate the joint default rate of different regions based on the different time periods according to the system equations based on the combination of the estimation of each parameter and the residual term. According to the previous model settings, the macroeconomic factors that affect the default rate are independent of each other, so that we can conduct the stress testing of each economic shock on the model through the simulated data of the Monte Carlo model with a single variable on the premise that other economic conditions (variables) remain unchanged.

This chapter selects the time fixed effect equation in the latest period to obtain the expected value of each macroeconomic factor for the next period and obtains the default rate in case of different extreme values simulated from the normal distribution based on the mean value and variance of each factor in the historical observation periods. The regression results of the vector autoregression model are shown in Table 4, and the simulated loss distribution of stress testing is shown in Table 5.

The regional stress testing in this chapter is targeted at the distribution in four major areas, and the expected values of different regions in the model are the mean provincial value in this region.

Table 4.   Regression results of the macroeconomic factors' vector autoregression model.

Variable	LnLoan	LnExcha	LnReAdd	LnGDP	F-S Index
Intercept	0.183***	0.485***	0.268***	0.135***	0.043***
	(7.033)	(4.048)	(12.027)	(7.908)	(11.344)
Lag Intervals	1.493***	0.895***	1.054***	1.534***	1.198***
(−1)	(34.04)	(19.593)	(24.930)	(37.834)	(20.382)
Lag Intervals	−0.504***	0.083*	−0.078*	−0.543***	−0.230***
(−2)	(−11.552)	(1.730)	(−1.881)	(−13.481)	(−4.023)
Year	2005–2016	2002–2016	1999–2016	2001–2016	2007–2016
Adj. R^2	0.997	0.926	0.993	0.998	0.995
F-statistic	67,394	2,887.6	38,558	161,197	29,746

Note: The figures in brackets are t-statistics. ***, **, and * indicate significance at the 1%, 5%, and 10% levels, respectively.

Based on the 10,000 Monte Carlo simulations, the loss distribution of regional stress testing is shown in Table 5.

First of all, the expected value of the default rate in each region is observed. It can be seen that the default rate of the middle region is at the highest level of 2.24 and that of the eastern region is at the lowest level of 1.01. However, stress testing intends to know more about what kind of shocks default risks will encounter when an extreme economic situation occurs. Throughout the four macroeconomic factors used for testing, the loan scale has the largest impact on the systemic risks or is the most sensitive to such risks, followed by the value added of the real estate industry, which means that in case of a sudden contraction in the scale of loans or a sudden drop in housing prices (we can obtain the corresponding range of drop according to the exponential values of the figures in Table 5), it will lead to varying degrees of default, thereby resulting in a systemic risk. For example, in the real estate market of the eastern region under the circumstances of 1% extreme loss, when the LnRed value is 4.75, the default rate of commercial banks will reach 6.31, which indicates that for the regulatory authorities, the default rate of the commercial banks is likely to reach a high-risk level of 6.31% when the scale of the value added of the real estate industry in an eastern province shrinks to the exponential value of 11.558 billion yuan with the LnRed value

Table 5. Distribution table of regional losses of macroeconomic shock stress testing.

Stress testing	Df.	LnLoan	Df.	LnExcha	Df.	LnReAdd	Df.	F-S Index
The eastern region of China								
Expected value	1.01	10.88	1.01	12.71	1.01	7.60	1.01	0.90
10% Extreme loss	4.99	9.67	3.90	15.10	3.88	6.06	1.93	0.70
5% Extreme loss	6.23	9.28	4.66	15.73	4.71	5.61	2.23	0.63
1% Extreme loss	9.00	8.43	5.91	16.77	6.31	4.75	2.56	0.56
The middle region of China								
Expected value	2.24	10.38	2.24	11.70	2.24	7.06	2.24	0.76
10% Extreme loss	4.75	9.61	4.47	13.55	4.47	5.87	2.84	0.63
5% Extreme loss	5.65	9.33	4.98	13.97	5.11	5.52	3.01	0.60
1% Extreme loss	6.98	8.92	6.38	15.13	6.10	4.99	3.25	0.54
The western region of China								
Expected value	2.10	9.74	2.10	10.47	2.10	5.82	2.10	0.67
10% Extreme loss	7.02	8.24	5.12	12.97	5.49	4.00	3.02	0.47
5% Extreme loss	8.07	7.92	5.87	13.59	6.56	3.42	3.26	0.41
1% Extreme loss	10.40	7.20	7.45	14.91	8.36	2.46	3.78	0.30
The northeastern region of China								
Expected value	1.91	10.15	1.91	11.38	1.91	6.62	1.91	0.74
10% Extreme loss	4.75	9.28	4.22	13.29	3.97	5.52	2.51	0.61
5% Extreme loss	5.54	9.04	4.81	13.78	4.52	5.22	2.68	0.57
1% Extreme loss	7.05	8.58	6.04	14.80	5.66	4.61	3.02	0.50

Note: Df. indicates default rate.

of 4.75. The impact of the loan scale on the financial systems in China is most uncontrollable in the macro-impact factors shown in Table 5. We can see that the non-performing loan ratio, triggered by the impact of the 1% extreme value of the factor, is at a very high default level (the minimum value is 6.98 for the middle region and the maximum value is 10.4 for the western region), which far exceeds the warning level that we set before. Furthermore, it is found that the two indicators of loan scale and housing price are the most sensitive in the western and eastern regions, while they are relatively stable in the middle and northeastern regions. Next, we observe the impact of the financial security environment in different regions on the default rate. Since the F-S Index is a composite index, there will be no significant fluctuations on the indicator in terms of the extreme value simulation. But, from the perspective of distribution, we can still find some regional differences. Taking the value of the F-S Index in case of 10% extreme loss as an example, the extreme conditions of financial security in the western region (the worst financial environment) have the greatest impact on the default rate, which is 3.02, followed by 2.84 in the middle region, 2.51 in the northeastern region, and 1.93 in the eastern region. The same sequence is shown in case of 5% and 1% catastrophic losses. It reflects the instability of the financial environment in the middle and western regions and indirectly verifies our previous conclusion that the eastern region has better financial security environment, but the excellent financial security environment in the eastern region highlights the hidden dangers and possible bubbles in the housing prices and the scale of loans.

This section mainly discusses the extreme impact of macroeconomic factors and the financial security index on systemic risk. From the perspective of individual macro-factors, the systemic risk caused by the contraction of loan scale is the most harmful and the risk in the western region is the most uncontrollable. Systematic risk caused by a shrinking real estate market also causes a tremendous damage. The western region still shows the biggest, uncontrollable risky situation followed by the eastern region, which implies that once the house price falls, the systematic risk caused may trigger economic panic. Our results also indicate that the risks from the price bubbles of financial assets are well managed in China at present. According to the stress test of financial security index, the risk of deterioration of financial environment in the western region is largest, followed by the middle, northeastern, and eastern regions.

5. Concluding Remarks and Policy Proposals

In this chapter, we focus on the non-performing loan rate of commercial banks to discuss the systemic risk of China. Through abundant data analysis, the systemic risk in China is closely related to credit scale, real estate markets, and financial asset prices. We design and calculate a composite index of financial security, which is composed of various macro-factors that significantly affect the non-performing loan rate of commercial banks. The objective of the index is to show that the financial environment assessment it represents is not only a comprehensive display of key macroeconomic factors but also a prediction of possible systemic risks. Compared with the previous studies on financial security index conducted by Chinese scholars, the index constructed in this chapter has dynamic characteristics and presents regional differences. According to the requirements of government financial supervision, we give the boundaries of "excellent", "good", and "low", which represent the different financial safety margins. Policymakers can take the requisite intervention measures to manage the corresponding levels of risks.

We test extreme value stress based on regional differences through the three indicators of systemic risk, namely credit scale, real estate prices, and financial asset prices. Taking 5% extreme value shocks as an example, assume that the non-performing loan rate exceeding 5% is the upper limit of regulatory capacity. The research conclusion states that the credit scale has the greatest impact on China's systemic risk, and the extreme consequences are beyond the scope of regulatory capacity in all regions, which is liable to trigger financial crisis. The real estate market has the second biggest impact on systemic risk, and the extreme risks also express greater harmfulness. The western and middle regions are beyond the scope of regulatory control. The extreme impact of financial asset price bubbles on systemic risks demonstrates that they are not beyond regulatory capacity except for the western region (which is very close to the regulatory threshold). For the four regions, the western region is the most exposed area to all the indicators. In addition, the eastern region has a higher credit risk, while the middle region has a higher real estate market risk.

According to the stress test of the financial security index composed of the other macroeconomic factors, the most sensitive to the deterioration of the macroeconomic environment is the western region, followed by the middle region, the northeastern region, and the eastern region.

Based on the analysis discussed in this chapter, we draw the following main conclusions. We should attach importance to the loan scale management of commercial banks and prudently use the tight credit policy. Slow credit expansion can prevent the rapid expansion of the credit bubble. China's real estate market has reached a certain scale, and further expansion needs to be carefully considered in combination with financial supervision. China's financial capital market still has flexible development space. China can be more in line with international financial markets, expand derivatives markets, and encourage diversified forms of capital flows, thus promoting faster maturity of China's financial markets. The western region of China has great potential financial risks, which need more detailed analysis of the relevant reasons, and has attracted the attention of the regulatory authorities.

The relevant policy proposals are as follows: it is necessary to establish a dynamic comprehensive evaluation system and regulatory system on financial security in China. The development of economic and financial markets involves complicated macro-environment, it is necessary to set up specific regulatory requirements according to the specific economic and financial conditions and to set up a supporting regulatory system that is flexible, prudent, and highly effective. We should lay more emphasis on a differentiated financial risk management in various regions and enhance the overall early-warning mechanism of the relevant financial institutions. There are significant differences in China in terms of regional development and financial development. In view of the characteristics of regional development and the different policies for regional development in China, we should strengthen the overall early-warning mechanism from the perspective of financial institutions themselves, rather than excessively relying on the stress on the management functions of the central bank. In other words, we should establish appropriate regional financial instruments concerning financial risk management and innovation, which are used by the local governments. Macroeconomic and financial control policies should be adopted in a moderate and appropriate manner. Macroeconomic policies and financial policies play different regulatory roles in different periods, and their effectiveness varies in different regions. They should be used taking into account regional economic development, the orientation of economic objectives, and different regulatory requirements.

Appendix A. Parameter Estimation of Mixed Section–Time Fixed Effect Model for Panel Data

The specific expression of the mixed section–time fixed effect model of panel data is shown in Equation (A.1).

$$y_{it} = m + x'_{it}\beta + Y_t + \mu_{it}, \quad i = 1, 2, \ldots, N, \ t = 1, 2, \ldots, T. \quad (A.1)$$

The parameters are estimated as follows:

$$\hat{\beta}_{FE} = \left[\sum_{i=1}^{N} \sum_{t=1}^{T} (x_{it} - \bar{x}_l \bar{x}_t + \bar{x})(x_{it} - \bar{x}_l \bar{x}_t + \bar{x})' \right]^{-1}$$

$$\left[\sum_{i=1}^{N} \sum_{t=1}^{T} (x_{it} - \bar{x}_l \bar{x}_t + \bar{x})(y_{it} - \bar{y}_l - \bar{y}_t + \bar{y})' \right]^{-1}, \quad (A.2)$$

$$\hat{m} = \hat{y} - \bar{x}' \hat{\beta}_{FE}, \quad (A.3)$$

$$\hat{Y}_t = (\bar{y}_t - \bar{y}) - (\bar{x}_t - \bar{x})' \hat{\beta}_{FE}, \quad (A.4)$$

where

$$\bar{x}_i - \frac{1}{T} \sum_{t=1}^{T} x_{it}, \quad \bar{y}_i = \frac{1}{T} \sum_{t=1}^{T} y_{it}, \quad \bar{x} = \frac{1}{NT} \sum_{i=1}^{N} \sum_{t=1}^{T} x_{it},$$

$$\bar{y} = \frac{1}{NT} \left(\sum_{i=1}^{N} \sum_{t=1}^{T} y_{it} \right), \quad \bar{x}_t = \frac{1}{N} \left(\sum_{i=1}^{N} x_{it} \right),$$

and

$$\bar{y}_i = \frac{1}{T} \left(\sum_{t=1}^{T} y_{it} \right).$$

Acknowledgment

This study was supported by the National Natural Science Foundation of China [Grant Nos. 71473137 and 71773058].

References

Acharya, V. V., Pedersen, L. P., Philippon, T. and Richardson, M. (2009). "Measuring Systemic Risk," *Mimeo*, New York University.

Adrian, T. and Shin, H. Y. (2010). "Money, Liquidity and Monetary Policy," *American Economic Review*, **99**(2), 600–605.

Adrian, T. and Brunnermeier, M. (2009). "CoVar." Federal Reserve Bank of New York Staff Report, 348.

Alessandri, P., Gai, P., Kapadia, S., Mora, N. and Puhr, C. (2009). "A Framework for Quantifying Systemic Stability," *International Journal of Central Banking*, **5**(3), 48–81.

Allen, F. and Gale, D. (2000). "Financial Contagion," *Journal of Political Economy*, **108**, 1–33.

Bank of England (2011). "Instruments of Macroprudential Policy." Bank of England Discussion Paper.

Bhattacharya, S. A. B. and Thakor, A. (1998). "The Economics of Bank Regulation," *Journal of Money, Credit and Banking*, **30**, 745–770.

Borio, C. (2009). "The Macroprudential Approach to Regulation and Supervision," http://www.voxeu.org/index.php?q$=$$node/3445.

Brownlees, C. and Engle, R. (2015). "SRISK: A Conditional Capital Shortfall Index for Systemic Risk Measurement," *Mimeo*, New York University.

Butzbach, O. (2016). "Systemic Risk, Macro-prudential Regulation and Organizational Diversity in Banking," *Policy and Society*, **35**(3), 239–251.

De Nicolo, G. and Kwast, M. I. (2002). "Systemic Risk and Financial Consolidation: Are They Related," *Journal of Banking and Finance*, **26**(5), 861–880.

Dewatripont, M. and Tirole, J. (1993). *The Prudential Regulation of Banks*, MIT Press, Boston.

Drehmann, M. (2008). "Macroeconomic Stress Testing Banks: A Survey of Methodologies," in M. Quagliariello (ed.), *Stress Testing the Banking System: Methodologies and Applications*, Cambridge University Press, Cambridge, pp. 59–62.

Elsinger, H., Lehar, A. and Summer, M. (2006). "Risk Assessment for Banking Systems," *Management Science*, **52**(9), 1–41.

Fan, X. Y., Fang, Y. and Wang, D. P. (2013). "Systemic Risk and Systematically Important Financial Institutions of China's Bank Section — An Analysis Based on CCA and DAG," *Journal of Financial Research*, **11**, 82–95 (in Chinese).

Freixas, X., Laeven, L. and Peydró, J.-L. (2015). *Systemic Risk, Crises, and Macroprudential Regulation*, MIT Press, Boston, MA.

Freixas, X., Parigi, B. and Rochet, J.-C. (1997). *Microeconomics of Banking*, MIT Press, Boston.

Freixas, X., Parigi, B. and Rochet, J.-C. (2000). "Systemic Risk, Interbank Relations and Liquidity Provision by the Central Bank," *Journal of Money, Credit and Banking*, **32**(3), 611–638.

Freixas, X. and Rochet, J.-C. (2008). *Microeconomics of Banking*, 2nd edn., MIT Press, Boston.

FSB, IMF, and BIS (2011). *Macroprudential Policy Tools and Frameworks*.

Goodhart, C., Sunirand, P. and Tsomocos, D. (2005). "A Risk Assessment Model for Banks," *Annals of Finance*, **25**(1), 197–224.

Kiyotaki, N. and Moore, J. (1997). "Credit Cycles," *Journal of Political Economy*, **105**(2), 211–248.

Lin, Y. E., Chen, X. L. and Chi, X. X. (2014). "Does Mutual Fund Flow Have Information Content?," *Economic Research Journal*, **S1**, 176–188 (in Chinese).

Liu, L. K., Zhang, D. S. and Zou, H. F. (2012). "Review of Latest Developments of Study on Measurement of Financial Systemic Risk," *Journal of Financial Research*, **11**, 31–43 (in Chinese).

Nie F. Q. and Zhou Y. Q. (2017). "The Assessment of Financial Security State Based on the Coordinate of Industry Financing Structure," *Economic Modelling Science Journal*, **2**, 53–61, 126 (in Chinese).

Peng, Y. C. and Fang, Y. (2016). "Structural Monetary Policy, Industrial Structure Upgrade and Economic Stability," *Economic Research Journal*, **7**, 29–42, 86 (in Chinese).

Peng, H. F. and Tan, X. Y. (2017). "RMB Internationalization: Degree Measurement and Determinants Analysis," *Economic Research Journal*, **2**, 125–139 (in Chinese).

Pesaran, M. H., Schuerman, T., Treutler, B. J. and Weiner, S. M. (2006). "Macroeconomic Dynamics and Credit Risk: A Global Perspective," *Journal of Money, Credit and Banking*, **28**(5), 1211–1262.

Rochet, J.-C. and Tirole, J. (1996). "Interbank Lending and Systemic Risk," *Journal of Money, Credit and Banking*, **28**(4), 733–762.

Virolainen, K. (2004). "Macro Stress Testing with a Macroeconomic Credit Risk Model for Finland." Bank of Finland Discussion Papers.

Wang, B. and Fan, X. Y. (2017). "Imbalance Adjustment, Macroeconomic Stability and Financial Risk Prevention," *Economic Research Journal*, **7**, 200–204 (in Chinese).

Wang, J. (2017). "Analysis of the Influence of Monetary Policy on Financial Security in China and Countermeasures Under the New Normal of Economy," *Theoretical Investigation*, **5**, 116–120 (in Chinese).

Wang, W. (2016). "On the Establishment of the Rule of Law System for National Financial Security," *Comparative Economics — Society System*, **4**, 192–203 (in Chinese).

Wilson, T. C. (1997a). "Portfolio Credit Risk (I)," *Risk*, September (reprinted in Shimko, D. (2004). *Credit Risk Models and Management*, 2nd edn., Risk Books).

Wilson, T. C. (1997b). "Portfolio Credit Risk (II)," *Risk*, October (reprinted in Shimko, D. (2004). *Credit Risk Models and Management*, 2nd edn., Risk Books).

Xiao, B. Q., Yan, J. Y., Yang, Y. and Zhang, P. (2015). "Modeling and Empirical Study of China's Financial Security Monitoring and Early Warning System: Based on BPNN," *International Business (Journal of University of International Business and Economics)*, **6**, 97–106 (in Chinese).

Zhang, W., Wei, L. J., Xiong, X., Li, G. and Ma, Z. X. (2011). "Discrimination of Cross-Market Price Manipulations in Stock Index Futures Market: Evidences from Volatility and Liquidity," *Management Review*, **7**, 163–170, 176 (in Chinese).

Chapter 8

Fiscal Sustainability of China's Provincial Governments: A Non-Stationary Panel Data Analysis

Vinh Q. T. Dang[*], Kenneth S. Chan[†], and Erin P. K. So[‡]

[*]*Nanjing University of Finance and Economics, China*
[†]*McMaster University, Canada*
[‡]*Hong Kong Baptist University, Hong Kong*

Applying non-stationary panel data approach to the expenditures and revenues of China's provincial governments for the period 1994–2013, we investigate whether there exists a long-run relationship between these two budget variables that would limit fiscal deficits and, consequently, debt, to a sustainable level. Considering the tax-sharing system instituted in 1994, we also include transfers from and to the central government in the analysis. Results from recent second-generation panel unit root and cointegration tests that account for cross-sectional dependence suggest that provinces in the central and western regions do not achieve fiscal sustainability on their own or even with central government transfers. Provinces in the more developed eastern region overall achieve fiscal sustainability in the weak form. Only the government budget in Jiangsu, Tianjin, Zhejiang, and, to a lesser extent, Shanghai is strictly sustainable on its own. These results bear important policy implications for China's macroeconomic stability.

1. Introduction

After three decades of fast growth that elevated China's economy to the second largest in the world, the current slowdown is a major concern for its trading partners. The single most serious challenge facing China now is probably an increasing burden of debt accumulated from many years of investment-oriented and, to a lesser extent, export-oriented growth strategy.[1] Most of the debt has been generated by state-owned enterprises (SOEs), through their preferential access to state-owned banks, and by local governments, through off-balance-sheet financing activities that proliferated under the auspices of the stimulus program in 2009. Years of frenzied investment from these entities have resulted in acute overcapacity and debt overhang. The amount of non-performing loans in commercial banks, particularly state-owned banks, has multiplied in the last decade. A systemic default in these debts will likely trigger a financial crisis that can once again engulf the world economy.

Motivated by this important development, we examine fiscal sustainability of provincial governments in China by testing if their behavior is consistent with an inter-temporal budget constraint. Since consistent and reliable time series data on local governments' debt and off-balance-sheet finance are not available, we investigate whether there exists a long-run relationship between local revenues and expenditures that would limit fiscal deficits and, consequently, debt, to a sustainable level.[2] Considering the "tax-sharing" system instituted in 1994, we also include central government transfers in the analysis.

Our study contains the following contributions. First, although sustainability of public finances has always been an important research topic, particularly after the 2008 financial crisis when large fiscal stimuli were widely used around the world, most studies focus on OECD countries (Afonso and Jalles, 2015; Gosh *et al.*, 2013; Westerlund and Prohl, 2010).[3] Our focus on China, an emerging market economy and the largest trading partner of many countries in the world, can contribute significant insights to the literature. To our best

---

[1]Bloomberg News on March 2, 2016 reported that the amount of debt in China rose to record-high 250% of GDP at the end of 2015 and that, as a result, Moody's cut China's credit rating from "stable" to "negative".

[2]China's first audit of local government debt was conducted in 2010 by National Audit Office, which has since published some statistics for 2010, 2012, and 2013.

[3]Afonso (2005) provides a useful summary of earlier research.

knowledge, there is no study on the fiscal sustainability of China's local governments using panel data of revenues and expenditures.

Second, the analysis in our study can also be considered as a review of the long-term impact of China's 1994 fiscal centralization on the local governments' budget. Before 1994, provincial governments collected most of the tax revenues and were responsible for most of their local budgetary expenditures. Under the tax-sharing system institutionalized in 1994, local governments must remit a much larger portion of their excise intakes to the central government while remaining responsible for most local expenditures. The central government, under its own discretion and various policy objectives (for example, reducing regional economic disparities), then makes some transfers across provinces. Forbidden to issue bonds or borrow directly from commercial banks, local governments have resorted to land sales and various off-balance-sheet activities in an attempt to offset recurring imbalances that have been rising since 1994. Our study, covering the period 1994–2013, therefore also checks the viability of China's 1994 fiscal arrangement and sheds light on the provinces' dependence on the central government transfers and off-budget finance.[4]

Our study differs from a few recent studies, such as those by Zhang and Barnett (2014) and Lu and Sun (2013), that examine the amount of debt accumulated through local government financing vehicles (LGFVs).[5] Data on off-balance-sheet activities such as LGFVs are not readily available and their estimation requires numerous assumptions and judgment, creating a considerable degree of

---

[4]Some studies, such as that by Huang and Chen (2012), investigate whether the central government transfers achieve the intended effect of reducing regional income disparities. The results of our analysis, on the contrary, shed light on the effect of the tax-sharing system on fiscal sustainability of provincial governments.
[5]To partly compensate for the decline in local budgetary revenue brought by the tax-sharing arrangement, the central government also redesignated revenues from land-use right to the local governments; these revenues have since become a major source of financing. As the 1994 budget law forbids local governments from running a deficit or raising debt directly, land-based transactions can only be conducted through LGFVs. The amount of local government debt, based on recent estimates of LGFVs, has reached an alarming level.

uncertainty surrounding the estimates (Zhang and Barnett, 2014). There is also the challenge of defining the boundary of quasi-fiscal activities; for example, whether the debt of local SOEs should be counted as part of the local governments' debt is a matter subject to debate. Consequently, these few studies primarily rely on descriptive statistics of data that are available only for the last few years to bring forth the important issue of LGFVs. Our study, on the contrary, focuses on formal, regular, and well-documented budgetary revenue and expenditure items to examine fiscal sustainability in a much longer term. Therefore, our analysis can also provide a useful baseline reference for future studies on shadow financing activities.

Lastly, we apply recent advances in the econometrics of non-stationary panel data. More specifically, instead of simply assuming cross-section independence in our panel data, we explicitly test for this data feature. Then, we perform recent second-generation panel unit root and cointegration tests to account for correlation among cross-section units (provinces here). We show that failing to properly account for this correlation will result in misleading inferences and therefore policy implications.

In Section 2, we discuss the methodology and data. The empirical results are reported in Section 3. We offer some concluding remarks in Section 4.

2. Methodology and Data

A common approach to testing sustainability of public finances in the literature is to examine whether the government's inter-temporal budget constraint is satisfied (Afonso, 2005; Afonso and Jalles, 2015; Westerlund and Prohl, 2010).[6] The government's one-period constraint is given by

$$\tilde{G}_t - (1 + r_t)B_{t-1} = R_t + B_t, \qquad (1)$$

where $\tilde{G}_t$, R_t, and B_t are government expenditures excluding interest payments, revenues, and debt, respectively, at time t. These variables

---

[6]These studies were in turn based on Hakkio and Rush (1991), Hamilton and Flavin (1986), Quintos (1995), and Trehan and Walsh (1991).

are expressed in terms of local GDP to account for economic size and growth. r_t is the growth-adjusted interest rate levied on government debt; it is assumed to be stationary around mean r.

By forward substitution and letting $E_t = \tilde{G}_t + (r_t - r)B_{t-1}$ and $G_t = \tilde{G}_t + r_t B_{t-1}$, the inter-temporal budget constraint can be written as follows:

$$G_t - R_t = \sum_{j=0}^{\infty} \left(\frac{1}{1+r}\right)^{j-1} (\Delta R_{t+j} - \Delta E_{t+s})$$

$$+ \lim_{j\to\infty} \left(\frac{1}{1+r}\right)^{j+1} B_{t+s}. \qquad (2)$$

Under the transversality condition (no-Ponzi scheme), which restricts the second term on the right-hand side to be zero, and assuming government spending including interest payment G_t and revenue R_t are $I(1)$, G_t and R_t must be cointegrated for the above budget constraint to hold. Therefore, assessing the sustainability of public finances involves testing if this cointegrating relationship exists[7]:

$$R_t = \alpha + \beta G_t + \varepsilon_t. \qquad (3)$$

According to Hakkio and Rush (1991) and Quintos (1995), the government budget is strongly sustainable when R_t and G_t are cointegrated with $\beta = 1$. The sustainability is weak if there is cointegration and $0 < \beta < 1$. In the absence of cointegration, there is no long-term relationship that binds government revenue and spending, and they will diverge. Fiscal sustainability is not tenable in this case.

We use different issues of Finance Yearbook of China (Ministry of Finance) and China Statistical Yearbook (National Bureau of Statistics) to extract data covering 29 provinces for 1994–2013.[8] We focus on the main budgetary revenue and expenditure items for each

---

[7]Another approach to testing sustainability hypothesis, also derived from Equation (2), is to check if the first difference of the stock of public debt (ΔB_t) is stationary, in which case the non-Ponzi scheme condition is satisfied. This approach, however, is not feasible here since reliable time series data on Chinese local governments' public debt are not available.

[8]Tibet and Chongqing are excluded because of data unavailability.

province; these "above-the-line" items are regular and well documented. We ignore extra-budgetary revenue and expenditure items as these "below-the-line" items, except transfers from and to the central government, are not available for all provinces and tend to have missing or unreliable values.[9] For each province, we scale the revenues and expenditures by GDP to account for the size and growth of its economy. Taking into account the tax-sharing system, we also consider central government transfers. Two versions of revenue and expenditure variables are defined as follows:

R_1 = total budgetary revenues/GDP,
G_1 = total budgetary expenditures/GDP,
R_2 = sum of total budgetary revenues and transfers from the central government/GDP, and
G_2 = sum of total budgetary expenditures and transfers to the central government/GDP.

China's economic development landscape varies considerably from one region to another. Moreover, under the 1994 fiscal centralization, the central government transfers a large portion of overall tax revenue remitted from the local economies across provinces to even out regional economic disparities. Therefore, we also group the provinces into three regions and examine them separately. The most developed eastern region consists of Beijing, Fujian, Guangdong, Hainan, Hebei, Jiangsu, Liaoning, Shandong, Shanghai, Tianjin, and Zhejiang. The central region includes Anhui, Heilongjiang, Henan, Hubei, Jiangxi, Jilin, and Shanxi. The least-developed western region consists of Gansu, Guangxi, Guizhou, Inner Mongolia, Ningxia, Qinghai, Shaanxi, Sichuan, Xinjiang, and Yunnan.

The above discussion of the theoretical framework suggests our testing procedure. We first examine the degree of integration in the

---

[9]Interested readers are referred to 2012 final account of budgetary revenue and expenditure for Beijing municipality. In this year, the "above-the-line" total budgetary revenues and expenditures (in 100 million yuan) are 3314.93 and 3685.31, respectively; the transfers from and to the central government (in 100 million yuan) are 568.41 and 56.1, respectively.

data series via unit root tests. If the government revenue and expenditure series are stationary, $I(0)$, then there is no need to check for cointegration since the fiscal budget is considered sustainable. If, on the contrary, these two variables are integrated of different orders, then fiscal budget is not sustainable as there can be no long-run relationship between them. When the two fiscal variables are $I(1)$, then we proceed to test if they are cointegrated.

Univariate unit root tests, such as the ADF test, suffer from low power, particularly for short data series, and result in a high non-rejection rate of the null hypothesis of unit root. To fully utilize the information in the data set and thereby improve the power of the test, we adopt panel unit root tests for our data. Early commonly used tests such as Levin *et al.*, (LLC) (2002) and Im *et al.*, (IPS) (2003), also referred to as first-generation tests, assume data are cross-sectionally independent (Breitung and Pesaran, 2008).

In China, provincial governments' top officials are appointed directly by the central government, which also drafts economic policies and sets GDP growth target for the whole country. Therefore, provinces in China are exposed to similar political and economic shocks. Moreover, there is a "political tournament" effect in that local officials strive to achieve high economic growth for their provinces to compete for further advancement of their political career (Su *et al.*, 2012). Consequently, government spending on infrastructure in one province will not be completely independent of that in other provinces. Lastly, central government transfers based on the tax-sharing system partly redistribute tax revenues from more to less developed provinces. Hence the assumption of cross-section independence in the first-generation non-stationary panel methods is probably not applicable to our revenue and expenditure data. Empirical and simulation studies have shown that the first-generation panel unit root tests exhibit a severe size distortion if cross-section dependence exists in the data (Breitung and Das, 2005; Gengenback *et al.*, 2010; O'Connell, 1998).

Since erroneous assumption of cross-section independence can produce misleading inferences, we formally test if this feature is present in our data sample with Pesaran (2004) cross-section dependence (CD) test. It is based on an average of pairwise correlation coefficients of OLS residuals from individual (province i) ADF regressions in the panel for each data series x:

$$\Delta x_{it} = \rho_i x_{it-1} + \alpha_i D_{it} + \sum_\tau \gamma_{i\tau} \Delta x_{it-\tau} + \varepsilon_{it}, \tag{4}$$

where D_{it} represents a vector of deterministic variables. Pesaran (2004) CD test statistic is calculated as

$$CD = \sqrt{\frac{2T}{K(K-1)}} \left(\sum_{i=1}^{K-1} \sum_{j=k+1}^{K} \hat{\pi}_{ij} \right), \tag{5}$$

where

$$\hat{\pi}_{ij} = \sum_{t=1}^{T} \hat{\varepsilon}_{it} \hat{\varepsilon}_{jt} \bigg/ \left(\sum_{t=1}^{T} \hat{\varepsilon}_{it}^2 \right)^{1/2} \left(\sum_{t=1}^{T} \hat{\varepsilon}_{jt}^2 \right)^{1/2}, \tag{6}$$

and K and T are cross-section and time dimensions of the panel, respectively. Under the null hypothesis of no cross-section dependence, $CD \sim N(0,1)$.[10]

Pesaran (2007) proposes a panel unit root test that accounts for cross-section dependence. He suggests augmenting the ADF regressions in Im *et al.* (2003) with the lagged cross-sectional mean and its first-difference means to capture cross-section dependence that arises in a single-factor model:

$$\Delta x_{it} = \rho_i x_{it-1} + c_i \bar{x}_{t-1} + \alpha_i D_{it} + \sum_\tau \delta_{i\tau} \Delta \bar{x}_{it-\tau}$$

$$+ \sum_\tau \gamma_{i\tau} \Delta x_{it-\tau} + \varepsilon_{it}. \tag{7}$$

The t-statistics on the coefficient of the lagged value x_{it-1} (called CADF) are averaged across the provinces to obtain the CIPS statistic, which is used in our study to test if each data series contains a

---

[10]Pesaran CD test is valid under a variety of models, including stationary and unit root dynamic heterogeneous panels or panels containing multiple structural breaks. It also has satisfactory performance for small data panels such as those with cross-section and time series dimensions $K = 5$ and $T = 20$.

unit root:

$$\text{CIPS} = \frac{1}{K} \sum_{i=1}^{K} \text{CADF}_i. \tag{8}$$

Next, to test if revenues and expenditures are cointegrated, we apply the error correction-based panel test developed by Westerlund (2007). The model can be written as

$$R_{it} = \delta'_i d_t + \psi_i (R_{it-1} - \beta'_i G_{it-1}) + \sum_\tau \psi_{i\tau} \Delta R_{it-\tau}$$

$$+ \sum_\tau \gamma_{i\tau} \Delta G_{it-\tau} + v_{it}, \tag{9}$$

where d_t contains the deterministic components. The parameter ψ_i is the error correction term; $\psi_i < 0$ if government revenues and expenditures are cointegrated and $\psi_i = 0$ if they are not. Westerlund (2007) proposes two pairs of test statistics. In the first pair, called group-mean test statistics G_τ and G_α, the null hypothesis of no cointegration H_0: $\psi_i = 0$ for all i is tested against an alternative hypothesis H_1^G: $\psi_i < 0$ for at least one i. In the second pair, called panel test statistics P_τ and P_α, the alternative hypothesis is H_1^P: $\psi_i = \psi < 0$ for all i. Cross-sectional dependence is explicitly accounted for by bootstrapping of the residuals. We perform 1,000 bootstrap replications and present the bootstrapped p-values for all four test statistics in addition to asymptotic p-values in the results.

Finally, if there is evidence of cointegration between government revenues and expenditures in a particular region from the above test, we then distinguish between the weak and strong forms of fiscal sustainability by estimating the cointegrating coefficient β for the region and its individual provinces. To this end, we use Pesaran (2006) common correlated effects mean group (MG) estimator. This estimator is particularly apt for our data sample as it can account for unobserved common factors (for example, local spillover effects and/or global shocks such as the financial crisis of 2008) that give rise to cross-section dependence. The regression specification between revenues and expenditures is augmented with their cross-section means as follows:

$$R_{it} = \theta_i + \beta_i G_{it} + \mu_1 \bar{R}_t + \mu_2 \bar{G}_t + \mu_{it}. \qquad (10)$$

3. Results

In Table 1, we report the provincial governments' expenditures and revenues as a fraction of their GDP, averaged over 1994–2013. For all provinces, revenues ($R_1 = 0.0773$) are about half of expenditures ($G_1 = 0.1596$). The gap is smallest in the eastern region ($R_1 = 0.0860$ and $G_1 = 0.1208$) and widens considerably in the central ($R_1 = 0.0653$ and $G_1 = 0.1403$) and western ($R_1 = 0.0771$ and $G_1 = 0.2177$) regions because local GDP is much lower in less developed provinces. Central government transfers appear to close these gaps as the average revenue and expenditure ratios for all the provinces are 0.1631 and 0.1639. These summary statistics, however, cannot reveal the dynamic relationship between the two budget variables. For this reason, our data will be subject to a more rigorous analysis.

The results of Pesaran (2004) cross-section dependence (CD) test for all-province, eastern, central, and western panels and for both versions of the fiscal variables are shown in Table 2. The CD statistic is significant at the 1% level across all panels and variables, suggesting very high cross-province correlation. The estimated correlation ranges between 0.866 and 0.980. We will therefore use panel unit root and cointegration tests that explicitly account for this important data feature.

We perform Pesaran (2007) panel unit root test and report the results in Table 3. To check robustness of the results, the test is done at 1 lag and 2 lags. Moreover, the test is performed for two specifications, with and without a linear trend, for data in levels. First-differenced data are tested without a linear trend. In each cell, $Z[t\text{-bar}]$ statistic is shown, followed by its p-value. In the all-province, eastern, and central panels, the null hypothesis of unit root is not rejected for all data series in levels. It is rejected for the first differences. In the western region panel, the unit root hypothesis is rejected for R_1 series in levels in both specifications at 1 lag and

Table 1. Provincial government expenditure and revenue as a fraction of GDP: 1994–2013 average.

	R_1	G_1	R_2	G_2
Eastern region	0.0860	0.1208	0.1288	0.1285
Beijing	0.1317	0.1539	0.1689	0.1641
Fujian	0.0687	0.0976	0.1012	0.1024
Guangdong	0.0858	0.1057	0.1106	0.1087
Hainan	0.0920	0.1858	0.1851	0.1870
Hebei	0.0550	0.1019	0.1051	0.1057
Jiangsu	0.0686	0.0869	0.0941	0.0949
Liaoning	0.0862	0.1386	0.1478	0.1480
Shandong	0.0588	0.0835	0.0865	0.0859
Shanghai	0.1373	0.1609	0.1830	0.1821
Tianjin	0.0937	0.1261	0.1395	0.1396
Zhejiang	0.0687	0.0873	0.0955	0.0946
Central region	0.0653	0.1403	0.1434	0.1438
Anhui	0.0698	0.1440	0.1455	0.1496
Heilongjiang	0.0642	0.1515	0.1558	0.1552
Henan	0.0531	0.1104	0.1120	0.1131
Hubei	0.0613	0.1235	0.1306	0.1293
Hunan	0.0603	0.1296	0.1343	0.1326
Jiangxi	0.0680	0.1483	0.1511	0.1489
Jilin	0.0627	0.1594	0.1598	0.1621
Shanxi	0.0831	0.1554	0.1581	0.1597
Western region	0.0771	0.2177	0.2164	0.2190
Gansu	0.0701	0.2359	0.2306	0.2364
Guangxi	0.0707	0.1544	0.1564	0.1552
Guizhou	0.0907	0.2416	0.2427	0.2425
Inner Mongolia	0.0717	0.1737	0.1724	0.1763
Ningxia	0.0785	0.2483	0.2518	0.2494
Qinghai	0.0684	0.3430	0.3376	0.3441
Shaanxi	0.0757	0.1667	0.1670	0.1676
Sichuan	0.0716	0.1569	0.1592	0.1580
Xinjiang	0.0753	0.2143	0.2104	0.2155
Yunnan	0.0986	0.2426	0.2363	0.2447
All provinces	0.0773	0.1596	0.1631	0.1639

Note: R_1 is the total budgetary revenues/GDP, G_1 is the total budgetary expenditures/GDP, R_2 is the (total budgetary revenues + transfer from the central government)/GDP, G_2 is the (total budgetary expenditures + transfer to the central government)/GDP.

Table 2. Pesaran cross-section dependence (CD) test.

	CD statistic	p-Value	Correlation
All provinces			
R_1	81.87	0.000	0.909
G_1	85.28	0.000	0.946
R_2	83.82	0.000	0.930
G_2	82.65	0.000	0.917
Eastern			
R_1	30.14	0.000	0.909
G_1	30.74	0.000	0.927
R_2	30.53	0.000	0.921
G_2	28.72	0.000	0.866
Central			
R_1	21.57	0.000	0.911
G_1	23.19	0.000	0.980
R_2	23.10	0.000	0.976
G_2	22.90	0.000	0.968
Western			
R_1	27.51	0.000	0.917
G_1	28.38	0.000	0.946
R_2	27.73	0.000	0.924
G_2	28.09	0.000	0.936

Note: Under the null hypothesis of cross-section independence, the CD test statistic follows the standard normal distribution.

with-trend specification at 2 lags; this series appears to be $I(0)$. Other series in the western region panel are $I(1)$. As a further robustness check, we perform Hadri (2000) panel unit root test where the data series is assumed to be stationary in the null hypothesis. The results are shown in Table A.1. Hadri (2000) test confirms the results from Pesaran (2007) test except R_1 in the western region for which the former suggests it is $I(1)$. On this note, we will consider all data series as $I(1)$.[11]

---

[11]Westerlund (2007) test later shows no evidence of cointegration between R_1 and G_1 in the western region panel, and therefore, treating R_1 as $I(1)$ here does not lead to any inconsistency.

Table 3. Pesaran panel unit root test. Null hypothesis: Unit root.

	1 lag			2 lags		
	Levels		Differences	Levels		Differences
	Trend	No trend	No trend	Trend	No trend	No trend
All						
R_1	1.329	1.310	-11.942^a	1.529	2.412	-4.688^a
	(0.908)	(0.905)	(0.000)	(0.937)	(0.992)	(0.000)
G_1	0.313	1.795	-12.700^a	2.326	3.727	-5.271^a
	(0.623)	(0.964)	(0.000)	(0.990)	(1.000)	(0.000)
R_2	-1.079	1.939	-13.509^a	0.550	3.420	-6.222^a
	(0.140)	(0.974)	(0.000)	(0.709)	(1.000)	(0.000)
G_2	0.160	1.574	-15.719^a	2.343	3.790	-6.032^a
	(0.564)	(0.942)	(0.000)	(0.990)	(1.000)	(0.000)
Eastern						
R_1	2.303	1.841	-6.306^a	2.568	2.470	-1.421^c
	(0.989)	(0.967)	(0.000)	(0.995)	(0.993)	(0.078)
G_1	0.934	1.307	-5.712^a	2.381	1.702	-1.615^c
	(0.825)	(0.904)	(0.000)	(0.991)	(0.956)	(0.053)
R_2	0.038	1.635	-7.731^a	1.513	3.456	-3.138^a
	(0.515)	(0.949)	(0.000)	(0.935)	(1.000)	(0.001)
G_2	0.789	0.479	-8.609^a	2.026	1.658	-2.908^a
	(0.785)	(0.684)	(0.000)	(0.979)	(0.951)	(0.002)
Central						
R_1	-0.510	0.189	-6.205^a	-0.121	0.120	-2.138^a
	(0.305)	(0.575)	(0.000)	(0.452)	(0.548)	(0.016)
G_1	-0.629	-0.008	-6.713^a	0.346	0.428	-3.414^a
	(0.265)	(0.497)	(0.000)	(0.635)	(0.666)	(0.000)
R_2	-0.230	1.283	-7.716^a	-0.299	0.715	-2.830^a
	(0.409)	(0.900)	(0.000)	(0.382)	(0.763)	(0.002)
G_2	-0.800	0.072	-8.961^a	-0.077	0.892	-3.982^a
	(0.212)	(0.529)	(0.000)	(0.469)	(0.814)	(0.000)
Western						
R_1	-3.565^a	-1.917^a	-6.977^a	-2.911^a	-0.737	-4.917^a
	(0.000)	(0.000)	(0.000)	(0.002)	(0.231)	(0.000)
G_1	-0.659	1.798	-7.897^a	1.179	3.808	-3.689^a
	(0.255)	(0.964)	(0.000)	(0.881)	(1.000)	(0.000)
R_2	-0.778	1.367	-8.293^a	1.157	3.263	-4.469^a
	(0.218)	(0.914)	(0.000)	(0.876)	(0.999)	(0.000)
G_2	-0.632	1.787	-8.389^a	1.170	3.772	-3.754^a
	(0.264)	(0.963)	(0.000)	(0.879)	(1.000)	(0.000)

Note: Contained in each cell is $Z[t\text{-bar}]$ statistic; p-value is included in the parentheses. ^{a}denotes p-value < 0.01, $^b p$-value < 0.05, and $^c p$-value < 0.10.

As both versions of revenues and expenditure are non-stationary, fiscal sustainability of the local governments can only be achieved if they are also cointegrated. Results from Westerlund (2007) group and panel test statistics are reported in Table 4. Due to limited time series observations, the panel error correction model is estimated with maximum three lags; the exact lag for each province is selected by the Akaike information criterion (AIC). For robustness check, we repeat Westerlund (2007) test with 2 lags and 1 lead, the results shown in Table A.2 are similar. Contained in each cell of Table 4 are the test statistic, followed by two p-values in parentheses. The first p-value is based on the asymptotic distribution; the second p-value is the robust one-sided p-value based on the bootstrapped distribution

Table 4. Westerlund panel cointegration test. Null hypothesis: No cointegration.

	R_1 and G_1		R_2 and G_2	
	Constant	Constant and trend	Constant	Constant and trend
All provinces	1.832	4.831	-3.081	-5.841
G_τ	(0.967)	(1.000)	$(0.001)^a$	$(0.000)^a$
	(0.695)	(0.966)	(0.186)	(0.183)
	1.256	5.899	-2.053	2.256
G_α	(0.895)	(1.000)	$(0.020)^b$	(0.988)
	(0.274)	(0.994)	$(0.063)^c$	(0.367)
	1.094	5.125	-2.647	-0.988
P_τ	(0.863)	(1.000)	$(0.004)^a$	(0.162)
	(0.561)	(0.947)	(0.180)	(0.451)
	-2.986	3.216	-3.217	2.758
P_α	$(0.001)^a$	(0.999)	$(0.001)^a$	(0.997)
	$(0.016)^b$	(0.846)	$(0.097)^c$	(0.800)
Eastern	-1.034	$-0.35-0$	-4.093	-4.369
G_τ	(0.150)	(0.363)	$(0.000)^a$	$(0.000)^a$
	(0.236)	(0.492)	$(0.004)^a$	$(0.031)^b$
	-1.332	2.185	-2.273	0.695
G_α	$(0.091)^a$	(0.986)	$(0.012)^b$	(0.756)
	$(0.037)^b$	(0.587)	$(0.012)^b$	(0.119)
	-0.983	1.507	-2.082	-1.080
P_τ	(0.163)	(0.934)	$(0.019)^b$	(0.140)
	(0.197)	(0.746)	$(0.063)^c$	(0.210)
	-3.661	1.190	-4.395	0.027
P_α	$(0.000)^a$	(0.883)	$(0.000)^a$	(0.511)
	$(0.025)^b$	(0.600)	$(0.004)^a$	(0.192)

Table 4. (*Continued*)

	R_1 and G_1		R_2 and G_2	
	Constant	Constant and trend	Constant	Constant and trend
Central	1.887	3.486	0.341	−4.029
G_τ	(0.970)	(1.000)	(0.634)	(0.000)[a]
	(0.805)	(0.952)	(0.714)	(0.239)
	2.577	4.081	−0.214	1.633
G_α	(0.995)	(1.000)	(0.415)	(0.949)
	(0.948)	(1.000)	(0.442)	(0.729)
	1.360	3.561	−0.904	−0.826
P_τ	(0.913)	(1.000)	(0.183)	(0.205)
	(0.726)	(0.953)	(0.402)	(0.558)
	−1.193	2.063	−1.930	1.436
P_α	(0.116)	(0.980)	(0.027)[b]	(0.925)
	(0.113)	(0.877)	(0.169)	(0.834)
Western	2.517	5.477	−1.258	−1.761
G_τ	(0.994)	(1.000)	(0.104)	(0.039)[b]
	(0.857)	(0.995)	(0.427)	(0.596)
	1.231	4.104	−0.920	1.653
G_α	(0.891)	(1.000)	(0.179)	(0.951)
	(0.460)	(0.996)	(0.160)	(0.541)
	1.087	3.411	−1.628	−0.588
P_τ	(0.862)	(1.000)	(0.052)[c]	(0.278)
	(0.643)	(0.922)	(0.236)	(0.508)
	−0.893	2.158	−1.625	1.805
P_α	(0.186)	(0.985)	(0.052)[c]	(0.965)
	(0.164)	(0.863)	(0.192)	(0.838)

Notes: Due to the limited number of observations, we set the maximum lag order of 3; the exact lag for each province (group) is selected by AIC. For semi-parametric correction, the Bartlett kernel window width is set according to $4(T/100)^{2/9}$. Contained in each cell is the test statistic, followed by two p-values in parentheses. The first p-value is based on asymptotic distribution. The second p-value is a robust one-sided p-value based on bootstrapped distribution (1,000 replications) to account for cross-section correlation. [a] denotes p-value < 0.01, [b] p-value < 0.05, and [c] p-value < 0.10.

of the residuals from 1,000 replications to account for cross-section correlation.[12] The panel error correction model in (9) is estimated

---

[12] For consistency, the null hypothesis of no cointegration is imposed when bootstrapped samples are generated.

with two specifications of deterministic terms. The first one includes a constant; the second one includes a constant and a trend, which is less applicable to our variables as revenues and expenditures are expressed in terms of GDP.

For the western region panel, based on both p-values, the null hypothesis of no cointegration between revenues and expenditures is not rejected when central government transfers are not included. When the transfers are considered, based on the asymptotic distribution of the residuals, the null hypothesis is rejected at the 10% level and 5% level for the "constant" (the asymptotic p-value of both P_τ and P_α is 0.052) and "constant and trend" (the asymptotic p-value of G_τ is 0.039) specifications, respectively. Similar results are obtained for the more developed central region, except that the null hypothesis can be rejected at 5% and 1% levels. If only the asymptotic distribution of the residuals is considered, one may infer that with central government transfers, fiscal sustainability is achieved, at least in the weak form, for these two regions. The earlier results from Pesaran (2004) test, however, show very strong evidence of cross-section correlation in the sample. Consequently, the standard errors based on asymptotic distribution in Westerlund (2007) test are probably too low, exhibiting a severe size distortion as documented in the literature (Breitung and Das, 2005; Gengenback *et al.*, 2010; O'Connell, 1998). The p-values derived from the bootstrapped distribution clearly confirm this is the case for our sample as none of the test statistics just discussed is significant even at the 15% level. The difference highlights the importance of accounting for cross-section dependence to avoid misleading inferences. For this reason, we focus on the results based on bootstrapped p-values only. Overall, for both central and western regions, local revenues and expenditures are not cointegrated, implying no fiscal sustainability, regardless of whether central government transfers are included or not.

In the eastern region, local revenues and expenditures without central government transfers are cointegrated when the error correction model includes only the constant term; the bootstrapped p-values of G_α and P_α are 0.037 and 0.025, respectively. The evidence is stronger when central government transfers are included because the null hypothesis of no cointegration is rejected by all four test statistics; the bootstrapped p-values of P_τ, G_α, P_τ, and P_α are 0.004, 0.012, 0.063, and 0.004, respectively. In the less applicable specification of constant and trend, evidence of cointegration is not as strong. The results for the panel of all the provinces are very similar to those for the eastern panel; the former also appears to be driven by the latter as the eastern region is the only panel in which cointegration is found.

Based on the cointegration results, we use Pesaran (2006) approach to estimate the cointegrating coefficient β for the all-province and eastern panels. In Table 5, the results of the mean group estimation indicate that the magnitude of β is far below 1

Table 5.   Mean group estimate of $R_{it} = \theta_i + \beta_i G_{it} + \mu_1 \bar{R}_t + \mu_2 \bar{G}_t + \mu_{it}$.

	β (p-value)	μ_1 (p-value)	μ_2 (p-value)	χ^2 test of $\beta = 1$ (p-value)	CD test (p-value)
All provinces					
R_1 & G_1	0.382	0.948	−0.300	78.73	0.85
	(0.000)	(0.000)	(0.000)	(0.000)	(0.395)
R_2 & G_2	0.792	0.975	−0.807	22.86	3.04
	(0.000)	(0.000)	(0.000)	(0.000)	(0.002)
Eastern					
R_1 & G_1	0.632	1.056	−0.651	18.88	−1.46
	(0.000)	(0.000)	(0.000)	(0.000)	(0.145)
R_2 & G_2	0.707	1.062	−7.56	23.74	−2.28
	(0.000)	(0.000)	(0.000)	(0.000)	(0.022)
Central					
R_1 & G_1	0.470	0.955	−0.489	15.98	−0.28
	(0.000)	(0.000)	(0.000)	(0.000)	(0.778)
R_2 & G_2	0.731	1.009	−0.752	12.75	−2.20
	(0.000)	(0.000)	(0.000)	(0.000)	(0.028)
Western					
R_1 & G_1	0.156	1.055	−0.156	171.95	−2.07
	(0.016)	(0.000)	(0.003)	(0.000)	(0.038)
R_2 & G_2	0.918	0.970	−0.894	2.06	−1.38
	(0.000)	(0.000)	(0.000)	(0.152)	(0.167)

Table 6. Mean group estimate of cointegrating coefficient β for eastern region provinces.

	R_1 and G_1		R_2 and G_2	
	β (*p*-value)	χ^2 test of $\beta = 1$ (*p*-value)	β (*p*-value)	χ^2 test of $\beta = 1$ (*p*-value)
Beijing	0.419	12.66	0.494	26.56
	(0.000)	(0.000)	(0.000)	(0.000)
Fujian	0.374	84.59	0.290	148.69
	(0.000)	(0.000)	(0.000)	(0.000)
Guangdong	0.650	9.27	0.767	2.70
	(0.000)	(0.002)	(0.000)	(0.101)
Hainan	0.583	15.23	0.665	13.24
	(0.000)	(0.000)	(0.000)	(0.000)
Hebei	0.470	7.22	0.663	6.64
	(0.017)	(0.007)	(0.000)	(0.010)
Jiangsu	0.976	0.05	0.941	0.56
	(0.000)	(0.821)	(0.000)	(0.453)
Liaoning	0.109	36.22	0.724	9.04
	(0.461)	(0.000)	(0.000)	(0.003)
Shandong	0.791	2.13	0.842	5.14
	(0.000)	(0.000)	(0.000)	(0.023)
Shanghai	0.822	3.58	0.574	13.66
	(0.000)	(0.058)	(0.000)	(0.000)
Tianjin	0.693	2.41	0.915	0.41
	(0.000)	(0.121)	(0.000)	(0.521)
Zhejiang	1.068	0.19	0.900	0.39
	(0.000)	(0.661)	(0.000)	(0.532)
Eastern	0.632	18.88	0.707	23.74
	(0.000)	(0.000)	(0.000)	(0.000)

for both panels; for example, β is estimated to be 0.707 for R_2 and G_2 in the eastern panel. Chi-squared test statistic rejects the null hypothesis of $\beta = 1$ for the eastern region irrespective of whether central government transfers are included ($\chi^2 = 23.74$) or not ($\chi^2 = 18.88$). This suggests that although fiscal budget in this region overall is sustainable, it is not strongly so. For comparison, we also present the estimate of β for the central and western panels in Table 5. The difference in the magnitude of β between the two definitions of fiscal variables is the largest in the western region

(0.156 versus 0.918).[13] The gap is lower in the central region (0.470 versus 0.731) and lowest in the eastern region (0.632 versus 0.707). This highlights the critical role of the central government transfers in the local government budget in less developed regions.

Given the evidence of cointegration between revenues and expenditures in the eastern panel, we estimate β for each province in this region in Table 6. For R_1 and G_1, out of 11 provinces, the null hypothesis of $\beta = 1$ is not rejected at 10% for Jiangsu, Tianjin, and Zhejiang and at 5% for Shanghai, suggesting the government budget in these provinces is strongly sustainable on its own. When central government transfers (R_2 and G_2) are considered, the null hypothesis of $\beta = 1$ is not rejected for Guangdong, Jiangsu, Tianjin, and Zhejiang.

4. Concluding Remarks

Sustainability of public finances has always been a crucial component of macroeconomic stability and long-term growth, particularly after the widespread exercise of fiscal stimulus in response to the financial crisis of 2008. In this study, we examine fiscal sustainability of provincial governments in China, the second-largest economy and the biggest trading partner of many countries in the world. Instead of using traditional time series techniques to look at each province separately, we employ recent advances in the econometrics of nonstationary panel data to not only increase the power of the test but also effectively account for cross-section dependence in the data.

Our empirical analysis shows that provinces in the less developed central and western regions do not achieve fiscal sustainability on their own or even with central government transfers since government expenditures and revenues are not cointegrated. On the whole, provinces in the eastern region, owing to their better economic development and growth, achieve fiscal sustainability in the weak form. In

---

[13]Note since R_2 and G_2 in the western region are not cointegrated, we do not interpret the non-rejection of the null hypothesis of $\beta = 1$ as evidence of strong sustainability of public finances in this region.

this region, the government budget in Jiangsu, Tianjin, Zhejiang, and
probably Shanghai can be strictly sustained on its own. With central
government transfers, Guangdong can also achieve sustainability.

There are important policy implications of our findings. First,
that only a few most developed provinces in China achieve fiscal
sustainability is a cause for concern, particularly in the new phase
of lower growth, in which revenue from land sales, a major source of
funding for local governments, will be significantly reduced. Although
central government transfers reduce very large and persistent deficits
in most provinces, this cannot be sustained indefinitely because local
revenues must either be raised via higher taxes or expenditures must
be pared down at some point in the future.

Next, there should be a reform in the budget law governing public finances of local governments in China. At least some provisions
ought to be created to allow the local authorities to issue bonds to
fund well-justified investment projects or social programs, as in many
other countries. The bonds can be auctioned with proper disclosure
standards in public offerings where private investors can participate
and have adequate opportunity to judge the quality of the underlying
assets.[14] By allowing the issuance of municipal bonds, local government's borrowings and debt can be standardized for easy monitoring and management (Xu and Li, 2014). Currently, without such a
recourse, less developed provinces rely heavily on central government
transfers, some of which are drawn from tax revenues collected in
more developed provinces. The effectiveness of such transfers in creating a more even economic landscape across China has been called
into question as some of the large components of the transfers are
not rule-based and therefore subject to political influence (Huang
and Chen, 2012).

On this note, the tax-sharing program instituted in 1994 should
also be reformulated to return greater fiscal autonomy to the
provinces so that they can be responsible for balancing both sides
of the budget instead of facing recurring mismatch in revenues and

---

[14]In 2015, local governments were allowed to directly issue municipal bonds but
mostly to swap out debt accumulated under local government financing vehicles.

expenditures. Moreover, resources from the private sector across the country can be mobilized for investment in less developed provinces via different tax incentives to, in the meantime, complement and, eventually, supplant most public investment.

Lastly, owing to either limited self-financing options or perverse incentives to overinvest for career advancement or both, local government officials have for the last several years resorted to off-budget financing activities. Although our analysis only examines regular and well-documented budgetary items in the data, it provides a reference and motivation for current and future studies on off-balance-sheet financing activities such as LGFVs. The concern of fiscal unsustainability in the long term suggested by our analysis would likely be upgraded to a major threat to China's macroeconomic stability even in the short term once LGFVs are considered. These ill-defined and shadow financing entities have recently grown very quickly, and their accurate estimates are not available. Our study therefore also calls for better data collection, through more frequent audits or proper reporting standards, of local governments' off-balance-sheet activities to accommodate timely research and prudential policy responses.

Appendix A.

Table A.1. Hadri panel unit root test. Null hypothesis: Stationarity.

	Levels		1st-differences
	Trend	No trend	No trend
All provinces			
R_1	34.99^{a}	19.63^{a}	1.06
	(0.000)	(0.000)	(0.144)
G_1	37.81^{a}	18.91^{a}	−0.01
	(0.000)	(0.000)	(0.504)
R_2	40.45^{a}	16.04^{a}	−1.08
	(0.000)	(0.000)	(0.860)
G_2	37.27^{a}	17.44^{a}	0.50
	(0.000)	(0.000)	(0.309)

(*Continued*)

Table A.1. (*Continued*)

| | Levels | | 1st-differences |
	Trend	No trend	No trend
Eastern			
R_1	24.39^{a}	14.75^{a}	2.05^{b}
	(0.000)	(0.000)	(0.02)
G_1	22.31^{a}	13.61^{a}	0.84
	(0.000)	(0.000)	(0.200)
R_2	19.32^{a}	12.15^{a}	0.56
	(0.000)	(0.000)	(0.287)
G_2	17.35^{a}	11.26^{a}	0.86
	(0.000)	(0.000)	(0.196)
Central			
R_1	17.99^{a}	9.61^{a}	-0.41
	(0.000)	(0.000)	(0.658)
G_1	20.32^{a}	8.10^{a}	-0.28
	(0.000)	(0.000)	(0.609)
R_2	20.71^{a}	9.22^{a}	-0.69
	(0.000)	(0.000)	(0.756)
G_2	16.47^{a}	6.74^{a}	0.00
	(0.000)	(0.000)	(0.500)
Western			
R_1	11.57^{a}	7.16^{a}	-0.46
	(0.000)	(0.000)	(0.676)
G_1	23.61^{a}	14.73^{a}	-0.08
	(0.000)	(0.000)	(0.532)
R_2	23.37^{a}	13.50^{a}	-0.385
	(0.000)	(0.000)	(0.650)
G_2	23.59^{a}	13.94^{a}	-0.26
	(0.000)	(0.000)	(0.604)

Notes: Cross-sectional mean is subtracted from the series to reduce the impact of cross-sectional dependence. In addition, the test statistic is robust to heteroscedasticity across panel. p-value is included in the parentheses. [a]denotes p-value < 0.01, [b]p-value < 0.05, and [c]p-value < 0.10.

Table A.2. Westerlund panel cointegration test. Null hypothesis: No cointegration; 2 lags and 1 lead.

	R_1 and G_1		R_2 and G_2	
	Constant	Constant and trend	Constant	Constant and trend
All provinces	1.785	2.441	−2.681	−4.843
G_τ	(0.963)	(0.993)	(0.004)[a]	(0.000)[a]
	(0.702)	(0.876)	(0.265)	(0.449)
	1.180	5.366	−2.470	1.858
G_α	(0.881)	(1.000)	(0.007)[a]	(0.968)
	(0.220)	(0.979)	(0.051)[c]	(0.413)
	1.094	5.125	−2.647	−0.988
P_τ	(0.863)	(1.000)	(0.004)[a]	(0.162)
	(0.555)	(0.961)	(0.193)	(0.571)
	−2.986	3.216	−3.217	2.758
P_α	(0.001)[a]	(0.999)	(0.001)[a]	(0.997)
	(0.023)[b]	(0.866)	(0.103)	(0.861)
Eastern	−1.034	−0.350	−3.031	−3.621
G_τ	(0.150	(0.363)	(0.001)[a]	(0.000)[a]
	(0.230)	(0.449)	(0.033)[b]	(0.259)
	−1.332	2.185	−3.091	0.482
G_α	(0.091)[c]	(0.986)	(0.001)[a]	(0.685)
	(0.023)[a]	(0.579)	(0.009)[a]	(0.177)
	−0.983	1.507	−2.082	−1.080
P_τ	(0.163)	(0.934)	(0.019)[b]	(0.140)
	(0.220)	(0.708)	(0.070)[c]	(0.649)
	−3.661	1.190	−4.395	0.027
P_α	(0.000)[a]	(0.883)	(0.000)[a]	(0.511)
	(0.015)[b]	(0.579)	(0.008)[a]	(0.462)
Central	1.798	3.154	0.341	−3.025
G_τ	(0.964)	(0.999)	(0.634)	(0.001)[a]
	(0.795)	(0.958)	(0.726)	(0.406)
	2.432	3.779	−0.214	1.241
G_α	(0.993)	(1.000)	(0.415)	(0.893)
	(0.916)	(0.998)	(0.455)	(0.621)
	1.360	3.561	−0.904	−0.826
P_τ	(0.913)	(1.000)	(0.183)	(0.205)
	(0.739)	(0.947)	(0.390)	(0.535)
	−1.193	2.063	−1.930	1.436
P_α	(0.116)	(0.980)	(0.027)[b]	(0.925)
	(0.140)	(0.869)	(0.173)	(0.820)

(*Continued*)

Table A.2.   (*Continued*)

	R_1 and G_1		R_2 and G_2	
	Constant	Constant and trend	Constant	Constant and trend
Western	2.517	1.703	−1.692	−1.744
G_τ	(0.994)	(0.956)	$(0.045)^{\text{b}}$	$(0.041)^{\text{b}}$
	(0.862)	(0.876)	(0.384)	(0.689)
	1.231	3.467	−0.773	1.549
G_α	(0.891)	(1.000)	(0.220)	(0.939)
	(0.441)	(0.978)	(0.206)	(0.612)
	1.087	3.411	−1.628	−0.588
P_τ	(0.862)	(1.000)	$(0.052)^{\text{c}}$	(0.278)
	(0.656)	(0.927)	(0.215)	(0.502)
	−0.893	2.158	−1.625	1.805
P_α	(0.186)	(0.985)	$(0.052)^{\text{c}}$	(0.965)
	(0.152)	(0.857)	(0.181)	(0.833)

Note: [a]Denotes p-value < 0.01, [b]p-value < 0.05, and [c]p-value < 0.10.

References

Afonso, A. (2005). "Fiscal Sustainability: The Unpleasant European Case," *FinanzArchiv*, **61**(1), 19–44.

Afonso, A. and Jalles, J. T. (2015). "Fiscal Sustainability: A Panel Assessment for Advanced Economies," *Applied Economics Letters*, **22**(11), 925–929.

Breitung, J. and Das, S. (2005). "Panel Unit Root Tests Under Cross Sectional Dependence," *Statistica Neerlandica*, **59**(4), 414–433.

Breitung, J. and Pesaran, M. H. (2008). "Unit Roots and Cointegration in Panels," in L. Matyas and P. Sevestre (eds.), *The Econometrics of Panel Data*, Springer: Berlin, Heidelberg, pp. 279–322.

Gengenback, C., Palm, F. and Urbain, J. P. (2010). "Panel Unit Root Tests in the Presence of Cross-sectional Dependencies: Comparison and Implications for Modelling," *Econometric Review*, **29**(2), 111–145.

Ghosh, A. R., Kim, J. I., Mendoza, E. G., Ostry, J. D., and Qureshi, M. S. (2013). "Fiscal Fatigue, Fiscal Space and Debt Sustainability in Advanced Economies," *Economic Journal*, **123**(February), F4–F30.

Hadri, K. (2000). "Testing for Stationarity in Heterogeneous Panel Data," *Econometr. J.*, **3**(2), 148–161.

Hakkio, C. S. and Rush, M. (1991). "Is the Budget Deficit Too Large?" *Economic Inquiry*, **29**(3), 429–445.

Hamilton, J. and Flavin, M. A. (1986). "On the Limitations of Government Borrowing: A Framework for Empirical Testing," *American Economic Review*, **76**(4), 808–819.

Huang, B. and Chen, K. (2012). "Are Intergovernmental Transfers in China Equalizing?" *China Economic Review*, **23**(3), 534–551.

Im, K. S., Pesaran, M. H. and Shin, Y. (2003). "Testing for Unit Roots in Heterogeneous Panels," *Journal of Econometrics*, **115**(1), 53–74.

Levin, A., Lin, C. F. and Chu, C. S. J. (2002). "Unit Root Tests in Panel Data: Asymptotic and Finite-sample Properties," *Journal of Econometrics*, **108**(1), 1–24.

Lu, Y. and Sun, T. (2013). "Local Government Financing Platforms in China: A Fortune or Misfortune?" International Monetary Fund Working Paper No. 13/243.

O'Connell, P. G. J. (1998). "The Overvaluation of Purchasing Power Parity," *Journal of Intelligence Economics*, **44**(1), 1–19.

Pesaran, M. H. (2007). "A Simple Panel Unit Root Test in the Presence of Cross-section Dependence," *Journal of Applied Econometrics*, **22**(2), 265–312.

Pesaran, M. H. (2006). "Estimation and Inference in Large Heterogeneous Panels with a Multifactor Error Structure," *Econometrica*, **74**(4), 967–1012.

Pesaran, M. H. (2004). "General Diagnostic Tests for Cross Section Dependence in Panels." Cambridge Working Papers in Economics No. 435.

Quintos, C. (1995). "Sustainability of the Deficit Process with Structural Shifts," *Journal of Business & Economic Statistics*, **13**(4), 409–417.

Su, F., Tao, R., Xi, L. and Li, M. (2012). "Local Officials' Incentives and China's Economic Growth: Tournament Thesis Reexamined and Alternative Explanatory Framework," *China World Economy*, **20**(4), 1–18.

Trehan, B. and Walsh, C. (1991). "Testing Intertemporal Budget Constraints: Theory and Applications to U.S. Federal Budget and Current Account Deficits," *Journal of Money, Credit and Banking*, **23**(2), 206–223.

Westerlund, J. (2007). "Testing for Error Correction in Panel Data," *Oxford Bulletin of Economics and Statistics*, **69**(6), 709–748.

Westerlund, J. and Prohl, S. (2010). "Panel Cointegration Tests of the Sustainability Hypothesis in Rich OECD Countries," *Applied Economics*, **42**(11), 1355–1364.

Xu. S. and Li, W. (2014). "Fiscal System and Local Government Behavior," in Yuan, Z. (ed.), *Economic Transition in China: Long-run Growth and Short-run Fluctuations*, World Scientific, Singapore, pp. 321–356.

Zhang, Y. S. and Barnett, S. (2014). "Fiscal Vulnerabilities and Risks from Local Government Finance in China." International Monetary Fund Working Paper No. 14/4.

Chapter 9

Size Matters After All: Evidence from the Chinese Stock Market

Kin-Yip Ho[*,§], Jiyoun An[†,¶], and Zhaoyong Zhang[‡,‖]

*College of Business and Economics,
The Australian National University, Australia
†College of International Studies,
Kyung Hee University, South Korea
‡School of Business & Law,
Edith Cowan University, Australia
§kin-yip.ho@anu.edu.au
¶ja256@khu.ac.kr
‖Zhaoyong.zhang@ecu.edu.au

This chapter explores the relation between the size anomaly and a variety of asset pricing factors in the Chinese stock market. Our main finding indicates that the size anomaly is still significant after taking into account the impact of various asset pricing factors, such as idiosyncratic volatility, liquidity, and the book-to-market ratio.

1. Introduction

The Chinese stock market has experienced remarkable growth since its two exchanges were established in the early 1990s, although its performance has often been described as irrational, uneven, and irregular. Despite its rapid growth in listings and market capitalization, China's stock market retains its reputation as a casino, dominated by retail investors and subject to frequent regulatory interventions and significant restrictions on the tradability of shares. Many researchers consider the Chinese stock market an anomaly in itself (An *et al.*, 2015; Yao *et al.*, 2019; Ye *et al.*, 2019; Zhang *et al.*, 2019). In contrast to other developed stock markets, the Chinese government used to divide the stock market into several segments catering to different investor groups (Wang and Jiang, 2004; Ho and Zhang, 2012; Tong and Yu, 2012; Ho *et al.*, 2014, 2016; Azzi and Suchard, 2019). These segments comprise the A-shares, B-shares, H-shares, and Red-Chips; in particular, the domestic retail investors used to dominate the A-share market and it was only in 2011 that the government relaxed the rules to allow Qualified Foreign Institutional Investors (QFII) to participate in that segment. Similarly, the B-share segment also witnessed an increase in domestic investor participation after 2011. Despite the fact that the government introduced more recent changes to the different segments (Huang *et al.*, 2019), the Chinese stock market still remains relatively segmented and investors currently face several challenges, such as problems of liquidity and short-selling constraints (Wang and Jiang, 2004; Tong and Yu, 2012). These challenges could have contributed to the significance of several asset pricing anomalies, such as size, in the Chinese stock market (Liu *et al.*, 2019).

In this chapter, we explore the significance of the size anomaly in the Chinese stock market and its relation to a variety of asset pricing factors (Liu *et al.*, 2019). Our main finding indicates that the size anomaly is still significant after taking into account the impact of various asset pricing factors, such as idiosyncratic volatility, liquidity, and the book-to-market ratio.

The rest of the chapter is organized as follows. Section 2 discusses data and characteristics of the Chinese stock market data. Section 3 outlines the econometric methodology. Section 4 discusses the significance of the size anomaly and the impact of various asset pricing factors on this anomaly. The final section concludes.

2. Data and Key Variables

2.1. *Data construction*

Our datasets, which are obtained from Chinese Stock Market and Accounting Research Database (CSMAR), comprise all the listed firms in the Shanghai and Shenzhen A-share markets. The sample period of our datasets ranges from January 1995 to December 2015. We select firms based on the following criteria: (1) their prices, market values, book values and return data must exist for at least three consecutive years; (2) their market values must be higher than 3 Chinese Yuan to avoid too small stocks; (3) observations with book-to-market ratios at the extreme top 1% and bottom 0.5% and with negative book value are dropped. Using the various frequency data, we construct key variables in the analysis: one-year ahead returns, Fama–French three factors, book-to-market (BM) ratio, market capitalization (SIZE), idiosyncratic volatility (IVOL), and Amihud's (2002) illiquidity measure (ILLIQ). The final data sample for the analysis consists of 15,553 firm-year observations.

The one-year ahead (future) returns is raw returns excluding the well-known Fama–French three-factors effects (hereafter, the FF3 abnormal returns, RESY). By applying the FF3 abnormal returns, the predictability of key variables (SIZE, BM, IVOL, and ILLIQ) on future returns is better identified by taking into account market risk and other two factors beforehand. First, we calculate the monthly Fama–French three factors (MKT, HML, and SMB) in the Chinese market by following Fama and French (1993) description. After having these factors, individual stock raw returns are regressed on the Fama–French three factors across time and the residuals from these regressions are the FF3 abnormal returns. Using the monthly returns, we calculate one-year ahead returns by annualizing it by annualizing monthly returns. For example, future RESY as of June 2011 is annualized from July 2011 to June 2012. In addition to these abnormal returns, the following key variables are computed: idiosyncratic volatility (IVOL) and Amihud's (2002) illiquidity measure (ILLIQ). The first variable IVOL is calculated by following Ali *et al.* (2003). Firstly, we regress the daily returns of the firms on a value-weighted market index over a one-year period immediately preceding the holding period. Subsequently, we compute the variance of the residual term from the regression as a proxy for IVOL. To compute ILLIQ, we calculate the annual mean of the average ratio of the daily absolute return to the trading volume on that day.

2.2. *Descriptive statistics*

Table 1 presents summary statistics of the yearly FF3 abnormal returns (RESY), BM, market capitalization (SIZE, billion Yuan), IVOL, and ILLIQ of the entire sample. The median of yearly returns is 1%, and the mean and median of BM are 0.41 and 0.35, respectively. Compared with the results reported for the US market in Ali *et al.* (2003), the BM of the Chinese stock market is lower. The estimated mean of IVOL is 32%, which falls within the range of values (22–51%) computed by Ang *et al.* (2009) for other developed countries. High value of IVOL (or ILLIQ) indicates that stocks are highly volatile (or illiquid). Our estimated mean of ILLIO (multiplied by 10^6) is 0.25, and its standard deviation is 0.81.

Figure 1 examines the time-series trend of key variables: SIZE, BM, IVOL, and ILLIQ. The black lines indicate the equal-weighted averages and the gray lines indicate the value-weighted averages using last year's firm market capitalization. When using the value-weighted average, ILLIQ shows a big gap in 2005, which implies that large firms were highly illiquid during the year. ILLIQ and firm size is closely related. During 2007–2008, BM and IVOL increased due to the Global Financial Crisis. Firm's market value dropped and volatility increased.

Table 1. Descriptive statistics.

Variable	N	Mean	Stdev	5th Pctl	25th Pctl	50th Pctl	75th Pctl	95th Pctl
RESY	15,553	0.17	0.60	−0.44	−0.25	0.01	0.40	1.34
BM	15,553	0.41	0.26	0.11	0.22	0.35	0.54	0.94
SIZE	15,553	5,504	8,857	929	1,786	2,978	5,512	18,500
IVOL	15,553	0.32	0.09	0.18	0.25	0.32	0.39	0.49
ILLIQ	15,553	0.25	0.81	0.01	0.05	0.11	0.30	0.87

Note: Stdev is the standard deviation and 5th Pctl is the data point at 5% distribution.

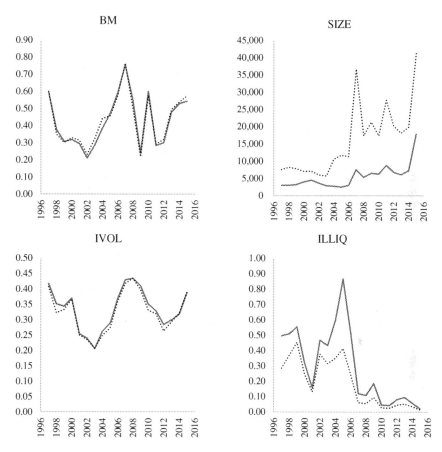

Figure 1. Time-series trends of equal-weighted (black line) and value-weighted (dotted line) averages: BM, SIZE, IVOL, and ILLIQ.

3. Econometric Methodology

3.1. *Future returns and key variables*

Table 2 presents the matrix of correlation coefficients among the different variables. As indicated by the table, BM is significantly negatively related to IVOL (-0.13) and ILLIQ (-0.06) but significantly positively related to SIZE (0.06). These relations are generally consistent with those noted by Ali *et al.* (2003) for the US market. More specifically, Ali *et al.* (2003) show that the BM effect

Table 2. Correlations matrix.

	BM	SIZE	IVOL	ILLIQ
SIZE	0.058 (0.031)*			
IVOL	−0.126 (0.051)**	−0.076 (0.034)**		
ILLIQ	−0.059 (0.034)*	−0.683 (0.024)***	0.017 (0.032)	
RESY	0.061 (0.025)**	−0.186 (0.030)***	−0.090 (0.023)***	0.143 (0.041)***

Note: This table shows the time-series averages of pairwise Spearman correlation coefficients. ( ) reports the standard errors of the annual coefficients. ***$p < 0.01$,**$p < 0.05$,*$p < 0.1$.

is more pronounced for stocks with high transaction costs and high IVOL. Table 2 also indicates that SIZE exhibits a negative relation with ILLIQ (−0.68). In general, big firms are more liquid than small firms. The variables BM and ILLIQ show significantly positive relations with future returns. In contrast, the variables SIZE and IVOL are negatively related to future returns. These significant relations suggest that our four variables could predict future returns.

3.2. *Fama–MacBeth (1973) cross-sectional regressions*

In this section, Fama–MacBeth (1973) cross-sectional regressions are introduced to examine the incremental role of different factors. The regression approach requires two steps. In the first step, a cross-sectional regression is conducted. For example, if we examine the relation between future returns and BM, the following regression model is estimated in each time period (here, each year):

$$\text{RESY}_{i,t+1} = \alpha_t + \beta_t \text{BM}_{i,t} + \varepsilon_{i,t}. \tag{1}$$

If the number of years is 20 years, Equation (1) produces 20 coefficients. In the second step, the time-series average of coefficients and R^2 are reported. To avoid heteroscedasticity and autocorrelation, Newey-West (1987) standard errors with one-year lag are reported. If BM is a significant asset pricing factor or predicts future returns, the average of β_t, $\bar{\beta}$, will be a statistically positive coefficient. Thus, stocks with higher BM values induce higher future FF3 abnormal returns. By extending Equation (1), we also examine the incremental roles of other factors such as SIZE in predicting future returns by BM. Equation (2) includes the interaction term between BM and SIZE in Equation (1).

$$\text{RESY}_{i,t+1} = \alpha_t + \beta_{1,t}\text{BM}_{i,t} + \beta_{2,t}\text{BM}_{i,t} \times \text{SIZE}_{i,t} + \eta_t\text{SIZE}_{i,t} + \varepsilon_{i,t}. \quad (2)$$

After rearranging Equation (2), $(\beta_{1,t} + \beta_{2,t}\text{SIZE}_{i,t})$ shows that the coefficient of the interaction term, $\beta_{2,t}$, represents the partial effects by $\text{SIZE}_{i,t}$ on the BM effects. The coefficients on the interaction terms in Equation (2) demonstrate how the BM effect varies cross-sectionally with the different variables (such as SIZE). Following Ali *et al.* (2003), the variables are also included by themselves to capture their main effects on future returns. Otherwise, the coefficients on the interaction terms may be biased. Other things being equal, a significantly positive coefficient $(\bar{\beta}_2)$ on BM $\times$ SIZE would indicate that SIZE contributes to the cross-sectional variation in the BM effect. Likewise, Equations (1) and (2) models can be applied to other variables: SIZE, IVOL, and ILLIQ.

4. Findings

4.1. *Including interaction terms*

Table 3 reports the regression estimates of Equation (1) and extended version of Equation (2) for SIZE and BM variables. The first column in Table 3 presents the results of a model with BM as the main explanatory variable. As shown in Table 3, the variable BM has a significantly positive effect on future returns (0.072). Equation (2) is similar to Equation (1), except that it analyzes the interaction of BM with other variables. As shown in the second column of Table 3, when SIZE, IVOL, and ILLIQ are included as interaction variables, the coefficient of BM becomes negative and insignificant, suggesting that the BM effects are affected by other asset pricing factors. The coefficient of SIZE is found to be always significant with a negative sign.

Table 3. Fama–MacBeth cross-sectional regressions: BM and SIZE with inter-action terms.

Dep. var.	Future returns RESY	BM RESY	Dep. var.	Future returns RESY	SIZE RESY
BM	0.072**	−0.071	SIZE	−0.058***	−0.037**
	(0.03)	(0.56)		(0.01)	(0.01)
BM × SIZE		−0.002	SIZE × BM		0.028
		(0.04)			(0.03)
BM × IVOL		0.476	SIZE × IVOL		−0.083*
		(0.37)			(0.04)
BM × ILLIQ		0.024	SIZE × ILLIQ		−0.003
		(0.11)			(0.03)
SIZE		−0.060***	BM		−0.388
		(0.02)			(0.38)
IVOL		−0.511***	IVOL		0.934
		(0.10)			(0.67)
ILLIQ		0.056*	ILLIQ		0.094
		(0.03)			(0.36)
Constant	−0.025	1.044***	Constant	0.864***	0.655***
	(0.02)	(0.25)		(0.15)	(0.21)
Observations	15,277	15,277	Observations	15,277	15,277
Avg. R^2	0.011	0.074	Avg. R^2	0.037	0.074
# of years	19	19	# of years	19	19

Note: Standard errors in parentheses; ***$p < 0.01$, **$p < 0.05$,*$p < 0.1$.

We then assess the incremental roles of IVOL and ILLIQ with interaction terms in predicting the future returns. Table 4 reports the regression results. The first column in the left panel of Table 4 presents the results of a model with IVOL as the main explanatory variable, and the right panel shows the results with ILLIQ as the main explanatory variable. As it can be seen in Table 4, the variable IVOL has a significantly negative effect on future returns, while ILLIQ has a significantly positive effect. However, when other variables are included as interaction variables, the results in the second column of Table 4 show that the sign of the coefficient of IVOL changes from negative to positive while ILLIQ remains positive, though both are statistically significant. The findings suggest

Table 4. Fama–MacBeth cross-sectional regressions: IVOL and ILLIQ with interaction terms.

Dep. var.	Future returns RESY	IVOL RESY	Dep. var.	Future returns RESY	ILLIQ RESY
IVOL	−0.255**	1.962*	ILLIQ	0.116*	0.611*
	(0.11)	(1.11)		(0.06)	(0.33)
IVOL × BM		0.326	ILLIQ × BM		−0.184
		(0.28)			(0.13)
IVOL × SIZE		−0.153*	ILLIQ × SIZE		−0.019
		(0.07)			(0.02)
IVOL × ILLIQ		−0.939*	ILLIQ × IVOL		−0.757
		(0.54)			(0.48)
SIZE		−0.015	SIZE		−0.052***
		(0.02)			(0.01)
BM		−0.063	BM		0.077*
		(0.09)			(0.04)
ILLIQ		0.361	IVOL		−0.196
		(0.22)			(0.16)
Constant	0.091*	0.319	Constant	−0.009	0.834***
	(0.05)	(0.27)		(0.02)	(0.11)
Observations	15,277	15,277	Observations	15,277	15,277
Avg.R^2	0.012	0.075	Avg. R^2	0.014	0.075
# of years	19	19	# of years	19	19

Note: Standard errors in parentheses; ***$p < 0.01$, **$p < 0.05$, *$p < 0.1$.

that the IVOL effects are affected by the marginal effects from BM, SIZE, and ILLIQ.

4.2. *Subsamples*

We examine further the potential driving forces behind asset pricing factors by using different subsamples. In this subsample approach, we investigate in which group the factor effects are strong and which variable strongly influences other factor effects.

Table 5 reports the average coefficients of BM in Equation (1). Each column indicates the subsample. SIZE1 (SIZE5) is the smallest (largest) quintile group; likewise, other IVOL–1.5, ILLIQ–1.5. Similarly, we report the results for the average coefficients of SIZE, IVOL, and ILLIQ, respectively, in Tables 6–8.

Table 5.   BM regression models (EW Fama–MacBeth) for each quintile group sample.

	Small SIZE1	SIZE2	SIZE3	SIZE4	Large SIZE5
BM	0.180	0.131*	0.099	0.033	0.131***
	(0.14)	(0.07)	(0.06)	(0.04)	(0.04)
	Low IVOL1	IVOL 2	IVOL3	IVOL4	High IVOL5
BM	0.026	0.011	0.133**	−0.002	0.077
	(0.07)	(0.04)	(0.05)	(0.05)	(0.07)
	Low ILLIQ1	ILLIQ2	ILLIQ3	ILLIQ4	High ILLIQ5
BM	0.191**	0.043	0.065*	0.100**	−0.015
	(0.08)	(0.04)	(0.03)	(0.04)	(0.03)

Note: Standard errors in parentheses; ***$p < 0.01$, **$p < 0.05$, *$p < 0.1$.

Table 6.   SIZE regression models (EW Fama–MacBeth) for each quintile group sample.

	Low BM1	BM2	BM3	BM4	High BM5
SIZE	−0.061***	−0.056***	−0.092***	−0.042*	−0.053***
	(0.01)	(0.01)	(0.03)	(0.02)	(0.01)
	Low IVOL1	IVOL2	IVOL3	IVOL4	High IVOL5
SIZE	−0.049***	−0.069***	−0.068***	−0.069***	−0.078***
	(0.01)	(0.02)	(0.02)	(0.02)	(0.01)
	Low ILLIQ1	ILLIQ2	ILLIQ3	ILLIQ4	High ILLIQ5
SIZE	−0.020*	−0.046***	−0.087***	−0.048***	−0.071***
	(0.01)	(0.01)	(0.03)	(0.02)	(0.02)

Note: Standard errors in parentheses; ***$p < 0.01$, **$p < 0.05$, *$p < 0.1$.

As it can be seen in Table 5, the BM effects are strong in the largest (lowest) quintile group in terms of SIZE (ILLIQ). This finding is consistent with the results in Table 3. Once SIZE and ILLIQ are included, the significance of BM coefficient is gone. The results in Table 6 show that SIZE effects are strong in each subsample group, and the stronger the effect, the lower the quintile group. In contrast,

Table 7. IVOL regression models (EW Fama–MacBeth) for each quintile group sample.

	Low BM1	BM2	BM3	BM4	High BM5
IVOL	−0.261*	−0.399***	−0.308	−0.211	−0.188
	(0.14)	(0.08)	(0.18)	(0.18)	(0.18)
	Small SIZE1	SIZE2	SIZE3	SIZE4	Large SIZE5
IVOL	−0.047	−0.107	−0.381**	−0.327**	−0.284**
	(0.27)	(0.40)	(0.14)	(0.12)	(0.11)
	Low ILLIQ1	ILLIQ2	ILLIQ3	ILLIQ4	High ILLIQ5
IVOL	−0.238***	−0.356**	−0.133	−0.241**	−0.457***
	(0.08)	(0.13)	(0.27)	(0.11)	(0.15)

Note: Standard errors in parentheses; ***$p < 0.01$, **$p < 0.05$, *$p < 0.1$.

Table 8. ILLIQ regression models (EW Fama–MacBeth) for each quintile group sample.

	Low BM1	BM2	BM3	BM4	High BM5
ILLIQ	0.134**	0.168*	0.162	0.156*	0.146
	(0.05)	(0.09)	(0.11)	(0.08)	(0.11)
	Small SIZE1	SIZE2	SIZE3	SIZE4	Large SIZE5
ILLIQ	0.071	−0.049	0.051	−0.002	0.130
	(0.05)	(0.03)	(0.07)	(0.05)	(0.09)
	Low IVOL1	IVOL2	IVOL3	IVOL4	High IVOL5
ILLIQ	0.337*	0.281**	0.219*	0.231*	0.065
	(0.17)	(0.13)	(0.11)	(0.13)	(0.04)

Note: Standard errors in parentheses; ***$p < 0.01$, **$p < 0.05$, *$p < 0.1$.

the results in Table 7 indicate that the stronger the effect of IVOL, the larger the SIZE and higher the ILLIQ. The results confirm the previous findings, suggesting that there are incremental roles from SIZE and ILLIQ in the IVOL effects. The results in Table 8 show that ILLIQ effects are gone in any SIZE group, which imply that ILLIQ effects are corresponding to SIZE effects.

5. Conclusion

This chapter examines the dynamic interrelationships between different firm-level predictors (such as idiosyncratic volatility, liquidity size, and value) and future stock returns in the Chinese stock market. Unlike most papers that focus partially on one predictor without considering the impact of the other predictors, we consider the potential linkages amongst the different predictors by using multiple portfolio sorting and cross-sectional regression analysis. Cross-sectional regressions indicate that BM ratio and idiosyncratic volatility are intimately linked. Illiquidity is related to size. Furthermore, the predictability of the size factor is highly significant. Once size is controlled for, the illiquidity factor is no longer significant. These results are robust across different regression specifications. Our findings have important implications for how to better understand the dynamic relationships of the firm-level predictors, including size, liquidity, BM ratio, and idiosyncratic volatility, and how liquidity influences future stock returns and market dynamics in the Chinese financial markets.

References

Amihud, Y. (2002). "Illiquidity and Stock Returns: Cross-section and Time Series Effects," *Journal of Financial Markets*, **5**, 31–56.

Amihud, Y., Hameed, A., Kang, W. and Zhang, H. (2015). "The Illiquidity Premium: International Evidence," *Journal of Financial Economics*, **117**, 350–368.

Ali, A., Hwang, L. S. and Trombely, M. A. (2003). "Arbitrage Risk and the Book-To-Market Anomaly," *Journal of Financial Economics*, **69**, 355–373.

An, J., Ho, K. and Zhou, L. (2015). "The Book-To-Value Anomaly in the Chinese Stock Market," *East Asian Economic Review*, **19**, 223–241.

Ang, A., Hodrick, R. J., Xing, Y. and Zhang, X. (2009). "High Idiosyncratic Volatility and Low Returns: International and Further US Evidence," *Journal of Financial Economics*, **91**, 1–23.

Azzi, S. and Suchard, J. (2019). "Crouching Tigers, Hidden Dragons: Private Equity Fund Selection in China," *Pacific-Basin Financial Journal*, **53**, 236–253.

Fama, E. F. and MacBeth, J. (1973). "Risk, Return and Equilibrium: Empirical Tests," *Journal of Political Economy*, **81**, 607–636.

Ho, K. and Zhang, Z. (2012). "Dynamic Linkages Among Financial Markets in the Greater China Region: A Multivariate Asymmetric Approach," *World Economics*, **35**, 500–523.

Ho, K., Shi, Y. and Zhang, Z. (2014). "Volatility and Correlation Dynamics of the Mainland China and Hong Kong Markets: Evidence from the A-, B-, H- and Red Chip Markets," *Journal of Wealth Management*, **17**, 55–67.

Ho, K., Shi, Y. and Zhang, Z. (2016). "It Takes Two to Tango: A Regime-switching Analysis of the Correlation Dynamics Between the Mainland Chinese and Hong Kong Stock Markets," *Scottish Journal of Political Economy*, **63**, 291–312.

Huang, Y., Li, M. and Chen, C. (2019). "Financial Market Development, Market Transparency, and IPO Performance," *Pacific-Basin Financial Journal*, **55**, 63–81.

Liu, J., Stambaugh, R. and Yuan, Y. (2019). "Size and Value in China," *J. Fin. Econ.*, https://doi.org/10.1016/j.jfineco.2019.03.008.

Newey, W. K. and West, K. D. (1987). "Hypothesis Testing with Efficient Method of Moments Estimation," *International Economic Review*, **28**, 777–787.

Tong, W. and Yu, W. (2012). "A Corporate Governance Explanation of the A-B Share Discount in China," *Journal of International Money and Finance*, **31**, 125–147.

Wang, S. and Jiang, L. (2004). "Location of Trade, Ownership Restrictions and Market Illiquidity: Examining Chinese A- and H-shares," *Journal of Banking and Finance,*, **28**, 1273–1297.

Yao, S., Wang, C., Cui, X. and Fang, Z. (2019). "Idiosyncratic Skewness, Gambling Preference and Cross-section of Stock Returns: Evidence from China," *Pacific-Basin Finance Journal*, **53**, 464–483.

Ye, Q., Wu, Y. and Liu, J. (2019). "Institutional Preferences, Demand Shocks and the Distress Anomaly," *The British Accounting Review*, **51**, 72–91.

Zhang, R., Xian, X. and Fang, H. (2019). "The Early-warning System of Stock Market Crises with Investor Sentiment: Evidence from China," *International Journal of Finance and Economics*, **24**, 361–369.

Chapter 10

Can "Active Portfolio Weight Change" of Institutional Investor Make the Stock Market Stable?

Zhaohui Wang, Xiangqun Zhang*, and Hongya Li

Ningbo University, Business School,
818 Fenghua Road, Ningbo, 315211, China
*wiskik@qq.com

The aim of the review is to study whether the institutional investor's active portfolio weight change can make the stock market stable. It is different from previous studies, which mainly focus on the effect of the whole institutional investor's portfolio weight change on the stock market. Based on the weekly data of 111 hybrid funds from 2006 to 2015, we use Granger causality test, vector autoregressive (VAR) model, and generalized autoregressive conditional heteroscedasticity (GARCH) model to empirically study it. The results show that the institutional investor's active portfolio weight change directly affects the returns of the stock market and enlarges the stock market volatility. It indicates that the institutional investor cannot be a stock market stabilizer as well.

1. Introduction

In June 2015, China's stock market experienced the most tragic "cliff-like" decline. Many people attribute the sharp decline of the stock market to the irrational investment structure of individual investors as the investment proportion of individual investor accounts for about 99.71% in the whole stock market.[1] Therefore, developing

---

[1] The data come from CSI database.

the institutional investors seems to be an effective way to reduce stock market volatility. However, can the institutional investors really be the "stabilizers" to promote the healthy development of the stock market?

This issue has been extensively studied, but no consistent conclusion has been reached. There are at least two different opinions about it. The supporters think that the institutional investor is rational people who holds much larger number of stocks than the individual investor and often adopt "buy and hold" investment strategy to save the transaction costs. Therefore, the institutional investors can play a "shock volatility absorption" role and they are good for the stock market (Hirshleifer *et al.*, 1994). However, from the opinions of "herding effect" (Wermers, 1999) and "short-sighted behavior" (Scharfstein and Stein, 1990), the opponents argue that the institutional investors cannot be the "stabilizers". Because the institutional investors mostly have the same information, particularly under the pressure of fierce competition and the social evaluation, the "herding effect" and "short-sighted behavior" of the institutional investors are stronger than those of individual investors, and the institutional investors would become the booster of stock market volatility. From the perspective of the empirical studies, there are also no consistent results on it. Cohen *et al.* (2002) as well as Barber and Odean (2008) find that institutional investors play a role in stabilizing stock prices in the United States. There are also some similar studies which find that the development of institutional investors is conducive to stabilizing the stock market in China (Qi *et al.*, 2006; Hu and Jin, 2007; Zhou and Peng, 2007). On the contrary, Sias (1996) finds that the greater the share held by the institutional investors in a stock, the stronger the volatility of the stock price. Dennis and Strickland (2002) find that institutional investors will further aggravate stock market volatility when the stock market fluctuates greatly. Xie *et al.* (2008) and Chen *et al.* (2010), as well as Shi and Wang (2014) show that the proportion of fund holdings by institutional investors aggravates the stock market volatility; thus, it denies "shock absorption" effect of institutional investors in the stock market.

The above literatures are very useful to understand the effects of the institutional investor's behaviors on the stock market volatility. However, there are still things that can be studied further. The main contributions to the related literatures in our study are the following.

First and foremost, in our study, we distinguish the institutional investor's active portfolio weight change (i.e. the portfolio weight change operated by the institutional investor) and passive portfolio weight change (i.e. even if the institutional investor keeps the same portfolio without adjusting the portfolio weight, the portfolio weight can also be changed due to the change of the stock market itself). The portfolio weight change is the reflection of market information and represents the expectation of institutional investors. The size and change of portfolio weight can be used as indicators for the investors to judge the trend of the future stock market development. In previous studies, many authors used the whole portfolio weight change of the institutional investor to judge institutional investor's behavior, which fails to capture the differences between the institutional investor's active portfolio weight change and the portfolio weight change caused by the market itself or passive portfolio weight change. The former cannot really reflect the expectation of the institutional investor while the latter can predict the behavior of the institutional investor which is more important. In our study, we distinguish them, provide the measurement for the institutional investor's active portfolio weight change, and study the effect of the institutional investor's active portfolio weight change on the stock market volatility, which is different from the previous studies.

Second, the data and the methods used in our study are different from others. The data used by most studies are directly from the quarterly reports, which have a long time span and are difficult to keep up with the rapidly changing stock market. In this study, we use weekly data of the portfolio weight change calculated from the database as our sample, which can be better for capturing the changing of the stock market. The methods used in the study including the Granger causality test, vector autoregressive (VAR) model, and generalized autoregressive conditional heteroscedasticity (GARCH) model, show that the results from different methods are consistent, and the institutional investor's active portfolio weight change directly affects the returns of the stock market and enlarges the stock market volatility.

The remaining structure of this chapter is organized as follows: Section 2 presents the data. In Section 3, we provide the measurement of the institutional investor's active portfolio weight change. Section 4 empirically studies the effect of the institutional investor's active portfolio weight change on the return of the stock market. Section 5 empirically studies the effect of the institutional investor's active portfolio weight change on the stock market volatility. Section 6 concludes the chapter and puts forward some relevant policy recommendations.

2. Data

As one of the main representatives of the institutional investors, China's securities investment fund has experienced a rapid development since 2006. In 2007–2015, two large bull markets had happened in China's stock market. Therefore, in this study, we select the period including 519 weeks from January 6, 2006 to December 31, 2015 as our sample period.

In this study, the open-ended hybrid funds are selected as the research objects, because they are less constrained by policy. After deleting those funds listed after 2006 and those funds delisted before 2015, we get the sample including 111 hybrid funds. According to the weekly data of the net value of the fund unit, we calculate the portfolio weight change and the active portfolio weight change. We use the CSI 300 index weekly to represent the stock market. The data of the net value of the fund unit and the stock index come from the WIND database.

3. Measurement of Active Portfolio Weight Change

3.1. *Overall portfolio weight change and active portfolio weight change*

Portfolio weight change refers to the proportion of market value of the stock held by the fund to its net asset value. The theory of portfolio weight change measurement can be traced back to Sharpe (1992), who puts forward a fund investment style analysis theory based on income. Due to shortage of the portfolio weight change measurement research, the articles related to portfolio weight change estimation models are considered confidential and not disclosed. This study follows the methods of Qu *et al.* (2014) to measure the overall portfolio weight change of the hybrid funds every week. The calculation process is as follows:

- The returns of each fund are compared with the China Securities Index (CSI) 100, 200, and 500 index returns weekly, and the rolling linear regressions are carried out in 20 weeks. In this study, we set up the following models:

$$r_{j,t} = \beta_{100,j,t} r_{I100,t} + \varepsilon_{100,j,t}, \tag{1}$$

$$r_{j,t} = \beta_{200,j,t} r_{I200,t} + \varepsilon_{200,j,t}, \tag{2}$$

$$r_{j,t} = \beta_{500,j,t} r_{I500,t} + \varepsilon_{500,j,t}, \tag{3}$$

where $r_{j,t}$ refers to the return of fund j at tth week; $r_{I100,t}$, $r_{I200,t}$, and $r_{I500,t}$ refer to the CSI 100, 200, and 500 index return, respectively; and $\varepsilon_{100,j,t}$, $\varepsilon_{200,j,t}$, and $\varepsilon_{500,j,t}$ are the random error terms. Based on the regressions of the above three models, we can get $\beta_{100,j,t}$, $\beta_{200,j,t}$, and $\beta_{500,j,t}$. The three coefficients are weighted equally with the ratio of each fund's net asset, then three data series independent of each fund can be calculated and denoted as fundA$_t$, fundB$_t$, and fundC$_t$. The overall portfolio weight change is the weighted average of the above three items. We can see from formula (4), where the value of α_A, α_B, α_C are determined by minimizing the function in formula (5) under constraints: $\alpha_A + \alpha_B + \alpha_C = 1, 0 \leq \alpha_A, \alpha_B, \alpha_C \leq 0.95$.[2]

$$\text{fund}_t = \alpha_A \text{fundA}_t + \alpha_B \text{fundB}_t + \alpha_C \text{fundC}_t, \tag{4}$$

---

[2] The fund's investment in the stock market shall not exceed 95% of its net assets.

$$Q(\alpha_A, \alpha_B, \alpha_C)$$

$$= \sum_t \left(\begin{array}{l} \alpha_A \dfrac{\text{fundA}_t \times r_{I100,t} - \text{fundA}_{t-1} \times r_{I100,t-1}}{\text{fundA}_{t-1} \times r_{I100,t-1}} \\[2ex] + \alpha_B \dfrac{\text{fundB}_t \times r_{I200,t} - \text{fundB}_{t-1} \times r_{I200,t-1}}{\text{fundB}_{t-1} \times r_{I200,t-1}} \\[2ex] + \alpha_C \dfrac{\text{fundC}_t \times r_{I500,t} - \text{fundC}_{t-1} \times r_{I500,t-1}}{\text{fundC}_{t-1} \times r_{I500,t-1}} - r_t \end{array} \right). \tag{5}$$

- Portfolio weight change can be divided into two parts. One part is due to fund managers actively increasing or reducing stock shares; while another part is due to the stock market itself, i.e. when managers remain unchanged shares, market fluctuations can also lead to change in portfolio weight. The former is the active portfolio weight change, the latter is the passive portfolio weight change. Assuming that fund assets consist of only stock and cash, we can get the measurement of the active portfolio weight change from formula (6) to formula (8):

$$\Delta\text{fund}_t = \text{fund}_t - \text{fund}_{t-1}, \tag{6}$$

$$\Delta\text{fund}_{p,t} = \frac{\text{fund}_{t-1} \times (1 + r_{I300,t})}{\text{fund}_{t-1} \times (1 + r_{I300,t}) + (1 - \text{fund}_{t-1})} - \text{fund}_{t-1}, \tag{7}$$

$$\Delta\text{fund}_{a,t} = \Delta\text{fund}_t - \Delta\text{fund}_{p,t}. \tag{8}$$

- In formula (6), Δfund_t measures the overall portfolio weight change; in formula (7), $\Delta\text{fund}_{p,t}$ measures the passive portfolio weight change, where $r_{I300,t}$ is CSI 300 index return. Therefore, in formula (7), $\Delta\text{fund}_{a,t}$ can measure the active portfolio weight change.

3.2. *Portfolio weight change measurement results and analysis*

According to the preceding calculation, we get the overall portfolio weight change, active portfolio weight change, and passive portfolio weight change from June 16, 2006 to December 31, 2015. In order to test the measurement results of the fund's portfolio weight change,

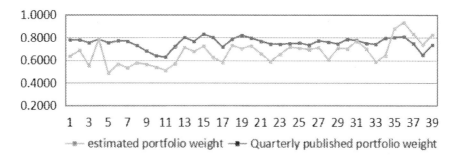

Figure 1. Open-ended hybrid fund portfolio weight changes.

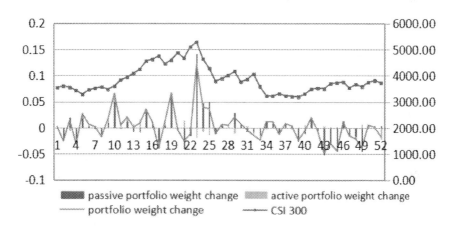

Figure 2. Open-ended hybrid fund active portfolio weight changes in 2015.

they are compared with the real value published by the fund quarterly reports. Figure 1 shows the comparison of 39 data from the second quarter of 2006 to the fourth quarter of 2015. Although there is difference between the fitted value and true value, most of the fitted portfolio weight changes are below the real portfolio weight changes, they have the same peaks and valleys, and the change direction of each sample point is basically the same. The correlation coefficient between them is 0.84. Therefore, it is reasonable to study the effect of the fund's active portfolio weight change on the market by means of the fitted value.

Figure 2 shows the overall portfolio weight change, active portfolio weight change, passive portfolio weight change, and the CSI 300 index. Active and passive portfolio weight changes varied between -5% and 15%. And the direction of the active portfolio weight change is in line with the change direction of the CSI 300 index. In particular, starting from the 5th week of 2015, with the fund actively increasing portfolio weight, CSI 300 index climbed to the highest at 5283 points at the 23rd week, then fell down with the fund actively reducing the portfolio weight. It indicates that the active portfolio weight change and stock movements have a strong correlation.

4. Estimation of the Effect of Active Portfolio Weight Change on Stock Market Returns

In the analysis of the impact of active portfolio weight change on the stock market returns, this chapter mainly studies the impact of the change of the active portfolio weight change on the CSI 300 index return $r_{I300,t}$. $\Delta\text{fund}_{a,t} > 0$ means that the fund actively increases the portfolio weight, and $\Delta\text{fund}_{a,t} < 0$ means that the fund actively reduces the portfolio weight.

In order to avoid spurious regression, the augmented Dicky Fuller (ADF) unit root test is used to test the unit root on the active portfolio weight change $\Delta\text{fund}_{a,t}$ and the CSI 300 return $r_{I300,t}$, respectively. Table 1 shows that at the 5% significance level, the time series $\Delta\text{fund}_{a,t}$ and $r_{I300,t}$ are stationary. Therefore, the two pairs Granger

Table 1. Active portfolio weight change and index returns ADF test results.

Index	Test form	ADF	P Value
$\Delta\text{fund}_{a,t}$	(C, 0, 0)	-13.14529	0.0000**
$r_{I300,t}$	(C, T, 0)	-20.88107	0.0000**

Notes: (1) **Indicates that the null hypothesis is rejected at the 5% significance level, and the variable is considered to be stationary at the 5% significance level. (2) The ADF unit root test form is (C, T, K), where C is the constant term, T is the time trend term, and K is the lag order selected according to the Schwarz information criterion (SIC).

Table 2. Granger causality test results.

Lag stage	Original hypothesis	F-statistic	P Value
1	$r_{I300,t}$ is not the Granger cause of $\Delta\text{fund}_{a,t}$	5.80398	0.0164
	$\Delta\text{fund}_{a,t}$ is not the Granger cause of $r_{I300,t}$	1380.64	0.0000*
2	$r_{I300,t}$ is not the Granger cause of $\Delta\text{fund}_{a,t}$	0.55256	0.5758
	$\Delta\text{fund}_{a,t}$ is not the Granger cause of $r_{I300,t}$	831.281	0.0000*
3	$r_{I300,t}$ is not the Granger cause of $\Delta\text{fund}_{a,t}$	1.24811	0.2917
	$\Delta\text{fund}_{a,t}$ is not the Granger cause of $r_{I300,t}$	558.487	0.0000*
4	$r_{I300,t}$ is not the Granger cause of $\Delta\text{fund}_{a,t}$	1.18354	0.3172
	$\Delta\text{fund}_{a,t}$ is not the Granger cause of $r_{I300,t}$	417.784	0.0000*

Note: *Indicates that the original hypothesis is rejected at the 1% significance level.

causality test can be carried on the series $\Delta\text{fund}_{a,t}$ and $r_{I300,t}$ directly. Table 2 shows the Granger causality test results. When the lag length is set to be 1, 2, 3, and 4 separately, the null hypothesis of "$\Delta\text{fund}_{a,t}$ is not the Granger cause of $r_{I300,t}$" is rejected at the 1% significance level, but the null hypothesis of "$r_{I300,t}$ is not the Granger cause of $\Delta\text{fund}_{a,t}$" is accepted. The results reflect that the active portfolio weight change is the Granger cause of the CSI 300 return, but the CSI 300 return is not the Granger cause of the active portfolio weight change, which implies that the CSI 300 return is affected by the active portfolio weight change. In addition, this study also conducts the two pairs Granger causality test respectively on the overall portfolio weight and the CSI 300 return, the overall portfolio weight change and the CSI 300 return, and the passive portfolio weight change and the CSI 300 return. The results show that none of the three is the Granger cause of the change in the CSI 300 return. Thus, it provides further evidence that the index return is caused by the fund's active portfolio weight change rather than the passive portfolio weight change.

In order to further analyze the dynamic impact of $\Delta\text{fund}_{a,t}$ on $r_{I300,t}$, the impulse response function is analyzed by using 3-lagged VAR model. The results are shown in Figure 3. In the current period, giving the active portfolio weight change a standard deviation of the

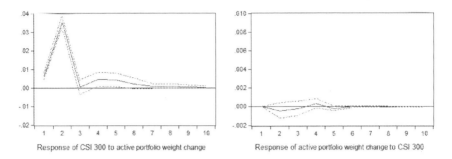

Response of CSI 300 to active portfolio weight change   Response of active portfolio weight change to CSI 300

Figure 3. The impulse response results.

positive impact of the innovation, its positive impact on the CSI 300 index return is small, but at the second period the positive impact reaches the highest, and at the fourth period the positive impact reaches the secondary peak, then positive impact is gradually going down and approaches 0 at the seven period. On the contrary, giving the current CSI 300 index a standard deviation of the positive impact of the innovation, the result is not significant. It implies that the active portfolio weight change has a positive impact on the index return in lagged periods, but not vice versa.

The above analysis from the perspective of the return provides the empirical evidence that the behavior of institutional investor actively adjust portfolio weight will enhance the market fluctuations.

5. Estimation of the Effect of Active Portfolio Weight Change on Stock Market Volatility

The stock market volatility is generally characterized by the variance or standard deviation. The market return usually exhibits the volatility-clustering properties, the larger changes cluster together for a period of time and then follow smaller changes during another period of time. The ARCH model (Engle, 1982) is originally proposed to describe these characteristics of distribution. Bollerslev (1986) proposes a more widely used GARCH model on the basis of Engle's linear expansion and innovation of heteroscedastic representations. The purpose of this chapter is to study the influence of the proportion of the active portfolio weight change on the volatility of the stock market. Therefore, the active portfolio weight change variable $\Delta\text{fund}_{a,t}$ is added to the variance equation. We set up the GARCH model as follows:

$$r_{I300,t} = \alpha_0 + \varepsilon_t; \tag{9}$$

$$\sigma_t^2 = \beta_0 + \beta_1 \varepsilon_{t-1}^2 + \beta_2 \sigma_{t-1}^2 + \beta_3 \Delta\text{fund}_{a,t}. \tag{10}$$

Table 3 provides the estimation results based on GARCH model. In the variance equation, the fund's active portfolio weight change has a positive effect on the volatility of the stock market at the 10% significance level. Therefore, institutional investor's active portfolio weight change increases the stock market volatility and enhances the risk of the stock market.

Why can the behavior of China's institutional investors increase the volatility of stock market? First, because China's securities market has not been so much mature, excessive speculation and herding behavior are more serious and common. Institutional investors tend to have stronger herd effects because of their higher mutual understanding and fiercer horizontal performance competition. Shi (2001) as well as Tang and Peng (2014) empirically analyze the herding effect of China's institutional investors, and the results show that there are significant herding effects among China's institutional investors, which aggravate the volatility of China's stock market. Second, under the mechanism of "a small assessment every quarter and a large assessment every year" among China's public funds, institutional investors are facing fiercer competition pressure and eager to

Table 3. GARCH model estimation results.

Variable	Coefficient	Std. Error	z-Statistic	Prob.
C	0.000898	0.001576	0.569801	0.5688
	Variance equation			
C	2.44E-05	1.75E-05	1.393270	0.1635
RESID$(-1)^\wedge 2$	0.096326	0.028165	3.420039	0.0006
GARCH(-1)	0.890704	0.033398	26.66904	0.0000
$\Delta\text{fund}_{a,t}$	0.004939	0.002928	1.687017	0.0916

exceed their peers and have more serious short-sighted operational thinking. Hence, once the stock in the portfolio cannot rise in the short term, fund managers have the opportunity to sell it, which will lead the institutional investors to constantly change their portfolio and increase the stock market volatility.

6.   Conclusions

In order to verify whether institutional investors have played a role in stabilizing the market, it is necessary to find a reasonable proxy variable to measure the behavior of institutional investors. This study designs an active portfolio weight change, which can accurately capture the specific operational behavior of institutional investors and empirically study the effects of the institutional investor's active portfolio weight change on the stock market. Granger causality test shows that the institutional investor's active portfolio weight change has a significant positive impact on the stock market returns in the next 1–4 periods. The GARCH model estimations show that institutional investor's active portfolio weight change has a positive impact on stock market volatility. Therefore, the behavior of institutional investors directly affects stock market returns and aggravates market volatility, the institutional investors cannot be the market stabilizers.

In order to make the institutional investors play the role in stabilizing the market, it is necessary to reduce the herding effects of institutional investors. According to our study, we provide some corresponding policy recommendations as follows.

First, the government should reduce the direct regulations on the securities market and let the market mechanism play a fundamental role in the resource allocation. China's securities market is known as the policy market. The government often adjusts the transaction stamp tax to restrict the supply of stocks and even directly intervenes in the market by administrative means. The government's actions will directly affect the behavior of investors. Investors must keep in line with the government in order to avoid adverse effects. This will lead to conformity behavior affected by norms, which may lead to market ups and downs. Therefore, the regulatory authorities should maintain the healthy operation of the securities market and avoid direct regulation in the market index.

Second, it ought to strengthen the information disclosure, strictly prohibit the behaviors of manipulation of stock prices, and promote the rational investment. Price is the reflection of information. Price fluctuation based on false information will lead to herd behavior affected by information. Therefore, information disclosure should be true, accurate, complete, and timely, and market manipulation should be strictly monitored so as to form a reasonable market pricing, guide market expectations, advocate value investment, and improve the stability of market operation.

Finally, it ought to develop the financial derivatives and hedge funds. The financial derivatives and hedge funds designed can control risk and stabilize the market.

Acknowledgement

This work was supported by the National Natural Science Foundation of China (NSFC) (Grant No. 71373135).

References

Barber, B. M. and Odean, T. (2008). "All that Glitters: The Effect of Attention and News on the Buying Behavior of Individual and Institutional Investors," *The Review of Financial Studies*, **21**, 785–818.

Bollerslev, T. (1986). "Generalized Autoregressive Conditional Heteroskedasticity," *Journal of Econometrics*, **31**, 307–327.

Chen, G. J., Zhang, Y. J. and Liu, C. (2010). "Are Institutional Investors Boosters of the Stock Market Boom and Bust?" *Journal of Financial Research*, **11**, 45–59 (in Chinese).

Cohen, R. B., Gompers, P. A. and Vuolteenaho, T. (2002). "Who Under-reacts to Cash-flow News?" *Journal of Financial Economics*, **66**, 409–462.

Dennis, P. J. and Strickland, D. (2002). "Who Blinks in Volatile Markets, Individuals or Institutions?" *The Journal of Finance*, **57**, 1923–1950.

Engle, R. F. (1982). "Autoregressive Conditional Heteroskedasticity with Estimates of the Variance of UK Inflation," *Econometrica*, **50**, 987–1008.

Hirshleifer D., Subramanyam, A. and Titman, S. (1994). "Security Analysis and Trading Patterns When Some Investors Receive Information Before Others," *The Journal of Finance*, **49**, 1665–1697.

Hu, D. and Jin, S. N. (2007). "Empirical Analysis of the Proportion of Fund Holdings and the Volatility of a Stock Market Returns," *Journal of Financial Research*, **4**, 129–142 (in Chinese).

Qi, B., Huang, M. and Chen Z. S. (2006). "Institutional Investors and Volatility of Stock Market," *Journal of Financial Research*, **9**, 54–64 (in Chinese).

Qu, R. H, Ma, L. Y., Zhan, C. Z. and Tong, X. W. (2014). "A Smoothing Model for Fund Position Estimation," *Journal of Mathematics and Statistic Research*, **5**, 35–45 (in Chinese).

Scharfstein, D. S. and Stein J. C. (1990). "Herd Behavior and Investment," *Journal of American Economic Review*, **80**, 465–479.

Sharpe, W. F. (1992) "Asset Allocation: Management Style and Performance Measurement," *Journal of Portfolio Management*, **2**, 7–19.

Shi, D. H. (2001). "Trading Behavior of Securities Investment Funds and its Market Impact," *Journal of World Economics*, **10**, 26–31 (in Chinese).

Shi, Y. L. and Wang, J. L. (2014). "Do Chinese Institutional Investors Really Stabilize the Market?" *Economics Research Journal*, **12**, 100–112 (in Chinese).

Sias, R. W. (1996). "Volatility and Institutional Investors," *Journal of Financial Analysis*, **3**, 13–20.

Tang, C. A. and Peng, G. (2014). "The Estimated Downward and Upward Bounds and the Impact Factors of Herding Level of Chinese Funds," *Journal of China Soft Science*, **9**, 135–146 (in Chinese).

Wermer, R. (1999). "Mutual Fund and the Impact on Stock Prices," *The Journal of Finance*, **54**, 581–620.

Xie, C., Zhang, T. Y. and Yu, X. (2008). "The Effects of Investment Behavior of Securities Investment Funds on the Volatility of Chinese Stock Market," *Social Sciences in China*, **3**, 68–78 (in Chinese).

Zhou, X. N. and Peng, D. (2007). "An Empirical Study on the Impact of Institutional Investors on Volatility of China's Stock Market," *Journal of Systems Engineering*, **12**, 58–62 (in Chinese).

Part III

Innovation and Sustainable Growth in the Chinese Economy

Chapter 11

Technology Level, Market Competition, and Firms' Innovation Behavior: Evidence from Chinese High-Tech Enterprises

Hui-hong Liu and Xin-miao Zhou*

Business School of Ningbo University,
Ningbo, 315211, China
*zhouxinmiao@nbu.edu.cn

The relationship between firms' innovation and market competition is an important focus in economic research. We categorize firms into three types, i.e. the leaders, the followers, and the neck-and-neck firms, with respect to their technology levels. This study is based on the competition and stepwise innovation model in Aghion *et al.* However, in contrast to their assumption that the leader firms do not innovate, we argue that it is possible for them to innovate. Furthermore, a game theory analysis can then be performed of the innovation options that can be made by all firms and the overall industry, and of the relationship between innovation and competition Based on the theoretical model and the annual survey data of Chinese high-tech enterprises, we find that the relationship varies with regard to their technology levels. We therefore propose that (i) the leader's market competition and its innovation constitutes an inverted-U shape relation; (ii) the follower's market competition suppresses its innovation; and (iii) the neck-and-neck firm's competition correlates positively with its innovation. As a whole, the relationship between market competition and the innovation of the industry is an inverted-U curve. Finally, we make some suggestions on how to encourage firms, especially the leader firms, to innovate.

1. Introduction

China enters an era of New Economic Normality, one characteristic of which is the turn from a factors-driven and investment-driven economy to an innovation-driven one. To achieve an innovation-driven economic development, a firm needs, first of all, enough innovative power, which means more incentive is required to promote innovation. Since China is a latecomer, it needs to enhance its industrial innovative power to catch up. As the gap between China and the world's leading technology decreases, little room is left for Chinese firms to innovate by learning technology overflow. More innovations instead are introduced on the basis of the original technology. Therefore, to catch up with the world's leading technology, it is imperative to encourage domestic technology leaders to innovate. Competition in the product market is a constant external environment factor. A firm's innovation choice is usually the response to the market structure. At this stage, government at all levels in China pay attention to the positive effects a highly concentrated market structure has on innovation, so they prioritize non-market forces to centralize innovation resources to large-scale firms and adopt policies to restrict new firms to enter and strengthen intellectual property rights protection. By all means, they try to protect the technological innovations of the large-scale firms in the current highly centralized market structure, in order to realize China's goal of innovation-driven growth and technological catch-up. Can the highly concentrated market structure promote technology innovation of Chinese firms, especially that of the technology leaders? The answer to this question will help us to explore ways to promote firms' innovation by drawing on the relationship between market competition and firms' innovation.

The relationship between competition and innovation has long been of interest to economists and the literature is vast. Opinions are divided. The "Depression theory" holds that a firm's innovative power correlates positively with its scale and market clout. In other words, market competition depresses innovation ability (Schumpeter, 1950; Grossman and Helpman, 1991; Aghion and Howitt, 1992). The

"Promotion theory", nevertheless, argues that under certain circumstances, competitive industries generate more R&D incentives than do monopoly industries, which means market competition is conducive to innovation (Arrow, 1962; Nickell, 1996; Blundell *et al.*, 1999; Carlin *et al.*, 2004; Blazsek and Escribano, 2016). As pointed out in the state-of-the-art, the relationship between market competition and innovation is not monotonous, an inverted-U shape curve may hold between the two (Aghion *et al.*, 2005; Philippe *et al.*, 2013; Aamir, 2013) or market competition may even not affect innovation (Tabacco, 2015). Studies of the Chinese market on the relationship between competition and innovation have also launched a lot of discussions. Scholars conducted studies on this relationship by classifying firms in accordance to their scale, business objective, property characteristics, or technical content, but no conclusion has yet been reached. Some studies conclude that market competition can promote firms' innovation (Zhang *et al.*, 2009; Wang and Huang, 2013), others think that the market competition depresses firms' innovation (Wu, 2012), and some papers find that market competition stimulates some innovation activities, but inhibits others, depending on different determinants (Liu *et al.*, 2014).

Previous studies classified firm types by scale, performance, developmental stage, and so on and examined the relationship between innovation and competition on this basis. However, there is little research on the relationship between market competition and innovation behavior of firm with various technology levels. Most scholars discussed the relation for the developed economies, but few analyzed the relationship for emerging economies such as China. Moreover, the model developed by Aghion *et al.* discussed the innovation choice made by firms with different technology levels, but it was assumed that the industry leader would not innovate. However, the leader may innovate to maximize profits and maintain market clout. So how market competition may affect a firm's innovation is not entirely clear and the theoretical model needs improvement.

The contribution of this study is twofold. Theoretically, we will show that the hypothesis that the leader firms do not innovate, posited in Aghion *et al.*, does not hold. Under conducive circumstances, a leader firm may innovate. This study enriches the theory of competition and innovation. Empirically, the firm-level panel data of Chinese high-tech enterprises will be used in analyzing the relationship between market competition and innovation behavior of firms with various technology levels, which has never been attempted before.

The rest of the chapter is organized as follows. In section 2, we develop a model of effects by market competition on the innovation of firms and industry. Section 3 is the explanation of empirical model, variables, data, and methods. Section 4 discusses the empirical results. Section 5 concludes this chapter and some suggestions are made.

2. Theoretical Model

We follow Aghion's competition and gradual innovation growth model. The industry's state is fully characterized by a pair of integers (l, m), where l is the technology level of the leader and m is the technology gap between the leader and the follower. We define π_m and π_{-m}, respectively, as the equilibrium profit flow of a firm being m steps ahead of or behind its rival. We assume that if a leader firm innovates, the follower firm will automatically learn to copy the leader's previous technology and thereby remain only one step behind. Thus, at any point of time, there will be two intermediate states in the economy: (i) the level or neck-and-neck sectors, where both firms are on a technological par with one another, so that $m = 0$; and (ii) the unlevel sectors, where one firm (the leader) runs one step ahead of its competitor (the follower) in the same industry, so that $m = 1$.

2.1. *Duopoly competition and income*

Assuming that there are two firms in the industry and its state is characterized by (l, m). The firm with the technical level l can use per unit elements to produce γ^l units of output, where $\gamma > 1$. The firms in the industry compete through pricing, implying a Bertrand duopoly. In the Bertrand competitive market, every firm i faces a discontinuous demand function:

$$Q_i(p_1, \ldots, p_n) = \begin{cases} Q(p_i), & p_i < \min\{p_j | j \neq i\} \\ Q(p_i)/k, & p_i = \min\{p_j | j \neq i\} \\ 0, & p_i > \min\{p_j | j \neq i\}, \end{cases} \tag{1}$$

where Q_i is the demand function of firm i, Q is the demand function of the industry, p_i is the product pricing of firm i, and k is the number of firms whose product pricing is $\min\{p_j | j \neq i\}$. If the firm's product pricing is lower than others', it will win the entire market; if more than one firm offers the lowest price in the market, they will share the market. The firm will lose the market as long as more than one firm's product pricing is lower than what it offers.

The marginal cost c_i of every firm is not exactly the same in the unlevel industry, and we assume $c_1 < c_2 \leq \cdots \leq c_n$. Then the Nash equilibrium of the Bertrand market is that: firm 1 prices its product at the marginal cost of firm 2, i.e. $p_1 = c_2$, yields $Q(p_1)$ to occupy the entire market and earns $\pi_1 = p_1 Q(p_1) - c_1 Q(p_1)$. Any other firm j prices $p_j \geq c_2$, $j \neq 1$, yields zero and earns zero.

Assuming that the industry is a facing a homogeneous consumer and the consumer decision-making is

$$\max u = \ln \left(\sum_i x_i \right),$$

$$\text{s.t.} \quad \begin{cases} \sum_i x_i p_i = 1 \\ x_i \geq 0. \end{cases} \tag{2}$$

In the unlevel duopoly industry, it is easy to get the pricing of the leader with technical level l as $p = \gamma^{1-l}$, and its profit is $\pi_1 = 1 - 1/\gamma$. The profit of the follower is $\pi_{-1} = 0$.

The firms cannot get a collusion in the unlevel industry. If the leader and the follower collusive price at $p' < c_2 = \gamma^{1-l}$, the follower will loss as long as it produces, so the follower has no motive of collusion. If their collusive price at $p' > c_2 = \gamma^{1-l}$, the potential entrants will enter the industry, learn to copy the leader's technology through the study, and copy to achieve the technology level of $l - 1$ and price p''. If only $p' > p'' > c_2 = \gamma^{1-l}$, the potential entrants can obtain the whole market, then the leader faces the demand, which would be 0, and its profit would be 0, which is lower than the profit without collusion. So, the leader has no motive of collusion.

In the level industry, the marginal cost c_i of every firm remains the same. Under the condition of complete competition, obviously any price p' which is higher than the marginal cost may not be the equilibrium price because any firm can use a lower price to obtain the whole market when others are priced at p'. On the contrary, any price p'' which is lower than the marginal cost cannot be the equilibrium price because the price p'' will make all firms lose. Then we get the Nash equilibrium: all firms price at the marginal cost, $p = c = \gamma^{-l}$, and the income is $\pi_i = cQ(c)/k - cQ(c)/k = 0$, $i = 1, \ldots, n$. So under the condition of complete competition, in the oligopoly-level industry, the price is $p = c = \gamma^{-l}$ and the revenue is $\pi_0 = 0$.

The firms have some motivation to collude in the level industry. The firm can make a profit $\pi_0 = p'Q(p')/2 - cQ(p')/2 > 0$ as long as the collusive price satisfies $p' > c = \gamma^{-l}$. The collusive price p' is affected by ε, which is the degree of the collusion between firms. When $\varepsilon = 0$, monopoly firms fully compete and their incomes are 0. When $\varepsilon = 1$, monopoly firms fully cooperate and make collusive price as high as possible. Due to the fact that potential entrants can achieve the technology level of $l - 1$ by imitation and learning, if the incumbents' collusive price stays at $p' > \gamma^{1-l}$, the potential entrants can obtain the whole market at price p'', which satisfies $p' > p'' > c_2 = \gamma^{1-l}$. It makes the revenue of the incumbents' bill at 0. So the firms who get full collusion will price at $p' = \gamma^{1-l}$, and the revenue of each is $\pi_0 = (1 - 1/\gamma)/2$.

Therefore, the profit of the firm in the duopoly-level industry is $\pi_0 = \varepsilon \pi_1/2$, where ε is the degree of collusion and it can also be used as the reverse measure of the degree of competition.

In short, in the industry whose highest technology level is l, $\pi_{-1} \leq \pi_0 < \pi_1$ is secured.

2.2. *Game analysis of firms' innovation choice*

In the competition and stepwise innovation model in Aghion *et al.*, the assumption of automatic catch-up renders the leader no more benefits through innovation, so the innovation of the leader would be 0 in the unlevel industry. But this assumption fails to capture the reality. Although in reality there are leaders who, for lack of innovation motivations, are overtaken by other firms in their industry (for example, the Sony Corp., once the leader in consumer electronics, was overtaken by the Apple Inc., due to a lack of innovation), there are also other cases that leaders still keep their leading position by innovating, such as Huawei and Haier, which, respectively, are leaders of the communications industry and home appliances industry in China, and both continue to innovate to stay ahead. The assumption is also theoretically self-contradictory. Wang and Huang (2013) use the competition and stepwise innovation model in Aghion *et al.* as their theoretical tool. Based on the "automatic catch-up assumption" that the leader's innovation is 0, they derived the result that "leaders' motivation to lead the technology innovation in their industry is very strong" (Wang and Huang, 2013), which is obviously at odds with the assumption. Therefore, the assumption that the leader in the unlevel industry would not carry out the innovation needs to be revised.

Firms can improve their skills through innovation, change their position in the industry, and increase their income. However, the firms' innovation costs are not the same so they will carry on the innovation decision, taking into account their revenues, innovation costs, and their rivals' innovation decision. If the firm in the level industry innovates, it can obtain the leading position of technology and become a leader in the unlevel industry, which allows it to capture the entire market and increase its revenue. In order to maximize the revenue, the firms in the level industry will inevitably innovate. In the unlevel industry, the income of the follower is 0. If the follower innovates, it can catch up with the industry leader and become the neck-and-neck firm in the level industry, which increases its income in the condition of incomplete competition. So, the follower is also motivated to innovate. The assumption of automatic catch-up makes the leader unable to widen the technology gap between itself and the follower through innovation. But the leader still has an incentive to innovate. If the leader does not innovate, it may be overtaken by the follower who innovates and become the neck-and-neck firm in the level industry which reduces its income. In order to prevent such a situation, the leader will also keep innovating, so the innovation of the leader in the unlevel industry is not necessarily 0.

When the innovation choice of the firm is n_i, the innovation cost should be $n_i^2/2$. Then the leader or the neck-and-neck firm ($i = 1$ or 0) would innovate successfully with the probability of n_i, while due to imitation and learning from the leader, the follower would innovate successfully with the probability of $n_{-1} + h$, where h is the level of learning. Whether the firms innovate or not affects the characteristics of the industry and the profit of the firms. The profits of the firms are only affected by the relative position of technology but have nothing to do with the absolute level of technology. The relative position of technology is only affected by the current technology status and innovation of the firms and, is independent of the innovation before. Therefore, we only analyze the current innovation decision by using static analysis in this chapter.

Given the innovation choices of the leader, the follower, and the neck-and-neck firm at n_1, n_{-1}, and n_0, respectively, we get the expected return of the innovation of different firms according to the duopoly income and the probability of successful innovation. Firms make their own innovation decisions to maximize their returns. According to the extreme conditions, the expressions for n_1, n_{-1}, and n_0 can be obtained.

In order to analyze the impact of competition on firms, we introduce the competitive degree measure ε into the optimal innovation choice of firms. The substitution of $\pi_0 = \varepsilon\pi_1/2$ can result in:

$$n_1 = \frac{\pi_1^2\varepsilon^2 + 2(h\pi_1 - \pi_1^2)\varepsilon - 4h\pi_1}{\pi_1^2\varepsilon^2 - 2\pi_1^2\varepsilon - 4}, \tag{3}$$

$$n_{-1} = \frac{h\pi_1^2\varepsilon^2 + 2(\pi_1 - h\pi_1^2)\varepsilon}{-\pi_1^2\varepsilon^2 + 2\pi_1^2\varepsilon + 4}, \tag{4}$$

$$n_0 = (\varepsilon\pi_1 - \pi_1)/(2\varepsilon\pi_1 - 2\pi_1 - 1). \tag{5}$$

See Appendix A for the proof.

In regard to the relationship between leader's innovation and competition, we can prove Theorem 1 and thus get Hypothesis 1.

Theorem 1. *As to the relationship between leader's innovation and competition,*

(a) *If $\pi_1 \geq 1/h - h$, then $\partial n_1/\partial \varepsilon < 0$, which means collusion suppresses the leader's innovation whereas competition encourages innovation.*

(b) *If $\pi_1 < 1/h - h$, when $0 \leq \varepsilon < 2(h\pi - 1 + \sqrt{1 - h^2 - h\pi})/(h\pi)$, then $\partial n_1/\partial \varepsilon > 0$, which means competition prevents the leader from innovating; when $2(h\pi - 1 + \sqrt{1 - h^2 - h\pi})/(h\pi) < \varepsilon < 1$, then $\partial n_1/\partial \varepsilon < 0$, which means competition encourages the leader to innovate.*

Hypothesis 1. *When the leader's profit is relatively higher than the level of learning, competition encourages leader innovation. And when the leader firm's profit is relatively lower to the level of learning, the relationship between leader's innovation and competition forms an inverted U curve.*

Therefore, in theory, competition inhibits the leader's innovation only when competition is strong and the leader's revenue is low. In other words, the high concentration of the market structure in most cases will not promote innovation of the technology leader.

In regard to the relationship between follower's innovation and competition, we can prove Theorem 2 and thus get Hypothesis 2.

Theorem 2. *As to the relationship between follower's innovation and competition, it is easy to get $\partial n_{-1}/\partial \varepsilon > 0$, which means that collusion is conducive to the follower's innovation while competition is detrimental.*

Hypothesis 2. *Competition inhibits innovation by the follower.*

In regard to the relationship between neck-and-neck firm's innovation and competition, we can prove Theorem 3 and thus get Hypothesis 3.

Theorem 3. *As to the relationship between neck-and-neck firm's innovation and competition, it is easy to get $\partial n_0/\partial \varepsilon < 0$, which means that collusion is detrimental to the neck-and-neck firm's innovation while competition is conducive.*

Hypothesis 3. *Competition encourages innovation by the neck-and-neck firms.*

2.3. *Impact of competition on industry innovation*

Competition encourages the neck-and-neck firm to innovate but hinders the follower's innovation. And the impact of competition on the leader is uncertain. Whether it stimulates or inhibits innovation depends on the leader's income π_1, the level of learning h, and the degree of competition ε. On average, the influence of the product market competition on the growth of the total productivity is not clear. We assume that there are two different groups: the even group and uneven groups. The even group is composed of neck-and-neck firms, while the uneven group is composed of leader firms and follower firms. The effect on the growth will depend on comparative result between even and uneven groups under the steady state. But this steady state is endogenous, because it depends on the balance of the innovation of two groups. We further analyze the effects of competition on innovation of the industry.

Let μ_1 and μ_0, respectively, be the steady-state probability of the even group and uneven group. Combining with the condition that the transfer probability between even groups and uneven groups is inevitably equal in a steady state, we can obtain and express the innovation intensity of these two groups and finally get the total innovation flow of the industry as follows:

$$I = \mu_1(1 - (1 - n_1)(1 - n_{-1} - h)) + \mu_0(1 - (1 - n_0)^2). \quad (6)$$

The total innovation flow I is more complex, so it is difficult to obtain the explicit formulas of the derivative and the collusion degree for it. In order to analyze the effect of competition on the total innovation flow, we simulate the total innovation flow with a different level of competition and explore the relationship between competition and the total innovation flow from the simulation results. The total innovation flow and simulation can be found in Appendix B. Then we get Hypothesis 4.

Hypothesis 4. *In the industry, when the leader's profit is higher to relative the level of learning, competition provides an incentive to innovation. And when the leader's profit is relatively lower to the level of learning, the relationship between innovation and competition is an inverted U.*

Therefore, theoretically speaking, only when the leader's income is lower will high competition level suppress innovation. That is to say, the high-concentration market structure is not conducive to the industrial technology innovation in most cases.

3. Empirical Analysis

This section demonstrates the relationship between innovation and competition of enterprises and industries with different technological levels. In our hypothesis, the relationships between the competition and the innovation of the leader, follower, neck-and-neck firms, and industry are not the same so they need to be verified. There are three types of relationships between the competition and the innovation: positive correlation, negative correlation, and the inverted U relation. Thus, we use the linear regression and polynomial regression to test the relationship between the competition and the innovation. We then calculate the corresponding AIC and SC criteria and choose the appropriate model to verify the relations of the competition and the innovation variable, accordingly.

The linear regression equation is

$$Innov_{it} = \alpha_{0i} + \alpha_1 comp_{it} + \beta X_{it} + \mu_{it}. \tag{7}$$

The binomial regression equation is

$$Innov_{it} = \alpha_{0i} + \alpha_1 comp_{it} + \alpha_2 comp_{it}^2 + \beta X_{it} + \mu_{it}. \tag{8}$$

Innov is firm innovation, *comp* is market competition, and X indicates control variables.

3.1. *Variable definition*

Looking at the variables in the regression equation, the dependent variable is our measure of firm innovation (Innov). At present, the methods scholars mainly adopt to measure the level of technological innovation are as follows. First, the innovation input is used to measure the innovation, such as per capita spending on R&D and ratio of research investment to sales. Second, the innovation output is used to measure the innovation, such as number of patents and sales of new products. Due to innovation risks, investment does not necessarily bring in success of innovation, and the market competition is more related to innovation output. Sometimes a firm cannot convert its innovations into patented products. So we use the ratio of the sales of new products to the main business income to measure a firm's innovation. In order to test the robustness of the conclusions, we also use the number of patents as a measure in the empirical analysis.

Our main explanatory variable is market competition (comp). The Lerner index is commonly used as the measure of product market competition. According to Aghion (Aghion *et al.*, 2005), this measure is better than the market share or the Herfindahl index. Unfortunately, the marginal cost of a firm is difficult to obtain, so that the Lerner index of each firm cannot be calculated. Considering that the profit rate and the Lerner index share some similarities and that firm profits are negatively related to the degree of market competition according to the above analysis of duopoly competition and income, we follow the common practice of measuring market competition with the industry average profit rate, which is the ratio of the sum of total profits of all firms in the industry to the sum of the main business income of all firms in the industry. This is actually a reverse index of the market competition measure.

In order to more accurately report the relationship between firm innovation and market competition and eliminate the endogeneity between them, we, like others, select enterprise characteristics, input of R&D, industry characteristics, and so on as control variables. The specific control variables are as follows: capital-intensive degree (cap), which is measured as the logarithm of the ratio of the net assets of the firms to the number of employees; scale of a firm (scale), which is measured as the logarithm of the main business income; tax force (tax_f), which is measured as the ratio of the tax a firm pays to the main business income. Property of high-tech enterprises (hightec), which is a dumb variable (it is 1 if the firm is a high-tech enterprise, else 0); research organization (reas_o), which is also a dummy variable (it is 1 if the firm has the research organization such as an R&D center, laboratory, technical center, and so on, otherwise it is 0); full-time R&D employee number (re_p), which is measured as the ratio of the number of full-time R&D employees to the number of employees; input force of R&D (rd_f), which is measured as the ratio of the total R&D input to the main business income; and aggregation of the market (agg), which is measured as the ratio of the sum of the sales of the four largest sales firms to the sum of the sales of all firms in the industry, which is CR4.

Our research also needs to define variables at the industry level. We use the two-digit SIC codes as the standard to classify the industries. The more than 400 firms included in the annual survey database of Chinese high-tech enterprises are categorized into 39 different industries. At the industry level, firm innovation (Innov), capital intensive (cap), scale of firm (scale), tax force (tax_f), full-time R&D employees (re_p) and input force of R&D (rd_f) are denoted as the average values of all firms in the industry, while market competition (comp) and aggregation of the market (agg) are the same values as the firm level. Property of high-tech enterprises (hightec) and research organization (reas_o) would not be applied at the industry level.

Considering the above variables, innovation and competition relationship in Hypotheses 1–4 are shown in Table 1.

Table 1. Expected symbols of innovation and competition.

	Hypothesis 1 (leader)	Hypothesis 2 (follower)	Hypothesis 3 (neck-and-neck)	Hypothesis 4 (industry level)
Comp	+	+	−	+
Comp^2	−	0	0	−

3.2. *Data specification*

The empirical analysis in this chapter is based on the annual survey database of Chinese high-tech enterprises, which includes the main financial indicators (such as main business income, number of employees, enterprise value added, profits, and so on) and the input and output index of R&D (such as total R&D investment, number of full-time R&D employees, sales of new products, patent number, and so on) of more than 400 firms from 2008 to 2011.

We take an example of sample selection. If there is only one firm in the industry, the industry is classified into unlevel industry, and it is a leader. In that case, the follower has no earnings so that it gives up production.

Based on the statistical properties of the data we collected, the following firm classification methods are proposed. We calculate the maximum, minimum, average, and standard deviation of the profit rate of all firms in the industry in which there are a number of firms. If the maximum value is less than the sum of the average and 0.125 times the standard deviation and the minimum value is more than the difference of the average and 0.125 times the standard deviation, it means that the profit rates of all the firms in the industry are about the same. So the industry is a level industry, and the firms in the industry are neck-and-neck firms.

The rest of the industries are regarded as unlevel industries because the profit rates of the firms are quite different. The firm, whose profit rate is more than the average profit rate of the industry, is the leader firm. And the firm whose profit rate is less than the average profit rate of the industry is the follower firm.

3.3. *Methodology*

Some firms' technology identities did not change, but other firms changed their identities during 2008–2011 because the innovation behavior of firms may change their technology identity. For that reason, the set of leader firms, the set of follower firms, and the set of the neck-and-neck firms are not exactly the same in different years. In consideration of the unbalanced panel data we obtained, we use the pooled regression model, fixed-effects model, and random-effects model for the unbalanced panel data to analyze the firm-level data. The panel data at the industry level are balanced, so we use the normal pooled regression model, fix-effects model, and random-effects model to analyze the data at the industry level. Finally, we select the most appropriate model, depending on the results of the F test, LM test, and Hausman test.

4. Result of Empirical Analysis

All these empirical analyses are calculated by stata12.0 and the empirical results are shown in Table 2. Models (1), (3), (5), and

Table 2.   Empirical results.

Model	Leader firms		Follower firms	
	(1) Pool	(2) Pool	(3) FE	(4) FE
	(a)			
comp	1.783***	1.930***	0.285**	0.293**
	(2.65)	(2.82)	(2.41)	(2.47)
comp2	—	−0.293*	—	0.013
	—	(1.69)	—	(0.94)
cap	0.066**	0.069***	0.041***	0.042***
	(2.37)	(2.68)	(5.54)	(5.56)
scale	0.037**	0.035**	0.030***	0.030***
	(2.15)	(2.00)	(4.34)	(4.29)
tax_f	0.107	0.209	0.156**	0.122
	(0.29)	(0.55)	(1.95)	(1.38)
hightec	0.116**	0.115**	0.011	0.011
	(2.08)	(2.07)	(1.11)	(1.10)
reas_o	0.007	0.007	0.017*	0.017*
	(0.14)	(0.15)	(1.73)	(1.73)
rd_p	0.097	0.093	0.007	0.007
	(0.58)	(0.56)	(0.17)	(0.16)
rd_f	0.031	0.076	0.047	0.032
	(0.14)	(0.34)	(0.93)	(0.60)
agg	0.715***	0.721***	−0.828***	−0.829***
	(3.39)	(3.42)	(−34.32)	(−34.33)
AIC	−1.3652	−1.3659	−5.4330	−5.4323
SC	−0.8871	−0.8937	−3.6405	−3.6347

(*Continued*)

Table 2. (*Continued*)

| Model | Neck-and-neck firms | | Industry | |
	(5) Pool	(6) Pool	(7) FE	(8) FE
		(b)		
comp	−14.538*	−16.025	0.641***	1.242***
	(−1.64)	(−1.53)	(2.96)	(3.19)
comp2	—	6.023	—	−2.248**
	—	(0.31)	—	(−1.98)
cap	0.331	0.182	−0.035	−0.031
	(0.67)	(0.25)	(−1.00)	(−0.88)
scale	0.195	0.331	−0.023	−0.021
	(0.46)	(0.53)	(−0.70)	(−0.66)
tax_f	−4.357	−3.652	−0.647	−0.756
	(−0.86)	(−0.63)	(−1.22)	(−1.43)
hightec	−6.841	−8.916	—	—
	(−0.18)	(−0.22)	—	—
reas_o	0.555	0.499	—	—
	(0.51)	(0.43)	—	—
rd_p	−0.851	−0.401	0.272	0.315
	(−0.17)	(−0.07)	(0.81)	(0.94)
rd_f	−0.200	2.506	0.112	0.123
	(−0.01)	(0.06)	(0.76)	(0.84)
agg	9.269**	9.058**	−0.656***	−0.635***
	(2.45)	(2.25)	(−4.79)	(−4.67)
AIC	−0.6209	−0.5597	−4.1791	−4.1944
SC	0.1165	0.2252	−3.2478	−3.2499

(7) are the linear regression model results, and models (2), (4), (6), and (8) are polynomial regression results. Pool means the pooled regression estimation is considered, and FE means that the fixed-effects estimation is selected. The choices are suggested by the result of the significant tests.

First, we have a look at the results of the leader firm. According to Hypothesis 1, we find an inverted U-shaped relationship between the innovation of the leader and market competition. This means that in the case of low level of competition, leader firms will innovate to maintain their leadership position. Because, when market competition is weak, with the increase of competition, the gap between the profit of the leader and the neck-and-neck firms becomes larger and the expected loss of the leader also increases if it loses the leading position. In order to avoid being overtaken by the follower who innovates, the maintaining-status effect drives the leader to innovate. However, when leader firms face increased competition, it will not bring innovation. When market competition is strong, with the increase of competition, the gap between the profit of the follower and the neck-and-neck firms becomes narrowed and the expected income of the innovation of the follower decreases, which decreases the initiative of the follower to innovate and the probability of the leader to be overtaken. So the maintaining-status effect becomes weak and the innovation of the leader becomes less. The empirical results show that a high concentrated market structure cannot promote the leader to innovate.

Compared with the linear regression model, the AIC and SC values of the polynomial regression model are smaller, so we choose polynomial regression model (2) for the leader firms. The empirical results show that there is an inverted U-shaped relationship between a firm's innovation and market competition. Although we use the reverse measure of market competition, it does not affect the inverted U-shaped relationship between the firms' innovation and market competition. Therefore, Hypothesis 1 is validated. The motivation for the leader to innovate is to maintain its leading position.

From Theorem 1, we can find that the inverted U-shaped relationship only occurs when $\pi_1 < 1/h - h$, which means the income of the leader is low as compared with the given level of learning. Because the income of the leader is $\pi_1 = 1 - 1/\gamma$, to a certain extent, γ denotes the ability of the firms to translate technology into productivity. That the income of the leader is low means Chinese firms do not have enough ability to translate technology into productivity. So when encouraging innovation, the firms need some strategies, such as increasing workers' labor skills and improving the matching of the organization and new technology, to improve their abilities of assimilating the innovation and translating it into productivity. In addition, the inverted U-shaped relationship is usually accompanied by a low level of learning ($h < (\sqrt{5} - 1)/2$). So it also shows that the technology learning ability of Chinese firms is low, and the ability of assimilating the technology spillover needs to be improved.

The degree of capital intensity and scale of firm both have significantly positive effects on the leader's innovation. High-tech firms are inclined to innovate because they need more new technology. If the capital-intensive degree is higher and the scale of a firm is larger, it is more possible to provide the quality and quantity of investment funds and personnel for technological innovation, which makes the output of the innovation higher. The degree of market concentration also has a significantly positive effect on the innovation of the leader. The reason is that the higher degree of market concentration produces larger percentage of leader's sales in the industry total sale because the leader firm is generally the large firm in the industry. So the output of the innovation is higher.

The other control variables have no significant effect on the innovation of the leader. The reason for that R&D investment has no significant impact on the firms' technological innovation probably because the output of innovation is used to measure the firm's innovation. Even if the firm invests on R&D, the outcome whether the innovation is successful or not is random. It is also affected by other factors (such as the degree of effort by R&D personnel, the degree of difficulty of innovation, and so on). So the relationship between the innovation output and investment in R&D is not a simple linear relationship, which gives R&D investment no significant effect on innovation.

Second, we will discuss the situation of follower firms. According to Hypothesis 2, we find that there is a negative correlation between innovation and market competition because the motive of the follower to innovate is the catch-up effect, to catch up with the leader which is to achieve neck-and-neck firm status. With the degree of competition increasing, the yield of the neck-and-neck firms decreases and the difference of the yield between the neck-and-neck firms and the follower also decreases. That lessens the expected income of the innovation of the follower. So the incentive of the catch-up effect on the follower to innovate declines.

AIC and SC value of the linear regression model are smaller, so the linear regression model (3) is chosen for the follower. The coefficient of the market competition in the model is positive and significant. Due to the reverse measure of market competition, the market competition inhibits the follower to innovate, and hence, Hypothesis 2 is validated.

The effects of control variables on the follower are similar to the effects on the leader, which supports the results of the other scholars. In particular, the market concentration has a significant negative effect on the follower to innovate. The reason is that the higher degree of market concentration causes more percentage of the leader's sale in the industry total sale and less percentage of the follower's sale so that the capacity of the follower to innovate becomes less.

Third, we will see neck-and-neck firms. According to Hypothesis 3, we find that there is a positive correlation between innovation and market competition. Because, the motivation to drive the neck-and-neck firms to innovate depends more on the difference of the income after the innovation and the income before the innovation, and innovation can help the neck-and-neck firms to stand out from the competition to obtain higher returns of the leader. When the degree of competition increases, the gap of the income between the leader and the neck-and-neck firms becomes larger, and the incentive of the shake-off-competition effect drives the neck-and-neck firms to innovate more.

In consideration of AIC and SC values again, the linear regression model (5) should be used for the neck-and-neck firms. In the model, the coefficient of market competition is negative, the corresponding p-value of the t-test is just 0.1. Due to the reverse measure of market competition, the market competition encourages innovation of the neck-and-neck firms, but it is not significant enough. Hypothesis 3 has been largely verified.

The effect of the market concentration on the neck-and-neck firms' innovation is significantly positive. The reason is that the neck-and-neck firms are well-matched in the ability so that the higher degree of market concentration results in larger percentage of some neck-and-neck firms' sale in the industry total sale and the more innovation ability of these firms. Thus, the aggregate innovation power of the neck-and-neck firms is stronger, of course.

The relationship between innovation and market competition is not apparently significant, and most of the control variables do not have significant effects on the innovation, but it may not be true. The number of the neck-and-neck firms which can be chosen in the database is relatively small (10 firms in 2008, 6 firms in 2009, 8 firms in 2010, 10 firms in 2011, among which only 4 firms are always neck-and-neck firms during 4 years), and this may be the reason why the regression in the model (5) is not significant.

Finally, we focus on the results at the industry level. According to Hypothesis 4, we find that there is an inverted U-shaped relationship between industry innovation and market competition. The reason for this inverted U-shaped relation is that the innovation of the industry depends on the innovations of the different departments in it. On the one hand, when competition is weak, the even group which includes the neck-and-neck firms is larger, so when the degree of the competition increases, the raise of the shake-off-competition effect of the neck-and-neck firms has more probability to exceed the reduction of the catch-up effect of the follower. In addition, there exists maintaining-status effect of the leader. Therefore, the competition drives the firms to innovate. On the other hand, with competition being strong, the uneven group is larger in the equilibrium of the industry. When the competition becomes more intense, the reduction of the catch-up effect of the follower more likely exceeds the raise of the shake-off-competition effect of the neck-and-neck firms. Moreover, the maintaining-status effect of the leader gets less. So the competition depresses the innovation. At last, the empirical results show that the high-concentration market structure is not conducive to promoting technological innovation in the industry.

The polynomial regression model (8) is chosen for the industry because the AIC and SC of the linear regression model are larger. The innovation is the quadratic function of the market competition, the quadratic term's coefficient is negative and the coefficient of the primary item is positive, so the curve is a parabola opening down and the market competition is positive at the apex. It means that there is an inverted U-shaped relationship. We use the reverse measure of market competition, but it does not affect the inverted U-shaped relationship between innovation and market competition. Hypothesis 4 is attested.

The inverted U-shaped relationships between market competition and innovation of the industry and the firms mainly occur at the same time. So the inverted U-shaped relationship between market competition and innovation of the industry implies that the ability of Chinese firms to learn technology or translate it into productivity is low.

The market concentration has a significant negative effect on the industry innovation. With the degree of market concentration getting higher, the leader gets more percentage of the sales in the industry total sales and the other firms get less percentage of the sales. That is, most of the firms cannot innovate because of a lack of ability even if they have a strong will to innovate. On the contrary, the possibility of the leader to be overtaken decreases and the maintaining-status effect of the leader weakens, which reduces the innovation of the leader. So, this is obviously not conducive to innovation of the whole industry.

In addition, by using the authorized patent number to measure the firms' innovation, for the relationship between the innovation and the competition, we also find there is an inverted U-shaped relation for the leader, a negative relation for the follower, and an inverted U-shaped relation for the industry. Moreover, the relations are significant. Although the relation for neck-and-neck firms is not significant, it is still a positive relation. For other control variables, the empirical analysis can also get similar results. Thus, the relationship between competition and innovation in this paper is robust.

5.　Conclusion

This study considers the innovative possibilities of the leader firms to improve the competition and stepwise innovation model described by Aghion *et al.* According to the technical level, we divide the firms into the leader, the follower, and the neck-and-neck groups. This study enriches the theory of competition and innovation. We analyzed these relations based on the firm-level panel data of Chinese high-tech enterprises. The results show that the relationships vary with technology levels. First, we find the relations between the competition and the innovation of the firms with different technology levels. The market competition stands in an inverted-U relationship with the innovation of the leader. It can be explained that when competition is low, competition promotes innovation of leading enterprises, and when competition intensifies, more competition will not bring innovation. The results also indicate competition prevents the follower from innovating and encourages the neck-and-neck firms to innovate.

Second, we calculate that the relationship between market competition and industry innovation forms an inverted-U relationship. It shows that competition encourages innovation in the case of low level of competition, while competition is not helpful to innovation in the case of high level of competition.

At this stage, the policy of high-concentrated market structure promoted by the Chinese government does not improve the innovation. How can we let the market play its role in empowering a firm's technological innovation such that it becomes an innovation-driven firm that matches its competitor in technology? According to this study, we propose some suggestions for policymakers: keep competition in moderation. When competition is low, it provides an incentive for firms to innovate. Government agencies are therefore suggested to relax control of enterprises, remove administrative barriers of entering the industry, break up monopoly, and introduce competition into the market. However, when competition is intense, it inhibits innovation. Government agencies are supposed to let small and medium-sized enterprises grow bigger and encourage them to set up industry association and reduce competition. Suggested by the inverted U-shaped relationship between the leader's innovation and market competition, governments should create an environment for leader firms to maintain competition in moderation by fully considering the specific internal and international environments. Caution is advised for the formation of large enterprises or groups. Some industrial policies, which are formulated and implemented by each level of Chinese government in recent years, advocate larger and stronger enterprises and corporate groups such that more profits can be made by sheer scale and innovation power can be boosted. However, letting enterprises becoming ever bigger is not conducive to keep competition in moderation, as it stifles a firm's innovation. In addition, the concentration of industry inhibits innovation in the industry, so the formation of large enterprises or groups should be controlled. But this is not to say that we are necessarily opposed to the formation of large enterprise or enterprise groups. When scales of all firms in the industry are small, being bigger and stronger can help firms combat competition, which is conducive to innovation. Moreover, the formation of large enterprises through mergers and acquisitions may produce a more synergistic effect to internalize unnecessary dissipation of the rent. Improve firm's capability of learning and translating technology into productivity. The empirical results show that the learning ability of Chinese firms is relatively low. However, as firms' learning ability gets stronger, total innovation and the leader's innovation are also growing, which help boost innovation of Chinese firms to transform themselves into innovation-driven growth models and to stay abreast of technology leaders. To improve the learning ability of the firms, government agencies are also suggested to weaken IPR protection, foster a healthy environment for corporate innovations, and improve staff training. The findings also show that the ability of Chinese firms to translate technology into productivity is not enough, so it is an important task to enhance the ability to translate technology into productivity. When firms are encouraged to innovate, it is also necessary to improve the supporting measures, such as enhancing the labor skills of direct labor, improving the match of the organization and new technology, in order to enhance the ability to assimilate technology and translate it into productivity, increase the income of the leader firms, and ultimately help firms to innovate.

Acknowledgments

The author gratefully acknowledges support from the Liu Kong Aiju Education Fund in Ningbo University, the National Natural Science Foundation of China (NSFC) (Grant Nos. 71473137 and 71773058).

Appendix A: Proof of Innovative Choice Expressions

If the leader successfully innovates, it can maintain the leading position. If the innovation of the leader and the follower both fail, they keep their original position. If the leader's innovation fails but the follower succeeds, they both become neck-and-neck firms. So the expected return of the leader is.

$$ER_1 = n_1\pi_1 + (1 - n_1)(1 - n_{-1} - h)\pi_1$$
$$+ (1 - n_1)(n_{-1} + h)\pi_0 - n_1^2/2. \qquad (A.1)$$

If the follower does not innovate successfully, it stays at the backward position. If the innovations of the follower and the leader both succeed, they keep their original position. If the follower innovates successfully but the leader's innovation fails, they both become neck-and-neck firms. So the expected return of the follower is

$$ER_{-1} = (1 - n_{-1} - h)\pi_{-1} + n_1(n_{-1} + h)\pi_{-1}$$
$$+ (1 - n_1)(n_{-1} + h)\pi_0 - n_{-1}^2/2,$$

that is

$$ER_{-1} = (1 - n_1)(n_{-1} + h)\pi_0 - n_{-1}^2/2. \qquad (A.2)$$

If both the neck-and-neck firms succeed or fail in their innovations, they only can keep their original position. If one neck-and-neck firm successfully innovates while the other fails, the former will become the leader and the latter will become the follower in the unlevel industry. So the expected return of the neck-and-neck firm is

$$ER_0 = n_0^2\pi_0 + (1 - n_0)^2\pi_0 + n_0(1 - n_0)\pi_1$$
$$+ n_0(1 - n_0)\pi_{-1} - n_0^2/2,$$

that is

$$ER_0 = (1 - 2n_0 + 2n_0^2)\pi_0 + n_0(1 - n_0)\pi_1 - n_0^2/2. \qquad (A.3)$$

The firm makes its innovation choice to maximize its revenue. Based on the conditions of the extreme value, let the first derivative of the innovation choice for the expected income of the leader, the follower, and the neck-and-neck firm be 0, then we can get the following formulas:

$$n_1 = (n_{-1} + h)(\pi_1 - \pi_0). \tag{A.4}$$

$$n_{-1} = (1 - n_1)\pi_0. \tag{A.5}$$

$$n_0 = (2\pi_0 - \pi_1)/(4\pi_0 - 2\pi_1 - 1). \tag{A.6}$$

From formulas (A.4) and (A.5), we can get

$$n_1 = (\pi_0 + h)(\pi_1 - \pi_0)/(1 + \pi_0(\pi_1 - \pi_0)). \tag{A.7}$$

$$n_{-1} = \pi_0(1 - h(\pi_1 - \pi_0))/(1 + \pi_0(\pi_1 - \pi_0)). \tag{A.8}$$

In order to analyze the effect of competition on the firms' innovation, we will incorporate the measure of the competition degree ε into the analysis of the optimal innovation choice. By substituting the value $\pi_0 = \varepsilon\pi_1/2$ into the formulas (A.7), (A.8) and (A.6), we can get the expression of innovation choice.

Appendix B: Total Innovation Flow and Simulation

When the leader does not innovate and the follower innovates, the uneven group will change to even group and the steady-state probability of the transfer is $\mu_1(1 - n_1)(n_{-1} + h)$. When one neck-and-neck firm innovates and the other does not, the even group will change to uneven group and the steady-state probability of the transfer is $2\mu_0 n_0(1 - n_0)$. In the steady state, the two probabilities must be equal, i.e.

$$\mu_1(1 - n_1)(n_{-1} + h) = 2\mu_0 n_0(1 - n_0). \tag{B.1}$$

With $\mu_1 + \mu_0 = 1$, the steady-state probabilities μ_1 and μ_0 can be calculated and be written as follows:

$$\mu_1 = 2n_0(1 - n_0)/((1 - n_1)(n_{-1} + h) + 2n_0(1 - n_0)). \tag{B.2}$$

$$\mu_0 = (1 - n_1)(n_{-1} + h)/((1 - n_1)(n_{-1} + h) + 2n_0(1 - n_0)). \tag{B.3}$$

The innovation of the uneven group and even group, respectively, is $\mu_1(1 - (1 - n_1)(1 - n_{-1} - h))$ and $\mu_0(1 - (1 - n_0)^2)$, so the total innovation flow of the industry is

$$I = \mu_1(1 - (1 - n_1)(1 - n_{-1} - h)) + \mu_0(1 - (1 - n_0)^2). \qquad \text{(B.4)}$$

When $h = 0.8$, let $\pi_1 = 0.6$ for $\pi_1 > 1/h - h$, let $\pi_1 = 0.45$ for $\pi_1 = 1/h - h$ and let $\pi_1 = 0.3$ for $\pi_1 < 1/h - h$. Then we get the effects of competition on innovations of the leader, the follower, the neck-and-neck firm, and the industry as shown in Figure B.1.

If $h = (\sqrt{5} - 1)/2$, then $\pi_1 = 1$ because of $\pi_1 = 1/h - h$. So when $h < (\sqrt{5}-1)/2$, it is only that $\pi_1 < 1/h-h$. Let $\pi_1 = 0.9$ and $h = 0.3$ or $h = 0.2$, we get the effects of the competition on the innovations of the leader, the follower, the neck-and-neck firm, and the industry as shown in Figure B.2.

Comparing the subfigures in Figure B.1, we find that the more the leader gains, the more the total innovation flow is. Comparing the subfigures in Figure B.2, we find that the higher the learning level is, the more the total innovation flow is. By comparing each subfigure of Figures B.1 and B.2, we find that the relationship between the total innovation flow and the competition is similar to the relationship between the leader's innovation and competition.

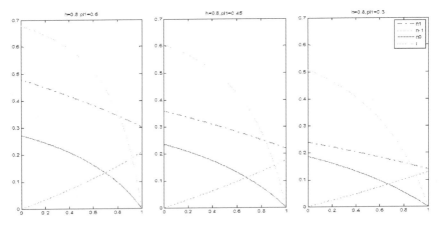

Figure B.1. The relationship between innovation and competition (collusion degree) at a high learning level.

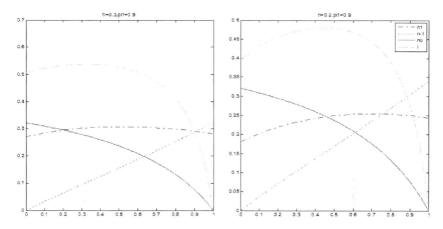

Figure B.2. The relationship between innovation and competition (collusion degree) at a low learning level.

When the leader's profit is relatively higher, there is a positive correlation between the total innovation flow and competition. Nevertheless, when the leader firm's profit is relatively lower, there is an inverted-U shaped relationship between the total innovation flow and the competition. Therefore, we get Hypothesis 4.

References

Aamir, R. H. (2013). "Competition and Innovation: The Inverted-U Relationship Revisited," *Review of Economics and Statistics*, **95**(5), 1653–1668.

Aghion, P. and Howitt, P. (1992). "A Model of Growth Through Creative Destruction," *Econometrica*, **60**(2), 323–351.

Aghion, P., Bloom, N., Blundell, R., Griffith, R. and Howitt, P. (2005). "Competition and Innovation: An Inverted-U Relationship," *Quarterly Journal of Economics*, **120**(2), 701–728.

Arrow, K. J. (1962). *Economic Welfare and the Allocation Resources for Inventions*, Princeton University Press, Princeton.

Blazsek, S. and Escribano, A. (2016). "Patent Propensity, R&D and Market Competition: Dynamic Spillovers of Innovation Leaders and Followers," *Journal of Econometrics*, **191**, 145–163.

Blundell, R., Griffith, R. and Reenen, J. V. (1999). "Market Share, Market Value and Innovation in a Panel of British Manufacturing Firms," *Review of Economic Studies*, **66**(3), 529–554.

Carlin, W., Schaffer, M. and Seabright, P. (2004). "A Minimum of Rivalry: Evidence from Transition Economies on the Importance of Competition for

Innovation and Growth," *B.E. Journal of Economic Analysis and Policy*, **2004**(3), 1–42.

Grossman, G. M. and Helpman, E. (1991). "Quality Ladders in the Theory of Growth," *The Review of Economic Studies*, **58**(4), 43–61.

Liu, X. H., Ian, R. H. and Chuang, F.-M. (2014). "Foreign Competition, Domestic Knowledge Base and Innovation Activities: Evidence from Chinese High-tech Industries," *Research Policy*, **43**(2), 414–422.

Nickell, S. J. (1996). "Competition and Corporate Performance," *Journal of Political Economy*, **104**(4), 724–746.

Philippe, A. Christophe, C. and Delphine, I. (2013). "Competition, R&D, and the Cost of Innovation: Evidence for France," *Oxford Economic Papers*, **2013**(65), 293–311.

Schumpeter, J. (1950). *Capitalism, Socialism and Democracy*, Harper, New York.

Tabacco, G. A. (2015). "Does Competition Spur Innovation? Evidence from Labor Productivity Data for the Banking Industry," *Economics Letters*, **132**, 45–47.

Wang, B.-H. and Huang H.-J. (2013). "The Research on the Technology Innovation Effect of the Oligopoly Market," *Economic Review*, 513–521 (in Chinese).

Wu, J. (2012). "Technological Collaboration in Product Innovation: The Role of Market Competition and Sectoral Technological Intensity," *Research Policy*, **41**(2), 489–496.

Zhang, J. F., Scott, H., Anthony, D. B., Richard, A. L. and Arvind, P. (2009). "What Contributes to the Enhanced Use of Customer, Competition and Technology Knowledge for Product Innovation Performance? A Survey of Multinational Industrial Companies' Subsidiaries Operating in China," *Industrial Marketing Management*, **38**(2), 207–218.

Chapter 12

Macroeconomic Costs and Potentials of CO$_2$ Emission Reduction: A Case Study of Zhejiang Province, China

Lin-Ju Chen and Cong-Lei Tan

Ningbo University, Business school,
818 Fenghua Road, Ningbo, Zhejiang 315211 China
chenlinju@nbu.edu.cn

This study employs multi-objective programming combined with input–output analysis to estimate the macroeconomic costs and potentials of CO$_2$ emission reduction in Zhejiang province, China. The genetic algorithm is applied to solve the programming problem. Several conclusions have been obtained in the study: (1) Zhejiang's abatement cost in 2020 is between 1507 and 3505 RMB/ton CO$_2$ according to different GDP growth rate. (2) As the intensity of emission reduction increases, the macroeconomic loss is also greater. (3) Several industrial sectors have huge potential to reduce carbon emissions, such as textile, general, and special machinery industry. (4) When the rate of GDP growth is more than 7%, marginal carbon emissions increases obviously with the economic growth.

1. Introduction

China's rapid development is based upon a large amount of energy consumption. China has surpassed the United States and become the world's largest greenhouse gas emitter since 2006. At the Paris Climate Conference in 2015, the Chinese government has pledged to cut carbon dioxide emission per unit of domestic production (GDP) by 60–65% from the 2005 levels by 2030 and to peak Chinese carbon dioxide emission by around 2030. Specifically, total energy consumption will be limited to 5 billion tons of standard coal, and energy consumption per unit of GDP will be 15% lower than that of 2015 by 2020. Carbon dioxide emission per unit of large power generation groups will be limited to 550 g of carbon dioxide/kWh. China will strive to install 340 million kW of conventional hydropower, 200 million kW of wind power, 100 million kW of photovoltaic power, 58 million kW of nuclear power, and 30 million kW or more of capacity under construction. China will strengthen the building of a smart energy system, promote energy conservation and low-carbon power dispatch, and increase the consumption capacity of non-fossil energy sources (NDRC, 2016).

Zhejiang province, located in the southeast region of China, is an important strategic area for China's newly proposed "Yangtze River Economic Belt". In 2016, Zhejiang's gross GDP was 4725.1 billion yuan, ranking the fourth among 31 provinces. However, it has consumed 20.276 million tons of standard coal, showing a 4.3% rise a year earlier. In order to actively respond to the national energy conservation and environmental protection policies, Zhejiang province plans to reduce its carbon intensity by 20.5% by the year 2020 compared with that in the year 2015 for the "13th Five-Year Plan" (ZPDRC, 2016a).

Admittedly, reducing carbon emission inevitably has an impact on economic growth. In the past two decades, many studies paid attention to the causal relationship between CO_2 emission and economic growth (Franklin and Ruth, 2012; Riti *et al.*, 2017; Schandl *et al.*, 2016; Yang *et al.*, 2017; Zhang and Da, 2015). In the context of China, Ma *et al.* (2016) investigated the relationship between Chinese household CO_2 emission and economic growth based upon the Logarithmic Mean Divisia Index structure model. Li *et al.* (2017) set up the energy–environment–economy model to simulate China's long-term CO_2 emission and economic development under fossil fuel supply constraints toward 2050. Zhang and Ren (2011) adopted the statistical data of Shandong province in China between 1980 and 2008 to explore the relationship between energy consumption and economic growth. These studies show that energy consumption and economic growth are positively correlated and economic growth has highly depended on energy consumption.

In 2017, the urbanization rate in Zhejiang province was 68%, which was lower than that of developed countries (ZPDRC, 2016b). In addition, Zhejiang had a per capita GDP of 13,634 dollars (Zhejiang Statistical Bureau, 2018a), which is far below the GDP per capita in developed countries. It means that Zhejiang province has to accelerate economic development and raise people's disposable income. However, it is really difficult to balance the contradiction between economic growth and emission reduction.

Therefore, this study mainly aims to estimate the macroeconomic costs and greenhouse gas emission potential in Zhejiang by 2020 in a feasible way. We set up an input–output model based upon multi-objective programming to simulate the two objectives of economic growths and carbon reduction. The outcomes of this study also provide some useful recommendations for policymakers.

The structure of this chapter is as follows. Section 2 shows the literature relevant to this study. Section 3 presents the research method and data used for this study. In Section 4, estimation results are discussed. The last section provides the conclusion of the study.

2. Literature Review

2.1. *Studies on the macroeconomic costs of CO_2 abatement*

With more and more attention to the climate change and global warming issues, numerous academics focusing on the relationship of CO_2 abatement and economic costs have published studies, especially in the context of China (Du *et al.*, 2015; Höglund-Isaksson *et al.*, 2012; Peng *et al.*, 2018; Van den Bergh and Delarue, 2015). The research on macroeconomic cost of greenhouse gas emission can be divided roughly into two categories in terms of research methods: static research methods (Fan *et al.*, 2010; Li *et al.*, 2018) and dynamic research methods (Kober *et al.*, 2016; Qi *et al.*, 2018).

A few studies employed input–output table and energy balance table to decompose the CO_2 emission and GDP of various industries.

Fan *et al.* (2010) estimated the macroeconomic costs of China's CO_2 emission reduction employing the input–output analysis with multi-objective programming. The results of their study showed that carbon emission abatement has a negative impact on China's economy and the estimated macroeconomic costs of reducing CO_2 emission in 2010 for China are approximately 3,100–4,024 RMB/ton. Similarly, Li *et al.* (2018) used the input–output analysis method with multi-objective programming to estimate the macroeconomic costs of carbon emission reduction in Beijing. The results of the study concluded that the abatement cost varies between \$259.97 and \$535.46/ton in different rates of economic growth, and a higher abatement target can induce economic costs.

Static input–output model is simple and easy to apply, but it can only reflect the economic development and structure at a certain point. The real production and consumption system structure is a dynamic process of constant change and development, which limits the application of the static model (Liu *et al.*, 2009). Therefore, some academics used dynamic models to estimate the impact of emission reduction on macroeconomy in the long term. For example, Qi *et al.* (2018) used the Computable General Equilibrium model to analyze the economic impacts of differentiated carbon reduction targets in Tianjin. The results showed that compared with the BAU scenario, the GDP in Tianjin would achieve the highest growth rate if the carbon intensity reduction target was set at 65% in Tianjin whereas 55% in the rest of China. In the Latin American context, Kober *et al.* (2016) employed the energy and economy model to estimate the macroeconomic consequences of CO_2 emission reduction. The study concluded that a decrease in consumer spending is restricted if the carbon prices reach around \$15/ton CO_2 up to 2030.

2.2. *Studies on the impact of policy instrument*

Many scholars have investigated the impact of introducing policy instrument's such as carbon tax on the reduction of carbon dioxide emission (Jin *et al.*, 2018; Mardones and Flores, 2018; Tapia

Granados and Spash, 2019; Zhang and Zhang, 2018). In recent literature, Yahoo and Othman (2017) employed a static Computable General Equilibrium model to explore the impacts of introducing a carbon tax and enforcing command-and-control measures with repeal petroleum product subsidies on energy use. The study found that levying carbon tax would be the cost efficient in increasing the cost of emission-intensive commodities and is conducive to the reallocation of economic resources. In the Austria context, Kirchner *et al.* (2019) used the macroeconomic model DYNK[AUT] to study the impacts of carbon tax schemes on greenhouse emission under different tax rates and revenue recycling options. The results found that CO_2 taxes can contribute to significant reductions in CO_2 emission in a short term. However, a low-income family would be more negatively affected by this tax policy compared with the high-income counterpart. In the Latin American context, Mardones and Baeza (2018) used the environmental extension of the input–output model to study the economic and environmental effects of setting disparate carbon tax rates. The study concluded that CO_2 tax would contribute to a decrease in the CO_2 emission in three Latin American countries (Brazil, Mexico, and Chile), but at the same time, it would increase the Consumer Price Index. Wei *et al.* (2017) studied the macroeconomic impacts of 22 greenhouse gas policy options on the Climate Action Plan through a state-of-the-art regional macroeconomic model in Baja, California. The results revealed that the 22 greenhouse gas policy bundles in this region have effective impacts on the state economy. For example, there is an increase in the employment with a mean of 1680 new jobs every year.

2.3. Studies on the greenhouse gas emission in different industries

Since industrial sector is the largest emitter of greenhouse gas in China, Zhang *et al.* (2017) studied how to achieve the 2030 CO_2 emission reduction target of China's industrial sector by combining the proposed scheme with the extended Logarithmic Mean Divisia

Index model and Monte Carlo simulation method. The results of this study indicated that the Chinese government adjusts the industrial structure and industrial enterprises improve energy efficiency to reach the goal in 2030. In addition, Zhou *et al.* (2015) analyzed the shadow price of CO_2 emission for Shanghai industrial sectors. The outcomes of the study confirmed that the overall weighted average of shadow price is estimated between 394.5 and 1906.1 yuan/ton. And they also identified that a negative relationship exists between the shadow price of CO_2 emissions and carbon intensities and that heavy industries with high carbon intensity tend to have lower shadow prices. Lin and Lei (2015) evaluated the changes in CO_2 emissions from energy use in China's food industry from 1986 to 2010 based on Logarithmic Mean Divisia Index method. They found that the enterprise size in food industry is generally small to accelerate cluster; therefore, the government should reduce the number of small workshops that run with a high cost and the food sectors should use more electricity instead of coal to reduce CO_2 emissions. Pinto *et al.* (2018) evaluated the potential and costs for mitigating CO_2 emissions in Brazil's steel-making industry. The results of their study showed that the increase in charcoal usage in pig iron production from 23.0% to 32.5% can reduce the total CO_2 emissions by 11.3% in 2050.

In the tertiary sectors, transport emits roughly 30% of the total energy-related CO_2 emissions in the EU. Karkatsoulis *et al.* (2017) simulated transition toward low-carbon transportation in EU until 2050 to evaluate the macroeconomic impacts. The study showed that transport restructuring affects the economy through investment in infrastructure, the purchasing and manufacturing of new technology vehicles, and production of alternative fuels.

3. Methods and Data

3.1. *Objective functions*

There are two objective functions in the model, representing the maximized GDP (Z_{GDP}, the aggregation of GDP of each sector) and the minimized carbon emission ($Z_{\mathrm{CO_2}}$, the sum of carbon emission over sector):

$$\text{Max } Z_{\text{GDP}} = \sum_{i=1}^{n} V_i {}^* X_i, \tag{1}$$

$$\text{Min } Z_{\text{CO}_2} = \sum_{i=1}^{n} P_i {}^* X_i, \tag{2}$$

where X_i indicates the outputs of each sector, which serves as the decision variable; V_i represents the added value coefficients of the sectors i. Similarly, P_i refers to the emission coefficient of every sector i; $n = 32$ because there are 32 sectors in total.

3.2. Constraint functions

The model has four types of constraints, that is, general equilibrium constraints, water resource constraints, sector expansion constraints, and non-negativity constraints. The general equilibrium constraints mean that the sum of output and import for each sector should be equal to the sum of its final consumption demand and intermediate demand from the other sectors. Water resource constraints require that the total water demand of each sector should be no more than the maximum supply of water resource. Sector expansion constraints limit the magnitudes of sector adjustments. And non-negativity constraints are required for the practical significance of the decision variable.

General equilibrium constraints:

$$F = (I - A + M) \cdot X_i \geq Fn. \tag{3}$$

Water resource constraints:

$$\sum_{i=1}^{n} r_i \cdot X_i \leq W_{\text{max}}. \tag{4}$$

Sector expansion constraints:

$$X_i^L \leq X_i \leq X_i^U \quad (i = 1, 2, 3, \ldots, n). \tag{5}$$

Non-negativity constraints:

$$X_i \geq 0 \quad (i = 1, 2, 3, \ldots, n). \tag{6}$$

In the constraints above, F is the final demand for all sectors ($n\times1$ matrix) in the year of planning (2020); I is an identity matrix; A is a $n\times n$ matrix of intermediate consumption coefficients; M is the $n\times n$ import coefficients diagonal matrix; X_i is the output vector for the n sectors ($n\times1$ matrix); F_n is the final consumption demand for all sectors in the year n ($n\times1$ matrix); r_i is the water utilization coefficient for sector i; $W_{\max}$ is the upper bound for water resource supply; X_i^{L} and X_i^{U} are the lower and upper bounds for the output expansion of sector i.

3.3. *Genetic algorithms*

In 1975, Holland proposed a genetic algorithm (GA), which is a kind of stochastic search method. GA takes all individuals in a population as objects and uses randomization technique to search an encoded parameter space efficiently. And selection, crossover, and mutation operation constitute the basic operations of a genetic algorithm. In addition, parameter coding, initial population setting, fitness function design, genetic operation design, and control parameter setting constitute the core content of a GA.

Traditionally, there are several methods to solve the multi-objective optimization problem, such as step-by-step method, efficacy coefficient method, and multi-objective weighted method. These methods transform the multi-objective problem into a single-objective problem. Meanwhile, they can only get one solution of the multi-objective problem. However, GA could get a number of Pareto optimal solutions because of optimization of the entire group of operations, and also it focuses on the individual set (Li *et al.*, 2018).

3.4. *Data*

The research data were collected from several sources. Data on economic sectors were sourced from the 2012 Input-Output Table of Zhejiang (Zhejiang Statistical Bureau, 2018b). GDP, energy consumption, and Energy Balance Table were taken from the 2018 Zhejiang Statistical Yearbook (Zhejiang Statistical Bureau, 2018a). CO_2 emission coefficients for each sector were provided by the IPCC report (Eggleston *et al.*, 2006). Water consumption coefficients were estimated by using the method suggested by the Researching Group of Chinese Input-Output Association (RGCIOA, 2007). Water supply data were sourced from the National Development and Reform Commission (RGAMR, 2004).

4. Results and Disscussions

The process of determining the optimum solution in this model is divided into two steps. First, this study employed GA to find the optimum solution of each objective function. The maximum value of GDP is 7.66 trillion RMB, and the minimum value of the carbon emission is 1.699 billion tons. That is to say, when Zhejiang province develops its social economy with the idea of only considering economic growth and allowing CO_2 emission at will, the maximum value of GDP is 7.66 trillion RMB. On the contrary, carbon emission can be capped to 1.699 billion tons. However, these two optimal values cannot be achieved simultaneously. Therefore, it is essential to change the sector variables to revise the objective functions so that they can be close to optimum values. The multi-objective programming model is transformed into nonlinear solutions as follows:

$$\min d = [W_1 \cdot (Z_{\text{GDP}} - Z_{\text{GDP}}^*)^2 + W_2(Z_{\text{CO}_2} - Z_{\text{CO}_2}^*)]^{1/2}, \quad (7)$$

$$W_1 = \frac{W_1}{W_1 + W_2}, \quad (8)$$

$$W_2 = \frac{W_2}{W_1 + W_2}, \quad (9)$$

where W_1, W_2 represent the corresponding weights of the GDP and carbon emission targets, and $W_1 + W_2 = 1$. Through changing the corresponding weights of the GDP and carbon emission, the non-inferior solutions for the multi-objective programming model can be estimated.

If $W_1 = 1$ ($W_2 = 0$), it means that the government only pays attention to the economic growth and ignores the target for the carbon reduction. Under this circumstance, the GDP is 7.67 trillion RMB and CO_2 emission load is 2.198 billion tons. If the value of

W_1 is adjusted to 0.875, 0.75, 0.625, 0.5, 0.375, 0.25, 0.125, respectively, it shows that the government gradually relaxes the targets of maximizing GDP and pays more attention to carbon abatement. This study obtained an array of non-inferior solutions of Z_{GDP}, Z_{CO_2}: 7.14 trillion RMB, 1.873 billion tons; 7.11 trillion RMB, 1.832 billion tons; 7.00 trillion RMB, 1.816 billion tons; 6.86 trillion RMB, 1.808 billion tons; 6.78 trillion RMB, 1.806 billion tons; 6.55 trillion RMB, 1.786 billion tons; and 6.49 trillion RMB, 1.780 billion tons.

If $W_2 = 1$ ($W_1 = 0$), it means that the government only seeks to maximize the reduction of carbon dioxide emission and ignores the target for the GDP growth. In this situation, the GDP is 5.70 trillion RMB and CO_2 emission load is 1.699 billion tons. The values are shown in Figure 1. This study uses polynominal curve to simulate the relationship between Z_{GDP} and Z_{CO_2} as follows:

$$Z_{co_2} = 0.2317 Z_{GDP}^3 - 4.4823 Z_{GDP}^2 + 28.894 Z_{GDP} - 60.286.$$

Goodness of fit of the above function for the nine points is 0.9949. The part of curve can be treated as the relationship between carbon emission and GDP growth when Z_{GDP} is more than 5.70 trillion RMB.

Figure 1 illustrates the relationship between GDP and carbon emission. A positive pattern that emerges from this figure is that the faster the economic growth, the more greenhouse gas is released. In particular, when GDP is between 5.70 and 7.00 trillion RMB,

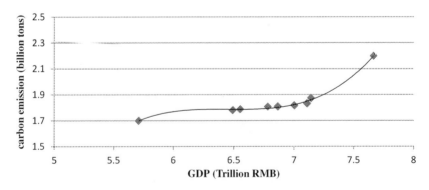

Figure 1.   Non-inferior solutions for the multi-objective programming model and curve fitting.

the marginal growth of carbon emission becomes less steep. And it means changing the industrial structure can effectively slow down the growth rate of CO_2 emission. However, when the GDP is more than 7.00 trillion RMB, the GDP growth leads to an increase of the marginal carbon emission. That is to say, over-quick economic expansion will lead to a dramatic increase in carbon emission.

Based on Zhejiang's socioeconomic conditions and its 13th five-year plan, this study put forward five scenarios according to the average annual GDP growth rate for Zhejiang from 2012 to 2020 (denoted as S1, S2, S3, and S4): 7%, 8%, 9%, and 10%, respectively. The GDP will be in 2020. And according to the curve in Figure 1, the corresponding CO_2 emission is 1.776, 1.779, 1.852, and 2.21 billion tons, respectively. From this, it can be seen that different economic growth rates relate to different greenhouse emission levels. In other words, reducing carbon dioxide emissions comes at the cost of slowing economic growth. The highest GDP is estimated as 7.67 trillion RMB when the government pays full attention to economic development and $W_1 = 1$. At the same time, this study sets the S4 (an annual GDP growth rate of 10%) as baseline to calculate the macroeconomic costs of CO_2 emission abatement. When the GDP growth rate dips from 10% (S4) to 9% (S3), carbon dioxide emission will be reduced by 0.358 billion tons and the macroeconomic cost is 0.54 trillion RMB. This indicates that the average emission abatement cost is 1507.699 RMB/ton. With further reducing the GDP growth rate to 8% (S2), carbon emission will be reduced by 0.431 billion tons and the macroeconomic cost will be 1.25 trillion RMB, implying the macroeconomic cost will be 2898.63 RMB/ton. Suppose that the annual GDP growth rate sharply decreases to 7% (S1). The carbon emission abatement will increase substantially to 0.434 billion tons, with the macroeconomic cost of 1.52 trillion RMB. It also means that the average emission abatement cost increases to 3505.58 RMB/ton.

From Table 1, we can conclude that the higher the carbon abatement target, the greater the macroeconomic losses. Specifically, when GDP rate decreases from 8% to 7%, the greenhouse emission abatement only increases 0.003 billion tons but the macroeconomic loss

Table 1. Potential CO$_2$ emission reduction and the macroeconomic cost of Zhejiang in 2020.

Scenario	Annual GDP growth rate (%)	Emission abatement potential (billion tons)	Macroeconomic loss (trillion RMB)	Emission abatement cost (RMB/ton CO$_2$)	The decrease of carbon intensity (%)
S1	7	0.434	1.52	3505.575	12.3
S2	8	0.431	1.25	2898.663	17.1
S3	9	0.358	0.54	1507.699	24.9
S4	10				

Note: The decrease of carbon intensity is calculated by taking 2010 as the base year.

increases from 1.25 to 1.52 trillion RMB. And the carbon emission abatement cost increases visibly according to the different GDP growth rates. If the GDP rate decreases from 9% to 7%, macro-economic cost will grow 1.7 times and reach 3505 per unit. In addition to this, the carbon intensity is not significantly lower than that in 2010.

The relationship between carbon abatement and economic sector output can have rich implications for modifying the industrial structure. Figures 2 and 3 illustrate the GDP and carbon emission contributions of each economic sector under the scenario, which balances the relationship between economic development and carbon emission reduction. In other words, the value of W_1 is 0.5.

From Figure 2, the proportion of output of 17 economic sectors has fallen in the year 2020. Under the carbon emission constraint, these sectors are mainly concentrated in the secondary industries, which are the largest source of carbon emission. Meanwhile, the percentage of carbon emission in these industries accordingly decreased by about 0.1–0.5%. It is worth noting that the chemical industry emits 20% CO$_2$ but contributes only 10% of the production value. A similar situation occurs in the papermaking, printing, stationery,

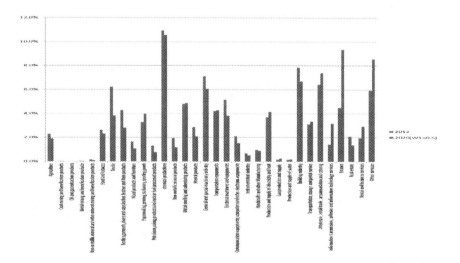

Figure 2.   Percentage of output value of each industrial sector in 2012 and 2020.

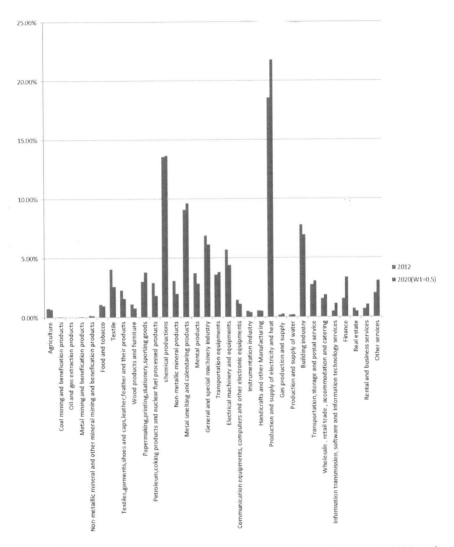

Figure 3. Percentage of carbon emission of each industrial sector in 2012 and 2020.

and sporting goods industries. In contrast to the base year, the percentage of GDP of the electrical machinery, equipment, and general and special machinery equipment industries decreased by 1.33% and 1.06%, which are the two slowest growing industries during this planning period. However, the percentage of papermaking, printing, stationery, and sporting goods industries increased to 3.98%, with a 0.69 % increase.

On the contrary, the share of most service industries for the value of output has been increasing by 2020. Compared with the base year, the sectors with a certain percentage increase are finance, wholesale, retail trade, accommodation and catering, information transmission, software and information technology services, rental and business services, and other services. In particular, the finance will rise from 4.53% to 9.33 % over 2012, with a 4.83% increase. Real estate, however, is the only service sector to witness a 0.7% decline for the period from 2012 to 2020.

5. Conclusions and Suggestions

There is in a sense of contradiction between economic development and carbon abatement. This study attempts to explore the relationship between economic growth and carbon abatement and to estimate the macroeconomic costs and potentials of CO$_2$ emission reduction. We set up an input–output model based upon multi-objective programming to simulate the two objectives of economic growth and carbon reduction, employing Zhejiang province, China as a case. The results show that Zhejiang's highest GDP can be up to 7.67 trillion RMB with 2.21 billion tons of carbon emission by 2020 under a GDP-first scenario. In contrast, the lowest CO$_2$ emission can be 1.699 billion tons, but the GDP is only 5.70 trillion RMB under a carbon abatement-first scenario. And Zhejiang's emission abatement costs in 2020 are between 1507 and 3505 RMB/ton CO$_2$ according to the hypothesized different GDP growth rate.

This study provides some important policy implications. First, maintaining a 7% of medium-speed economic growth will not only help accelerate the transformation of the way of economic development but also balance the relationship between economic growth and carbon emission. Second, it is important to adjust the industrial structure to achieve CO$_2$ structural emission reduction. Textile, general, and special machinery industries and building industry are suggested to slow down their expansion to reduce the greenhouse emission. Third, this research finds that sectors such as non-metallic mineral products, papermaking, printing, stationery and sporting goods, and chemical productions emit a large amount of greenhouse gas but contribute only small amounts of output. Therefore, these industries could be an area to reduce carbon emission first.

This study still has limitations. The input–output analysis implied in this study is static, without considering the change of direct consumption coefficient caused by the dynamic change of industrial structure. A dynamic input–output analysis is expected to be discussed in future research.

References

Du, L., Hanley, A. and Wei, C. (2015). "Estimating the Marginal Abatement Cost Curve of CO_2 Emissions in China: Provincial Panel Data Analysis," *Energy Economics*, **48**, 217–229.

Eggleston, S., Buendia, L., Miwa, K., Ngara, T. and Tanabe, K. (2006). *2006 IPCC Guidelines for National Greenhouse Gas Inventories*, Vol. 5, Hayama, Japan

Fan, Y., Zhang, X. and Zhu, L. (2010). "Estimating the Macroeconomic Costs of CO_2 Emission Reduction in China Based on Multi-objective Programming," *Advances in Climate Change Research*, **1**, 27–33.

Franklin, R. S. and Ruth, M. (2012). "Growing Up and Cleaning Up: The Environmental Kuznets Curve Redux," *Applied Geography*, **32**, 29–39.

Höglund-Isaksson, L., Winiwarter, W., Purohit, P., Rafaj, P., Schöpp, W. and Klimont, Z. (2012). "EU Low Carbon Roadmap 2050: Potentials and Costs for Mitigation of Non-CO_2 Greenhouse Gas Emissions," *Energy Strategy Reviews*, **1**, 97–108.

Jin, M., Shi, X., Emrouznejad, A. and Yang, F. (2018). "Determining the Optimal Carbon Tax Rate Based on Data Envelopment Analysis," *Journal of Cleaner Production*, **172**, 900–908.

Karkatsoulis, P., Siskos, P., Paroussos, L. and Capros, P. (2017). "Simulating Deep CO_2 Emission Reduction in Transport in a General Equilibrium Framework: The GEM-E3T model," *Transportation Research: Transport and Environment*, Part D, **55**, 343–358.

Kirchner, M., Sommer, M., Kratena, K., Kletzan-Slamanig, D. and Kettner-Marx, C. (2019). "CO_2 Taxes, Equity and the Double Dividend — Macroeconomic Model Simulations for Austria," *Energy Policy*, **126**, 295–314.

Kober, T., Summerton, P., Pollitt, H., Chewpreecha, U., Ren, X., Wills, W., Octaviano, C., McFarland, J., Beach, R., Cai, Y., Calderon, S., Fisher-Vanden, K. and Rodriguez, A. M. L. (2016). "Macroeconomic Impacts of Climate Change Mitigation in Latin America: A Cross-Model Comparison," *Energy Economics*, **56**, 625–636.

Li, N., Zhang, X., Shi, M. and Zhou, S. (2017). "The Prospects of China's Long-Term Economic Development and CO$_2$ Emissions Under Fossil Fuel Supply Constraints," *Resources, Conservation and Recycling*, **121**, 11–22.

Li, Y., Wei, Y., Shan, S. and Tao, Y. (2018). "Pathways to a Low-Carbon Economy: Estimations on Macroeconomic Costs and Potential of Carbon Emission Abatement in Beijing," *Journal of Cleaner Production*, **199**, 603–615.

Lin, B. and Lei, X. (2015). "Carbon Emissions Reduction in China's Food Industry," *Energy Policy*, **86**, 483–492.

Liu, H.-T., Guo, J.-E., Qian, D. and Xi, Y.-M. (2009). "Comprehensive Evaluation of Household Indirect Energy Consumption and Impacts of Alternative Energy Policies in China by Input–Output Analysis," *Energy Policy*, **37**, 3194–3204.

Ma, X.-W., Ye, Y., Shi, X.-Q. and Zou, L.-L. (2016). "Decoupling Economic Growth from CO$_2$ Emissions: A Decomposition Analysis of China's Household Energy Consumption," *Advances in Climate Change Research*, **7**, 192–200.

Mardones, C. and Baeza, N. (2018). "Economic and Environmental Effects of a CO$_2$ Tax in Latin American Countries," *Energy Policy*, **114**, 262–273.

Mardones, C. and Flores, B. (2018). "Effectiveness of a CO$_2$ Tax on Industrial Emissions," *Energy Economics*, **71**, 370–382.

NDRC (2016). *The 13th five-year plan for energy development*, from: ⟨http://www.ndrc.gov.cn/zcfb/zcfbtz/201701/t20170117_835278.html⟩.

Peng, J., Yu, B.-Y., Liao, H. and Wei, Y.-M. (2018). "Marginal Abatement Costs of CO$_2$ Emissions in the Thermal Power Sector: A Regional Empirical Analysis from China," *Journal of Cleaner Production*, **171**, 163–174.

Pinto, R. G. D., Szklo, A. S. and Rathmann, R. (2018). "CO$_2$ Emissions Mitigation Strategy in the Brazilian Iron and Steel Sector — From Structural to Intensity Effects," *Energy Policy*, **114**, 380–393.

Qi, Y., Dai, H., Geng, Y. and Xie, Y. (2018). "Assessment of Economic Impacts of Differentiated Carbon Reduction Targets: A Case Study in Tianjin of China," *Journal of Cleaner Production*, **182**, 1048–1059.

Riti, J. S., Song, D., Shu, Y. and Kamah, M. (2017). "Decoupling CO$_2$ Emission and Economic Growth in China: Is there Consistency in Estimation Results in Analyzing Environmental Kuznets Curve?," *Journal of Cleaner Production*, **166**, 1448–1461.

RGAMR (2004). "Analysis of Safety Factor of Water Resources in China in 2020 and Strategy Suggestion," *Macroeconomics*, **6**, 3–6 (in Chinese).

RGCIOA (2007). "Input–Output Analysis of Water Resources Consumption and Water Input Coefficient in National Economic Sectors: The Fifth of Researching Report Series on Input–outut Table of 2002," *Statistical Research*, **24**, 20–25.

Schandl, H., Hatfield-Dodds, S., Wiedmann, T., Geschke, A., Cai, Y., West, J., Newth, D., Baynes, T., Lenzen, M. and Owen, A. (2016). "Decoupling Global Environmental Pressure and Economic Growth: Scenarios for Energy Use, Materials Use and Carbon Emissions," *Journal of Cleaner Production*, **132**, 45–56.

Tapia Granados, J. A. and Spash, C. L. (2019). "Policies to Reduce CO_2 Emissions: Fallacies and Evidence from the United States and California," *Environmental Science & Policy*, **94**, 262–266.

Van den Bergh, K. and Delarue, E. (2015). "Quantifying CO_2 Abatement Costs in the Power Sector," *Energy Policy*, **80**, 88–97.

Wei, D., Brugués, A., Rose, A., De la Parra, C. A., García, R. and Martínez, F. (2017). "Climate Change and the Economy in Baja California: Assessment of Macroeconomic Impacts of the State's Climate Action Plan," *Ecological Economics*, **131**, 373–388.

Yahoo, M. and Othman, J. (2017). "Employing a CGE Model in Analysing the Environmental and Economy-Wide Impacts of CO_2 Emission Abatement Policies in Malaysia," *Science of the Total Environment*, **584–585**, 234–243.

Yang, L., Wang, J. and Shi, J. (2017). "Can China Meet its 2020 Economic Growth and Carbon Emissions Reduction Targets?," *Journal of Cleaner Production*, **142**, 993–1001.

Zhang, J. and Zhang, Y. (2018). "Carbon Tax, Tourism CO_2 Emissions and Economic Welfare," *Annals of Tourism Research*, **69**, 18–30.

Zhang, X., Zhao, X., Jiang, Z. and Shao, S. (2017). "How to Achieve the 2030 CO_2 Emission-Reduction Targets for China's Industrial Sector: Retrospective Decomposition and Prospective Trajectories," *Global Environmental Change*, **44**, 83–97.

Zhang, Y.-J. and Da, Y.-B. (2015). "The Decomposition of Energy-Related Carbon Emission and its Decoupling with Economic Growth in China," *Renewable and Sustainable Energy Reviews*, **41**, 1255–1266.

Zhang, Z. and Ren, X. (2011). "Causal Relationships between Energy Consumption and Economic Growth," *Energy Procedia*, **5**, 2065–2071.

Zhejiang Statistical Bureau (2018a). *Zhejiang Statistical Yearbook 2018*, China Statistics Press, Beijing.

Zhejiang Statistical Bureau (2018b). *Input and Output Table 2012*, China Statistics Press, Beijing.

Zhou, X., Fan, L. W. and Zhou, P. (2015). "Marginal CO_2 Abatement Costs: Findings from Alternative Shadow Price Estimates for Shanghai Industrial Sectors," *Energy Policy*, **77**, 109–117.

ZPDRC (2016a). *The 13th five-year plan for energy development in Zhejiang province*, from: ⟨http://www.360doc.com/content/18/0316/16/14202298_73 7549217.shtml⟩.

ZPDRC (2016b). *The 13th five-year plan for the development of new urbanization in Zhejiang province*, from: ⟨http://www.zjdpc.gov.cn/art/2016/12/9/ art_1709_1719179.html⟩.

Chapter 13

Does the Environmental Policy Stringency Gap between China and Its Trading Partners Affect Its Manufacturing Exports?

Limin Liu*, Minjie Wang, Ziyuan Xie, and
Malviskate Ekia Ambonaya

*Zhejiang Wanli University,
No. 8 Qian Hunan Road, Ningbo City,
Zhejiang Province, 315100, China*
*liulimin790@zwu.edu.cn

Using the gravity model of international trade, this study makes an empirical examination of the Pollution Haven Hypothesis (PHH) for China's manufacturing industry. First, with panel data of bilateral trade in manufacturing industries for China and selected countries from 2000 to 2011, a system GMM estimation of the effects of the environmental policy stringency gap on trade between China and its trading partners is conducted. Second, this study makes a group estimation of the effects on different industries (heavy-pollution industry, medium-pollution industry, and low-pollution industry). The results show that China's manufacturing industry can be regarded as a pollution haven. And the environmental policy stringency gap between China and its trading partners has a significant impact on gross export, net export, and domestic value added in exports of manufacturing. But the effects of environmental policies differ by industry. Environmental policies are found to be a comparative advantage for heavy-pollution industries, but a corresponding disadvantage for medium-pollution industries. And they will not necessarily reduce the international competitiveness in low-pollution industries. Therefore, tighter policies would be implemented gradually considering the stage of the manufacturing industry.

1.　Introduction

Across the world, environmental pollution, ecological destruction, and the growing scarcity of resources and energy are the severe challenges facing all countries. Strengthening environmental regulation, developing green clean production, and realizing sustainable development have become the international consensus. In response to global climate problems, many countries have gradually reduced their greenhouse gas emissions by the implementation of various environmental regulations and have actively promoted the global climate governance processes including the Paris Agreement. The report of the 19th National Congress of the Communist Party of China pointed out that it was necessary to speed up the reform of the ecological civilization system to achieve "Beautiful China". At the same time, China actively participates in global environmental governance and implements emission reduction commitments. According to the "Environmental Performance Index of 2018" jointly released by the Yale University, Columbia University, and the World Economic Forum, China scores 50.74, ranking 120th, still facing tremendous pressure of resources and environment. Against this background, China has enforced regulations in recent years, which also caused extensive discussions in the arena of researchers and entrepreneurs. Will the environmental policy stringency in China affect the exports of the manufacturing industry? Is there any difference of the effects in different industries? Academics have carried out a large number of related researches on these issues. However, due to the difficulty of evaluating the stringency of environmental policies across countries and time, those researches have not reached unified conclusion yet.

2.　Short Review of Literature

Regarding the effects of environmental policies on trade, there are three main perspectives in the academic world.

(1) Trade will be affected by more stringent environmental policies. This type of research is based primarily on the HOV model or the gravity model, using traditional comparative advantage theory

to explain effects of environmental policies on trade. For example, neoclassical economics believes that although enforcement of environmental policies can bring immediate effects on environmental protection, it cannot avoid the additional increase in production costs and will decrease the international competitiveness of enterprises, which will lead to a negative impact on economic growth. Therefore, in order to maintain the international competitiveness, countries have the motivation to compete to lower environmental standards or relax environmental regulations, the so-called "race to the bottom" phenomenon (Dua and Esty, 1997). Gray *et al.*, 1998 found that in the paper and pulp industry, environmental governance investments squeezed out productivity-enhancing investments. In addition, Copeland (1990) and some other scholars put forward the "Pollution Haven Hypothesis" (PHH), which argues that in the open economy, in order to avoid the effects of stringent environmental policies or reducing compliance costs, international differences in environmental standards or regulatory levels in trade and investment will promote cross-border (transnational) transfers in pollution industries (Millimet and Roy, 2016; Solarin *et al.*, 2017), which will lead to adjustments of the industrial structure in different countries and regions. The pollution haven effect has also been extensively validated in studies of trade, facility location, and foreign direct investment (Brunnermeier and Levinson, 2004; Raspiller and Riedinger, 2008; Kalamova and Johnstone, 2011; Kahouli *et al.*, 2014).

(2) Stricter environmental policies may lead to efficiency gains. The Porter Hypothesis holds that well-designed environmental policies could spur productivity and competitiveness gains in concerned companies (Porter, 1991; Porter and van der Linde, 1995). Although the Porter Hypothesis is not widely supported by empirical research (Koźluk and Zipperer, 2014; Ambec *et al.*, 2013; Albrizio *et al.*, 2014; Ramanathan *et al.*, 2017), there is evidence that environmental policies may stimulate innovations in specific clean sectors, which may lead to the improvement of export performance (Sauvage, 2014; Chen, 2010;

Wang *et al.*, 2010; Li *et al.*, 2012; Jefferson *et al.*, 2013; Li and Chen, 2013; Fan *et al.*, 2016).

(3) Environmental policies are not a major driver of international trade. Its effects on competitiveness are limited. Attempts to expand exports by lowering environmental standards will not achieve the desired results (Tobey, 1990; Grossman and Krueger, 1991; Xu, 2000; Harris *et al.*, 2000; Levinson and Taylor, 2002; Ederington and Minier, 2003; Busse, 2004; Lu, 2009; Xu, 2013; Ren and Huang, 2015; Tu and Yan, 2015; Xie and Liu, 2015). Based on the conclusion of the literature, Dechezlepretre and Sato (2017) pointed out that there was limited evidence that strengthening environmental regulation would hurt international competitiveness, and the effects of current environmental policies on trade and investment could be negligible compared to other factors such as market conditions and the quality of the local labor.

All the while, the analysis of effects of environmental policies on trade is a research hotspot. Empirical evidence on the validity of the PHH has been mixed. This study argues that from an empirical point of view, there are two main reasons for this situation:

(1) It is difficult to evaluate the stringency of environmental policies across countries and time. Such evaluation is challenging due to the large and increasing number of environmental issues and environmental policy instruments, as well as problems with the identification of effects. Also, there are many studies on whether domestic environmental regulation affects trade, but fewer studies on whether the environmental policy stringency gap between trading partner affects trade. In fact, the factors affecting a country's export include both domestic and foreign environmental regulations. As Ederington *et al.* (2005) pointed out, "the similarity of the level of environmental regulation between developed countries and the difficulty of migration of pollution-intensive industries themselves are the reasons why previous studies have not been able to show a significant relationship

between environmental regulation and trade". If the gap between the two countries is not large enough to offset the cost of the transfer of polluting industries, the effects of pollution haven may not be found. Therefore, it is not sufficient to only take domestic environment regulation into account in empirical research.

(2) Traditional data on trade often exaggerate the trade imbalance between China and its trade partners. Previous studies often estimate policy effects with gross trade flows or sometimes net trade flows. This is not appropriate for two reasons: first, since there is a large amount of intermediate input trade, it will lead to the problem of double counting if we focus on the cross-border trade flows only; second, traditional bilateral trade statistics also count the added value of intermediate inputs from third countries, so it is impossible to obtain the added value created by each production process directly (Kang and Xu, 2015). As Li and Xu (2013) pointed out: "the customs statistics based on the geographical concept cannot accurately reflect the actual added value of each country, which inevitably will lead to double counting in import and export statistics. This kind of double counting not only distorts the gross trade, but also distorts the trade dependence of countries and exaggerates the trade imbalance. In order to avoid double counting in international trade statistics, it is necessary to introduce the value-added accounting method into the international trade accounting system which can reflect the value-added distribution of different regions and different production processes in the global production chain more objectively."

Based on the considerations, taking China as an example to examine the impact of environmental policy stringency on bilateral exports, this study focuses on expanding the previous research in three ways. First, this analysis estimates the environmental policy stringency gap's effects, considering environment regulations both at home and abroad. Second, it estimates the model with new data on domestic value-added content in exports — the value that domestic firms add to exported goods — providing a more appropriate framework to analyze the PHH in light of global value chains.

Third, in order to explore the impacts in different industries, after estimating the impact on full sample, it makes a group estimation of the effects for three types of industries (heavy-pollution industry, medium-pollution industry, and low-pollution industry).

The chapter is organized as follows. Section 3 describes the empirical approach. It also defines the variables and gives a description of the data. Section 4 presents the estimation results with the full sample and a grouped sample for gross exports and domestic value-added content in exports, respectively, as well as their interpretation. Section 5 draws conclusions.

3. Model Specifications and Variable Description

3.1. Model specification

The classical gravity model of bilateral trade is as follows:

$$F_{ij} = \beta_0 M_i^{\beta_1} M_j^{\beta_2} D_{ij}^{\beta_3} A_{ij}^{\beta_4}. \tag{1}$$

F_{ij} is bilateral trade volume between country i and j. M_i and M_j represent gravity variables for the two countries (e.g. GDP). D_{ij} is the geographical distance between the partners. A_{ij} represents other variables which may affect bilateral trade volume. According to the purpose of the research, this paper takes the environmental policy stringency gap between China and its trading partners, human capital, and physical capital as new variables affecting the bilateral trade volume. In logarithmic form, the econometric model becomes:

$$EXP_{ijst} = \alpha + \beta_1 Gravity_{ijt} + \beta_2 Endowment_{it} + \beta_3 Endowment_{jt}$$
$$+ \beta_4 EPSgap_{ijt} + \theta_i + \theta_j + \theta_s + \theta_t + \varepsilon_{ijst}, \tag{2}$$

where i is the exporting country, j is the importing country, s is the sector, and t is the year. EXP_{ijst} stands for export; $Gravity_{ijt}$ denotes a set of gravity variables between export and import country; $Endowment_{it}$ is a set of variables at the country level, including variables that may affect comparative advantages following the HO model. They include the stock of physical capital per worker and human capital per worker; $EPSgap_{ijt}$ denotes the environmental policy stringency gap; θ_i, θ_j, θ_s, θ_t and ε_{ijst} are, respectively, exporter, importer, sector, and time fixed effects, included in the basic specification.

3.2. *Variables specification and data description*

(1) EXP_{ijst} is the USD value of the gross manufacturing exports going from country i to country j in a given year t for a given sector s. In this study, we adopt three indicators to represent EXP_{ijst}. The first is gross export ($GEXP_{ijst}$). The second is the net export ($NEXP_{ijst}$) (see Appendix A.1). The third is the domestic value-added content of gross exports ($VEXP_{ijst}$). The reason why $VEXP_{ijst}$ is adopted here is to avoid the problem of repeated counting on the re-entry part of the added value. And national environmental policies may have a greater impact on domestic production for export than that on the gross exports, which always contains large amounts of intermediate inputs from other countries.

(2) $Gravity_{ijt}$ denotes a set of gravity variables of country pair (i,j). This study takes two indexes as gravity variables, one is geographical distance between two capitals, and the other is GDP of each country over years.

(3) $Endowment_{it}$ and $Endowment_{jt}$ represent a series of resource endowment in exporting country i and importing country j, respectively. This study takes physical capital and human capital per capital and FDI as endowment variables (see Appendix A.2).

(4) $EPSgap_{ijt}$ is a proxy for the environmental policy stringency gap between exporter i (China) and the importer j in year t. It is computed as $EPSgap_{ijt} = EPS_{it} - EPS_{jt}$ (see Appendix A.3).

3.3. *Estimation issues*

First, in order to prevent the occurrence of "spurious regression without equilibrium relationship", the unit root tests of dependent variables, independent variables, and control variables are carried out before the system GMM estimation. The Levin–Lin–Chu tests were done, and the results show all variables are significant at least at the 1% level and there are no unit roots.

Second, we make the estimation by the GMM dynamic panel regression method. Some researches indicate that endogeneity is an important factor that impacts the empirical study. Serious endogeneity can lead to biased and inconsistent estimation results. Differences in environmental regulation intensity will affect exports, but in turn, some countries may take steps to lower the level of environment regulation to stimulate exports. Also, the dynamic change characteristics of exports imply that the estimation results obtained by the ordinary panel data regression method may be biased. So, we adopt the system GMM dynamic panel regression method to solve these problems. In doing so, this study takes the first-order lagged term of variables as the instrumental variable to estimate the equation to overcome the possible endogeneity. In addition, in order to ensure the reliability of the estimated results, the Hansen test, AR (2) test, and Wald test are used to check the consistency of the model and instrumental variables in GMM estimation. According to estimation results by GMM, the Arellano–Bond test revealed that at the 1% significance level, there is a first-order autocorrelation for the difference of the random error for all estimation models, but there is no second-order autocorrelation. P value of the Sargan test of overid shows we can accept the original hypothesis that overidentifying restrictions are valid therefore, the SYS-GMM estimation results in this study are consistent and reliable.

4. Estimation Results and Analysis

4.1. _Estimation of full sample_

The empirical results are shown in Table 1. Models (1)–(3) estimate the impact of environmental regulation on gross exports, net exports, and domestic value-added content of gross exports of the manufacturing industry with energy consumption per 10,000 yuan of GDP as the proxy variable for environmental regulation. Models (4)–(6) estimate the impact with the reciprocal of CO_2 emission intensity as the environmental variable.

The overall impact of environmental regulation difference between China and the importing countries on China's gross export, net

Table 1. SYS-GMM estimation results of impact of environmental regulation on manufacturing exports.

Model explained variable	(1) texp	(2) nexp	(3) vexp	(4) texp	(5) nexp	(6) vexp
$epsgap_1$	0.733***	0.0724***	0.636***			
	(0.0429)	(0.0020)	(0.0513)			
$epsgap_2$				0.257***	0.0202***	0.263***
				(0.0475)	(0.0006)	(0.0238)
$gdpi$	0.904***	0.0245***	0.814***	0.778***	0.0278***	0.729***
	(0.0172)	(0.0008)	(0.0195)	(0.0202)	(0.0005)	(0.0239)
$gdpe$	1.295***	0.0849***	1.007***	1.515***	0.0946***	1.224***
	(0.0511)	(0.0015)	(0.0669)	(0.0459)	(0.0005)	(0.0468)
hce	1.207***	-0.158***	1.287***	1.278***	-0.158***	1.353***
	(0.0389)	(0.0007)	(0.0358)	(0.0263)	(0.0005)	(0.0244)
pce	0.455***	0.121***	0.367***	0.433***	0.115***	0.374***
	(0.0256)	(0.0008)	(0.0180)	(0.0251)	(0.0004)	(0.0257)
$fdie$	1.077***	0.00468**	0.950***	1.337***	0.0233***	1.164***
	(0.0533)	(0.0020)	(0.0584)	(0.0356)	(0.0005)	(0.0447)

(*Continued*)

Table 1. (Continued)

Model explained variable	(1) texp	(2) nexp	(3) vexp	(4) texp	(5) nexp	(6) vexp
texp lag 1	0.308*** (0.0117)			0.389*** (0.0109)		
nexp lag 1		0.252*** (0.0060)			0.220*** (0.0024)	
vexp lag 1			0.337*** (0.0137)			0.392*** (0.0131)
CONS	−6.14*** (0.8720)	1.990*** (0.0177)	−10.9*** (1.1750)	−1.222 (0.8940)	1.951*** (0.0182)	−6.47*** (1.1520)
Observations	473	473	473	473	473	473
AR (1) test P value	0.0021	0.0003	0.0011	0.0001	0.0000	0.0001
AR (2) test P value	0.2931	0.2893	0.3631	0.1975	0.0011	0.1975
Sargan test P value	0.2039	0.1985	0.2424	0.2485	0.1974	0.2485

***Significant at 1% level.

export, and domestic value-added content of manufacturing industry is positive, whether energy consumption per 10,000 yuan of GDP is used as proxy variable or the reciprocal of CO_2 emission intensity is used. That is to say, the greater the environmental policy stringency gap between China and importing countries, the more exports of China's manufacturing industry. The results show that the effect of environmental regulatory is negative, and PHH is established in China as a whole. China is a successful exporter, compared with its trading partners in polluting and energy-inefficient activities.

According to this estimation, China's export performance is affected by environmental regulation and is also a function of — among other factors — the export specialization patterns of the Chinese economy and the comparative advantages and income levels of China and its trading partners. For example, the symbols of explanatory variables of gravity variables are consistent with expectations, indicating that the higher the level of economic development between China and the importing country, the stronger the attraction of trade between the two countries, and the greater the export of China's manufacturing industry. And among the factor endowment variables, the impact of China's material capital variables on exports is significantly positive, indicating that factor endowment is an important factor affecting the export of China's manufacturing industry. The effect of FDI on export is positive. As Wen *et al.* (2009) pointed out, China once encouraged export-oriented FDI and the expansion of foreign capital scale would inevitably promote China's export. In this study, we found FDI and exports were positively correlated.

4.2. *Estimation of grouped estimation*

In order to examine the impacts of environmental regulations on different industries, regression analysis is carried out once again after dividing the manufacturing industry into high-pollution industries, medium-pollution industries, and low-pollution industries referring to the research by Tomasz and Christina (2016). Table 2 reports the impact of the environmental regulations difference between China

Table 2. SYS-GMM estimation on the influence of the environmental regulation stringency gap on VEXP and TEXP of different manufacturing industries.

Model	(1)	(2)	(3)	(4)	(5)	(6)
	Export value added			Gross export		
Explained variable	High-pollution industry	Medium-pollution industry	Low-pollution industry	High-pollution industry	Medium-pollution industry	Low-pollution industry
epsgap	0.374	−0.961**	−0.435	0.382	−0.981**	−0.535
	(0.3930)	(0.4240)	(0.3540)	(0.5000)	(0.4250)	(0.4600)
gdpi	0.719***	0.679***	0.940***	0.772***	0.668***	1.061***
	(0.1280)	(0.1930)	(0.1540)	(0.1220)	(0.1950)	(0.2560)
gdpe	−0.945**	−1.512***	−0.316	−0.948**	−1.71***	−0.735
	(0.4690)	(0.4850)	(0.6490)	(0.4660)	(0.4390)	(0.5810)
hce	1.581***	1.233***	0.837**	1.655***	1.331***	0.647*
	(0.2270)	(0.2950)	(0.3590)	(0.2310)	(0.2860)	(0.3610)
pce	0.306*	0.341***	0.387***	0.183	0.284***	0.552***
	(0.1610)	(0.1090)	(0.1320)	(0.1740)	(0.1080)	(0.1600)
fdie	1.085***	1.398***	0.276	1.252***	1.683***	0.4
	(0.3700)	(0.4440)	(0.5730)	(0.3540)	(0.4010)	(0.5830)

(Continued)

Table 2. (*Continued*)

Model	(1)	(2)	(3)	(4)	(5)	(6)
	Export value added			Gross export		
Explained variable	High-pollution industry	Medium-pollution industry	Low-pollution industry	High-pollution industry	Medium-pollution industry	Low-pollution industry
High-pollution industry exports lag1	0.220** (0.0942)			0.151* (0.0794)		
Medium pollution industry exports lag1		0.467*** (0.1800)			0.476*** (0.1800)	
Low-pollution industry exports lag1			0.304*** (0.1100)			0.274* (0.1510)
CONS	−14.35 (8.7920)	0.503 (9.8030)	−23.04* (11.8300)	−16.47** (7.6770)	2.991 (8.8970)	−15.11 (12.0800)
Observations	473	473	473	473	473	473
AR (1) TEST *P* value	0.0031	0.004	0.0033	0.0085	0.0048	0.0112
AR (2) TEST *P* value	0.1724	0.1422	0.0691	0.1169	0.1459	0.0646
Sargan test *P* value	0.2153	0.2823	0.3224	0.2597	0.2949	0.2981

*Significant at 10% level.
**Significant at 5% level.
***Significant at 1% level.

and the other countries represented by EPSGAP1 on gross exports and domestic value-added content in different industries. Models (1)–(3) estimate the impact of environmental regulation on the domestic value-added content of high-polluting industries (HDI), medium-polluting industries (MDI), and low-polluting industries (LDI). Models (4)–(6) estimate the impact of environmental regulation on gross exports of different industries.

According to the estimation, the coefficients of EPSGAP1 for high-polluting industries are positive, while those for medium-polluting industries and low-polluting industries are negative, indicating that the greater the environmental regulation difference between China and the importing countries, the more polluting industries of China will export. In other words, other countries' "dirty" sectors shift their production to China. This is not the case in the medium-polluting and low-polluting industries. The greater the difference, the fewer exports of these sectors. That is to say, in industries with lower pollution levels, the higher the level of environmental regulation in China, the more exports of these industries. It can be concluded that the tightening of environmental regulation in the manufacturing industry will reduce the exports of high-polluting-industries and increase the exports of medium- and low-polluting industries.

The pollution haven effect differs in different manufacturing industries in China. A possible explanation is that the stringent environmental policies mean that investment for environmental pollution treatment needs to be increased. In the face of the same environmental constraints, compared with medium- and low-polluting industries, the environmental pollution control investment of heavy polluting industries accounts for a larger proportion of production costs, and the profits space is compressed. Enterprises may reduce the scale of production investment, and their motivation to develop new products and create new demand is not adequate, all of which contribute to loss of comparative advantage of industries and lower exports. However, for medium-polluting industries and low-polluting industries, the investment in environmental protection is relatively low, and there is an innovation compensation effect of environmental regulation. At the same time, the United States, Japan, and European Union are major export markets of China. They set strict environmental trade barriers to trading partners (e.g. China). With the improvement of environmental regulation and the development and application of clean production technology, product quality standards can be improved correspondingly, which can better meet the market demand of other countries, thus driving increased export performance.

During the sample period, the compensation effect of environmental regulation on innovation of medium- and low-pollution industries is still insufficient to offset the cost increase effect of high-pollution industries. One possible explanation is that on the one hand, heavy-pollution industries have always been the focus of government's environmental policies, and environmental policies have greater impact on heavy-pollution industries. On the other hand, technical progress of clean production in medium-pollution industries and low-pollution industries is a gradual process and takes time.

5. Main Conclusions and Policy Implications

With the dynamic panel data of China's manufacturing industry export to 43 countries from 2000 to 2011, this study makes an empirical analysis of the impacts of environmental regulation on China's manufacturing industry. It estimates the full and group sample with the GMM method. And it draws the main conclusions as follows: Firstly, environmental regulation will reduce the overall export scale of China's manufacturing industry. There is the pollution haven effect in China's manufacturing industry. The weak environmental regulation is still one of the important comparative advantages of China's export trade. With the improvement of environmental regulation level, China's gross export and net export of manufacturing industry will both decrease, while the import of heavy-pollution industries will increase; secondly, stringently environmental regulations have a negative effect on heavily polluting industries, a positive effect on medium-pollution industries and a not so significant effect on low-pollution industries. And in the short run, the promotion of the latter is not enough to offset the negative impact of the former.

In the context of the international division of the value chain and the increasingly severe environmental problems, this study analyzes the impact of environmental regulation on China's manufacturing exports and provides new clues for China to formulate trade and environment-related policies. Based on the results of empirical analysis, we obtain three implications.

First, we should establish an ecological environmental impact assessment mechanism for introducing foreign capital, estimate FDI and other investment projects' ecological security and environmental pollution, and assess the environmental benefits of projects.

Second, the formulation and implementation of environmental policies should follow the principle of graduality, which requires full consideration of the stage of economic development and the actual development of manufacturing industry.

Third, more economic incentive policies should be adopted to encourage manufacturing enterprises, especially those in medium- and low-pollution industries, to upgrade technology or develop clean technology, so as to promote the win–win situation of economic, social development, and environmental protection.

Acknowledgement

Fund Projects: Soft Science Project of Zhejiang Science and Technology Bureau, Research on the Realization Mechanism and Strategy of Zhejiang enterprises leading "One Belt and One Road" Regional Value Chain Based on Vertical Specialization Perspective (2018C35012); Soft Science Project of Zhejiang Science and Technology Bureau, Research on Green Transformation and Upgrading of Zhejiang Manufacturing Industry Embedded in GVC on Biased Technology Progress Perspective (2020C35030); Zhejiang Natural Science Foundation, Research on the Dynamic Mechanism of Green Technology Innovation of Zhejiang Industrial Enterprises under the SST Scope (LY19G030008)

Appendix

A.1. Net export

Since the value of net export may be both positive and negative, this study adopted a dimensionless process as follows: $y_{ij} = \frac{x_{ij}-x_{jmin}}{x_{jmax}-x_{jmin}}; y_{ij} = \frac{x_{jmax}-x_{ij}}{x_{jmax}-x_{jmin}}$. x_{jmin} and x_{jmax} are the minimum and maximum net exports of sector s for country i respectively. And then they were translated by $y_{ij}^* = y_{ij} + 0.5$ in order to get the logarithmic data.

A.2. The physical capital stock

Physical capital per capital is represented by the ratio of the physical capital stock in constant price to the number of employees, and human capital per capital is represented by the number of R&D personnel in millions of people. The physical capital stock in constant price is calculated with perpetual inventory method. The calculation formula is as follows: $K_{it} = (1 - \delta_{it})K_{it-1} + I_{it}$. In which K_{it} represents the physical capital stock of country i at the end of year t, taking 1999 as the base year, and δ_{it} is the depreciation rate with a fixed value of 9.6% (Zhang *et al.*, 2004). I_{it} is the total investment of country i in year t.

A.3. EPS

Considering the availability of data in various countries and robustness of the research conclusions, we adopt two indicators to measure the environmental policy stringency and carry out measurement and empirical analysis. The first indicator is the reciprocal of CO_2 emission intensity. The original unit is USD/kg. The larger the reciprocal of CO_2 emission intensity, the smaller the carbon emission per unit output and the higher the level of environmental regulation. The second indicator is energy efficiency, i.e. GDP per unit of energy consumption. The higher GDP per unit of energy consumption, the higher the energy efficiency and the higher the level of environmental regulation. The original data of the two indicators are converted into the constant price in 2010.

A.4. Data sources

The export data in this paper are taken from the Trade in Value Added (TiVA) database of OECD. This study matches all data from 2001 to 2011.[1] In total, 13 sectors of manufacturing industries were selected, including food products, beverages, and tobacco; textiles, wearing apparel, leather, and related products; wood and paper products; printing; chemicals and non-metallic mineral products; basic metals and fabricated metal products; computers, electronic and electrical equipment; machinery and equipment; transport equipment; other manufacturing industries; repair and installation of machinery and equipment. The OECD-TiVA database covers 34 major OECD member, 23 non-member economies, and other major economies in the world. Considering the availability of data and the coherence of samples, 44 countries[2] including China were selected as sample countries. Data of environmental regulation indicators come from the IEA statistical database. The distance data between countries is from CEPII database. The original data of GDP, human capital, and material capital are from WDI database. China's data come from China's Industrial Statistics Yearbook and China's Energy Yearbook. Table A.1 gives a detailed description of the calculation methods and data sources for each variable index.

Since the industry classification standard of China is different from that of other countries, this study matches industry classification of China with that of OECD-ViTA database as shown in Table A.2.

---

[1] https://stats.oecd.org/Index.aspx?DataSetCode=TIVA_2016_C1.

[2] The 44 sample countries are Australia, Austria, Belgium, Canada, Czech Republic, Denmark, Estonia, Finland, France, Germany, Greece, Hungary, Iceland, Ireland, Israel, Italy, Japan, Korea, Mexico, the Netherlands, New Zealand, Norway, Poland, Portugal, Slovak Republic, Slovenia, Spain, Sweden, Turkey, United Kingdom, the United States, Argentina, Brazil, Bulgaria, China, India, Indonesia, Latvia, Lithuania, Malaysia, Romania, Russian Federation, Singapore, Thailand.

Table A.1. Definition of the main variables and the calculation method.

Abbreviations for variables	Variable name	Description	Data sources
$texp_i$	Gross exports of industry i	China's gross exports of industry i to country j in year t	OECD-ViTA
$nexp_i$	Net export of sector i	China's net exports of industry i to country j in year t	OECD-ViTA author's calculation
$vexp_i$	Domestic value-added content of gross exports of industry i	China's domestic value-added content of gross exports of industry i to country j in year t	OECD-ViTA
$EPSgap_1$	Environmental regulation stringency gap	Differences in reciprocal of CO_2 emission intensity between China and the importing country j	WDI, China Energy Yearbook
$EPSgap_2$	Environmental regulation stringency gap	Difference in energy efficiency between China and the importing country j	WDI, China Energy Yearbook
gdp_i	GDP of each country		WDI
lab_e	Labor endowment of exporting countries	Number of R&D personnel in millions of people	WDI, China's Industrial Statistics Yearbook
pc_e	Capital endowment of exporting countries	Ratio of the physical capital stock in constant price to the number of employees	WDI, China's Industrial Statistics Yearbook, author's calculation
fdi_e	Foreign direct investment attracted	Foreign direct investment attracted by China in year t	WDI
DIS	Distance between the two countries	Distance between the capitals of the two countries	CEPII

Table A.2. Classification matching table.

Industry classification in China's statistical yearbook	Code	Product classification in OECD-VITA Database	Code
Agricultural and sideline food processing industry; food manufacturing; beverage manufacturing; tobacco manufacturing	C15 T16	Food products, beverages and tobacco	D10 T12
Textile industry; textile and garment, footwear manufacturing	C17	Textiles, wearing apparel, leather and related products	D13 T15
Wood processing and wood, bamboo, rattan, palm and grass products industries	C20	Wood and products of wood and cork	D16
Paper and paper products industry; reproduction of printing and recording media	C21	Paper products and printing	D17 T18
Petroleum processing, coking, and nuclear fuel processing	C23	Coke and refined petroleum products	D19
Rubber and plastic products	C24	Chemical and chemical products	D20 T21
Rubber products industry; plastic products industry	C25	Rubber and plastic products	D22
Non-metallic mineral products	C26	Other non-metallic mineral products	D23
Ferrous metal smelting and rolling processing industry; non-ferrous metal smelting and rolling processing industry; metal products	C27 C28	Basic metals and fabricated metal products	D24 T25
Communication equipment, computers, and other electronic equipment manufacturing	C29	Computer, electronic and optical equipment	D26 T27
Electrical machinery and equipment manufacturing industry	C30 T33X	Electronic equipment	D27

(Continued)

Table A.2. (*Continued*)

Industry classification in China's statistical yearbook	Code	Product classification in OECD-VITA Database	Code
General equipment manufacturing; special equipment manufacturing; instrumentation and culture, office machinery manufacturing	C31	Machinery and equipment, nec	D28
Transportation equipment manufacturing	C34 C35	Transport equipment	D29 T30

References

Albrizio, S., Tomasz, K. and Zipperer, V. (2014). "Empirical Evidence on the Effects of Environmental Policy Stringency on Productivity Growth," OECD Economics Department Working Papers No. 1179, http://dx.doi.org /10.1787/5jxrjnb36b40-en.

Ambec, S., Cohen, M. A., Elgie, S. and Lanoie, P. (2013). "The Porter Hypothesis at 20: Can Environmental Regulation Enhance Innovation and Competitiveness?" *Review of Environmental Economics and Policy*, **7**(1), 2–22.

Brunnermeier, S. B. and Levinson, A. (2004). "Examining the Evidence on Environmental Regulations and Industry Location," *Journal of Environment & Development*, **13**(1), 6–41.

Busse, M. (2004). "Trade, Environmental Regulations and the World Trade Organization: New Empirical Evidence," *World Bank Policy Research Working Paper*.

Chen, S. (2010). "Energy-Saving and Emission Reduction and the Win-Win Development of China's Industry: 2009–2049," *Economic Research*, (3), 129–143.

Copeland, B. R. (1990). "Strategic Interaction Among Nations: Negotiable and Non-negotiable Trade Barriers," *Canadian Journal of Economics*, **23**(1), 84–108.

Dechezlepretre, A. and Sato, M. (2017). "The Impacts of Environmental Regulations on Competitiveness," *Review of Environmental Economics & Policy*, **11**(2), 183–206.

Dua, A. and Esty, D. C. (1997). *Sustaining the Asia Pacific Miracle: Environmental Protection and Economic Integration*. Peterson Institute for International Economics, Washington D.C.

Ederington, J. and Minier, J. (2003). "Is Environmental Policy a Secondary Trade Barrier? An Empirical Analysis," *Canadian Journal of Economics*, **36**(1), 137–154.

Ederington, J., Levinson, A. and Minier, J. (2005). "Footloose and Pollution-Free," *Review of Economics & Statistics*, **87**(1), 92–99.

Fan Qingquan, Zhou Xianhua and Zhang Tongbin. (2016). "Dynamic Environmental Tax Externality, Pollution Accumulation Path and Long-Term Economic Growth — Also on the Issue of the Choice of Time Point for the Levy of Environmental Tax," *Economic Research*, (8), 116–128.

Gray, W. B., Shadbegian, R. J. and Ronald J. (1998). "Environmental Regulation, Investment Timing and Technology Choice," *The Journal of Industrial Economics*, **46**(2), 235–256.

Grossman, G. M. and Krueger, A. B. (1991). "Environmental Impacts of a North American Free Trade Agreements," *Social Science Electronic Publishing*, **8**(2), 223–250.

Harris, M. N., László, K. and László, M. (2000). "Modelling the Impact of Environmental Regulations on Bilateral Trade Flows: OECD 1990-96," *World Economy*, **25**(3), 387–405.

Jefferson, G. H., Tanaka, S. and Yin, W. (2013). "Environmental Regulation and Industrial Performance Evidence from Unexpected Externalities in China," *Mimeo*, Tufts University.

Kahouli, B., Omri, A. and Chaibi, A. (2014). "Environmental Regulations and Foreign Direct Investment: Evidence from Gravity Equations," IPAG Business School Working Paper Series No. 189.

Kalamova, M. and Johnstone, N. (2011). "Environmental Policy Stringency and Foreign Direct Investment," OECD Environment Working Papers No. 33, OECD Publishing, Paris.

Kang, Z. and Xu, P. (2015). "Analysis of Sino-Japanese Trade in the Era of Global Value Chain — Based on the Perspective of Value Added [J]," *International Trade Issues*, (4), 75–84.

Koźluk, T. and Zipperer, V. (2014). "Environmental Policies and Productivity Growth: A Critical Review of Empirical Findings," *OECD Journal: Economic Studies*, (1), 155–185.

Levinson, A. and Taylor, M. S. (2002). *Trade and the Environment: Unmasking the Pollution Haven Hypothesis*, *Mimeo*, University of Georgetown, Washington D.C.

Li, S. and Chen, G. (2013). "Environmental Regulation and Productivity Growth — Taking the Revision of APPCL2000 as an Example,"*Economic Research*, (1), 17–31.

Li, W. and Xu, Y. (2013). "Re-estimation of China's Foreign Trade Dependence and Unbalance — The Value-Added Trade in Global Production Chains," *Chinese Social Sciences*, (1), 29–55+205.

Li, X., Lu, X. and Tao, X. (2012). "Does the Intensity of Environmental Regulation Affect the Comparative Advantage of Trade in China's Industrial Sector," *World Economy*, (4), 62–78.

Lu, H. (2009). "Does Environmental Regulation Affect the Comparative Advantage of Trade in Pollution-Intensive Goods?" *Economic Research*, (4), 28–40.

Millimet, D. and Roy, J. (2016). "Empirical Tests of the Pollution Haven Hypothesis When Environmental Regulation is Endogenous," *Journal of Applied Econometrics*, **31**(4), 652–677.

Porter, M. E. (1991). "America's Green Strategy," *Scientific American*, **264**(4), 168, 193–246.

Porter, M. E. and Claas van der Linde (1995). "Toward a New Conception of the Environment-Competitiveness Relationship," *Journal of Economic Perspective*, **9**(4), 97–118.

Ramanathan, R., He, Q. L., Black, A., *et al.* (2017). "Environmental Regulations, Innovation and Firm Performance: A Revisit of the Porter Hypothesis," *Journal of Cleaner Production*, **155**(2), 79–92.

Raspiller, S. and Riedinger, N. (2008). "Do Environmental Regulations Influence the Location Behavior of French Firms?" *Land Economics*, **84**(3), 382–395.

Ren, L. and Huang, C. (2015). "The Impact of Environmental Regulations at Home and Abroad on China's Export Trade," *World Economy*, (5), 59–80.

Sauvage, J. (2014). "The Stringency of Environmental Regulations and Trade in Environmental Goods," OECD Trade and Environment Working Papers No. 2014/3.

Solarin, S. A., Al-Mulali, U., Musah, I., and Ozturk, I. (2017). "Investigating the Pollution Haven Hypothesis in Ghana: An Empirical Investigation," *Energy*, **124**, 706–719.

Tobey, J. A. (1990). "The Effects of Domestic Environmental Policies on Patterns of World Trade: An Empirical Test," *Kyklos*, **43**(2), 191–209.

Tomasz, K. and Christina, T. (2016). "Do Environmental Policies Affect Global Value Chains?" OECD Economics Department Working Papers No. 1282.

Tu, Z. and Yan, R. (2015). "Can the Emissions Trading Mechanism Achieve the Potter Effect in China?" *Economic Research*, (7), 160–173.

Wang, B., Wu, Y. R. and Yan, P. F. (2010). "Regional Environmental Efficiency and Environmental Total Factor Productivity Growth in China," *Economic Research*, (5), 95–109.

Wen, D., Xian, G. and Ma, J. (2009). "FDI, Changes in Industrial Structure and China's Export Competitiveness [J]," *Managcment World*, (4), 96–107.

Xie, R. and Liu, W. (2015). "Research on the Influence of Domestic Environmental Regulation on Vertical Specialized Division of Labor," *World Economics and Political Forum*, (1), 107–121.

Xu, M. (2013). "Leaf Peace Research on the Relationship between Environmental Regulation and Industrial Competitiveness under the Effect of Agglomeration — A Re-Test Based on "Porter Hypothesis"," *China Industrial Economy*, (3), 72–84.

Xu, X. (2000). "International Trade and Environmental Regulation: Time Series Evidence and Cross Section Test," *Environmental and Resource Economics*, **17**(3), 233–257.

Zhang, J. and Wang, Q. (2004). "Authority, Enterprise Performance and State-Owned Enterprise Reform," *China Social Sciences*, (05), 106–116, 207.

Chapter 14

Local Public Expenditure and Local Economic Growth: Evidence from Zhejiang Province of China

Yunhua Zhang[*,‡] and Dan Luo[†,§]

*Business School of Ningbo University,
Ningbo 315211, China
†Henley Business School, University of Reading Whiteknights,
PO Box 217, Reading Berkshire, United Kingdom RG6 6AH
‡zhangyunhua@nbu.edu.cn
§dan.luo@henley.ac.uk

Fiscal policy is always prioritized for stabilization policy within China due to the structure of a command economy. It is worth investigating how local government expenditures, which have the largest share of the local economy in China, react to cyclical economic downturns by adjusting fiscal expenditures. This chapter intends to address this concern and test whether these local government fiscal adjustments carry a substantial effect on local economic growth, consumption, and private investment. This chapter provides new evidence on the effects of a special local governmental fiscal policy in China. Through provincial-level data analysis in Zhejiang province, in this chapter we study how local economic growth, consumption, and private investment respond to local fiscal expenditure shocks. We find that, fiscal expenditure has no effect on local economic growth and consumption, but has a clear leading effect on private investment. Because Zhejiang is a province with a primarily private economy while most of China is still government managed, it is highly important that private investors always pay attention to current governmental activities and respond accordingly. Finally, we analyze the impact of different types of fiscal

expenditure on private investment, and we conclude that only
maintenance expenditures have a significant positive impact on
private investment in Zhejiang province. Security expenditures
have a negative impact, while other types of fiscal expenditures
have no significant impact on private investment.

1. Introduction

The Chinese government often exercises fiscal policy to guide the
economy particularly during periods of economic downturn. For
example, a 4 billion yuan governmental investment was injected
in 2008, and it is reported that the central government has trans-
ferred 40 billion yuan to local governments in order to stimulate
the economy in 2016. In Keynesianism, fiscal policy plays a crucial
role in adjusting revenues, fiscal expenditures, debt levels, and other
factors to achieve an optimal level of economic and social development. Keynesians believe that expansionary fiscal policy boosts
the demand and stimulates investment and consumption Hence, fiscal policy is effective. By contrast, the Neoclassical school argues
that governmental expenditures and purchases tend to "crowd out"
private investment and consumption Despite in-depth research and
repeated demonstration, economists have not reached a consensus.

Although the dispute on the efficacy and effectiveness of fiscal
policy has been a subject for decades, in practice, almost all governments resort to using fiscal policy as the central means to intervene and manage the economy and related aspects. In China, under
the current tax system, fiscal expenditure is used with relative flexibility, frequency, and breadth. Therefore, studying the effectiveness
of government expenditure is not merely a thought experiment but
also a key practical issue for China now. In the institutional context
of fiscal decentralization, Chinese local governments have enjoyed
a high independent authority to conduct fiscal policies. Local governments often allocate financial resources based on local development needs such that each area presents different fiscal expenditure
characteristics, and also because of the fiscal decentralization and
vertical management system. GDP remains the most important performance measure for the local government officials. However, most

local officials' goal is political promotion, and thus, when making policies they tend to care more about output or GDP growth rather than maximizing the welfare of local residents. Even in order to win a prize at "GDP competition", local officials are more concerned about short-term economic performance, disregarding the impact on long-term economic development. Thus, in China, local government fiscal expenditure is always increasing, regardless of the state of the local economy.

Zhejiang province is the biggest local economy in China and plays an important role in the national economy. During the last few decades Zhejiang has developed rapidly with continuous improvements in living standards. However, at the same time there also exist many internal problems such as an irrational industrial structure, unstable private investment, and a slowdown in economic growth. All these reflect the lack of local financial functions. It is a well-known fact that GDP growth has declined in China. Therefore, the Zhejiang provincial governmental fiscal policy has shifted its focus from "stable" to "positive." In 2015 alone, over 900 billion yuan fiscal investment flowed into the market within the Zhejiang province. With nearly a trillion renminbi being directed, a large-scale expansion of fiscal expenditure to stimulate the economy has begun to take place. The question then arises, in a private-sector dominant local economy, will the large amount of public investment crowd private capital investment out? Will the growth of government expenditure crowd local citizens' consumption out? These questions are widely discussed now in Zhejiang province.

In this chapter, we will use local macroeconomic data including per capita GDP growth, per capita consumption, private investment, and government expenditure collected from Zhejiang province since 1978. We apply statistical techniques such as HP filter, regression analysis, and Granger causality test. The aim is to analyze whether local governmental fiscal expenditure has the desired effectiveness as well as whether or not it crowds out private investment and aggregate consumption. Finally, we analyze the impact of different types of fiscal expenditure on private investment. Suggestions and references will be provided on how to determine the optimal method in

allocating resources to achieve a comprehensive, coordinated, and
sustainable development by adjusting the local fiscal expenditure.

2. Review on Theoretical Literature

2.1. *Fiscal expenditure's influence on economic growth*

Some scholars hold the view that fiscal expenditure has a negative
effect. Alchian (1972), Friedman (1979), Sowell (1980), and others
suggest that expansionary fiscal policy, that is, increasing expenditure and taxes, has a negative effect on economic growth. They
point out that due to the lack of price signals, competition, and
the profit motive, government intervention tends to distort the market system, exacerbate productivity costs, and thus impede real economic growth. Laudaw (1985), who analyzes the relationship between
government expenditure and real GDP growth rate in 16 developed
countries from 1952 to 1976, has obtained the empirical result that
the total government expenditure and real GDP growth rate are
correlated negatively. Aiyagari (1990), who uses panel data of 13
OECD countries, concludes that government expenditure has a negative effect on economic growth. In addition, Karras (1994), who
has analyzed the panel data of 37 countries from 1955 to 1984, also
supports the proposition that State expenditure has negative effects.

On the other hand, some scholars support the narrative that
government expenditure, has a positive effect on economic growth.
McDermott and Westcott (1996), who study 20 OECD countries
from 1970 to 1995, find that proper fiscal adjustment can promote
economic growth, with the successful fiscal result depending on a
suitable combination of amount and structure. Alesina and Perotti
(1997) maintain that reducing government expenditure is a superior
way to promote economic growth compared to expansionary "tax &
spend" policy. Adam and Bevan (2001) use panel data from 45 developing countries to analyze the relationship between fiscal deficit and
economic growth. They find that the budget deficit has an inverse
ratio with regards to economic growth with a threshold effect around
1.5%. A reduction of the deficit to 1.5% raises the rate of economic

growth, but a reduction to less than 1.5% leads to economic growth effects that are disappearing or even reversing.

2.2. *Fiscal expenditure's influence on private consumption*

It was relatively recent when researchers finally began to study the influence of governmental fiscal expenditure on private consumption. The seminal work by Brown and Jackson's (1990) on public economics states that, with the assumption of the same production functions adopted by all local governments, household consumption can be modelled as a function of government public expenditure (such as health, education, infrastructure investment, expenditure on culture, social security). The Brown–Jackson model suggests that the amount and structure of household consumption have a positive correlation with government subsidies for production. Bertola and Drazen (1993) demonstrate the extent and direction of private consumption in response to government expenditure shocks by assuming that government expenditure follows a stochastic process drift containing positive reaction. Their study has the following conclusion: when government expenditure is at a low level, increasing it further will diminish private consumption by imposing a crowding out effect; otherwise, when government expenditure is already at a high level, further increases can stimulate the private consumption. Sutherland (1997) proposes a model to demonstrate the response of personal consumption to sudden changes of fiscal deficit or public debt. When public debt is at a low level, current increases of debt levels will have a positive influence on personal wealth and consumption; otherwise, when public debt is already high, further increases will lead to a reduction of private wealth and consumption. Hristov (2013), who uses experience analysis of 16 OECD countries from 1974 to 2011, finds that when the economy is at full utilization of resources, expansion of fiscal expenditure by the government can be effective in stimulating aggregate demand. On the other hand, when the economy is in recession, this action may be counterproductive, as the government budget itself is not sufficient and is likely to fall into deficit. In addition, Schclarck (2005) uses analyse panel data from 19 industrial countries and 21 developing countries to empirically, the effect of fiscal expenditures on private consumption and finds that fiscal policy has Keynesian effects on private consumption in both the developing countries and the industrialized countries.

2.3. *Fiscal expenditure's influence on private investment*

Some scholars believe that fiscal expenditure has a positive impact on the private investment. Aschauer (1989), who studies the US labor productivity, stock price and government expenditure data, finds that the expansion of government expenditure will increase the market rate. He also points out that the net stock of public capital has played an important role in the economy's growth over the past 15 years, such that government expenditure not only reduces the level of investment but also has a significant crowding-in effect. Lopez (2006), using the theoretical framework of the crowding-out effect and panel data from regions of Spain from 1965 to 1997, reports that public investment in the education sector has the most visible effect in the context of private capital accumulation–public expenditure.

Some other scholars take the contrary view that government expenditure has a negative impact on private investment. Bairam and Ward (1993) test the impact of government expenditure on private investment by looking at annual time series data from 1958 to 1988 from 25 OECD countries. The final result supports the "accelerator principle" and the "crowding-out" hypothesis. By using a growth regression model and panel data, Fisher (1993) shows that inflation will retard economic growth by reducing the investment and lowering the productivity, that is, there is a positive correlation between budget surplus and private investment. By studying data from the US and Canada as well as private and public investment behavior based on neoclassical theory, Voss (2002) finds evidence that public investment has a crowding-out effect on private investment.

The main difference among various economic schools in public economics can be distilled to the question of whether government expenditure effect on economic growth matches the predicted Keynesian effects. Some theories suggest that the fiscal expenditures have Keynesian effects on economic growth and private consumption; that is, increases in government expenditure will stimulate private consumption and promote output. Other theories deem that fiscal policy has non-Keynesian effects on economic growth and private consumption with the implication that increasing government expenditure will reduce output, or at best have no impact on economic growth. Although researchers have performed various empirical studies, contrary to other macroeconomic phenomena, fiscal policy is a purely empirical question, which necessitates control over the specific circumstances of different subjects to be analyzed.

These findings based on other countries may not be applied to China due to China's unique institutional features, especially in the various situations of local governments, as every local governmental fiscal policy has its own features. Although Chinese scholars also address the effectiveness of fiscal policy through theoretical analysis and empirical tests, it is necessary to obtain useful results and meaningful guidance for the government through practical management and experience. Most of the existing studies tend to focus on the central government, but research and analysis of local and regional financial economic effects of fiscal policy are scarce. Zhejiang, being "special" by being the only primarily private economic province in China, requires alternate approaches to understand macroeconomic behavior. Therefore, besides learning from foreign research methods and ideas, it is essential to explore further the fiscal policy effect in the context of Chinese national conditions and the situation in Zhejiang.

3. Model and Data

3.1. *Model*

In order to verify the impact of fiscal expenditure on economic growth, private investment, and private consumption in Zhejiang province, this study constructs the following econometric model.

$$Y_j = \alpha + \beta X_i + \varepsilon_i \quad j = 1, 2, 3 \quad i = 1, 2, 3, 4, 5. \tag{1}$$

In formula (1), the explanatory variable Y_j denotes economic growth, private investment, and private consumption, X and X_i denote the total fiscal expenditure of Zhejiang province and the fiscal expenditure under categories, respectively, and ε_i is the perturbation item. β is the key parameter of this study. If β is positive to show that fiscal expenditure in Zhejiang province can promote economic growth, private investment, and private consumption, which means that fiscal expenditure efficiency is positive. On the contrary, if β is negative, it shows that fiscal expenditure efficiency in Zhejiang province is negative, and expansionary local fiscal policy cannot play a positive role in economic growth.

3.2. *Variables*

- **Fiscal expenditure** (represented by G): In this chapter, total local government expenditure rather than government investment expenditure will be used as the fiscal expenditure in Zhejiang province, as local governments in China always have a variety of other expenditures (extra-budgetary) in addition to the budget expenditure. The actual amount and the use of extra-budgetary expenses are very difficult to measure.
- **Economic growth** (represented by PGDP): Per capita GDP will be used as the measurement of economic growth in Zhejiang province.
- **Private consumption** (represented by PC): Per capita consumption expenditure will measure the consumption expenditure status.
- **Private investment** (represented by PI): Private investment expenditure will be used to measure the private enterprises' investment.

3.3. *Data*

Since 1978, which marked China's reform and opening up policy, Zhejiang has been one of the fastest growing and most active provinces in China, with the main economic indicators in the province demonstrating a leading position in China's economy. With the rapid development of the economy in Zhejiang province, local and regional fiscal expenditures have increased obviously.

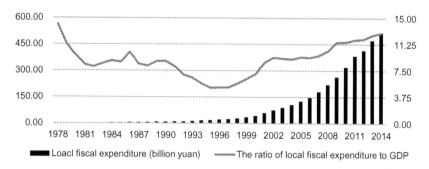

Figure 1. Total local fiscal expenditure and its ratio to GDP (secondary coordinates, right) in Zhejiang province, from 1978 to 2014.

Source: Data from Statistical Yearbook of Zhejiang province.

Figure 1 displays that from 1978 to 2014, the rate of the absolute value of the government expenditure has increased exponentially in Zhejiang province. Total expenditure increased from 1.74 billion yuan in 1978 to 515.96 billion yuan in 2014, indicating an average annual increase of nearly 14 billion yuan.

The ratio of local governmental expenditure to GDP in Zhejiang province can be divided into the following three stages. The first stage from 1978 to 1982 shows a slow economic growth in Zhejiang province with a total government expenditure of 18 billion yuan. The ratio of local governmental expenditure to GDP declined from 14.09% to 8.07%. In the second stage from 1983 to 1995, the size of local governmental expenditure slowly expanded and increased from 2.2 billion yuan in 1983 to 18 billion yuan in 1990, with a significant fluctuation in the expenditure as a share of GDP. Starting from in 8.53% 1983, it grew to 10.14% in 1986, with a sharp decline in 1990; finally, the ratio of expenditure to GDP was only about 5% in 1995. In the third stage, from 1996 to 2014, the amount of local governmental expenditure increased dramatically, surging from 21.3 billion yuan in 1996 to 515.9 billion yuan in 2014, while the share of GDP also increased from 5.10% to 12.84% during this time. Since the Asian financial crisis in 1998, both the absolute amount of fiscal expenditure and the relative share to GDP have shown a significant growth in Zhejiang province. The data show that in recent years, using fiscal policy to intervene in the local economy became more important for the government of Zhejiang, which resembles the pattern of central government of China. The province comprises the biggest private economy in the country. How does a strong fiscal intervention influence the private enterprises' investment? What happens to the expenditure of citizens? How does this affect the performance of the economy in Zhejiang?

Figure 2 shows the economic situation in Zhejiang (measured as per capita GDP, right axis) in the last 15 years. Both per capita consumption expenditure and private investment show a rapid growth except for a few years (as in 2009). Private capital investment maintains the same growth rate as per capita GDP growth, consistent with overall pattern of China, as Zhejiang is the largest private economic province in China.

In contrast, per capita consumption expenditure rose much more slowly in Zhejiang province, which seems contrary to it being one of the richest provinces in China; it's expected that consumer spending would always to be in direct proportion to the output (income). Is this because of regional governmental fiscal policy? Is the private

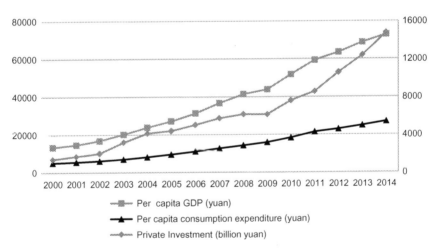

Figure 2. Per capita GDP, per capita consumption expenditure and private investment status (secondary coordinates, right) from 2000 to 2014 in Zhejiang province.

Source: Data from Statistical Yearbook in Zhejiang province.

consumption affected only by their income? At the same time, the GDP of Zhejiang province has achieved a phenomenal growth, from 123.0 billion yuan in 1978 to 4.02 trillion yuan, with an average annual growth rate of 12.40%. Does the local governmental fiscal policy make any contribution to this remarkable achievement? Further empirical analysis will try to answer the above series of questions.

Considering the data available, records of 37 years (except for private investment, which, according to official data released by the Statistics Bureau of Zhejiang province, is only currently available from 2000 to 2014; therefore, these 15-year data will be used for private investment crowding-into/out effect analysis) are available from 1978 to 2014 to carry out the time series data analysis.

4. An Empirical Analysis

4.1. *HP filtering process*

The main purpose of this study is to explore the impact of local government fiscal expenditure shocks on the economy and some related economic effects. Time series data often have their own trend in the process of economic growth. Therefore, we will first of all use the Hodrick–Prescott (HP) filtering method (Hodrick and Prescott,1980) to separate the time series data into two parts, namely trend component series and fluctuation component series, as follows[1]:

$$Y_t = Y_t^T + Y_t^C \quad t = 1, 2, \ldots, T, \tag{2}$$

where $\{Y_t\}$ is the original series data which include trend component series $\{Y_t^T\}$ and fluctuation component series $\{Y_t^C\}$.

Here our purpose is to remove the trend series $\{Y_t^T\}$ and obtain the component fluctuation component series $\{Y_t^C\}$:

$$Y_t^C = Y_t - Y_t^T \quad t = 1, 2, \ldots, T, \tag{3}$$

where $\{Y_t^C\}$ is a series to measure the absolute gap, that is, the local governmental "counter-cyclical" behavior including unexpected

---

[1]See the details in Appendix B

increases of fiscal expenditure as well as sudden cuts during the economic growth.

We will thereby investigate the correlation among them, that is how much impact a sudden fiscal expenditure shock will have on private investment, on consumption expenditure, and on economic growth.

4.2. *Unit root test*

Generally, to avoid spurious regression,time series data always need a stationary test before analysis. In this study, we use the above-mentioned HP filter method to separate and obtain the fluctuation component data series, marked as hpG, hpPGDP, hpPC, and hpPI. It is generally believed that the above four sets of sequences should be stationary after the trend is removed, but we still use the ADF stationary test to check the four groups of data series. Results are shown in Table 1.

The results in Table 1 show that at the 5% significance level, hpG, hpPGDP, hpPC, and hpPI are all stationary series, which meets the general expectations.

4.3. *Regression analysis*

We shall define hpG as an independent variable and hpPGDP, hpPC, and hpPI as the dependent variables to establish the respective regression models. Using fomula (1), we will study the dynamic relationship between local government expenditures and other economic variables through empirical analysis. There may be a certain time

Table 1. The results of ADF test on hpG, hpPGDP, hpPC, and hpPI.

Variables	Difference form	ADF value (5%)	t Value	P Value	Result
hpG	Level	-1.95	-2.18	0.03	Stable**
hpPGDP	Level	-1.95	-2.52	0.01	Stable***
hpPC	Level	-1.95	-2.61	0.01	Stable***
hpPI	Level	-1.97	-2.05	0.05	Stable**

Note: *Significant at 10%; **significant at 5%; ***significant at 1%.

Table 2. The regression results between hpG and hpPGDP, hpPC, and hpPI.

Variables	hpG	hpG (−1)	Variable (−1)	F Value	R^2
hpPGDP	8.05*** (3.64)	−5.60** (−2.15)	0.59*** (4.05)	16.81	0.57
hpPC	3.00*** (4.59)	−1.89** (−2.33)	0.69*** (5.46)	34.61	0.74
hpPI	−0.72 (−0.48)	3.81** (2.46)	0.82*** (3.69)	10.58	0.69

Notes: The *t*-test parameter values are provided in parentheses. *Significant at 10%; **significant at 5%; ***Significant at 1%. Variable (−1) represents the hysteresis endogenous variable.

lag taken into account as a result of the impact of local fiscal expenditure; thus, it is best to use the AIC criterion to determine that the optimal lag order is of order 1. The regression results are shown in Table 2.

For a local government, an unexpected (generally considered to be a counter-cyclical behavior of the government) increase of fiscal expenditure has a significant positive effect on the current economic growth and a significant negative effect on the economy in the next period. One can draw the conclusion that the local government fiscal expenditure has no effect on economic growth in the long run.

Very similar to the impact on economic growth, a sudden increase of local government expenditure can promote the current level of private consumption, but will lead to a decline in the next period, in line with the Ricardian equivalence theorem. It is deemed that local government fiscal expenditure has no long-term effect on private consumption.

Finally, local government expenditure has a negative effect on current private investment, though the effect is not very significant. However, there is a positive impact on the private investment in the next period. Thus, it can be determined that an increase in local government expenditure will lead to a growth of private investment, which is consistent with the causal observation made in China.

4.4. *Granger causality test*

To further define the relationship between local government fiscal expenditure and the other three economic variables, we conduct

Table 3. Granger causality tests results between hpG and hpPGDP, hpPC, and hpPI.

Variables	H$_0$ (original hypothesis)	F value	P Value	Results
hpPGDP	hpG does not Granger cause hpPGDP	0.37	0.55	Accepted
	hpPGDP does not Granger cause hpG	0.55	0.90	Accepted
hpPC	hpG does not Granger cause hpPC	1.01	0.32	Accepted
	hpPC does not Granger cause hpG	001	094	Accepted
hpPI	hpG does not Granger cause hpPI	14.86	0.00	Refused
	hpPI does not Granger cause hpG	2.45	0.15	Accepted

Granger causality tests between hpG and hpPGDP,hpPC,and hpPI. The results are show in Table 3.

Statistical analysis shows that local government fiscal expenditure does not, according to the test, cause local economic growth or expansion of private consumption expenditure, but it does cause additional private investment, which coincides with the above regression analysis.

In addition, the performance of government is based on financial expenditure, which determines the structure of financial expenditure. It is useful to analyze the impact of different types of expenditure on private investment. This issue will be analyzed now.

5. The Impact of Fiscal Expenditure Structure on Private Investment

Due to the reform of the government revenue and expenditure classification carried out by the Ministry of Finance in 2007, the components of fiscal expenditure in the Statistical Yearbook had changed. The analyses in this chapter, depend on the Ministry of Finance's "Solution to the Reform of Government Revenue and Expenditure Classification". And we follow the classification of Li Yongyou(2009), Wu Xiaoli, Huang Jiangfeng (2014), Chen Tianxiang, Zhao Hui (2016), and other scholars. We classify the components of expenditures into five categories according to their purposes before and after 2007, which are economic construction expenditure, science, education, culture and health expenditure, security expenditure, maintenance expenditure, and other expenditure, which are represented by ECOX, EDUX, SOCX, SECX, and OTHX respectively. Table 4 reports the details.

Table 4. Cassification of local financial expenditure in Zhejiang province.

Classification	Before 2007	After 2007
Economic construction expenditure	• Construction expenditure • Expenditure on tapping potential and transforming enterprises • Costs of science and technology • Operational expenses of agriculture, forestry, water conservancy departments • Industrial transportation and other departments' expenses	• (Industry) Business services, etc. • Agriculture, forestry, and water affairs • Transportation • Resources exploration, electricity information, etc. —
Science, education, culture, and health expenditure	• Art, sports, and broadcasting departments' expenses • Educational departments' expenses • Scientific departments' expenses • Health expenditure	• Education • Science and technology • Cultural, sports, and media • Medical and health work
Security expenditure	• Pensions and social welfare benefits expenditure • Retirement funds of administrative institutions • Social security subsidy expenditure	• Social security and employment — —

(*Continued*)

Table 4. (*Continued*)

Classification	Before 2007	After 2007
Maintenance expenditure	• Administrative expenses • Expenditure for the armed and police force • Public prosecution expenditure • Urban maintenance expenses • Foreign affairs expenditure	General public services Public safety — — —
Other expenditure	• Other expenditure	• Other expenditure

Table 5. The impact of different types of fiscal expenditure on private investment in Zhejiang province.

Variable Test Value	lnECOX	lnEDUX	lnSOCX	lnSECX	lnOTHX
β	−0.447	−0.180	−0.572	0.358	0.668
T Value	−1.223	−0.496	−2.959	4.109	1.056
p Value	0.249	0.631	0.014*	0.001***	0.315

Note: *Significant at 10%; **significant at 5%; ***significant at 1%.

In order to further measure the impact of different types of fiscal expenditure on private investment, we still use formula (1) to do the empirical research. In order to avoid the problem of heteroscedasticity caused by time series, we take the logs of various fiscal expenditures, defined as lnECOX, lnEDUX, lnSOCX, lnSECX, and lnOTHX. At the same time, we have conducted the ADF test to ensure the stationarity of the time series. The final results are reported in Table 5.

Results of the empirical analysis show that only maintenance expenditure has a significant positive impact on private investment, but security expenditure has a negative impact, while other types of fiscal expenditures have no significant impact on the private investment in Zhejiang province.

6. Conclusions and Policy Implications

6.1. *Conclusions*

The main purpose of this chapter is to study the impact of local and regional governmental fiscal expenditure shocks on economic growth, consumption, and private investment in the biggest private economy in China. We analyze the effects of local fiscal expenditures on the local economy. The primary conclusions are as follows.

First of all, since the implementation of the reform and trade liberalization policies of China from the year 1978, it appears that economic growth is almost irrelevant to government expenditure in Zhejiang province. That is to say, government expenditure does not directly stimulate economic growth (though indirect effects may certainly exist). Second, the government expenditure has neither a significant crowding-out effect on the private consumption nor a significant crowding-in effect. This means that changes in local government expenditure have very minimal impact on the private consumption. Therefore, under the current economic slowdown or even during recession, the Keynesian recommendation that the provincial government should stimulate economic growth by stimulating consumption seems impracticable. The reason is very simple. Compared to other provinces in China where the government can require state-owned enterprises to increase their expenditure by purchasing additional materials or equipment while simultaneously injecting funds to stimulate the local economic growth, Zhejiang has a relatively "hand-off" policy.

Another finding from both regression analysis and Granger causality shows that government expenditure shocks have a significant positive effect on private investment, implying that an increase in government expenditure can stimulate private investment in the next period. It seems that, as the country's biggest private economy province in the current economy of China, the investment field and direction of government funding serve as indicators for private capital, so when regional government expenditures increase, private capital will follow to increase investment as well.

As for current trends, in the second session of the National People's Congress of Zhejiang province, the government work report pointed out that in 2015 the gross regional product in Zhejiang province was expected to grow about 7.5%, while the general public budget expenditure was also expected to grow around 7.5%. At the same time, from January to September 2015, private investment in Zhejiang province amounted to 1.1414 trillion yuan, an increase of 8.1%. It can be seen that the two generally grow almost at the same rate, which is consistent with the conclusions of this study.

Finally, from the perspective of the impact of different types of fiscal expenditure on private investment, only maintenance expenditure has a significant positive impact on private investment in Zhejiang province This indicates that the increases in maintenance expenditure on urban maintenance, public services, public safety, etc., will stimulate private investment. In contrast, the increase of security expenditures such as pension and social welfare expenditure has a negative impact on private investment, while other types of financial expenditures have no significant impact. Compared with state-owned and collective capital, private capital is more sensitive and is more profit-seeking in the market. Local government's maintenance expenditure means that private capital can benefit more from the public resources conveniently in the future, thus promoting the increase of private investment.

But security expenditure implies that public resources tend to be the "vulnerable groups", which is a "bad" signal that public resources are occupied, thus inhibiting private investment. Besides, private capital is relatively insensitive to local government expenditures on economic construction, science, education, culture and health, and other types of financial expenditure.

6.2. *Research implications*

Since local government fiscal expenditures have no effect on the local economic growth and private consumption, fiscal investments of the provincial government should be primarily used as a stimulator. In recent years, private investment has become an essential part of economic development in Zhejiang province as a crucial force in driving economic growth. Thus, it is highly important to encourage the development of private investment, in particular the development of small-and medium-sized enterprises (SMEs). SMES are the main force of the economy of Zhejiang; they really drive the expansion of domestic demand, enhance corporate finance capabilities, revive the market environment, and enlarge total investment in Zhejiang province. There are two ways the local government is suggested to take action.

On the one hand, to encourage private investment, especially the development of SMEs, the local government can implement some policies including reduction of the tax burden on private enterprises, reducing the amount of investment in fixed assets, lowering the proportion of big project funds, and relaxing restrictions of private corporate bond. It may also be in the best regional interest to support the establishment of an SME credit guarantee system to ensure the steady development of the economy. In general, a freer market will draw more investors' attention to Zhejiang province as an ideal place to do business.

On the other hand, affirming the positive effects of fiscal policy and making different effective policies at different periods of time may prove beneficial. Great attention should be paid to the quantitative analysis of financial expenditure, and there should be a focus on refining the fiscal policy. When embarking on new local fiscal policies, the government should take full account of the guidance role of such expenditure on private capital, especially the positive effect of fiscal expenditure on maintenance. Thus, the local government can support and guide private capital investing to strategic industries, which can help the local government to achieve a sustainable economic development of the province.

Appendix

A.1. *Hodrick–Prescott filtering method*

The HP filtering method is used to separate the time series data into two parts, namely trend component series and fluctuation component series, as follows:

$$Y_t = Y_t^T - Y_t^C \quad t = 1, 2, \ldots, T, \tag{A.1}$$

where $\{Y_t\}$ is the original series data which includes trend component series $\{Y_t^T\}$ and fluctuation component series $\{Y_t^C\}$. To separate the unobserved trend series $\{Y_t^T\}$ from $\{Y_t\}$, it is usually defined as a problem to solve the following minimization problem:

$$\min \sum_{t=1}^{T} \{(Y_t - Y_t^T)^2 + \lambda[B(L)Y_t^T]^2\}, \tag{A.2}$$

where $B(L)$ is a polynomial delay operator

$$B(L) = (L^{-1} - 1) - (1 - L) \tag{A.3}$$

Substituting (A.3) in (A.2), we obtain

$$\min \left\{ \sum_{t=1}^{T}(Y_t - Y_t^T)^2 + \lambda \sum_{t=2}^{T-1}[(Y_{t+1}^T - Y_t^T) - (Y_t^T - Y_{t-1}^T)]^2 \right\}. \tag{A.4}$$

By making $y_1, y_2, \ldots, y_n$ the first-order derivatives, equal to zero in Equation (A.4), we get

$$g_1 : c_1 = \lambda(g_1 - 2g_2 + g_3)$$
$$g_2 : c_2 = \lambda(-2g_1 + 5g_2 - 4g_3 + g_4)$$
$$\vdots$$
$$g_t : c_t = \lambda(g_{t-2} - 4gt - 1 + 6g_t - 4gt + 1 + g_4)$$
$$\vdots$$
$$g_{n-1} : c_{n-1} = \lambda(g_{n-3} - 4gn - 2 + 5gn_1 - 2g_n)$$
$$g_n : c_n = \lambda(g_{n-2} - 2gn_1 + g_n)$$

In the form of a matrix, it is represented as follows:

$$c = \lambda F g,$$

where

$$
F = \begin{bmatrix}
1 & -2 & 1 & 0 & \cdots & & & & & 0 \\
-2 & 5 & -4 & 1 & 0 & \cdots & & & & 0 \\
1 & -4 & 6 & -4 & 1 & 0 & \cdots & & & 0 \\
0 & 1 & -4 & 6 & -4 & 1 & 0 & \cdots & & 0 \\
\cdots & & & & & & & & & \\
\cdots & & & & & & & & & \\
\cdots & & & & & & & & & \\
0 & & 0 & 1 & -4 & 6 & 4 & 1 & 0 \\
0 & & & 0 & 1 & -4 & 6 & 4 & 1 \\
0 & & & & 0 & 1 & -4 & 5 & -2 \\
0 & & & & & 0 & 1 & -2 & 1
\end{bmatrix}.
$$

Thus, we can get

$$
y - g = \lambda F g.
$$

So,

$$
g = (\lambda F + I)^{-1} y.
$$

And, in the F matrix, the sum of each column elements are zero. Therefore, the sum of short-term volatility is 0. That is,

$$
\sum_{t=1}^{n} c_t = 0.
$$

Here, we make the HP filtering problem minimize the loss function (4), using $[B(L)Y_t^T]^2$ to adjust the trend changes, and depending on the parameter λ, which is an *a priori* given parameter, in general experience, λ values are given as follows:

$$
\lambda = \begin{cases}
100, & \text{Annual data} \\
1600, & \text{Quarterly data} \\
14400, & \text{Monthly data.}
\end{cases}
$$

Here, our purpose is to remove the trend series $\{Y_t^T\}$ and obtain the component fluctuation component series $\{Y_t^C\}$

$$
Y_t^C = Y_t - Y_t^T \quad t = 1, 2, \ldots, T. \tag{A.5}
$$

Acknowledgements

Supported by the Natural Science Foundation of Zhejiang province (LY15G030009).

References

Aiyagari, S. R. *et al.* (1992). "The output, Employment, and Interest Rate Effects of Government Consumption," *J. Monetary Econ.*, 30(10), 73–86.

Aschauer, A. D. (2009). "Is Public Expenditure Productive?" *Ecnomics*, **41**, 913–919.

Bairam, Er. and Ward, B. (1993). "The Externality Effect of Government Expenditure on Investment in OECD Countries," *Appl. Econo.*, (25), 711–716.

Barro, R. (1989). "Economic Growth in a Gross Section of Countries," *Quarte. J. Econ.*, (104), 407–444.

Barro, R. (1990). "Government spending in a Simple Model of Endogenous Growth," *J. Polit. Econ.*, 103–117.

Cochrane, J. H. (2001). "Long term Debt and Optimal Policy in the Fiscal Theory of Price Level," *Econometrics*, 69–116.

Daniel, B. (2001). "The Fiscal Theory of the Price Level," *J. Monetary Econo.*, **48**, 293–308.

Easterly, W. (1993). "Fiscal Policy and Economic Growth — An Empirical Investigation," *Dep. Econ.* (24), 259–276.

Engle, R. F. and Granger, C. W. J. (1987). "Estimation and Testing," *Econometri. Cointegr. Error Repr.*, **55**, 119–139.

Evans, P. (1997). "Government Consumption and Growth," *Econo. Inq.*, 209–217.

Feldstein, M. (1980). "Fiscal Policy, Inflation and Capital Formation," *Am. Econ. Rev.*, **70**, 636–650.

Fischer, S. (1993). "The Role of Macroeconomic Factors in Growth," *Journal of Monetary Economics*, (32), 485–512.

Grier, G. T. (1989). "An Empirical Analysis of Gross-National Economic Growth," *J. Monetary Econ.*, 259–276.

Hodrick, R. and Prescott, E. C. (1980). *Post-war U.S. Business Cycles: An Empirical investigation*, mimeo, Pittsburch: Carnegie-Mellon University.

Keynes, J. M. (1936). "The General Theory of Employment," *Interest and Money* Commercial Publishing House.

Marcus, Ed. (1952). "The Effectiveness of Canadian Fiscal Policy," *The J. Fin.*, **7**(4), 559–579.

Marianne, B. (1993). "Fiscal Policy in General Equilibrium," *The Am. Econ. Rev.*, **83**(3), 315–334.

Martinez Lopez. D. (2006). "Linking Public Investment to Private Investment. The Case of Spanish Regions," *Int. Rev. Appli. Econ.*, **20**, 411–423.

Rater, J. B. (1983). "Government Capital and Production Function for U.S. Private Output," *Econ. Lett.*, (13), 213–217.

Vijverberg *et al.* (2009). "Public Capital and Private Productivity," *Rev. Econ. Statist.*, **79**, 267–278.

Voss, G. M. (2002). "Public and Private Investment in the United States and Canada," *Econ. Model.* **19**(4), 641–664.

Index

Printed in the United States
By Bookmasters